BIG ISLAND OF HAWAII

Welcome to the Big Island

Little did we realize that the emergence of a novel coronavirus in early 2020 would abruptly bring almost all travel to a halt. Although our Fodor's writers around the world have continued working to bring you the best of the destinations they cover, we still anticipate that more than the usual number of businesses will close permanently in the coming months, perhaps with little advance notice. We don't expect things to return to "normal" for some time. As you plan your upcoming travels to the Big Island of Hawaii, please confirm that places are still open and let us know when we need to make updates by writing to us at this address: editors@fodors.com.

TOP REASONS TO GO

★ **Hawaii Volcanoes National Park:** The world's most active volcano is an amazing sight.

★ **Fun Towns:** Humming Kailua-Kona, cowboy country Waimea, rainbow-streaked Hilo.

★ **Stargazing:** Maunakea's peak is the best place on Earth to stare out into space.

★ **Beaches:** The Big Island offers sand in many shades—black, white, and even green.

★ **Wildlife:** You can watch sea turtles on the beach and humpback whales in the waves.

★ **Kona Coffee:** Farm tours, smooth sips, and a coffee cultural festival are all memorable.

Contents

Fodor's Features

MAPS

Chapter 1

EXPERIENCE BIG ISLAND

17 ULTIMATE EXPERIENCES

Big Island of Hawaii offers terrific experiences that should be on every traveler's list. Here are Fodor's top picks for a memorable trip.

⟩n Maunakea

⟩rgazing at Maunakea's summit is outstanding. The visitor center (as far ⟩are allowed to go) offers free public stargazing four nights a week, but ⟩. *(Ch. 5)*

2 Tour a Kona Coffee Plantation

Local coffee farmers love to share their passion with the public, and most offer free tours. Our favorite is Lion's Gate Farm at mile marker 101 in Honaunau. *(Ch. 3)*

3 Be a Cowboy for a Day

Saddle up and get ready to ride the ranges, cliffs, and trails of the Big Island on horseback. It's one of the best ways to take in the island's beautiful scenery. *(Ch. 8)*

4 Hike to the Green Sand Beach

It's worth the effort to drive to the end of South Point Road and hike about three miles to a stunning olivine Papakolea Beach. Take lots of water. *(Ch. 7)*

5 Enjoy a Sunday Stroll in Kailua-Kona

On the third Sunday of every month, Kailua-Kona town closes off to car traffic for a local market, ending with a free Hawaiian concert. *(Ch. 3)*

6 Swim at Night With Manta Rays

These gracious, gentle giants feed on plankton in a spot called "Manta Village." An experienced diving outfitter can get you there. *(Ch. 8)*

7 Go Bowling on a Volcano

Kilauea Military Camp (KMC), within Hawaii Volcanoes National Park, was established in 1916 for military families, but the public is also welcome to bowl, eat, shop, and pump affordable gas. *(Ch. 7)*

8 Walk on a Solid Lava Lake

Although no lava is flowing at Kilauea, the Kilauea Iki Trail takes you to the floor of the crater, where you'll walk on a solidified lake of formerly red-hot lava flow. *(Ch. 7)*

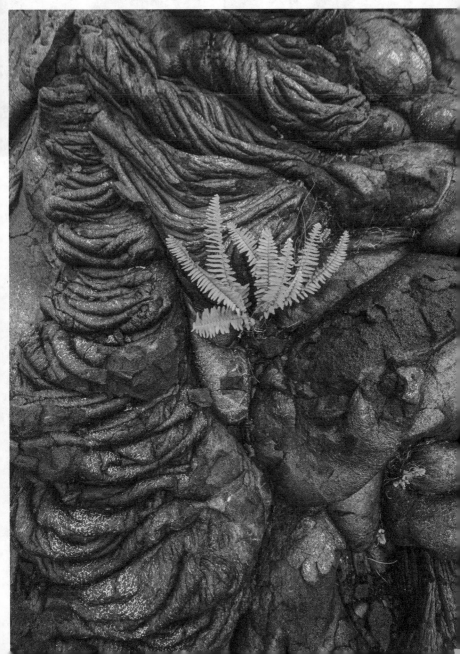

9 Sky Dive the Big Island

Jump out of a plane for a true bird's eye view of the incredible northern landscapes of the Big Island—even beginners can do it. You'll feel more like you are floating rather than freefalling. *(Ch. 8)*

10 Visit Kaloko-Honokohau

At this underrated national historic park, boardwalks take visitors past ancient fishponds and ruins in addition to beautiful beaches populated with interesting flora and fauna. *(Ch. 3)*

11 Go Whale Watching

From November through May, take a boat trip to watch migrating humpbacks from Alaska mate, give birth, and nurture their young in the waters off the Hawaiian Islands. *(Ch. 8)*

12 Tour a Royal Palace

Take a tour of the gorgeous Hulihee Palace, which is on the National Register of Historic Places and one of only three royal palace residences in the United States. *(Ch. 3)*

13 Explore Lava Tubes

Thurston Lava Tube in Hawaii Volcanoes National Park is convenient; Kula Kai Caverns and Kilauea Caverns of Fire are fascinating but require expert guides. *(Ch. 7, 8)*

14 Walk Down to Waipio Valley

This lush, waterfall-laden valley—surrounded by sheer, fluted 2,000-foot cliffs—was once a favorite retreat for Hawaiian royalty. *(Ch. 5)*

15 Sleep on the Volcano's Rim

The historic Volcano House hotel overlooks the Kilauea caldera and is the oldest hotel in Hawaii, offering great views of the crater. *(Ch. 7)*

16 Check out Sleeping Turtles at a Black Sand Beach

At Punaluu Black Sand beach, rows of endangered Hawaiian green sea turtles (honu) often bask on the hot sand in the sun. *(Ch. 7)*

17 Visit a 5-Star Beach

The Big Island's (and the state's) most beautiful white sand beaches flank the Kohala Coast, including beautiful Anaehoomalu Bay, Hapuna Beach, and Kaunaoa Beach. *(Ch. 4)*

WHAT'S WHERE

1 Kailua-Kona and the Kona Coast. This seaside town is packed with restaurants, shops, and a busy waterfront bustling with tourists along the main street, Alii Drive. The coast stretches a bit north of Kailua-Kona and much farther south, including gorgeous Kealakekua Bay. It's the place to take farm tours and taste samples of world-famous Kona coffee.

2 The Kohala Coast and Waimea. The sparkling coast is home to all those long, white-sand beaches and the expensive resorts that go with them. Ranches sprawl across the cool, upland meadows of Waimea, known as *paniolo* (cowboy) country.

3 The Hamakua Coast. Waterfalls, dramatic cliffs, ocean vistas, ancient hidden valleys, rain forests, and the stunning Waipio Valley are just a few of the treats here. Journey up 13,796-foot Maunakea for what's considered the world's best stargazing, with 13 telescopes perched on top.

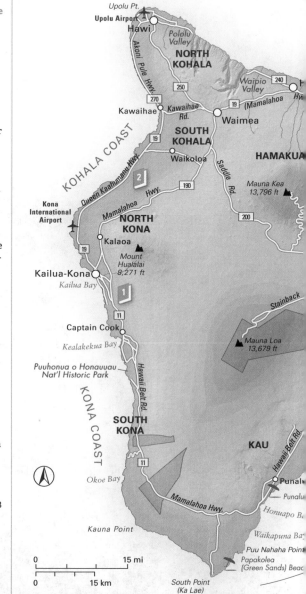

4 **Hilo.** Known as the City of Rainbows for all its rain, Hilo is often skipped by tourists in favor of the sunny Kohala Coast. But for what many consider the "real" Hawaii, as well as incredible rain forests, waterfalls, and the island's best farmers' market, Hilo can't be beat.

5 **Hawaii Volcanoes National Park, Puna, and Kau.** The spectacular Halemaumau Crater, now quiet, within Kilauea Caldera is not to be missed. The adjacent hamlet of Volcano Village provides a great base for exploring the park. The remote Puna district has the quirky, hippie town of Pahoa as well as the island's most recent lava flows. Round the southernmost part of the island to Kau for two of the Big Island's most unusual beaches: Papakolea (Green Sands Beach) and Punaluu Black Sand Beach.

Big Island Today

BACK-TO-BASICS AGRICULTURE

Emulating how the Hawaiian ancestors lived and returning to their simple ways of growing and sharing a variety of foods has become a statewide initiative. Hawaii boasts the natural conditions and talent to produce diversity in agriculture, from coffee, avocados, and dragon fruit to flowers, goat cheese, and wine. The seed of this movement thrives through various farmers' markets and partnerships between restaurants and local farmers. Localized efforts such as the Hawaii Farm Bureau Federation are collectively leading the organic and sustainable agricultural renaissance. From home-cooked meals and casual plate lunches to fine-dining cuisine, cooks, farmers, and chefs are blazing a trail of sustainability, helping to enrich the culinary tapestry of Hawaii.

TOURISM AND THE ECONOMY

Tourism, by far the state's most important industry, shows no signs of slowing down. In 2019, the arrival of 10.4 million visitors to the state surpassed a long-expected milestone. According to the Hawaii Tourism Authority, there were, on average, more than 250,000 visitors in the Islands on any given day, spending about $17.8 billion last year alone, up 1% from 2018. The Big Island experienced growing visitor arrivals, too, despite the three-month 2018 Puna eruption, which spurred cancellations and dampened arrivals for a short time. However, even as Big Island visitors increased, spending fell, as visitors seemed to favor lower-cost vacation rentals over hotels, cooked in more instead of eating out, and spent less money on pricey activities such as golf. With the 10 million visitor threshold met, concerns about overtourism in the state began to creep into statewide discussion, along with calls for balance.

SHORT-TERM VACATION RENTAL REGULATION

The explosive popularity of short-term vacation rentals (STRs) in Hawaii—and indeed, around the world—has had a major impact on the way visitors travel, very much in contrast to traditional hotel options. Not only are vacation rentals generally less expensive, but they can accommodate larger groups or families who can stay together and save money by cooking and eating in. Renters can also stay in uncrowded, rural areas of the island away from the hotel or resort scene. According to Hawaii Tourism Authority statistics, the Big Island had more than 200,000 unit nights available with a 71.8% occupancy rate for the month of December 2019. Unfortunately, with the increased number of STRs came significant community backlash. Residents who experienced high rents and housing shortages blamed vacation rentals, perhaps unfairly. Guests who partied or otherwise disrupted neighborhoods without oversight also got the attention of regulators. Bill 108 was introduced by the Hawaii County Council in 2018, becoming law in April 2019. Existing rentals not in approved resort zones could apply for a one-time permit to continue operations. All others, except hosted stays, were banned, but there is talk of also regulating hosted vacation rentals in upcoming legislation.

THIRTY METER TELESCOPE

The Thirty Meter Telescope (TMT) is the latest telescope project to be proposed for the summit of Maunakea, the best place in the world for astronomy. With a planned mirror size of a jaw-dropping 30 meters (98 feet) in diameter, the $1.4 billion TMT will be one of the strongest telescopes on the planet when it is completed in 2027, with three times the resolution of other large instruments.

With such power, astronomer teams from multiple nations and universities hope to peer back in time to study the evolution of the oldest, most distant structures in the universe. They will study the life cycle of supermassive black holes and detect faint, hard-to-see exoplanets that may rest within the "habitable zone." The TMT has been controversial, as some residents worry about the potential impact of further development on Maunakea and to native Hawaiian cultural and spiritual practices. In 2014, protests at the Maunakea access road delayed the project's ground breaking, and the original building permit was invalidated by the court. Following years of contested case hearings and an exhaustive process, in 2018, the Hawaii Supreme Court ruled in favor of the TMT, giving the green light to start. Before construction began in July of 2019, protesters once again gathered at the base of the mountain, chaining themselves to cattle grates and refusing to allow vehicles to pass. The protest garnered international media attention, leading to the arrest of 38 elders and others. As of this writing, the TMT is still negotiating with the protestors and working on a compromise plan moving forward.

INVASIVE SPECIES

The Big Island of Hawaii has a long history of imported invasive species devastating native flora and fauna, as well as crops such as coffee and macadamia nuts. Unfortunately, this affliction continues today. Although Hawaii has adopted strict regulations on imported species, some inevitably slip through the cracks. As you drive around the island at night, for example, you will encounter the infamous mating call of the coqui, a frog whose two-tone shriek can exceed 90 decibels. Originally from Puerto Rico, this teeny frog likely hitched a ride on nursery plants. With no natural predators, they were able to rapidly multiply throughout the island's lush forests, but now they are found most everywhere. It's only the latest in a long line of animals imported or who hitchhiked in and became difficult, if not impossible, to control as they spread throughout the rugged and inaccessible mountains and rain forests of Hawaii Island. Goats, wild boars, mongooses, feral cats, mosquitoes, and others have all wreaked havoc on local wildlife and the environment, including wiping out hundreds of species of endemic Hawaiian bird species.

THE LATEST VOLCANIC ERUPTIONS

In May 2018, startling changes began happening at Kilauea Volcano on the southeastern quadrant of the island. The cessation of the Puu Oo Vent, which had been continuously erupting since 1983, preceded a line of fissure eruptions in a remote neighborhood in Lower Puna, destroying dozens of homes. Meanwhile, back in Hawaii Volcanoes National Park, the lava lake at Halemaumau began receding quickly, creating ash plumes above the summit and steam explosions as it collapsed. The dramatic events claimed several beloved beaches in Lower Puna, including the Kapoho tide pools and the Ahalanui warm ponds. Those same destructive forces also created a brand-new black-sand beach, Pohoiki, which continues to expand as more black sand builds up on the shore. Hawaii Volcano Observatory (HVO) scientists have since declared this eruption over, but if it were to start up again, there would be lots of warning.

Best Big Island Beaches

PUNALUU BLACK SAND BEACH PARK

Along the desolate southeastern coast of the island, this pretty little beach park impresses with its shimmering black sands, a duck pond, coconut palms, and the stars of the show: plenty of turtles, both the Hawaiian green sea turtle and sometimes the highly endangered hawksbill.

ANAEHOOMALU BAY

Although less well known than its Kohala Coast cousins, this lovely stretch of beach, with its mature coconut palms and ancient fishponds, is just a stone's throw from two large resorts. It's a spectacular spot for swimming, snorkeling, stand-up paddleboarding, and spotting turtles.

HAPUNA BEACH STATE RECREATION AREA

This sugar-white stretch of perfect tropical glory evokes everyone's ideal fantasy of Hawaii and is consistently rated among the best beaches in the state. Glistening, aquamarine water guarantees idyllic conditions for swimming, snorkeling, wading, and sunbathing.

KEKAHA KAI STATE PARK

This treasure of a place is anything but off the beaten path. Down a bumpy, unimproved road, beachgoers will find their difficult journey rewarded with the soft sands of Mahaiula Beach. Turtles love to sun on this shore, but please retain a respectful distance. A moderately long hike along an *aa* (rocky lava) path takes you all the way to Kua Bay, on the other side of the park. Local surfers and body boarders love the challenge of the rough waves in winter.

PAPAKOLEA (GREEN SANDS BEACH)

This isolated beach at the southern tip of the island came into being thanks to a volcano. Olivine crystals, a semiprecious mineral born of volcanic eruptions, give the sand the famous green hue. Sure it's a 2½-mile hike (one way) from remote South Point Road, but where else are you going to experience a beach with green sand? Come prepared with water, wear sturdy, comfortable shoes, and swim only in the calmest of conditions.

KAMAKAHONU BEACH (KING KAM BEACH)

In the heart of Kailua-Kona, this gentle spot of sand and surf makes the perfect place for kids and babies. Sometimes known by locals as Kona's "baby beach," Kamakahonu means "eye of the turtle" and was named for a large rock formation now buried by the pier. It fronts the Courtyard King Kamehameha's Kona Beach Hotel.

HONOLII BEACH PARK

This scenic beach park is pure gold to east-side surfers. A couple miles north of Hilo, the cove is surrounded by lush tropical foliage. Because of its constant year-round swells (more vigorous in winter), Honolii regularly hosts local surf contests. It's not particularly favorable for swimming, however, due to murky waters fed by the nearby river mouth, as well as some strong rip currents and other dangerous conditions.

RICHARDSON OCEAN PARK

This black-sand beach park south of town is probably the best beach in the Hilo area. Not only are there protected sections of lava outcrops that make it a good spot for snorkeling, but the vistas from here are also superb. You can see Maunakea in the background as coconut palms line the beach area, giving it a postcard quality.

POHOIKI BLACK SAND BEACH

As the devastating Puna eruption made its way down to the treasured Puna coastline, it destroyed nearly all in its path, then set its sights on Pohoiki Bay, at that time a popular boat launch spot and picnic area. But then, the river of molten earth suddenly stopped, fingers of lava actually reaching only as far as the parking lot at next-door Issac Hale Beach Park, then a large black sand beach formed.

KAUNAOA (MAUNA KEA BEACH)

If you were given the job of painting a picture of the most scenic spot on the Big Island, your canvas might include this breathtaking crescent of white sand, lapped by extraordinarily clear waters and fronted by the Mauna Kea Beach Hotel, Autograph Collection.

Best Natural Wonders on the Big Island

KEALAKEKUA BAY STATE HISTORICAL PARK
One of the undisputed jewels of the entire state, Kealakekua Bay, a marine life conservation district, encompasses several miles of shimmering, crystal-clear aquamarine waters, bordered by a long, sloping *pali* (cliff) that ranges in color from emerald green to soft brown.

THURSTON LAVA TUBE
Estimated to be about 500 years old, this giant, easily accessible cavern presents a wonderful example of what happens when molten lava flows through a channel and then hardens around it, leaving a hollowed-out space. It's lush, porous, and damp inside, and the first portion is even lit.

WAILUKU RIVER STATE PARK
A short distance from downtown Hilo, 80-foot Rainbow Falls are part of the fearsome Wailuku River. Translating to "River of Destruction" in Hawaiian, this river is classified as a Class V rapid and is extremely dangerous.

AKAKA FALLS STATE PARK
Free-falling 442 feet into a deep gorge, Akaka Falls present some of the most dramatic and easily accessible waterfalls on Hawaii Island. A short, ½-mile hike through the lush rain forest offers unique views of the two different waterfalls.

HALEMAUMAU CRATER
This famous summit caldera, quiet since 2018, is home to an active lava lake that rises and falls over generations and sometimes even disappears. In early 2018, when all the lava withdrew within a month or two, a rift-zone eruption fired up in the Lower East Rift Zone, causing widespread destruction as well as expanding and deepening the crater.

MAUNAKEA
Reigning almost 14,000 feet above sea level, Maunakea invokes a plethora of superlatives. Not only is it the best place in the world for astronomy, but it's the tallest peak in the Hawaiian Islands. The mountain also boasts the state's only alpine lake, Lake Waiau. Only about 10 feet deep, it's replenished by permafrost from the last ice age, in which monstrous glaciers raked over the summit, leaving deep marks from passing rocks and stones.

MAUNA LOA
At 13,679 feet, Mauna Loa ("Long Mountain") is the largest active volcano on the planet, its flows comprising more than 50% of the Big Island's slopes. It's so huge and heavy that

it has created a sea floor depression in excess of 5 miles, just through its sheer mass. But for now, she rests.

POLOLU VALLEY

At the end of the Akoni Pule Highway, a steep, ½-mile hike leads to a fantastic black-sand beach, dotted with large boulders and surrounded by beautiful, sheer green cliffs. The beach has a contemplative quality, which is a good thing, because like all east-side beaches, the water is very rough and dangerous, while the scenery is beautiful.

2018 PUNA LAVA FLOWS

The island's newest land emerged in the middle of a quiet subdivision called Leilani Estates in May 2018. It is quite shocking to drive through what appears to be a dense, lush rain forest and suddenly come across a black, desolate landscape, replete with burned-out tree trunks and brush and with solid walls of lava blocking the road like a commanding fortress built by Pele herself, the Hawaiian volcano goddess.

WAIPIO VALLEY

Whichever way you choose to explore it—on horseback, in a four-wheel drive, or on foot—you'll discover that the Valley of the Kings, on the Hamakua Coast, is full of sky-high waterfalls, lush green cliffs, and a mystical quality that can't quite be described or rivaled.

What to Eat and Drink in Hawaii

SHAVE ICE

Shave ice is simple in its composition—fluffy ice drizzled in Technicolor syrups. Shave ice traces its roots to Hawaii's plantation past. Japanese laborers would use the machetes from their field work to finely shave ice from large frozen blocks and then pour fruit juice over it.

MUSUBI

Musubi are Hawaii's answer to the perfect snack. Portable, handheld, and salty, musubi are a great go-to any time of day. The local comfort food is a slice of Spam encased in packed white rice and snugly wrapped with nori, or dried seaweed. Available everywhere, musubi are usually just a few dollars.

MAI TAI

When people think of a Hawaiian cocktail, the colorful Mai Tai often comes to mind. It's the unofficial drink to imbibe at a luau and refreshingly tropical. This potent concoction has a rum base and is traditionally made with orange curaçao, orgeat, fresh squeezed lime juice, and simple syrup.

HAWAIIAN PLATE

The Hawaiian plate comprises the delicious, traditional foods of Hawaii, all on one heaping plate. You can find these combo meals anywhere from roadside lunch wagons to five-star restaurants. Get yours with the melt-in-your-mouth shredded kalua pig, pork, or chicken *laulau* (cooked in ti leaves) with *lomi* salmon (diced salmon with tomatoes and onions) on the side and the coconut-milk haupia for dessert. Most Hawaiian plates come with the requisite two scoops of white rice. Don't forget to try *poi*, or pounded and cooked taro. For an authentic plate, visit Helena's Hawaiian Food on Oahu; just be sure to get there early.

POKE

In Hawaiian, *poke* is a verb that means to slice and cut into pieces. It perfectly describes the technique Hawaiians have used for centuries to prepare poke the dish. The cubed raw fish, most commonly ahi, or tuna, is traditionally tossed with Hawaiian sea salt, imu kohu, seaweed, inamona, or crushed, roasted kukui nuts. Today, there are countless varieties of poke across the Islands. It's a must try when visiting Hawaii. On Oahu, Ono Seafood, a no-frills, take-out eatery serves made-to-order poke.

MANAPUA

When *kamaaina*, or Hawaii residents, are invited to a potluck, business meeting, or even an impromptu party, you'll inevitably see a box filled with manapua.

Inside these airy white buns are pockets of sweet char siu pork. Head to Oahu's Chinatown in Honolulu, and you'll find Chinese restaurants with manapua on their menus, as well as manapua take-out places serving a variety of fillings. There's sweet potato, curry chicken, *lup cheong* (or Chinese sausage), even sweet flavors such as custard and ube, a purple yam popular in Filipino desserts.

SAIMIN
This only-in-Hawaii noodle dish is the culinary innovation of Hawaii plantation workers in the late 1800s who created a new comfort food with ingredients and traditions from their home countries.

LOCO MOCO
Loco moco is one of Hawaii's classic comfort-food dishes. The traditional loco moco consists of white rice topped with a hamburger patty and fried eggs and generously blanketed in rich, brown gravy. Cafe 100 in Hilo on Hawaii Island is renowned as the home of the loco moco. The 74-year-old café's original loco moco is one of the most popular, and at the amazing price of $4.35.

KONA COFFEE
In Kona, on Hawaii Island, coffee reigns supreme. There are roughly 600 coffee farms dotting the west side of the island, each producing flavorful coffee grown in the rich, volcanic soil. Kona coffee is typically harvested from August to December.

MALASADA
Malasadas are a beloved treat in Hawaii. The Portuguese pastries are about the size of a baseball and are airy, deep-fried, and dusted with sugar. In Honolulu, on Oahu, Lenard's Bakery is a well-known purveyor of these delicious desserts.

Flora and Fauna in Hawaii

KUKUI

The kukui, or candlenut, is Hawaii's state tree. Hawaiians had many uses for kukui. Oil was extracted from its nuts and burned as a light source and also rubbed on fishing nets to preserve them. The juice from the husk's fruit was used as a dye. The small kukui blossoms and nuts also had medicinal purposes.

PLUMERIA

This fragrant flower is named after Charles Plumier, the noted French botanist who discovered it in Central America in the late 1600s. Plumeria come in shades of white, yellow, pink, red, and orange. The hearty, plentiful blossoms are frequently used in lei.

HUMPBACK WHALES

Each year, North Pacific humpback whales make the long journey to Hawaii from Alaska. With its warm waters, Hawaii's shores provide the ideal place for the marine mammals to mate, birth, and nurse their young. They arrive between November and May, and their presence is an anticipated event for many. You can see them up close during whale-watching boat tours.

GARDENIA

The gardenia is a favorite for lei makers because of its sweet smell. The plant is native to tropical regions throughout China and Africa, but there are also endemic gardenia in Hawaii. The nanu gardenia are found only in the Islands and have petite white blossoms.

HONU

The honu, or Hawaiian green sea turtle, is a magical sight. The graceful reptile is an endangered and protected species in Hawaii. It's easier to run across honu during a snorkeling or scuba diving excursion, but they occasionally can be spotted coming to the ocean's surface.

MONK SEAL
Known as the *ilio holo I ka uaua*, or, "dog that runs in rough water," monk seals are endemic to Hawaii and critically endangered. Most of these mammals, which can grow more than seven feet long and weigh up to 600 pounds, live in remote, uninhabited Northwestern Hawaiian Islands.

TROPICAL FISH
Approximately 25% of the fish species in the Islands are endemic. Snorkeling in Hawaii is a unique, fun opportunity to see colorful fish, big and small. Interestingly, Hawaii's state fish, the tongue-twister *humuhumunukunukuapuaa*, or reef trigger, is not endemic to the state.

NENE GOOSE
Pronounced *nay-nay*, the endemic nene goose (the state bird) is the rarest in the world. Thanks to preservation efforts, the goose, which is a descendent of the Canadian goose, has been bred back from the edge of extinction and reintroduced into the wild.

HIBISCUS
In 1923, the Territory of Hawaii passed a law designating hibiscus as Hawaii's official flower. While there are more than 30 introduced species of the large, colorful flowers throughout the Islands, there are five endemic types. In Hawaiian, the endemic hibiscus has yellow blossoms and is known as mao hau hele, which means the "traveling green tree."

PIKAKE
These small, delicate blossoms are known for their hypnotic sweet scent. The jasmine flower was introduced from India and was a favorite of Princess Kaiulani. Pikake, which is the Hawaiian word for the blossom as well as peacock—another favorite of the princess—is the subject of many mele or Hawaiian songs.

What to Buy in Hawaii

MACADAMIA NUT CANDY

Macadamia are native to Australia, but the gumball-sized nut remains an important crop in Hawaii. It was first introduced in the late 1880s as a windbreak for sugar cane crops. Today, mac nuts, as they are colloquially known, are a popular local food, especially in desserts. They are easily found at convenience and grocery stores.

LEI

As a visitor to Hawaii, you will likely receive a lei, either a shell, kukui nut, or the fragrant flower variety, as a welcome to the Islands. Kamaaina or Hawaii residents mark special occasions by gifting lei.

ALOHA WEAR

Aloha wear in Hawaii has come a long way from the cheap fabrics with the too bright and kitsch patterns (although those still exist). Local designers have been creating stylish, modern Aloha shirts, dresses, and more with soft, sleek prints that evoke Island botanicals, heritage, and tradition. Hawaii residents sport Aloha wear for everything from work to weddings.

LAUHALA

The hala tree is most known for its long, thin leaves and the masterful crafts that are created from them. Lauhala weavers make baskets, hats, mats, jewelry, and more, using intricate patterns.

JEWELRY

Island-inspired jewelry is a unique and personalized gift. There are several styles from which to choose, including pieces featuring Tahitian pearls, shells like the dainty orange and pink sunrise shell, and gold Hawaiian heirloom necklaces and bangles with black Old English lettering.

KONA COFFEE

Reminiscence about your wonderful Hawaii getaway each time you brew a cup of Kona coffee. Authentic Kona coffee is renowned throughout the world for its heady aroma and full-bodied flavor. Stores and cafés sell bags of varying sizes.

BIG ISLAND HONEY

With its temperate climate and bountiful foliage, honeybees love Hawaii. The island's unique ecosystem results in robust honey flavors, including the nutty macadamia nut blossom honey or the ohia lehua variety, made from the endemic tree.

KOA WOOD

If you're looking for an heirloom keepsake from the Islands, consider a Koa wood product. Grown only in Hawaii, the valuable Koa wood is some of the world's rarest and hardest wood. Hawaiians traditionally made surfboards and canoes from Koa trees.

HAWAIIAN SEA SALT

A long tradition of harvesting salt beds by hand continues today on the islands of Kauai and Molokai. The salt comes in various colors, including inky black and brick red; these distinctive colors come from the salt reacting and mixing with activated charcoal and alaea, or volcanic clay.

UKULELE

In Hawaiian, *ukulele* means "the jumping flea." The small instrument made its way to the Islands in the 1880s via Portuguese immigrants who brought with them the four-string, guitar-like machete. It is renowned as a solo instrument today, with artists like Jake Shimabukuro and Taimane Gardner popularizing it.

Kids and Families

With dozens of adventures, discoveries, and fun-filled beach days, Hawaii is a blast with kids. Even better, the things to do here don't appeal only to small fry. The entire family, parents included, will enjoy surfing, discovering a waterfall in the rain forest, and snorkeling with sea turtles. And there are plenty of organized activities for kids that will give parents time for a few romantic beach strolls.

CHOOSING A PLACE TO STAY

Resorts: Most of the big resorts make kids' programs a priority, and it shows. When you are booking your room, ask about "kids eat free" deals and the number of kids' pools at the resort. Also check out the size of the groups in the children's programs, and find out whether the cost of the programs includes lunch, equipment, and activities.

The Hilton Waikoloa Village is every kid's fantasy vacation come true, with multiple pool slides, a lagoon for snorkeling, and even a choice between riding a monorail or taking a boat to your room. Not to be outdone, the Four Seasons Resort Hualalai has a great program that will keep your little ones happy and occupied all day.

Condos: Condo and vacation rentals are a fantastic value for families vacationing in Hawaii. You can cook your own food, which is cheaper than eating out and sometimes easier (especially if you have a finicky eater in your group), and you'll get twice the space of a hotel room for about a quarter of the price. If you decide to go the condo route, be sure to ask about the size of the complex's pool (some try to pass off a tiny soaking tub as a pool) and whether barbecues are available. One of the best reasons to stay in your own place is to hold a sunset family barbecue by the pool or overlooking the ocean. New regulations apply for

vacation rentals now, so make sure the one you book is permitted.

Condos in Kailua-Kona (on or near Alii Drive) are the some of the best values on the Big Island. We like Casa de Emdeko for its oceanfront pool and on-site convenience store. On the Kohala Coast, the Vista Waikoloa complex provides extra-large condos and is walking distance to beautiful Anaehoomalu Bay. Affordable food is available at restaurants in Kona, if you are looking for a family night out or, even better, a date night.

OCEAN ACTIVITIES

On the Beach: Most people like being in the water, but toddlers and school-age kids tend to be especially enamored of it. The swimming pool at your condo or hotel is always an option, but don't be afraid to hit the beach with a little one in tow. There are lots of family-friendly beaches on the Big Island, complete with protected bays and pleasant white sand. As always, use your judgment, and heed all posted signs and lifeguard warnings.

Calm beaches to try include Kamakahonu Beach and Kahaluu Beach Park in Kailua-Kona; Spencer Beach Park and Waialea Bay in Puako; and Onekahakaha Beach Park in Hilo.

On the Waves: Surf lessons are a great idea for older kids. Beginner lessons are always on safe and easy waves. Most surf schools also offer instruction in stand-up paddleboarding.

For school-age and older kids, book a four-hour surfing lesson with Kahaluu Bay Surf and Sea and either join the kids out on the break or say aloha to a little parents-only time.

The Underwater World: If your kids are ready to try snorkeling, Hawaii is a great place to introduce them to the underwater world. Even without the mask and snorkel, they'll be able to see colorful fish darting this way and that below the surface of the water, and they may also spot turtles at many of the island's bays.

The easily accessible Kahaluu Beach, in Kailua-Kona, is a great introductory snorkel spot because of its many facilities. Protected by a natural breakwater, these shallow reefs attract large numbers of sea creatures, including the Hawaiian green sea turtle. These turtles feed on seaweed near shore and sometimes can be spotted basking on the rocks.

Near the southern tip of the island, Punaluu Black Sand Beach provides opportunities to see sea turtles up close. Though the water can be rough, hawksbill turtles nest here, and there are nearly always one or two napping on the beach. Please heed signs and don't get too close. These animals are endangered and protected. At nighttime, head to the Sheraton Kona Resort and Spa at Keauhou Bay or Huggo's on the Rocks in Kailua-Kona to view manta rays; each place shines a bright spotlight on the water to attract them. Anyone, but especially kids, could sit and watch them glide through the ocean in graceful circles for hours. No snorkel required!

Another great option is to book a snorkel cruise or opt to stay dry inside the Atlantis Submarine that operates out of Kailua-Kona. Kids love crawling down into a real-life submarine and viewing the ocean world through its little portholes.

LAND ACTIVITIES

In addition to beach experiences, Hawaii Island has easy waterfall hikes, botanical gardens, a zoo, and hands-on museums that will keep your kids entertained and out of the sun for a day.

Hawaii Volcanoes National Park is a must for any family vacation. Even phone-addicted teenagers will acknowledge the coolness of lava tubes, steaming volcanic craters, and a fiery nighttime lava show (when they happen).

On the Hilo side, the Panaewa Rain Forest Zoo is small but free and lots of fun for the little ones, with a small petting zoo on Saturday. Your kids might even get to hold a Hawaiian hawk. Just a few miles north, on the Hamakua Coast, the Hawaii Tropical Botanical Garden makes a beautiful and fun stop for kids, filled with huge lily pads and noisy frogs.

School-age and older kids will get a kick out of Hamakua Coast ATV tours with Maunkea ATV Trails and horseback rides past the waterfalls of Waipio Valley via Waipio on Horseback.

AFTER DARK

At night, younger kids get a kick out of attending a luau, and many of the shows incorporate young audience members, adding to the fun. Teens and adults alike are sure to enjoy the music and overall theatrical quality of all of the island's luau shows, which are produced by serious practitioners of all the Polynesian native dance styles.

Stargazing from Maunakea is another treat. The visitor center has telescopes set up for all visitors to use. If you'd rather leave the planning to someone else, book a tour with Hawaii Forest and Trail. Its unbelievably knowledgeable guides are great at sharing that knowledge in a narrative form that kids—and adults, for that matter—enjoy. And everyone enjoys the hot chocolate and cookies served during the star talk.

The History of Hawaii

Hawaiian history is long and complex; a brief survey can put into context the ongoing renaissance of native arts and culture.

THE POLYNESIANS

Long before both Christopher Columbus and the Vikings, Polynesian seafarers set out to explore the vast stretches of the open ocean in double-hulled canoes. They didn't just flail around and land here by accident; they understood the deep nuances of celestial navigation and were masters of the craft. From western Polynesia, they traveled back and forth between Samoa, Fiji, Tahiti, the Marquesas, and the Society Isles, settling on the outer reaches of the Pacific, Hawaii and Easter Island, as early as AD 300. The golden era of Polynesian voyaging peaked around AD 1200, after which the distant Hawaiian Islands were left to develop their own unique cultural practices and subsistence in relative isolation.

The Islands' symbiotic society was deeply intertwined with religion, mythology, science, and artistry. Ruled by an *alii*, or chief, each settlement was nestled in an *ahupuaa*, a pie-shaped land division from the uplands, through the valleys, and down to the shores. Everyone contributed, whether it was by building canoes, catching fish, making tools, or farming land, thereby developing a sustainable society.

A UNITED KINGDOM

When the British explorer Captain James Cook arrived in Kealakekua Bay in 1778, he was greeted by the Hawaiians as a person of important stature. With guns and ammunition purchased from subsequent foreign trading ships, the Big Island chief, Kamehameha the Great, gained a significant advantage over the other *alii* (chiefs). He united Hawaii into one kingdom in 1810, bringing an end to the frequent interisland battles that dominated Hawaiian life.

Tragically, the new kingdom was beset with troubles. Native religion was abandoned, and *kapu* (laws and regulations) were eventually abolished. The European explorers brought diseases with them, and within a few decades the Native Hawaiian population was decimated.

New laws regarding land ownership and religious practices eroded the underpinnings of pre-contact Hawaii. Each successor to the Hawaiian throne sacrificed more control over the Island kingdom. As Westerners permeated Hawaiian culture, so did social unrest.

MODERN HAWAII

In 1893, the last Hawaiian monarch, Queen Liliuokalani, was overthrown by a group of Americans and European businessmen and government officials, aided by an armed militia. This led to the creation of the Republic of Hawaii, and it became a U.S. territory for the next 60 years. The loss of Hawaiian sovereignty and the conditions of annexation have haunted the Hawaiian people since the monarchy was deposed.

Pearl Harbor was attacked in 1941, which engaged the United States immediately into World War II. Tourism, from its beginnings in the early 1900s, flourished after the war and naturally inspired rapid real estate development in Waikiki. In 1959, Hawaii officially became the 50th state.

HAWAIIAN CULTURAL
TRADITIONS HULA, LEI, AND LUAU

HULA: MORE THAN A FOLK DANCE

Hula has been called "the heartbeat of the Hawaiian people" and also "the world's best-known, most misunderstood dance." Both are true. Hula isn't just dance. It is storytelling.

Chanter Edith McKinzie calls it "an extension of a piece of poetry." In its adornments, implements, and customs, hula integrates every important Hawaiian cultural practice: poetry, history, genealogy, craft, plant cultivation, martial arts, religion, protocol. So when 19th-century Christian missionaries sought to eradicate a practice they considered depraved, they threatened more than just a folk dance.

With public performance outlawed and private hula practice discouraged, hula went underground for a generation. The fragile verbal link by which culture was transmitted from teacher to student hung by a thread. Even increasing literacy did not help because hula's practitioners were a secretive and protected circle.

As if that weren't bad enough, vaudeville, Broadway, and Hollywood got hold of the hula, giving it the glitz treatment in an unbroken line from "Oh, How She Could Wicky Wacky Woo" to "Rock-A-Hula Baby." Hula became shorthand for paradise: fragrant flowers, lazy hours. Ironically, this development assured that hundreds of Hawaiians could make a living performing and teaching hula. Many danced *auana* (modern form) in performance; but taught *kahiko* (traditional), quietly, at home or in hula schools.

Today, decades after the cultural revival known as the Hawaiian Renaissance, language immersion programs have assured a new generation of proficient chanters, songwriters, and translators. Visitors can see more, and more authentic, traditional hula than at any other time in the last 200 years.

Like the culture of which it is the beating heart, hula has survived.

Lei *poo*. Head lei. In *kahiko*, greenery only. In auana, flowers.

Face emotes appropriate expression. Dancer should not be a smiling automaton.

Shoulders remain relaxed and still, never hunched, even with arms raised. No bouncing.

Eyes always follow leading hand.

Lei. Hula is rarely performed without a shoulder lei.

Arms and hands remain loose, relaxed, below shoulder level—except as required by interpretive movements.

Traditional hula skirt is loose fabric, smocked and gathered at the waist.

Hip is canted over weight-bearing foot.

Knees are always slightly bent, accentuating hip sway.

Kupee. Ankle bracelet of flowers, shells, or foliage.

In kahiko, feet are flat. In auana, they may be more arched, but not tiptoes or bouncing.

BASIC MOTIONS

Speak or Sing

Moon or Sun

Grass Shack or House

Mountains or Heights

Love or Caress

At backyard parties, hula is performed in bare feet and street clothes, but in performance, adornments play a key role, as do rhythm-keeping implements such as the pahu drum and the *ipu* (gourd).

In hula *kahiko* (traditional style), the usual dress is multiple layers of stiff fabric (often with a pellom lining, which most closely resembles *kapa*, the paperlike bark cloth of the Hawaiians). These wrap tightly around the bosom but flare below the waist to form a skirt. In pre-contact times, dancers wore only kapa skirts. Men traditionally wear loincloths.

Monarchy-period hula is performed in voluminous muumuu or high-necked muslin blouses and gathered skirts. Men wear white or gingham shirts and black pants.

In hula *auana* (modern), dress for women can range from grass skirts and strapless tops to contemporary tea-length dresses. Men generally wear aloha shirts, but sometimes grass skirts over pants or even everyday gear.

SURPRISING HULA FACTS

■ Grass skirts are not traditional; workers from Kiribati (the Gilbert Islands) brought this custom to Hawaii.

■ In olden-day Hawaii, *mele* (songs) for hula were composed for every occasion—name songs for babies, dirges for funerals, welcome songs for visitors, celebrations of favorite pursuits.

■ Hula *mai* is a traditional hula form in praise of a noble's genitals; the power of the *alii* (royalty) to procreate gave mana (spiritual power) to the entire culture.

■ Hula students in old Hawaii adhered to high standards: scrupulous cleanliness, no sex, daily cleansing rituals, certain food prohibitions, and no contact with the dead. They were fined if they broke the rules.

WHERE TO WATCH

If you're interested in "the real thing," there are annual hula festivals on each island. Check the individual island visitors' bureaus websites at ⊕ *www.gohawaii.com*.

If you can't make it to a festival, there are plenty of other hula shows—at most resorts, many lounges, and even at certain shopping centers. Ask your hotel concierge for performance information.

ALL ABOUT LEI

Lei brighten every occasion in Hawaii, from birthdays to bar mitzvahs to baptisms. Creative artisans weave nature's bounty—flowers, ferns, vines, and seeds—into gorgeous creations that convey an array of heartfelt messages: "Welcome," "Congratulations," "Good luck," "Farewell," "Thank you," "I love you." When it's difficult to find the right words, a lei expresses exactly the right sentiment.

WHERE TO BUY THE BEST LEI

Most airports in Hawaii have lei stands where you can buy a fragrant garland upon arrival. Every florist shop in the Islands sells lei; you can also treat yourself to a lei while shopping for provisions at any supermarket or box store. And you'll always find lei sellers at crafts fairs and outdoor festivals.

LEI ETIQUETTE

■ To wear a closed lei, drape it over your shoulders, half in front and half in back. Open lei are worn around the neck, with the ends draped over the front in equal lengths.

■ Pikake, ginger, and other sweet, delicate blossoms are "feminine" lei. Men opt for cigar, crown flower, and ti leaf lei, which are sturdier and don't emit as much fragrance.

■ Lei are always presented with a kiss, a custom that supposedly dates back to World War II when a hula dancer fancied an officer at a U.S.O. show. Taking a dare from members of her troupe, she took off her lei, placed it around his neck, and kissed him on the cheek.

■ You shouldn't wear a lei before you give it to someone else. Hawaiians believe the lei absorbs your mana (spirit); if you give your lei away, you'll be giving away part of your essence.

ORCHID

Growing wild on every continent except Antarctica, orchids—which range in color from yellow to green to purple—comprise the largest family of plants in the world. There are more than 20,000 species of orchids, but only three are native to Hawaii—and they are very rare. The pretty lavender vanda you see hanging by the dozens at local lei stands has probably been imported from Thailand.

MAILE

Maile, an endemic twining vine with a heady aroma, is sacred to Laka, goddess of the hula. In ancient times, dancers wore maile and decorated hula altars with it to honor Laka. Today, "open" maile lei usually are given to men. Instead of ribbon, interwoven lengths of maile are used at dedications of new businesses. The maile is untied, never snipped, for doing so would symbolically "cut" the company's success.

ILIMA

Designated by Hawaii's Territorial Legislature in 1923 as the official flower of the island of Oahu, the golden ilima is so delicate it lasts for just a day. Five to seven hundred blossoms are needed to make one garland. Queen Emma, wife of King Kamehameha IV, preferred ilima over all other lei, which may have led to the incorrect belief that they were reserved only for royalty.

PLUMERIA

This ubiquitous flower is named after Charles Plumier, the noted French botanist who discovered it in Central America in the late 1600s. Plumeria ranks among the most popular lei in Hawaii because it's fragrant, hardy, plentiful, inexpensive, and requires very little care. Although yellow is the most common color, you'll also find plumeria lei in shades of pink, red, orange, and "rainbow" blends.

PIKAKE

Favored for its fragile beauty and sweet scent, pikake was introduced from India. In lieu of pearls, many brides in Hawaii adorn themselves with long, multiple strands of white pikake. Princess Kaiulani enjoyed showing guests her beloved pikake and peacocks at Ainahau, her Waikiki home. Interestingly, pikake is the Hawaiian word for both the bird and the blossom.

KUKUI

The kukui (candlenut) is Hawaii's state tree. Early Hawaiians strung kukui nuts (which are quite oily) together and burned them for light; mixed burned nuts with oil to make an indelible dye; and mashed roasted nuts to consume as a laxative. Kukui nut lei may not have been made until after Western contact, when the Hawaiians saw black beads from Europe and wanted to imitate them.

LUAU: A TASTE OF HAWAII

The best place to sample Hawaiian food is at a backyard luau. Aunts and uncles are cooking, the pig is from a cousin's farm, and the fish is from a brother's boat.

But even locals have to angle for invitations to those rare occasions. So your choice is most likely between a commercial luau and a Hawaiian restaurant.

Some commercial luau are less authentic; they offer little of the traditional diet and are more about umbrella drinks, spectacle, and fun.

For greater culinary authenticity, folksy experiences, and rock-bottom prices, visit a Hawaiian restaurant (most are in anonymous storefronts in residential neighborhoods). Expect rough edges and some effort negotiating the menu.

In either case, much of what is known today as Hawaiian food would be as foreign to a 16th-century Hawaiian as risotto or chow mien. The pre-contact diet was simple and healthy—mainly raw and steamed seafood and vegetables. Early Hawaiians used earth ovens and heated stones to cook seafood, taro, sweet potatoes, and breadfruit and seasoned their food with sea salt and ground kukui nuts. Seaweed, fern shoots, sweet potato vines, coconut, banana, sugarcane, and select greens and roots rounded out the diet.

Successive waves of immigrants added their favorites to the ti leaf–lined table. So it is that foods as disparate as salt salmon and chicken long rice are now Hawaiian— even though there is no salmon in Hawaiian waters and long rice (cellophane noodles) is Chinese.

AT THE LUAU: KALUA PORK

The heart of any luau is the *imu*, the earth oven in which a whole pig is roasted. The preparation of an imu is an arduous affair for most families, who tackle it only once a year or so, for a baby's first birthday or at Thanksgiving, when many Islanders prefer to imu their turkeys. Commercial luau operations have it down to a science, however.

THE ART OF THE STONE
The key to a proper imu is the *pohaku*, the stones. Imu cook by means of long, slow, moist heat released by special stones that can withstand a hot fire without exploding. Many Hawaiian families treasure their imu stones, keeping them in a pile in the backyard and passing them on through generations.

PIT COOKING
The imu makers first dig a pit about the size of a refrigerator, then lay down *kiawe* (mesquite) wood and stones, and build a white-hot fire that is allowed to burn itself out. The ashes are raked away, and the hot stones covered with banana and ti leaves. Well-wrapped in ti or banana leaves and a net of chicken wire, the pig is lowered onto the leaf-covered stones. Laulau (leaf-wrapped bundles of meats, fish, and taro leaves) may also be placed inside. Leaves—ti, banana, even ginger—cover the pig followed by wet burlap sacks (to create steam). The whole is topped with a canvas tarp and left to steam for the better part of a day.

OPENING THE IMU
This is the moment everyone waits for: The imu is unwrapped like a giant present and the imu keepers gingerly wrestle out the steaming pig. When it's unwrapped, the meat falls moist and smoky-flavored from the bone, looking just like Southern-style pulled pork, but without the barbecue sauce.

WHICH LUAU?
Most resort hotels have luau on their grounds that include hula, music, and, of course, lots of food and drink. Each island also has at least one "authentic" luau. For lists of the best luau on each island, visit the Hawaii Visitors and Convention Bureau website at ⊕ *www.gohawaii.com*.

MEA AI ONO: GOOD THINGS TO EAT.

LAULAU
Steamed meats, fish, and taro leaf in ti-leaf bundles: fork-tender, a medley of flavors; the taro resembles spinach.

LOMI LOMI SALMON
Salt salmon in a piquant salad or relish with onions and tomatoes.

POI
Poi, a paste made of pounded taro root, may be an acquired taste, but it's a must-try during your visit.

Consider: The Hawaiian Adam is descended from *kalo* (taro). Young taro plants are called "keiki"–children. Poi is the first food after mother's milk for many Islanders. Ai, the word for food, is synonymous with poi in many contexts.

Not only that, we love it. "There is no meat that doesn't taste good with poi," the old Hawaiians said.

But you have to know how to eat it: with something rich or powerfully flavored. "It is salt that makes the poi go in," is another adage. When you're served poi, try it with a mouthful of smoky kalua pork or salty lomi lomi salmon. Its slightly sour blandness cleanses the palate. And if you don't like it, smile and say something polite. (And slide that bowl over to a local.)

Laulau

Lomi Lomi Salmon

Poi

E HELE MAI AI! COME AND EAT!

Local-style Hawaiian restaurants tend to be inconveniently located in well-worn store-fronts with little or no parking, outfitted with battered tables and clattering Melmac dishes, but they personify aloha, invariably run by local families who welcome tourists who take the trouble to find them.

Many are cash-only operations and combination plates, known as "plate lunch," are a standard feature: one or two entrées, two scoops of steamed rice, one scoop of macaroni salad, and—if the place is really old-style—a tiny portion of coarse Hawaiian salt and some raw onions for relish.

Most serve some foods that aren't, strictly speaking, Hawaiian, but are beloved of ka-maaina, such as salt meat with watercress (preserved meat in a tasty broth), or *akubone* (skipjack tuna fried in a tangy vinegar sauce).

Weddings and Honeymoons

There's no question that Hawaii is one of the country's foremost honeymoon destinations. Romance is in the air here, and the white-sand beaches, turquoise water, swaying palm trees, soft Hawaiian music, balmy tropical breezes, and perpetual sunshine put people in the mood for love. It's easy to understand why Hawaii is a popular wedding destination as well, especially as the cost of airfare is often discounted, and new resorts and hotels entice visitors. You can plan a traditional ceremony in a place of worship followed by a reception at an elegant resort, or you can go barefoot on the beach and celebrate at a luau. There are almost as many wedding planners in the Islands as real estate agents, which makes it oh-so-easy to wed in paradise and then, once the knot is tied, stay and honeymoon as well.

THE BIG DAY

Choosing the Perfect Place. When selecting a location, remember that you really have two choices to make: the ceremony location and where to have the reception, if you're having one. For the former, there are beaches, bluffs overlooking beaches, gardens, private residences, resort lawns, and, of course, places of worship. As for the reception, there are these same choices, as well as restaurants and even a luau. If you decide to go outdoors, remember the seasons—yes, Hawaii has seasons. If you're planning a summer wedding outdoors, be sure you have a backup plan (such as a tent) in case it rains. Also, if you're planning an outdoor wedding at sunset—which is very popular—be sure you match the time of your ceremony to the time the sun sets at that time of year. If you choose an indoor spot, be sure to ask for pictures of the location when you're planning. You don't want to plan a pink wedding, say, and wind up in a room that's predominantly red. Or maybe you do. The point is, it should be your choice.

Finding a Wedding Planner. If you're planning to invite more than an officiant and your loved one to your wedding ceremony, seriously consider an on-island wedding planner who can help select a location; help design the floral scheme and recommend a florist and photographer; help plan the menu and choose a restaurant, caterer, or resort; and suggest Hawaiian traditions to incorporate into your ceremony. And more: Will you need tents, a cake, music? Maybe transportation and lodging? Many planners have relationships with vendors providing packages—which mean savings.

If you're planning a resort wedding, most have on-site wedding coordinators; however, there are many independents around the Islands and even those who specialize in certain types of ceremonies—by locale, size, religious affiliation, and so on. A simple "Hawaii weddings" Google search will reveal dozens. What's important is that you feel comfortable with your coordinator. Ask for references and call them. Share your budget. Get a proposal—in writing. Ask how long they've been in business, how much they charge, how often you'll meet with them, and how they select vendors. Request a detailed list of the exact services they'll provide. If your idea of your wedding doesn't match their services, try someone else. If you can afford it, you might want to meet the planner in person.

Getting Your License. The good news about marrying in Hawaii is that there is no waiting period, no residency or citizenship requirement, and no blood test or shots required. You can apply and pay the fee online; however, both the bride and groom must appear together in person before a marriage-license agent to receive the marriage license (the permit to get married). You'll need proof of age—the legal age to marry is 18. (If you're 19 or older, a valid driver's license will suffice; if you're 18, a certified birth certificate is required.) Upon approval, a marriage license is immediately issued and costs $60 plus a $5 portal fee. After the ceremony, your officiant will mail the marriage certificate (proof of marriage) to the state. Approximately four months later, you will receive a copy in the mail. Applications are good for one year. For more detailed information, visit ⊕ *marriage.ehawaii.gov.*

Also—this is important—the person performing your wedding must be licensed by the Hawaii Department of Health, even if he or she is a licensed officiant. Be sure to ask.

Wedding Attire. In Hawaii, basically anything goes, from long, formal dresses with trains to white bikinis. Floral sundresses, or *pareus,* are fine, too. For men, tuxedos are not the norm; a pair of solid-colored slacks with a nice aloha shirt is. In fact, tradition in Hawaii for the groom is a beautiful white aloha shirt (they do exist) with slacks or long shorts and a colored sash around the waist. If you're planning a wedding on the beach, barefoot is the way to go.

If you decide to marry in a formal dress and tuxedo, you're better off making your selections on the mainland and hand-carrying them aboard the plane. Yes, it can be a pain, but ask your wedding-gown retailer to provide a special carrying bag. After all, you don't want to chance losing your wedding dress in a wayward piece of luggage. And when it comes to fittings, again, that's something to take care of before you arrive in Hawaii.

Local Customs. The most obvious traditional Hawaiian wedding custom is the lei exchange, in which the bride and groom take turns placing a lei around the neck of the other—with a kiss. Traditional leis for both bride and groom are created of fragrant and rare *maile,* a green leafy garland that drapes around the neck and is open at the ends. *Maile* leis should be ordered in advance and can be expensive. Check with your florist well in advance, especially if your wedding coincides with the timing of local events such as graduation or hula festivals. Brides often also wear a *haku* lei—a circular floral headpiece. Other Hawaiian customs include the blowing of the conch shell, hula, chanting, and Hawaiian music.

THE HONEYMOON

Do you want champagne and strawberries delivered to your room each morning? A breathtaking swimming pool in which to float? A five-star restaurant in which to dine? Then a resort is the way to go. If, however, you prefer the comforts of a home, try a bed-and-breakfast. A small inn is also good if you're on a tight budget or don't plan to spend much time in your room. On the other hand, maybe you want your own private home in which to romp freely—or just laze around recovering from the wedding festivities. Maybe you want your own kitchen so you can whip up a gourmet meal for your loved one. In that case, a private vacation-rental home is the answer. Or maybe a condominium resort. That's another beautiful thing about Hawaii: the lodging accommodations are almost as plentiful as the beaches, and there's one that will perfectly match your tastes and your budget.

Big Island's Best Farmers' Markets

The Big Island boasts a wealth of farmers' markets, each offering a different range of goods, but all providing at the very least a good place to pick up fresh produce, jarred goods such as jams and salsas, and homemade local Hawaiian treats. Not surprisingly, locally grown mango, papaya, pineapple, passion fruit, coconut, and guava are available in abundance at good prices, but you can also find delicious avocados, organic peppers, fantastic goat cheese, and, of course, coffee. Local handmade gifts abound, too.

Hawaii's farmers are experimenting with dozens of varieties of exotic fruits such as dragon fruit, poha berries, bilimbis, and mamey sapotes. Due to state government restrictions, these fruits generally can't leave the island, so this is your only chance to sample them.

Markets listed from north to south.

ON THE WEST SIDE

Under the Banyan Hawi Farmers' Market. Fresh produce, seasonal fruit, plants, and craft items are sold at this market way up north in the village of Hawi. It's open Saturday from 8 to 2 and on Tuesday from noon to 5.

Waimea Homestead Association Farmers' Market. Check out the crafts sold here in the Kuhio Hale Building before heading to Waimea's more expensive stores. Produce, flowers, plants, and baked goods are also available. It's open 7 to noon every Saturday.

Keauhou Farmers' Market. Live music and plenty of local color permeate this down-home farmers' market held every Saturday from 8 to noon in the parking lot of the Keauhou Shopping Center.

Pure Kona Green Market. This popular market features coffee, baked goods, and local honey and jams. Located at Amy B.

H. Greenwell Ethnobotanical Garden in Captain Cook, it runs Friday and Sunday from 9 to 2.

Kau Farmers' Market. On a trip to South Point, stock up on local produce and freshly baked pastries at this market held in front of the Shaka restaurant in Naalehu. It's open every Saturday from 8 to noon.

ON THE EAST SIDE

Hamakua Harvest Farmers' Market. This good old-fashioned farmers' market in the midst of a charming old plantation town of Honokaa is a good stop during a drive up the Hamakua Coast. It opens at 9 on Saturday.

Hilo Farmers Market. The biggest and best of the farmers' markets on the island runs Wednesday and Saturday 6 to 4.

Makuu Farmers' Market. There is not only food and produce here, but also Hawaiian crafts, plants, jewelry, shells, books, and secondhand clothing. It's along the Keaau/Pahoa Highway and is open Sunday 8 to 2.

Uncle Awa Bar and the Kalapana Night Market. This great market, held in Kalapana at the end of Highway 137, offers local produce, prepared foods, coffee, clothing, and live music from 5 pm to 9 pm every Wednesday.

Volcano Village Farmers' Market. This market sells local produce, fresh flowers, prepared foods, and baked goods and hosts an occasional clothing swap. It's held in the Cooper Center from 6 to 10 am on Sunday.

Top 5 Big Island Outdoor Adventures

Getting out for active adventure is one of the top reasons people come to the Big Island. There are endless options here for spending time outside and enjoying the land, the ocean, or the highest points of mountains and volcanoes. Here are a few of our favorites.

BIKE KULANI TRAILS
Stands of 80-foot eucalyptus. Giant *hapuu* tree ferns. The sweet song of honeycreepers overhead. Add a single track of rock and root—no dirt here—and we're talking technical. Did we mention this is a rain forest near Hilo? That explains the perennial slick coat of slime on every possible surface. This is for advanced cyclists only, and a permit is required.

SNORKEL AT KEALAKEKUA BAY
Yes, the snorkeling here is tops for the Big Island. Visibility reaches depths of 80 feet, and you'll spot colorful creatures swimming among jagged pinnacles and pristine coral habitats. But, to be real, the draw here is the Hawaiian spinner dolphins that come to rest in the bay during the daytime. While it's enticing to swim with wild dolphins, getting too close can disrupt their sleep cycles. Observe from a distance and respect their space while still enjoying a fantastic experience communing with nature.

HIKE THROUGH A STEAMING CRATER AT HAWAII VOLCANOES NATIONAL PARK
Lava may not be flowing on the island at the moment, but there are still plenty of wondrous sights to see in Hawaii Volcanoes National Park. Kilauea Iki Crater, located in the center of the park, last erupted spectacularly in 1959, the cone shooting astonishing 1,900-foot lava fountains into the air. One of the best hikes in the park, it takes you through the 4-mile loop trail, down the crater walls, and across an otherwordly landscape of a long-still lava lake dotted with steaming vents and alien-looking fumaroles. You climb up the crater wall through a zigzagging trail, ending back at the overlook.

GO HORSEBACK RIDING IN WAIPIO VALLEY
The Valley of the Kings owes its relative isolation and off-the-grid status to the 2,000-foot-high cliffs bookending the valley. Really, the only way to explore this sacred place is on two legs—or four. We're partial to the sanctioned horseback rides that wend deep into the rain forest to a series of waterfalls and pools—the setting for a perfect romantic photo op.

WITNESS WATERFALLS ON THE HILO SIDE
The east side of the Big Island—also called the Hilo side (as opposed to the western-facing Kona side)—is essentially a rain forest, with an average rainfall of 130 inches a year. It's no wonder Hilo is called the City of Rainbows—and all that rain means tons of waterfalls. Some of our favorites include Peepee Falls (Boiling Pots) and Rainbow Falls, both easy to access from main roads just above downtown Hilo.

What to Read and Watch

HAWAIIAN MYTHOLOGY, BY MARTHA BECKWITH

This exhaustive work of ethnology and folklore was researched and collected by Martha Beckwith over decades and published when she was 69. *Hawaiian Mythology* is a comprehensive look at the Hawaiian ancestral deities and their importance throughout history.

HAWAII'S STORY BY HAWAII'S QUEEN, BY LILIUOKALANI

This poignant book, by Queen Liliuokalani, chronicles the 1893 overthrow of the Hawaiian monarchy and her plea for her people. It's an essential read to understand the political undercurrent and the push for sovereignty that exists in the Islands more than 125 years later.

MARK TWAIN'S LETTERS FROM HAWAII, BY MARK TWAIN

When Samuel Clemens was 31 in 1866, he sailed from California and spent four months in Hawaii. He eventually mailed 25 letters to the *Sacramento Union* newspaper about his experiences. Along the way, Twain sheds some cultural biases as he visits the Kilauea volcano, meets with Hawaii's newly formed legislators, and examines the sugar trade.

SHOAL OF TIME: A HISTORY OF THE HAWAIIAN ISLANDS, BY GAVAN DAWS

Perhaps the most popular book of this best-selling Honolulu author is *Shoal of Time*. Published in 1974, this account of modern Hawaiian history details the colonization of Hawaii and everything that was lost in the process.

MOLOKAI, BY ALAN BRENNERT

Alan Brennert's debut novel, set in the 1890s, follows a Hawaiian woman who contracts leprosy as a child and is sent to the remote, quarantined community of Kalaupapa on the island of Molokai where she then lives. The Southern California–based author was inspired to write the book during his visits to Hawaii.

THE DESCENDANTS

Based on the book by local author, Kaui Hart Hemmings, the film adaptation starring George Clooney and directed by Alexander Payne was filmed on Oahu and Kauai. It spotlights a contemporary, if not upper-class, family in Hawaii as they deal with family grief and landholdings in flux.

50 FIRST DATES

The majority of this 2004 Drew Barrymore–Adam Sandler rom-com was shot on Oahu. While the plot is simultaneously cute and cheesy, *50 First Dates* highlights the beauty of Hawaii. You can pick out several picturesque island places, including the rolling Kualoa Ranch and Waimanalo, Makapuu, and Kaneohe Bay, all on Oahu's rustic east side.

BLUE HAWAII

The 1961 musical features the hip-shaking songs and moves by Elvis Presley, who plays tour guide Chadwick Gates. Elvis famously sings *Ke Kali Nei Au*, or *The Hawaiian Wedding Song*, at the iconic and now-shuttered Coco Palms Resort on Kauai. (The resort has remained closed since 1992 following Hurricane Iniki.)

MOANA

The release of *Moana* in 2016 was celebrated by many in Hawaii and the Pacific for showcasing Polynesian culture. The now-beloved animated movie, which includes the story of the demigod Maui, features the voice talents of Aulii Cravalho and Dwayne Johnson. In 2018, *Moana* was re-recorded and distributed in Olelo Hawaii, or the Hawaiian language, with Cravalho reprising her role. It marked the first time a Disney movie was available in Hawaiian.

Chapter 2

TRAVEL SMART

Updated by
Karen Anderson

★ **MAJOR CITIES**
Kailua-Kona, Hilo

👥 **POPULATION:**
201,000 (Big Island); 1,416,589 (Hawaii)

💬 **LANGUAGES:**
English, Hawaiian

$ **CURRENCY:**
U.S. dollar

☎ **AREA CODE:**
808

⚠ **EMERGENCIES:**
911

🚗 **DRIVING:**
On the right

⚡ **ELECTRICITY:**
120–220 v/60 cycles; plugs have two or three rectangular prongs

🕐 **TIME:**
Five or six hours behind New York, depending on time of year

🌐 **WEB RESOURCES:**
GoHawaii.com, Hawaii.com, LoveBigIsland.com

✈ **AIRPORTS:**
Ellison Onizuka Kona International Airport (KOA); Hilo International Airport (ITO)

KAUAI

NIIHAU

OAHU

HONOLULU

MOLOKAI

LANAI

MAUI

KAHOOLAWE

Hawi

Hilo

Kailua-Kona

Pahoa

BIG ISLAND OF HAWAII

PACIFIC OCEAN

Know Before You Go

COVID-19

All tourism to Hawaii shut down for several months in early 2020 due to the COVID-19. It's likely that the impact to the local economy will continue through much of 2020 and perhaps into 2021.

DRIVING ON THE BIG ISLAND

The Big Island is big, which means the average drive to get from Point A to Point B can take some time. If you're on the Kona side and are planning a day-trip to Hawaii Volcanoes National Park, know that the round trip could take at least five hours of drive time. Conversely, if you're staying in Hilo and want to check out the best sand beaches on the island, you'll have to drive across "the Saddle" to the South Kohala resort beaches, which are a minimum 1½-hour drive away. Many visitors make the mistake of trying to cram too many sights into a week-long stay. Take a day or two to relax, unwind, and appreciate the offerings that are right in front of you instead of spending all your time in the car.

CAN I STILL SEE ACTIVE LAVA FLOWS?

The short answer is no, because all active lava flows from Kilauea Volcano came to a complete stop in summer 2018 after a months-long eruption that began in May 2018 and changed Lower Puna forever. This is a dramatic shift from the decades-long continuous eruption that began in 1983 from the Puu Oo Vent on Kilauea Volcano, when relatively slow-moving lava oozed down the southwestern flanks of the island into places like Kalapana and the Royal Gardens subdivision and into the ocean. During that span of time, lava viewing, whether by land, boat, or air, was a sight to behold, as was the lava lake at the summit, which awed visitors nightly for 10 straight years with an otherworldly glow that lit up the dark expanse of the Kilauea Caldera below the Jaggar Museum. There was a downside to all the activity, however. Although Pele's lava flows put on quite a show, the gases emitted from the craters also produced lots of vog (volcanic smog) that drifted westward and blanketed the Kona side with haze. Now that the lava has stopped for the foreseeable future, the upsides for Kona are the crystal-clear, vog-free, blue-sky days and glorious, clear-sky starry nights. Pele may have ceased her fiery show for now, but there are still plenty of steaming craters, steam vents, and sights to appreciate at Hawaii Volcanoes National Park, not to mention beautiful, unobstructed ocean views.

WEATHER

Of all the islands in the Hawaiian Islands chain, the Big Island is the most diverse in terms of weather. The variety of elevations and the vast expanse of differing topography produce a range of weather patterns that can vary from one town to the next on any given day. Take, for example, the seaside enclave of Puako near Kawaihae in South Kohala. Here, it can get searing hot and windy one moment, while just a 15-minute drive up the highway in Waimea, it could be "sweater weather." Some areas of the Big Island are incredibly rainy, like the entire town of Hilo, while other areas stay relatively arid, such as the resort zones in South Kohala. At the higher elevations, such as in Volcano, it can get downright bone-chilling, with temperatures dropping into the low 40s on some nights. Pack accordingly and bring layers.

POPULAR ACTIVITIES

The Big Island is well known for deep-sea fishing and is also a golfer's island. It's also popular for snorkeling, kayaking, and scuba diving; the visibility is amazing. If you book a nighttime manta-ray dive, you will likely see some majestic manta rays up close in Keauhou Bay.

In winter, you might see the spouts of migrating humpback whales just off the coast. All year round, spinner dolphins make their home close to shore. Turtle-watching is another exciting pursuit at beaches such as Punaluu Black Sand Beach in Kau.

FESTIVALS YEAR-ROUND

From the Kona Brew Fest and the Merrie Monarch Festival to the Kona Coffee Cultural Festival, Kona Chocolate Festival, Waimea Cherry Blossom Heritage Festival, and many more, festivals happen year-round on the Big Island and can be a highlight of a trip. One of the most prestigious annual events in the state of Hawaii, the Merrie Monarch Festival takes place in Hilo in mid-April and attracts thousands for hula competitions.

BEACH TREKS

Because of its rocky shorelines and lava-laden coasts, the Big Island of Hawaii has fewer sand beaches than Maui or Oahu. Fortunately, some of the Big Island's best beaches are also some of the best beaches in Hawaii. Reef walkers are essential for getting in and out of the water over potentially rocky entries, or for walking along the shoreline and exploring tide pools. Pack a rash guard that is lightweight and can protect you from harmful UV rays. Reef-safe sunscreen is also essential.

INSECTS, PESTS, AND MOSQUITOES

It's the tropics, so don't be surprised if you encounter an extra-large flying cockroach at night or the occasional mosquito buzzing around you during the day. Pack insect repellent and anti-itch spray. A rare but emerging disease in Hawaii, rat lungworm disease, can be contracted by accidental consumption of a slug or slug residue hidden in lettuce or other types of vulnerable produce. Never eat fruit that you pick up off the ground. Think twice about eating locally grown lettuce unless it was grown hydroponically. Rat lungworm disease is a devastating affliction.

VACATION RENTAL BILL

In 2019, the County of Hawaii passed a new piece of legislation that regulates non-hosted vacation rentals that operate outside of the resort zones. To continue to operate in these zones, the owners of non-hosted vacation rentals have had to obtain nonconforming-use permits (among other requirements) from the county. Now that the law is in place, there are still plenty of permitted vacation rentals across the Big Island, contrary to Internet rumors. Hosted rentals (owner-occupied) are exempt from this bill if the owner or site manager resides on the property. You can book directly from the owner or through the traditional online platforms. Booking directly with the vacation rental owner through Houfy or Homescape eliminates the intermediary fees.

TRAVELING WITH YOUNGER KIDS

Traveling with young children can be a challenge, especially when it comes to keeping them entertained. Fortunately, there are lots of kid-friendly places to go on the Big Island. A great home base for family vacations, Waikoloa Beach Resort is the most kid-friendly vacation destination on the Big Island. Queens' MarketPlace offers daily free activities for the family, plus there's an excellent food court for easy family fare. Whether it's the giant waterslide or the waterfall swimming pools at the Hilton Waikoloa Village, or a family-friendly 9-hole putting course at the Kings' Shops, the entire Waikoloa Beach Resort area features lots of fun stuff for the *keiki* (children).

GREEN GECKOS

With their green bodies and tails, bright circular spots, and funny little toes, Madagascar gold-dust day geckos have proliferated on the Big Island since the early 1990s and will beg for food. As its name suggests, the day gecko comes out during the day, while other species of geckos come out at night.

Getting Here and Around

Air

Flying time to the Big Island is about 10 hours from New York; eight hours from Chicago; five hours from Los Angeles, Seattle, San Francisco, Oakland, Portland, and San Diego; and 15 hours from London, not including layovers. Some of the major airline carriers serving Hawaii fly direct to the Big Island, allowing you to bypass connecting flights out of Honolulu and Maui. If you're a more spontaneous traveler, island-hopping flights depart daily every 90 minutes or so.

Serving Kona are Air Canada, Alaska Airlines, American Airlines, Delta Airlines, Hawaiian Airlines, Japan Airlines, Mokulele, Southwest, United Airlines, Virgin Atlantic, and Westjet. Hawaiian Airlines, Mokulele, Southwest, and United fly into Hilo. Airlines schedule flights seasonally, meaning the number of daily flights—and sometimes the carriers themselves— vary according to demand.

Should you wish to visit neighboring islands, Hawaiian Airlines, Mokulele, and Southwest offer regular service. Prices for interisland flights have increased quite a bit in recent years, while flight schedule availability has been reduced. Mokulele also serves Waimea. Planning ahead is your best bet.

Big Island Air, in addition to offering air tours of the Big Island, offers charter service between all the Islands via a Cessna Caravan. Nine passengers can ride comfortably, and the charter has plenty of room for luggage.

Although the Big Island's airports are smaller and more casual than Honolulu International, during peak times they can also get quite busy. Allow extra travel time getting to all airports during morning and afternoon rush-hour traffic periods. Due to increased security measures, TSA screening can often become backed up. Plan to arrive at the airport 90 minutes before departure for interisland or domestic flights. If your interisland flight is part of an international itinerary, then you must check in to your interisland flight at least two hours prior.

Plants and plant products are restricted by the U.S. Department of Agriculture upon both entering and leaving Hawaii. When you leave the Islands, both checked and carry-on bags will be screened and tagged at the airport's agricultural inspection stations. Pineapples and coconuts with the packer's agricultural inspection stamp pass freely; papayas must be treated, inspected, and stamped. All other fruits are banned for export to the U.S. mainland. Flowers pass except for gardenias, rose leaves, jade vines, and maunaloa. Also banned are insects, snails, soil, cotton, cacti, sugarcane, and all berry plants.

Pet policies vary depending on the airline. If specific pre- and post-arrival requirements are met, animals may qualify for a 30-day or five-day-or-less quarantine; this includes service animals. The provision allows for direct release of the pet at a number of airports around the Islands (Kona, on the Big Island; also Honolulu, Lihue, and Kahului) if all requirements are met upon inspection. Hilo Airport does not have a direct-release program.

AIRPORTS

Daniel K. Inouye International Airport (HNL) is the main gateway for most domestic and international flights into Hawaii. From Honolulu, interisland flights to the Big Island depart regularly from early morning through mid-evening. From Honolulu, the travel time is about 35 minutes. From Maui, it's about 20 minutes.

Those flying to the Big Island regularly land at one of two fields. Ellison Onizuka

Kona International Airport at Keahole, on the west side, serves Kailua-Kona, Keauhou, the Kohala Coast, North Kohala, Waimea, and points south. There are Visitor Information Program (VIP) booths by all baggage-claim areas to assist travelers. Additionally, the airport offers news and lei stands, Laniakea by Centerplate (a café), and a small gift and sundries shop. A modernization project launched in 2017 (and still ongoing at this writing) aims to join the two terminals (now separate) so that baggage and passenger screening can be streamlined and retail options enhanced.

Hilo International Airport is more appropriate for those planning visits based on the east side of the island. Here, you'll find VIP booths across from the Centerplate Coffee Shop near the departure lobby and in the arrival areas at each end of the terminal. In addition to the coffee shop, services include a Bank of Hawaii ATM, a gift shop, newsstands, and lei stands.

Waimea-Kohala Airport, called Kamuela Airport by residents, is used primarily for private flights between islands but offers daily flights via Mokulele Airlines.

AIRPORT TRANSFERS

Check with your hotel to see if it runs an airport shuttle. If you're not renting a car, you can choose from multiple taxi companies serving the Hilo Airport. The approximate taxi rate is $3 for the initial 1/8th mile, plus $3 for each additional mile, with surcharges for waiting time (40¢ per minute) and baggage ($1 per bag) for up to six people. Call or calculate online for fares to popular destinations. The local Hele-On county bus also services the Hilo airport.

At the Kona airport, taxis are available. SpeediShuttle also offers transportation between the airport and hotels, resorts, and condominium complexes from Waimea to Keauhou. Uber and Lyft have designated pickup areas at the Kona and Hilo airports.

🚌 Bus

Although public transportation isn't very practical for the average vacationer, depending on where you're staying, you can take advantage of the affordable Hawaii County Mass Transit Agency's Hele-On Bus, which travels several routes throughout the island. Mostly serving local commuters, the Hele-On Bus costs $2 per person (students and senior citizens pay $1). Just wait at a scheduled stop for the next bus. A one-way journey between Hilo and Kona takes about four hours. There's regular service in and around downtown Hilo, Kailua-Kona, Waimea, North and South Kohala, Honokaa, and Pahoa. However, some routes are served only once a day, so if you are planning on using the bus, be sure to study up carefully before assuming the bus serves your area.

Visitors staying in Hilo can take advantage of the Transit Agency's Shared Ride Taxi program, which provides door-to-door transportation in the area. A one-way fare is $2, and a book of 15 coupons can be purchased for $30. Visitors to Kona can also take advantage of free trolleys operated by local shopping centers.

🚗 Car

It's essential to rent a car when visiting the Big Island. As the name suggests, it's a very big island, and it takes a while to get from one destination to another.

Fortunately, when you circle the island by car, you are treated to miles and miles

Getting Here and Around

of wondrous vistas of every possible description. In addition to using standard compass directions such as east and west, Hawaii residents often refer to places as being either *mauka* (toward the mountains) or *makai* (toward the ocean).

It's difficult to get lost along the main roads of the Big Island. Although their names may challenge the visitor's tongue, most roads are well marked; in rural areas look for mile marker numbers. Free publications containing basic road maps are given out at car rental agencies, but if you are doing a lot of driving, invest about $4 in the standard Big Island map available at local retailers. GPS might be unreliable in remote areas.

⚠ **Driving the roads on the Big Island can be dangerous, as there's no margin for error to avoid a head-on collision. Distracted drivers are all too common. Most roads and main highways are two lanes with no shoulders; if there is a shoulder to access, it might be riddled with rocks, debris, and potholes. Speeding and illegal passing are frequent occurrences along winding, remote roads. In addition, most roads are not well lit at night. Fatalities can happen at a moment's notice, whether on the main highway from the airport to the resorts, the Saddle Road, the upper road from Waimea to Hawi, or on the Hawaii Belt Road that wraps around the island. During Ironman week, cyclists pose additional potential hazards on all roads in West Hawaii. Use extreme caution when driving on the Big Island, and of course, do not drive after drinking.**

For those who want to travel from the west side to the east side, or vice versa, the rerouted and repaved Saddle Road, now known as the Daniel K. Inouye Highway, is a nice shortcut across the middle of the island. This is especially convenient if you are staying on the west side of the island and wish to visit the east side.

Hazardous conditions such as fog and speeding are common.

Turning right on a red light is legal, except where noted. Hawaii has a strict seat-belt law that applies to both drivers and passengers. The fine for not wearing a seat belt is $102. Mobile phone use is strictly limited to talking on a hands-free mobile device, and only for those over 18. Many police officers drive their own cars while on duty, strapping the warning lights to the roof. Because of the color, locals call them "blue lights."

GASOLINE
You can count on having to pay more at the pump for gasoline on the Big Island than almost anywhere on the U.S. mainland except for California. Prices average about $4 per gallon. Prices tend to be higher in Kailua-Kona and cheaper in Hilo. Gas stations can be few and far between in rural areas, and it's not unusual for them to close early. If you notice that your tank is getting low, don't take any chances: keep your tank filled.

PARKING
Parking can be limited in Historic Kailua Village. A few municipal lots near Alii Drive offer convenient parking on an honor system. (You'll be ticketed if you don't pay.) There is one free county lot downtown. In Hilo, you'll find plenty of free parking along the scenic bayfront.

ROAD CONDITIONS
Roads on the Big Island are generally well marked and can be easily accessed. Most of the roads are two-lane highways with limited shoulders—and yes, even in paradise, there is traffic, especially during the morning and afternoon rush hours and before and after school. There are several lighted intersections in downtown Kona and Hilo that are notorious for backed-up traffic no matter the time of day, so give yourself extra time if you

Car Rental Resources

Automobile Associations		
American Automobile Association	☎ 315/797–5000	⊕ www.aaa.com
Local Agencies		
AA Aloha Cars-R-Us	☎ 800/655–7989	⊕ www.hawaiicarrental.com
Big Island Motorcycle Co.	☎ 866/886–2011	⊕ www.thrillseekershawaii.com
Harper Car and Truck Rental (Big Island)	☎ 800/852–9993	⊕ www.harpershawaii.com
Hawaiian Discount Car Rentals	☎ 800/955–3142	⊕ www.hawaiidrive-o.com
Major Agencies		
Alamo	☎ 844/354–6962	⊕ www.alamo.com
Avis	☎ 808/327–3000	⊕ www.avis.com
Budget	☎ 800/214–6094	⊕ www.budget.com
Dollar	☎ 800/800–5252	⊕ www.dollar.com
Enterprise	☎ 808/331–2509	⊕ www.enterprise.com
Hertz	☎ 808/329–2042	⊕ www.hertz.com
National Car Rental	☎ 888/826–6890	⊕ www.nationalcar.com
Thrifty	☎ 808/331–0531	⊕ www.thrifty.com

need to catch a flight. Jaywalking and bike riding are very common, so pay careful attention to the roads, especially while driving in rural areas. Also use caution during heavy downpours, especially if you see signs warning of flash floods and falling rocks. Stay clear of ponding or rising water on roadways and heed emergency weather advisories not to cross flooded roads.

RENTALS

Should you plan to sightsee around the Big Island, it is best to rent a car. With more than 260 miles of coastline—and attractions as varied as Hawaii Volcanoes National Park, Akaka Falls State Park, Puuhonua O Honaunau National Historic Park, and Puukohola Heiau National Historic Site—ideally you should split up your stay between the east and west coasts of the island. Even if all you want to do is

relax at your resort, you may want to hop in the car to check out one of the island's popular restaurants.

While on the Big Island, you can rent anything from an econobox to a sports car or a motorcycle. Rates are usually better if you reserve though a rental agency's website, and most sites allow you to reserve for free. It's wise to make reservations in advance and make sure that a confirmed reservation guarantees you a car, especially if visiting during peak seasons or for major events. It's not uncommon to find several car categories sold out during major events on the island, such as the Merrie Monarch Festival in Hilo in April or the Ironman World Championship triathlon in Kailua-Kona in October. Harper Car and Truck Rental, with offices in Hilo and Kona, is the *only*

Getting Here and Around

company that allows its vehicles to be driven to the summit of Maunakea.

If exploring the island on two wheels is more your speed, Big Island Motorcycle Company rents motorcycles and mopeds.

Rates begin at about $40 a day for an economy car with air-conditioning, automatic transmission, and unlimited mileage. This does not include the airport concession fee, general excise tax, rental vehicle surcharge, or vehicle license fee. When you reserve a car, ask about cancellation penalties and drop-off charges should you plan to pick up the car in one location and return it to another. Many rental companies in Hawaii offer coupons for discounts at various attractions.

In Hawaii, you must be 21 years of age to rent a car, and you must have a valid driver's license and a major credit card. Those under 25 pay a daily surcharge of $27 to $30. Request car seats and extras such as GPS when you book. Hawaii's Child Restraint Law requires that all children three years and younger be in an approved child safety seat in the backseat of a vehicle. Children ages four to seven must be seated in a rear booster seat or child restraint such as a lap and shoulder belt. Car seats and booster rentals range from $8 to $10 per day.

In Hawaii, a mainland driver's license is valid for a rental for up to 90 days.

Because the road circling the Big Island can be two-lane, narrow, and winding in places, allow plenty of time to return your vehicle so that you can make your flight. Traffic can be heavy during morning and afternoon rush hours, especially in the Kona area. Roadwork is ongoing and often unscheduled. ■TIP→ **Give yourself about three and a half hours before departure time to return your vehicle.**

CAR RENTAL INSURANCE

Everyone who rents a car wonders whether the insurance that the rental companies offer is worth the expense. No one—including us—has a simple answer. It all depends on how much regular insurance you have, how comfortable you are with risk, and whether or not money is an issue.

If you own a car and carry comprehensive car insurance for both collision and liability, your personal auto insurance probably covers a rental, but call your auto insurance company to confirm. If you don't have auto insurance, then you will need to buy the collision- or loss-damage waiver (CDW or LDW) from the rental company. The CDW allows you to walk away from most incidents, so it might be worth the peace of mind. Some credit cards offer CDW coverage, but it's usually supplemental to your own insurance and rarely covers SUVs, minivans, and luxury models. If your coverage is secondary, you may still be liable for loss-of-use costs from the car-rental company (again, read the fine print). But no credit card insurance is valid unless you use that card for *all* transactions, from reserving to paying the final bill.

■TIP→ **Diners Club offers primary CDW coverage on all rentals reserved and paid for with the card. This means that Diners Club's company—not your own car insurance—pays in case of an accident. It doesn't mean that your car insurance company won't raise your rates once it discovers you had an accident.**

You may also be offered supplemental liability coverage; the car-rental company is required to carry a minimal level of liability coverage insuring all renters, but it's rarely enough to cover claims in a really serious accident if you're at fault. Your own auto-insurance policy will protect you if you own a car; if you don't, you have to decide whether or not you are willing to take the risk.

U.S. rental companies sell CDWs and LDWs for about $15 to $25 a day; supplemental liability is usually more than $10 a day. The car-rental company may offer you all sorts of other policies, but they're rarely worth the cost. Personal accident insurance, which is basic hospitalization coverage, is an especially egregious rip-off if you already have health insurance.

ISLAND DRIVING TIMES

Before you embark on your day-trip, it's a good idea to know how long it will take you to get to your destination. Some areas, like downtown Kailua-Kona and Waimea, can become congested at certain times of day. For those traveling to South Kona, a bypass road between Keauhou and Kealakekua alleviates congestion considerably during rush hour. In general, you can expect the following average driving times.

Ride-Sharing

Both Uber and Lyft have designated pickup sites at the Hilo and Kona airports. Those who plan on traveling long distances may find that regular taxis are a bit cheaper, and you may have a longer wait for Uber and Lyft pickups beyond the airports.

Island Driving Times	
Kailua-Kona to Kealakekua Bay	14 miles/25 min
Kailua-Kona to Kohala Coast	32 miles/40 min
Kailua-Kona to Waimea	40 miles/1 hr
Kailua-Kona to Hamakua Coast	53 miles/1 hr, 40 min
Kailua-Kona to Hilo	75 miles/2½ hrs
Kohala Coast to Waimea	16 miles/20 min
Kohala Coast to Hamakua Coast	29 miles/55 min
Hilo to Volcano	30 miles/40 min

2

Travel Smart GETTING HERE AND AROUND

Essentials

Beaches

Don't believe anyone who tells you that the Big Island lacks beaches. It's just one of the myths about Hawaii's largest island that have no basis in fact. It's not so much that the Big Island has fewer beaches than the other islands, just that there's more island, so getting to the beaches can be slightly less convenient.

That said, there are plenty of those perfect white-sand stretches you think of when you hear "Hawaii," and the added bonus of black- and green-sand beaches, thanks to the relative young age of the island and its active volcanoes. New beaches appear and disappear regularly, created and destroyed by volcanic activity. In 1989, a black-sand beach, Kamoamoa, formed when molten lava shattered as it hit cold ocean waters; it was enjoyed for a few years before it was closed by new lava flows in 1992. It's part of the ongoing process of the volcano's creation-and-change dynamic.

Hawaii's largest coral reef systems lie off the Kohala Coast. Waves have battered them over millennia to create abundant white-sand beaches on the northwest side of the island. Black-, mixed-, and green-sand beaches lie in the southern regions and along the coast nearest the volcano. On the eastern side of the island, beaches tend to be of the rocky-coast–surging-surf variety, but there are still a few worth visiting, and this is where the Hawaii shoreline is at its most picturesque.

🍴 Dining

Resorts along the Kohala Coast have long invested in culinary programs offering memorable dining experiences that include inventive entrées, spot-on wine pairings, and customized chef's table options. But great food on the Big Island doesn't begin and end with the resorts. A handful of chefs have retired from the fast-paced hotel world and opened their own small bistros in upcountry Waimea or other places off the beaten track. Unique and wonderful restaurants have cropped up in Hawi, Kainaliu, and Holualoa, and on the east side of the island in Hilo.

In addition to restaurants, festivals devoted to island products draw hundreds of attendees to learn about everything from breadfruit and mango to avocado, chocolate, and coffee. Agritourism has turned into a fruitful venture for farmers as farm tours afford the opportunity to meet with and learn from a variety of local producers. Some tours conclude with a meal of items sourced from the same farms. From goat farms churning creamy, savory goat cheese to Waimea farms planting row after row of bright tomatoes and high-tech aquaculture operations at the Natural Energy Lab of Hawaii Authority (NEHLA), visitors can see exactly where their next meal comes from.

WITH KIDS
Keiki (kids') menus are offered at a majority of restaurants on the Big Island, the exceptions being a small handful of fine-dining restaurants that cater to adults.

SMOKING
Smoking is prohibited in all Hawaii restaurants and bars.

RESERVATIONS
Only a few restaurants on the Big Island require reservations. Nevertheless, always call ahead if you're bringing a large party or booking a special-occasion dinner.

HOURS AND PRICES

Though it might seem at first glance like the Big Island's dining scene consists of either high-end restaurants or hole-in-the-wall dives, there is in fact a fairly large middle ground of good restaurants that cater to both local and visiting families, with new places cropping up all the time. However, prices are generally higher than on the mainland. Tipping is similar to elsewhere in the country: 15%–20% of the bill or $1 per drink at a bar. Bills for large parties generally include an 18% tip, as do bills at some resort restaurants, so be sure to check before leaving extra.

Restaurant reviews have been shortened. For full information, visit Fodors. com.

What It Costs			
$	$$	$$$	$$$$
AT DINNER			
under $17	$17–$26	$27–$35	over $35

✚ Health and Safety

HEALTH

The Hawaii State Department of Health recommends that you drink 16 ounces of water per hour to avoid dehydration when hiking or spending time in the sun. Use zinc-based sunblock, wear UV-reflective sunglasses, and protect your head with a visor or hat for shade. If you're not acclimated to warm, humid weather, you should allow plenty of time for rest stops and refreshments. When visiting freshwater streams, be aware of the tropical disease leptospirosis, which is spread by animal urine and carried into streams and mud. Symptoms include fever, headache, nausea, and red eyes. If left untreated, it can cause liver and kidney failure,

respiratory failure, internal bleeding, and even death. To avoid this, don't swim or wade in freshwater streams or ponds if you have open sores and don't drink from any freshwater streams or ponds. Wash all locally grown leafy vegetables thoroughly to protect yourself against rat lungworm disease, which is rare but extremely serious.

The Islands have their share of bugs and insects that enjoy the tropical climate as much as visitors do. Most are harmless but annoying. When planning to spend time outdoors in hiking areas, wear long-sleeve shirts and pants and use mosquito repellent. In very damp or rocky places, you may encounter the dreaded local centipede. Blue or brown in color, centipedes can grow as long as eight inches. If surprised, they might sting, which can be painful and last for days. If you are stung by a centipede, be sure to wash the site of your bite thoroughly to prevent infection. When camping, shake out your sleeping bag before climbing in, and check your shoes in the morning, as centipedes like warm, moist places. If planning on hiking or traveling in remote areas, always carry a first-aid kit and appropriate medications for sting reactions.

COVID-19

Older adults, especially those over 65, have a greater chance of having severe complications from COVID-19. The same is true for people with weaker immune systems or those living with some types of medical conditions, including diabetes, asthma, heart disease, cancer, HIV/AIDS, kidney disease, and liver disease. Starting two weeks before a trip, anyone planning to travel should be on the lookout for some of the following symptoms: cough, fever, chills, trouble breathing, muscle pain, sore throat, new loss of smell or

Essentials

taste. If you experience any of these symptoms, you should not travel at all.

And to protect yourself during travel, do your best to avoid contact with people showing symptoms. Wash your hands often with soap and water. Limit your time in public places, and, when you are out and about, wear a cloth face mask that covers your nose and mouth. Indeed, a mask may be required in some places, such as on an airplane or in a confined space like a theater, where you share the space with a lot of people.

You may wish to bring extra supplies, such as disinfecting wipes, hand sanitizer (12-ounce bottles were allowed in carry-on luggage at this writing), and a first-aid kit with a thermometer.

Given how abruptly travel was curtailed in March 2020, it is wise to consider protecting yourself by purchasing a travel insurance policy that will reimburse you for any costs related to COVID-19 related cancellations. Not all travel insurance policies protect against pandemic-related cancellations, so always read the fine print.

SAFETY ISSUES

Hawaii is generally a safe tourist destination, but it's still wise to stick to the same commonsense safety precautions you would normally follow in your own hometown. Hotel and visitor-center staff can provide information should you decide to head out on your own to more remote areas. Because their models and colors are obvious, rental cars are magnets for break-ins, so don't leave any valuables in them, not even in a locked trunk. Thieves watch these areas and can pop your hood and be gone in 60 seconds. Avoid poorly lighted areas, beach parks, and isolated areas after dark as a precaution. When hiking, stay on marked trails, no matter how alluring the

temptation might be to stray; changing weather conditions can cause landscapes to become muddy, slippery, and tenuous, so staying on marked trails lessens the possibility of a fall or getting lost. This is especially true on the wetter, windward side. Heed warnings about dangerous currents in rivers and swimming holes.

Ocean safety is of the utmost importance when visiting any island destination. Visitors often get into trouble because the beach looks benign and they can't wait to get in the water, so they throw caution to the wind and jump in. We urge you to avoid swimming if the conditions seem rough or dangerous. Most beaches on the Big Island do not have lifeguards. Unfortunately, most of the drowning deaths that occur in Hawaii are visitors—and this is not by chance. Winter brings higher, more dangerous surf, so please exercise caution. Don't swim alone, and follow the international signage posted at beaches, which alerts swimmers to strong currents, man-of-war or box jellyfish, sharp coral, high surf, sharks, and dangerous shorebreaks. At coastal lookouts along cliff tops, heed the signs indicating that waves can climb over the ledges. If there are lifeguards, ask about current conditions, and if the red flags are up, or if a high surf advisory has been issued by civil defense agencies indicating swimming and surfing are not allowed, don't go in. Waters that look calm on the surface can harbor strong currents and undertows, and not a few people who were "just wading" have been dragged out to sea and never seen again. When in doubt, don't go out!

Women traveling alone are generally safe in Hawaii, but always follow the same safety precautions you would use in any major destination. When booking hotels, request rooms closest to the elevator, and always keep your hotel room door and balcony doors locked. Stay away from isolated areas after dark. If you stay out late at a nightclub or bar, use caution when exiting and returning to your car or lodging; most establishments will be glad to give you an escort to your car.

🛜 Internet

If you've brought your laptop or tablet with you to the Big Island, you should have no problem checking email or connecting to the Internet. Most hotels, resorts, and vacation rentals offer high-speed access in rooms or lobbies. You should check with your hotel in advance to confirm that access is wireless; also ask if the signal is strong in every room. In some cases, there will be an hourly or daily charge posted to your room. The latest unhappy trend is for the major hotels to charge a resort fee, a mandatory daily fee that is supposed to cover Wi-Fi and parking. It may range from $25 to $40.

🛏 Lodging

Consider staying at one of the upscale resorts along the Kohala Coast or in a condo in Kailua-Kona for half of your trip. Then, shift gears and check into a romantic bed-and-breakfast on the Hamakua Coast, South Kona, Hilo, or near the volcano. If you've got children in tow, opt for a vacation home or a stay at one of the island's many family-friendly hotels. On the west side, explore the island's most pristine beaches or try some of the fine-dining restaurants; on the east side, hike through rain forests, witness majestic waterfalls, or go for a plate lunch.

Some locals like to say that the east is "more Hawaiian," but we argue that King Kamehameha himself made Kailua-Kona his final home during his sunset years.

Another reason to try a bit of both: your budget. You can justify splurging on a stay at a Kohala Coast resort for a few nights because you'll spend the rest of your time paying one-third that rate at a cozy cottage in Volcano or a vacation rental on Alii Drive. And although food at the resorts is very expensive, you don't have to eat every meal there. Condos and vacation homes can be ideal for a family trip or for a group of friends looking to save money and live like *kamaainas* (local residents) for a week or two. Many of the homes also have private pools and hot tubs, lanai, ocean views, and more—you can go as budget or as high-end as you like.

If you choose a B&B, inn, or out-of-the-way hotel, explain your expectations fully to the proprietor and ask plenty of questions before booking. Be clear about your travel and location needs. Some places require stays of two or three days.

HOTELS AND RESORTS

The resorts—most clustered on the Kohala Coast—are expensive, no two ways about it. That said, many offer free nights with longer stays (fifth or seventh night free) and sometimes team with airlines or consolidators to offer package deals that may include a rental car, spa treatments, golf, and other activities. Some hotels allow children under 17 to stay for free. Ask about specials when you book, and check websites as well—many resorts have Internet-only deals.

CONDOS AND VACATION RENTALS

Renting a condo or vacation house gives you much more living space than the average hotel, plus the chance to meet more people (neighbors are usually friendly), lower nightly rates, and the option of cooking or barbecuing rather than eating out. When booking, remember that most properties are individually owned, with rates and amenities that

Essentials

differ substantially depending on the place. Some properties are handled by rental agents or agencies, while many are handled directly through the owner.

The booking agencies may specialize in various lodging types or locations, so be sure to call and ask questions before booking. Big Island Villas lists condos attached to a number of resorts. Hawaiian Beach Rentals is an excellent source for high-end homes. Keauhou Property Management has condos along the Kona Coast, as do Kona Coast Vacations and Knutson and Associates. Kona Hawaii Vacation Rental is known for affordable Kailua-Kona condos. Kolea Vacations lists high-end condos in Waikoloa, and Kona Vacation Rentals focuses on luxury Kohala Coast condos. Hawaii Vacation rentals has some properties in Puako, near the Kohala Coast resorts.

B&BS AND INNS

B&Bs and locally run inns offer a nice alternative to hotels or resorts in terms of privacy and location. Guests enjoy the perks of a hotel (breakfast and cleaning service), but without the extras that drive up rates.

Be sure to check industry association websites as well as property websites, and call to ask questions. There are still a few "B&Bs" that are really just dumpy rooms in someone's house, and you don't want to end up there. Members of the Big Island–based **Hawaii Island Bed and Breakfast Association** (⊕ www.stayhawaii.com) are listed with phone numbers and rates in a comprehensive online brochure. In order to join this network, B&Bs must be evaluated and meet fairly stringent minimum requirements, including a yearly walk-through by association officers, to maintain their membership. Another B&B association is **Hawaii's**

Best Bed and Breakfasts (☎ 808/885–4550 ⊕ www.bestbnb.com).

RESERVATIONS

You'll almost always be able to find a room on the Big Island, but you might not get your first choice if you wait until the last minute. Make reservations six months to a year in advance if you're visiting during the peak seasons (summer, Christmas holiday, and spring break). Major festivals and events affect availability too: during the week after Easter Sunday, for example, the Merrie Monarch Festival is in full swing, and most of Hilo's rooms are booked. Kailua-Kona is packed in mid-October during the Ironman World Championship triathlon. ■ TIP→ **September and February are great months to visit Hawaii; fares are lower, crowds are smaller, and accommodation prices are reduced.**

PRICES

Keep in mind that many resorts charge "resort fees" for things like parking, Internet, daily newspaper service, beach gear, and activities. Most condos and vacation rental owners charge an additional cleaning fee. Always ask about hidden fees as well as specials and discounts when you book. Look online for great package deals. *Hotel reviews have been shortened. For full information, visit Fodors.com.*

What It Costs			
$	$$	$$$	$$$$
FOR TWO PEOPLE			
under $180	$180–$260	$261–$340	over $340

Where to Stay on the Big Island

	Local Vibe	Pros	Cons
Kailua-Kona	A bustling little village; Alii Drive brims with hotels and condo complexes.	Plenty to do, day and night; everything within easy walking distance of most hotels; many grocery stores in the area.	More traffic than anywhere else on the island; limited number of beaches; traffic noise on Alii Drive.
South Kona and Kau	Popular Kealakekua Bay has plenty of B&Bs and vacation rentals; a few more are farther south in Kau.	Kealakekua Bay is popular for kayaking and snorkeling and has some good restaurants; Captain Cook and Kainaliu have coffee farms.	Few sandy beaches; not as many restaurant options; Kau is quite remote.
The Kohala Coast	Home to most of the Big Island's major resorts. Blue sunny skies prevail here, along with the island's best beaches.	Beautiful beaches; high-end shopping and dining; lots of activities for adults and children.	Pricey; long driving distances to Volcano, Hilo, and Kailua-Kona.
Waimea	Though it seems a world away, upcountry Waimea is only about a 15- to 20-minute drive from the Kohala Coast.	Striking scenery, *paniolo* (cowboy) culture; home to some exceptional local restaurants.	Can be cool and rainy year-round; nearest beaches are a 20-minute drive away.
The Hamakua Coast	A nice spot for those seeking peace, tranquility, and an alternative to the tropical-beach-vacation experience.	Close to Waipio Valley; foodie and farm tours in the area; good spot for honeymooners.	Beaches are an hour's drive away; convenience shopping is limited, as are lodging options.
Hilo	Hilo is on the wet and lush eastern side of the Big Island. It's less touristy than the west side but retains much local charm.	Proximity to waterfalls, rain forest hikes, museums, zoo, and botanical gardens; also many good restaurants.	The best white-sand beaches are on the other side of the island; noise from coqui frogs can be distracting at night.
Puna	Puna doesn't attract as many visitors as other regions, so you'll find good deals on rentals here.	A few black-sand beaches; off the beaten path and fairly wild; lava has flowed into the sea here in years past.	Few dining and entertainment options; no resorts or resort amenities; noisy coqui frogs at night.
Hawaii Volcanoes National Park and Vicinity	There are any number of enchanting B&B inns in fern-shrouded Volcano Village, near the park.	Great for hiking, nature tours, and bike riding; close to Hilo and Puna.	Just a few dining options; not much nightlife; can be cold and wet.

2

Travel Smart ESSENTIALS

Essentials

⍦ Nightlife

If you're the sort of person who doesn't come alive until after dark, you might be a little lonely on the Big Island. Blame it on the sleepy plantation heritage. People did their cane raising in the morning, and there was very limited late-night fun. Still, there are a few lively bars on the island. In addition, many resorts have bars and late-night activities and events and keep pools and gyms open late so there's something to do after dinner.

⊡ Packing

Hawaii is casual: sandals, bathing suits, and comfortable, informal clothing are the norm. Year-round, clothing of cotton or rayon proves very comfortable. Local women love to wear the *pareu*, or sarong. For men, you'll look right at home in T-shirts and board shorts.

One of the most important things to tuck in your suitcase is sunscreen. Recent research has indicated that some traditional sunscreens are harming coral reefs; statewide legislation now bans the sale of sunscreens that contain oxybenzone and octinoxate. So if you do want to use reef-safe sunscreen, buy products that are zinc-based or reef approved. Even better? Buy a long-sleeved rash guard, available at all major retailers. That way, you have no gunky lotions or harmful chemicals to deal with while out enjoying the reefs. Hats and sunglasses offer important sun protection, too. Both are easy to find in island shops, but if you already have a favorite packable hat or sun visor, bring it with you. All major hotels in Hawaii (and most small ones) provide beach towels.

As for clothing in the Hawaiian Islands, there's a saying that when a man wears a suit during the day, he's either going for a loan or he's a lawyer trying a case. Only a few upscale restaurants require a jacket for dinner. The aloha shirt is accepted dress in Hawaii for business and most social occasions. Shorts are acceptable daytime attire, along with a T-shirt or polo shirt. There's no need to buy expensive sandals on the mainland—here you can get flip-flops (called "slippers" by locals) for under $5. Golfers should remember that many courses have dress codes requiring a collared shirt; call courses you're interested in for details. If you're not prepared, you can pick up appropriate clothing at resort pro shops. If you're visiting in winter, bring a sweater or light- to medium-weight jacket. A polar fleece pullover is ideal and makes a great impromptu pillow.

If your vacation plans include Hilo, you'll want to pack a compact umbrella and a light poncho. And if you'll be exploring Hawaii Volcanoes National Park, make sure you pack appropriately, as weather ranges from hot and dry along the shore to chilly, foggy, and rainy at the 4,000-foot summit. Sturdy boots are recommended if you'll be hiking or camping in the park.

⊕ Passport

All visitors to the United States require a valid passport that is valid for six months beyond your expected period of stay.

▦ Performing Arts

A handful of great local playhouses, half a dozen or so movie houses (including those that play foreign and independent films), and plenty of musical entertainment can keep fans of the arts happy.

And let's not forget the luau. These fantastic dance and musical performances are combined with some of the best local food on the island and are plenty of fun for the whole family.

🛍 Shopping

Dozens of shops in Kailua-Kona offer a range of souvenirs from far-flung corners of the globe as well as many local coffee and foodstuffs to take home to everyone you left behind. Housewares and artworks made from local materials (lauhala, coconut, koa, and milo wood) fill the shelves of small boutiques and galleries throughout the island. Upscale shops in the resorts along the Kohala Coast carry high-end clothing and accessories, as do a few boutiques scattered around the island. Galleries and gift shops, many showcasing the work of local artists, fill historical buildings in Waimea, Kainaliu, Holualoa, Hilo, and Hawi. Hotel shops generally offer the most attractive and original resort wear, but, as with everything else at resorts, the prices run higher than elsewhere on the island.

HOURS

In general, stores on the Big Island open at 9 or 10 and close by 6. Hilo's Prince Kuhio Plaza stays open until 8 on weekdays and 9 on Friday and Saturday. In Historic Kailua Village and in Keauhou, most shopping plazas geared to tourists remain open until 9. Grocery stores such as KTA Superstore are open until 11.

📍 Spas

High prices are entirely too common at the island's resort spas, but a handful of unique experiences are worth every penny. Beyond the resorts, the Big Island is also home to independent massage therapists and day spas that offer similar treatments for lower prices, albeit usually in a slightly less luxurious atmosphere. In addition to the obvious relaxation benefits of any spa visit, the Big Island's spas have done a fantastic job incorporating local traditions and ingredients into their menus. Massage artists work with coconut or *kukui* (candlenut) oil, hot-stone massages are conducted with volcanic stones, and ancient healing techniques such as *lomilomi*—a massage technique with firm, constant movement—are staples at every island spa.

💲 Taxes

Businesses on the Big Island of Hawaii collect a 4.5% general excise tax on all purchases, including food and services. A hotel transient accommodations tax of 10.25%, combined with the excise tax, totals a 14.75% rate added to your room bill. Even vacation rentals and B&Bs are required to collect this tax. A $3-per-day road tax is also assessed on each rental vehicle, in addition to an airport concession recovery tax and other fees that are not technically taxes but are tacked on to the base rate.

🕐 Time

Hawaii is on Hawaii Standard Time, five hours behind New York, two hours behind Los Angeles, and 10 hours behind London.

When the U.S. mainland switches to daylight saving time, Hawaii does not, so add an extra hour of time difference between the Islands and U.S. mainland destinations.

Essentials

Tipping

Tipping is not only common but expected: Hawaii is a major vacation destination and many people who work at the hotels and resorts rely on tips to supplement their wages. Give $1 to bartenders and bellhops and $2 to cleaners, but tip more in an expensive luxury resort. Tip 15%–20% in restaurants and in taxis.

Visa

Except for citizens of Canada and Bermuda, most visitors to the United States must have a visa. If you are from one of the 39 designated members of the Visa Waiver Program, then you only require an Electronic System for Travel Authorization (ESTA) as long as you are staying for 90 days or less. You must have an e-passport to use the Visa Waiver Program.

Visitor Information

Before you go, visit Hawaii Tourism Authority's website (⊕ www.gohawaii. com) for a plethora of helpful advice and to request a free official vacation planner with information on accommodations, transportation, sports and activities, dining, arts and entertainment, and culture. The site includes a calendar section that shows which local events will coincide with your visit. ■TIP➔ **To experience the aloha spirit firsthand, connect the old-fashioned way—by phone.**

The Hawaii Island Chamber of Commerce has links to dozens of museums, attractions, B&Bs, and parks on its website. The Kona-Kohala Chamber of Commerce lists local activities.

Tipping Guides for the Big Island	
Bartender	$1–$5 per round of drinks, depending on the number of drinks
Bellhop	$1–$5 per bag, depending on the level of the hotel
Coat Check	$1–$2 per coat
Hotel Concierge	$5 or more, depending on the service
Hotel Doorstaff	$1–$5 for help with bags or hailing a cab
Hotel Cleaner	$2–$5 a day (in cash, preferably daily since cleaning staff may be different each day you stay)
Hotel Room Service Waitstaff	$1–$2 per delivery, even if a service charge has been added
Porter at Airport or Train Station	$1 per bag
Restroom Attendants	$1 or small change
Skycap at Airport	$1–$3 per bag checked
Spa Personnel	15%–20% of the cost of your service
Taxi Driver	15%–20%
Tour Guide	10%–15% of the cost of the tour, per person
Valet Parking Attendant	$2–$5, each time your car is brought to you
Waitstaff	15%–20%, with 20% being the norm at high-end restaurants; nothing additional if a service charge is added to the bill

Contacts

✈ Air

MAJOR AIRLINE CONTACTS Air Canada.
☎ 888/247–2262 ⊕ www.
aircanada.com. **Alaska
Airlines.** ☎ 800/252–7522
⊕ www.alaskaair.
com. **American Airlines.**
☎ 800/433–7300 ⊕ www.
aa.com. **Delta Airlines.**
☎ 800/221–1212 for U.S.
reservations ⊕ www.del-
ta.com. **Hawaiian Airlines.**
☎ 800/367–5320 ⊕ www.
hawaiianair.com. **Japan
Airlines.** ☎ 800/525–3663
⊕ www.jal.com. **Southwest
Airlines.** ☎ 800/435–9792
⊕ www.southwest.com.
United Airlines. ☎ 800/864–
8331 for U.S. reservations,
800/241–6522 arrival and
departure information
⊕ www.united.com. **Virgin
Atlantic.** ☎ 800/862–8621
⊕ www.virginatlantic.com.
Westjet. ☎ 888/937–8538
⊕ www.westjet.com.

INTERISLAND CONTACTS Mokulele Airlines.
☎ 866/260–7070 ⊕ www.
mokuleleairlines.com.

**CHARTER CONTACTS Big
Island Air.** ☎ 808/329–4868
⊕ www.bigislandair.com.

**AIRPORTS Daniel K. Inouye
International Airport (HNL).**
✉ 300 Rodgers Blvd.,
Honolulu ☎ 808/836–6413
⊕ hawaii.gov/hnl. **Ellison
Onizuka Kona International
Airport at Keahole (KOA).**
☎ 808/327–9520 ⊕ hawaii.
gov/koa. **Hilo International

Airport (ITO).** ☎ 808/961–
9300 ⊕ hawaii.gov/ito.
**Waimea-Kohala Airport
(MUE).** ☎ 808/887–8126
⊕ hawaii.gov/mue.

**AIRPORT TRANSFERS
SpeediShuttle.** ☎ 877/242–
5777, 808/329–5433
⊕ www.speedishuttle.
com.

🚍 Bus

CONTACTS Hele-On Bus.
☎ 808/961–8744 ⊕ www.
heleonbus.org.

🛏 Lodging

**CONTACTS Big Island
Villas.** ☎ 808/936–3870,
808/443–6991 ⊕ www.
bigislandvillas.com.
Hawaiian Beach Rentals.
☎ 844/261–0464 ⊕ www.
hawaiianbeachrentals.
com. **Hawaii Vacation
Rentals.** ☎ 808/882–7000
⊕ www.vacationbigisland.
com. **Keauhou Property
Management.** ☎ 808/326–
7053 ⊕ www.konacondo.
net. **Knutson and Asso-
ciates.** ☎ 808/329–1010
⊕ www.konahawaiiren-
tals.com. **Kolea Vacations.**
☎ 888/565–3244 ⊕ www.
koleavacations.com.
Kona Coast Vacations.
☎ 808/329–2140 ⊕ www.
konacoastvacations.com.
**Kona Hawaii Vacation
Rentals.** ☎ 808/326-4137
⊕ www.konahawaii.com.

Kona Vacation Rentals.
☎ 886/456–4252 ⊕ www.
konarentals.com. **South
Kohala Management.**
☎ 808/883–8500 ⊕ www.
southkohala.com.

📍 Visitor Information

**CONTACTS Hawaii Island
Chamber of Commerce.**
☎ 808/935–7178
⊕ www.hicc.biz. **Island
of Hawaii Visitors Bureau.**
☎ 800/648–2441 ⊕ www.
gohawaii.com/islands/
hawaii-big-island. **Kona-Kohala Chamber of Commerce.**
☎ 808/329–1758 ⊕ www.
kona-kohala.com.

Hawaiian Vocabulary

Although an understanding of Hawaiian is by no means required on a trip to the Aloha State, a *malihini,* or newcomer, will find plenty of opportunities to pick up a few of the local words and phrases. Traditional names and expressions are widely used in the Islands. You're likely to read or hear at least a few words each day of your stay.

Simplifying the learning process is the fact that the Hawaiian language contains only seven consonants—H, K, L, M, N, P, W, and the silent *'okina,* or glottal stop, written '—plus one or more of the five vowels. All syllables, and therefore all words, end in a vowel. Each vowel, with the exception of a few diphthongized double vowels such as *au* (pronounced "ow") or *ai* (pronounced "eye"), is pronounced separately. Thus *'Iolani* is four syllables (ee-oh-la-nee), not three (yo-la-nee). Although some Hawaiian words have only vowels, most also contain some consonants, but consonants are never doubled.

Pronunciation is simple. Pronounce *A* "ah" as in *father; E* "ay" as in *weigh; I* "ee" as in *marine; O* "oh" as in *no; U* "oo" as in *true.*

Consonants mirror their English equivalents, with the exception of *W.* When the letter begins any syllable other than the first one in a word, it is usually pronounced as a *V. 'Awa,* the Polynesian drink, is pronounced "ava," *'ewa* is pronounced "eva."

Almost all long Hawaiian words are combinations of shorter words; they are not difficult to pronounce if you segment them. *Kalaniana'ole,* the highway running east from Honolulu, is easily understood as *Kalani ana 'ole.* Apply the standard pronunciation rules—the stress falls on the next-to-last syllable of most two- or three-syllable Hawaiian words—and Kalaniana'ole Highway is as easy to say as Main Street.

Now about that fish. Try *humu-humu nuku-nuku āpu a'a.*

The other unusual element in Hawaiian language is the *kahakō,* or macron, written as a short line (ˉ) placed over a vowel. Like the accent (´) in Spanish, the kahakō puts emphasis on a syllable that would normally not be stressed. The most familiar example is probably *Waikīkī.* With no macrons, the stress would fall on the middle syllable; with only one macron, on the last syllable, the stress would fall on the first and last syllables. Some words become plural with the addition of a macron, often on a syllable that would have been stressed anyway. No Hawaiian word becomes plural with the addition of an *S,* since that letter does not exist in the language.

The Hawaiian diacritical marks are not printed in this guide.

PIDGIN

You may hear pidgin, the unofficial language of Hawai'i. It is a Creole language, with its own grammar, evolved from the mixture of English, Hawaiian, Japanese, Portuguese, and other languages spoken in 19th-century Hawai'i, and it is heard everywhere.

GLOSSARY

What follows is a glossary of some of the most commonly used Hawaiian words. Hawaiian residents appreciate visitors who at least try to pick up the local language.

'a'ā: rough, crumbling lava, contrasting with *pāhoehoe,* which is smooth.

'ae: yes.

aikane: friend.

āina: land.

akamai: smart, clever, possessing savoir faire.

akua: god.

ala: a road, path, or trail.

ali'i: a Hawaiian chief, a member of the chiefly class.

aloha: love, affection, kindness; also a salutation meaning both greetings and farewell.

'ānuenue: rainbow.

'a'ole: no.

'apōpō: tomorrow.

'auwai: a ditch.

auwē: alas, woe is me!

'ehu: a red-haired Hawaiian.

'ewa: in the direction of 'Ewa plantation, west of Honolulu.

hala: the pandanus tree, whose leaves (*lau hala*) are used to make baskets and plaited mats.

hālau: school.

hale: a house.

hale pule: church, house of worship.

hana: to work.

haole: foreigner. Since the first foreigners were Caucasian, *haole* now means a Caucasian person.

hapa: a part, sometimes a half; often used as a short form of *hapa haole*, to mean a person who is part-Caucasian.

hau'oli: to rejoice. *Hau'oli Makahiki Hou* means Happy New Year. *Hau'oli lā hānau* means Happy Birthday.

heiau: an outdoor stone platform; an ancient Hawaiian place of worship.

he mea iki or **he mea 'ole:** you're welcome.

holo: to run.

holoholo: to go for a walk, ride, or sail.

holokū: a long Hawaiian dress, somewhat fitted, with a yoke and a train. It was worn at court, and at least one local translates the word as "expensive mu'umu'u."

holomū: a post–World War II cross between a *holokū* and a mu'umu'u, less fitted than the former but less voluminous than the latter, and having no train.

honi: to kiss; a kiss. A phrase that some tourists may find useful, quoted from a popular hula, is *Honi Ka'ua Wikiwiki:* Kiss me quick!

honu: turtle.

ho'omalimali: flattery, a deceptive "line," bunk, baloney, hooey.

huhū: angry.

hui: a group, club, or assembly. A church may refer to its congregation as a *hui* and a social club may be called a *hui.*

hukilau: a seine; a communal fishing party in which everyone helps to drive the fish into a huge net, pull it in, and divide the catch.

hula: the dance of Hawai'i.

iki: little.

ipo: sweetheart. Commonly seen as "ku'uipo," or "my sweetheart."

ka: the. This is the definite article for most singular words; for plural nouns, the definite article is usually *nā.* Since there is no *S* in Hawaiian, the article may be your only clue that a noun is plural.

Hawaiian Vocabulary

kahuna: a priest, doctor, or other trained person of old Hawai'i, endowed with special professional skills that often included prophecy or other supernatural powers.

kai: the sea, saltwater.

kalo: the taro plant from whose root *poi* (paste) is made.

kamā'aina: literally, a child of the soil; it refers to people who were born in the Islands or have lived there for a long time.

kanaka: originally a man or humanity, it is now used to denote a male Hawaiian or part-Hawaiian, but is occasionally taken as a slur when used by non-Hawaiians. *Kanaka maoli* is used by some Native Hawaiian rights activists to embrace part-Hawaiians as well.

kāne: a man, a husband. If you see this word (or kane) on a door, it's the men's room.

kapa: also called by its Tahitian name, *tapa,* a cloth made of beaten bark and usually dyed and stamped with a repeat design.

kapakahi: crooked, cockeyed, uneven. You've got your hat on *kapakahi.*

kapu: keep out, prohibited. This is the Hawaiian version of the more widely known Tongan word *tabu* (taboo).

kēia lā: today.

keiki: a child; *keikikāne* is a boy, *keikiwahine* a girl.

kōkua: to help, assist. Often seen in signs like "Please *kōkua* and throw away your trash."

kona: the leeward side of the Islands, the direction (south) from which the *kona* wind and *kona* rain come.

kula: upland.

kuleana: a homestead or small plot of ground on which a family has been installed for some generations without necessarily owning it. By extension, *kuleana* is used to denote any area or department in which one has a special interest or prerogative. You'll hear it used this way: "If you want to hire a surfboard, see Moki; that's his *kuleana.*"

kupuna: grandparent; elder.

lā: sun.

lamalama: to fish with a torch.

lānai: a porch, a balcony, an outdoor living room.

lani: heaven, the sky.

lau hala: the leaf of the *hala,* or pandanus tree, widely used in handicrafts.

lei: a garland of flowers.

lōlō: feeble-minded, crazy.

luna: a plantation overseer or foreman.

mahalo: thank you.

mahina: moon.

makai: toward the ocean.

mālama: to take care of, preserve, protect

malihini: a newcomer to the Islands.

mana: the spiritual power that the Hawaiians believe inhabits all things and creatures.

manō: shark.

manuahi: free, gratis.

mauka: toward the mountains.

mauna: mountain.

mele: a Hawaiian song or chant, often of epic proportions.

Mele Kalikimaka: Merry Christmas (a transliteration from the English phrase).

Menehune: a Hawaiian pixie. The *Menehune* were a legendary race of little people who accomplished prodigious work, such as building fishponds and temples in the course of a single night.

moana: the ocean.

muʻumuʻu: the voluminous dress in which the missionaries enveloped Hawaiian women. Culturally sensitive locals have embraced the Hawaiian spelling but often shorten the spoken word to "muʻu." Most English dictionaries include the spelling "muumuu."

nani: beautiful.

nui: big.

ʻohana: family.

ʻono: delicious.

pāhoehoe: smooth, unbroken, satiny lava.

palapala: document, printed matter.

pali: a cliff, precipice.

pānini: prickly pear cactus.

paniolo: a Hawaiian cowboy, a rough transliteration of *español*, the language of the Islands' earliest cowboys.

pau: finished, done.

pilikia: trouble. The Hawaiian word is much more widely used here than its English equivalent.

pū: large conch shell used as trumpet before start of luau and other special events.

puka: a hole.

pule: prayer, blessing. Often performed before a meal or event.

pupule: crazy, like the celebrated Princess Pupule. This word has replaced its English equivalent in local usage.

puʻu: volcanic cinder cone.

tūtū: grandmother

waha: mouth.

wahine: a female, a woman, a wife, and a sign on the ladies' room door; the plural form is *wāhine*.

wai: freshwater, as opposed to saltwater, which is *kai*.

wailele: waterfall.

wikiwiki: to hurry, hurry up (since this is a reduplication of *wiki*, quick, neither *W* is pronounced as a *V*).

Great Itineraries

Road Trip: Best of the Big Island in a Week

Experiencing the best of the Big Island requires some drive time, plus some downtime.

DAY 1: HISTORIC KAILUA VILLAGE

Start your first day in Kailua-Kona with a stroll around Historic Kailua Village. Eat breakfast or brunch at one of the ocean-front restaurants along Alii Drive. Stroll the seaside village's many gift stores, art galleries, and apparel boutiques. Historic landmarks include royal **Hulihee Palace** and the oldest Christian church in Hawaii, **Mokuaikaua Church.** In the afternoon, take a ride on the **Atlantis Submarine,** or take a sunset dinner sail with **Body Glove Cruises.**

Logistics: The village is walkable. There are paid and free lots behind the stores on the *mauka* (mountain) side of Alii Drive.

DAY 2: BEST KOHALA BEACHES

Head north to the beautiful sand beaches of the Kohala Coast. Check out **Anae-hoomalu Bay** in Waikoloa Beach Resort. Not only can you rent beach amenities including kayaks or stand-up paddle-boards, you'll also be near Queens' MarketPlace with its restaurants and shops. For lunch, try **Lava Lava Beach Club,** right on the beach at Anaehoomalu Bay. Head north to Kawaihae and visit **Puukohola Heiau National Historic Site,** where King Kamehameha I oversaw the building of a great temple. On the way back, make a stop at **Hapuna Beach State Recreation Area.**

Logistics: Parking is easy at Waikoloa Beach Resort. Distance and time traveled: 35 miles one-way, 40 minutes one-way, starting in Kailua-Kona. Car, via Queen Kaahumanu Highway.

DAY 3: KEALAKEKUA BAY

In South Kona, **Kealakekua Bay State Historical Park** attracts visitors to this marine conservation district frequented by spinner dolphins. The **Captain James Cook Monument,** a white obelisk on a wharf, marks where the navigator was slain in 1779. Guided kayak tours are available, and snorkeling here is excellent. In the afternoon, visit the historic **St. Benedict Painted Church** and **Puuhonua O Honaunau National Historical Park.** On your way back north, stop at **Greenwell Farms** in Kealakekua for a Kona coffee farm tour.

Logistics: Take the lower bypass road from Keauhou or the upper road from Kailua-Kona, and head down Napoopoo Road to the end. Distance and time traveled: 44 miles round-trip, 35 minutes one-way, starting in Kailua-Kona. Car, via Highway 11.

DAY 4: HAWAII VOLCANOES NATIONAL PARK

It's a long drive from Kona to **Hawaii Volcanoes National Park,** so leave early to get to the park by 11 am. Begin at the **Kilauea Visitor Center,** where you can review maps, buy trail-guide booklets, or talk to the rangers. Stroll along a boardwalk to the **sulfur banks** and **steam vents.** Along the way, stop at **Volcano Art Center** to view fantastic local art. Drive to the Steaming Bluffs and walk to an overlook with views of Halemaumau Crater and Kilauea Caldera. Then drive down Chain of Craters Road to visit **Thurston Lava Tube** and the adjacent **Kilauea Iki Trail.** Afterward, stop by **Volcano House** and eat lunch or dinner at **The Rim.**

Logistics: The park is open 24/7, but entrance fees are charged during normal visiting hours. Distance from Kailua-Kona one-way: 90 miles. Time traveled one-way: 2½ hours.

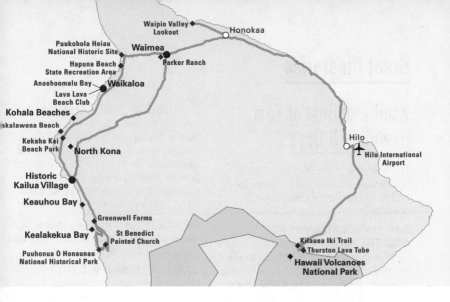

A map showing locations including Waipio Valley Lookout, Honokaa, Puukohola Heiau National Historic Site, Waimea, Parker Ranch, Hapuna Beach State Recreation Area, Anaehoomalu Bay, Waikaloa, Lava Lava Beach Club, Kohala Beaches, Makalawena Beach, Kekaha Kai Beach Park, North Kona, Historic Kailua Village, Keauhou Bay, Greenwell Farms, St Benedict Painted Church, Kealakekua Bay, Puuhonua O Honaunau National Historical Park, Hilo, Hilo International Airport, Kilauea Iki Trail, Thurston Lava Tube, and Hawaii Volcanoes National Park.

DAY 5: WAIMEA AND UPCOUNTRY

At the foothills of Maunakea, the small upcountry town is home to **Parker Ranch,** one of the country's largest privately owned cattle ranches. You can book several activities in town, including horseback riding and tours of two historic homes. Waimea has great restaurants, including **Merriman's** and **Big Island Brewhaus.** Not far from Waimea, **Waipio Valley** is a beautiful destination best explored by horseback or guided tour. The nearby town of **Honokaa** still feels like a slice of the old sugar plantation days.

Logistics: Waimea can be reached from Kona via the upper road, or up Kawaihae Drive from the lower road. Distance from Kailua-Kona: 39 miles one-way.

DAY 6: KEAUHOU BAY

Keauhou is just south of Kailua-Kona on Alii Drive. Here you'll find lots of recreational activities, including tennis, golf, and stand-up paddleboarding. **Keauhou Shopping Center** has movie theaters, restaurants, and cafés. The **Sheraton Kona Resort and Spa at Keauhou Bay** has the bayfront **Rays on the Bay,** open for dinner. One of the island's most popular activities is a nighttime manta ray tour with operators who depart nightly from Keauhou Harbor.

Logistics: You'll need your car to drive around the area. Distance from Kailua-Kona: 5 miles one-way on Alii Drive. Time traveled one-way: 10 minutes.

DAY 7: NORTH KONA

Two of the best beaches near Kailua-Kona take some time to get to. **Kekaha Kai State Park—Mahaiula Side** is down a long gravel road that winds through a lava field on the way to a wonderful white-sand beach. About a 20-minute walk south across a lava field from Kekaha Kai State Park, **Makalawena Beach** is a true gem and worth the hike. If you go to Makalawena, pack lots of water, a shade umbrella, food, and sunscreen. End your trip with a great dinner.

Logistics: On Wednesday, the park is closed. Distance from Kailua-Kona: 17 miles one-way.

Great Itineraries

Road Trip: Best of East Hawaii in 5 Days

The east side of the Big Island offers spectacular scenery, hidden attractions, must-see destinations, and Hilo's thriving downtown.

DAY 1: VOLCANO VILLAGE AND THE NATIONAL PARK

From your home base at **Volcano House** or other hotel, drive to tiny, artsy Volcano Village for breakfast at **Lava Rock Cafe.** Explore **Kilauea Kreations** for local souvenirs and handmade Hawaiian quilts, and check out **2400 Fahrenheit** gallery; **Volcano Garden Arts** offers more locally crafted items. Notice the old homes and lodges, including historic **Kilauea Lodge.** Arrive at Hawaii Volcanoes National Park by 11 am, so you can explore the steam vents, sulfur banks, **Thurston Lava Tube,** and **Kilauea Iki Trail,** a 2-mile (one-way) trek into the still-steaming crater. Have dinner at **The Rim** at Volcano House, which features views of Halemaumau Crater. After dinner, visit the arcade and bowling alley at **Kilauea Military Camp.**

Logistics: Distance traveled: 4–5 miles round-trip via Highway Belt Road from the park to Volcano Village, and Crater Rim Drive inside the park.

DAY 2: HAWAII VOLCANOES NATIONAL PARK

Head to **Kilauea Visitor Center** to talk to the rangers and to learn about ranger-led programs. Visit **Devastation Trail,** an area strewn with cinder that descended from towering lava fountains in 1959. One of the park's most fascinating hikes is **Mauna Ulu Trail** (2½-mile round-trip) off **Chain of Craters Road.** Purchase a trail guide at the center about the Mauna Ulu lava flow of 1969–74. Allow about two hours for the hike with stellar views of Mauna Loa

and Maunakea. After, continue driving Chain of Craters Road to its end, and take in the view of the sea arch from the viewing station. After lunch back at **Volcano House,** wander along the Earthquake Trail and Waldron Ledge just outside of the hotel. Don't miss **Volcano Art Center,** which presents works by Hawaii artists.

Logistics: Distance and time traveled: about 40 miles round-trip, starting in park via Chain of Craters Road.

DAY 3: HILO AND VICINITY

From Volcano, take a 40-minute drive to Hilo and have breakfast at a local restaurant. Wander around the Hilo bayfront to visit the many galleries, cafés, and shops, including **Sugar Coast Candy.** If you are in Hilo on a Wednesday or Saturday, the **Hilo Farmers Market** is in full swing with Hawaii-made products like honey, mochi, goat cheese, and crafts. Across the way on Banyan Drive, **Liliuokalani Gardens** offers a serene Japanese setting with arched bridges and gazebos. At noon, the daily "Skies Above Hawaii" takes place at the **Imiloa Astronomy Center** planetarium. Afterward, head back to town (2 miles away) for lunch and more exploring. Then drive up the road a mile above town and visit **Rainbow Falls** and, a bit farther away, **Boiling Pots.** Take a walk by Reeds Bay along Banyan Drive, shaded by a canopy of 50 enormous banyan trees, followed by a first-rate dinner at **Hilo Bay Cafe.**

Logistics: You'll need a car to travel between sights, though you can walk around downtown Hilo. Distance and time traveled: 30 miles, 45 minutes one-way. Car, via Highway 11 starting in Volcano.

DAY 4: HAMAKUA COAST, HONOKAA, WAIPIO VALLEY

The longest drive of your itinerary takes you back through Hilo to the opposite side of the island on the Hamakua Coast.

It's a 22-minute drive from Hilo to **Akaka Falls State Park** on the Hamakua Coast, with its two cascading waterfalls. Then drive to the historic town of **Honokaa** and browse the galleries and shops downtown. Afterward, follow the signs to **Waipio Valley** lookout at the end of the Hamakua Heritage Corridor. If you brought your hiking or tennis shoes and water, the steep walk in and out of the valley is worth the effort. On your way back, stop at **Laupahoehoe Point Beach Park** for breathtaking ocean views. Treat yourself to dinner in Hilo before driving back to Volcano.

Logistics: The descent into Waipio Valley by car is restricted to four-wheel-drive vehicles. Distance and time traveled: 78 miles; 1 hour, 50 minutes one-way, starting in Volcano. Car, via Highway 19.

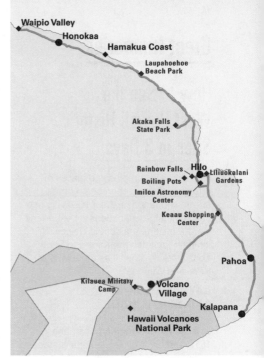

DAY 5: LOWER PUNA, PAHOA, KALAPANA

It's a 31-mile drive from Volcano to the Big Island's most offbeat destination, **Pahoa.** This funky, historic village has escaped destruction twice: in 2014 and more recently in 2018, when the eruption destroyed nearby neighborhoods. Explore the hippie boutiques and cafés of Pahoa Town, eat lunch, and visit the **Lava Zone Museum** to learn about the area's eruption history. Drive 14 miles down Hawaii Route 130 or 137 to see what's left of the village of **Kalapana,** which was inundated by lava beginning in 1986. Here you'll find **Uncle Robert's Awa Bar and Farmers Market,** a family-run venue that also hosts live music. Grab a quick bite to eat at **Keaau Shopping Center** before heading to your home base.

Logistics: Gas up for the round trip to this destination. Distance and time traveled: 31 miles, 42 minutes one-way, starting from Volcano. Car, via Highway 11 and Highway 130.

Tips

Even on sunny mornings, bring a light hooded jacket and umbrella: rain showers can happen anytime.

Affordable local-style "plate lunch" eateries are abundant on the east side: try one.

Plan your time carefully if you want to hike in the Waipio Valley; this is a long driving day.

Great Itineraries

How to See the West Hawaii Historic Sites in 3 Days

From ancient temples and places of refuge to historic churches, homes, farms, and ranches, West Hawaii is rich in fascinating destinations for experiencing the bygone eras of old Hawaii. This itinerary includes the Kona and South Kohala areas, as well as the towns of Hawi and Waimea.

DAY 1: KAILUA-KONA AND SOUTH KONA

The first capital of the Hawaiian Kingdom established by King Kamehameha in 1812, the town of Kailua-Kona is steeped in history. Stroll the grounds of the **Courtyard King Kamehameha's Kona Beach Hotel,** the site where the king spent his last years at **Kamakahonu,** the royal compound. Inside the hotel, historic artifacts and exhibits are displayed in the lobby. A restored temple, **Ahuena Heiau,** sits sentry at the entrance to Kailua Bay by the pier. Kamehameha I met with advisors here, and passed away here in 1819. Nearby, **Hulihee Palace** is one of three royal palaces in the state. Docents lead guided tours, which showcase antique koa furnishings and artifacts of the day. Across the street, **Mokuaikaua Church** is the first Christian church in the state of Hawaii. It features a history room documenting the arrival of the first missionaries to Hawaii.

Drive south on Highway 11 to the Kona Historical Society in upcountry Kealakekua on Mamalahoa Highway. The destination includes the **H. N. Greenwell Store Museum.** This area is a peaceful place to linger awhile, as there are coffee farm tours and tasting at the adjacent

Greenwell Farms. A couple miles south down Mamalahoa Highway, the **Kona Coffee Living History Farm** in Captain Cook highlights farm life in the 1920s on a still-active coffee farm. Your next stop is **Puuhonua O Honaunau National Historical Park,** overlooking Honaunau Bay. This ancient sacred site offers self-guided walking tours through the royal compounds that once served as a refuge for lawbreakers and warriors fleeing battle. ■TIP→ **Before heading to the historical park, stop at ChoiceMart in Captain Cook and buy picnic items. The oceanfront picnic grounds at the park include barbecues, picnic tables, tide pools, and hiking trails.**

Logistics: You can walk around Kailua-Kona but will need a car for South Kona sites. When traveling south from Keauhou to Captain Cook, take the bypass road. Distance and time traveled: 44 miles round-trip, 35 minutes one-way, starting in Kailua-Kona. Car, via Highway 11.

DAY 2: SOUTH KOHALA

Pack your bags for a beach day while you also explore some ancient sites of old Hawaii. While in downtown Kailua-Kona, have breakfast and drive to nearby Honokohau Harbor. At the farthest end of the parking lot, a beach access trail takes you to a sandy cove inside **Kaloko-Honokohau National Historical Park.** Swim the pristine bay or walk the boardwalk to see ancient petroglyphs. Drive north on Queen Kaahumanu Highway and grab a gourmet lunch to go at **Pine Tree Cafe** before heading to the popular **Hapuna Beach State Recreation Area** for the afternoon. After spending time at Hapuna, explore the nearby **Puukohola Heiau National Historic Site,** home to the last major temple built by Kamehameha I. Ruins of the massive temple are still intact, and there's a small bay where black-tipped reef sharks pass over a submerged temple. For dinner, head back south down the highway to the **Shops at Mauna Lani,** where restaurants offer options for dinner. **Queens' MarketPlace** in Waikoloa has a food court with locally owned eateries.

Logistics: A car is needed. Distance and time traveled: 44 miles round-trip, 35 minutes one-way, starting in Kailua-Kona. Car, via Queen Kaahumanu Highway.

DAY 3: NORTH KOHALA AND WAIMEA

Start your day with breakfast at the **Kings' Shops,** where early-morning fare is served at several places at this lakeside retail and dining center in Waikoloa Beach Resort. Head north past the harborside town of Kawaihae to **Lapakahi State Historical Park,** site of an ancient fishing village revealing remnants of canoe houses, dwellings, and temples. Farther up the highway before the town of Hawi, turn west at the Upolu Airport turnoff and drive left of the airfield to King Kamehameha's birthplace, marked by a plaque. Park your car and hike south down the dirt road about a mile to the mysterious ruins of **Mookini Heiau,** which dates back to AD 480 and was known for human sacrifices. An eerie vibe emanates from the moss-laden rock walls that occupy windswept cliffs above the ocean. During winter, this is a great spot to watch migrating humpback whales. Drive into the artists' town of Hawi and eat lunch, then browse the galleries and stores. Just north of Hawi, the town of Kapaau is home to the original **King Kamehameha statue**; it towers above the highway on the grounds of the Kohala Information Center.

Take the scenic Kohala Mountain Road (Highway 250) to Waimea, in the heart of *paniolo* (cowboy) country. Two historic homes on **Parker Ranch** host visitor tours. Mana Hale is an all-koa wood home built

Tips

You can drive this loop itinerary in either direction, starting in Waimea if you wish.

Remember: "Kona" is the district, "Kailua-Kona" is the town, even though many people incorrectly use the terms interchangeably.

Respectful behavior is essential at sacred historic sites.

by John Parker Palmer in 1879 that sits just below a "Hawaiian Victorian" manor house built in 1862. The manor house was the family home of six generations of Parkers, the last of whom was actor Richard Smart, who outfitted it with art, family portraits, and treasures from his world travels. The houses can be toured on weekdays. Another historic site in Waimea, **Anna Ranch Heritage Center,** offers tours of the historic home that belonged to the legendary female equestrian and rancher Anna Lindsey Perry-Fiske. Before heading back home, eat dinner at one of Waimea's acclaimed restaurants.

Logistics: This day involves some scenic driving. Factor about 35 miles from Waikoloa Beach Resort to Kapaau, and 22 miles from Kapaau to Waimea. It's about a 15-minute drive from Waimea to the Kohala Coast resorts, and an hour or so drive back to Kailua-Kona.

Best Tours

A guided tour can be a hassle-free way to see lots of attractions on the Big Island (and other islands) without having to worry about the logistics and details yourself. Taking a tour can also be a great way to make new friends. Tour operators offer all kinds of itineraries to Hawaii, from general trips that include a variety of sights and experiences to more focused trips that hone in on anything from biking to nature. Keep in mind that Hawaii is a popular destination, and trips can book up well in advance.

General-Interest Tours

If you want to cover the ground efficiently while seeing a variety of sights, a general-interest tour is a good bet. These trips can include several islands. Often, visits to Hawaii Volcanoes National Park are included.

Aloha Hawaiian Vacations. Among other trips to the Islands, this company offers an all-inclusive, six-day adventure to the Big Island that includes a luau, beachfront buffets, half-day expeditions, a rental car, bellman tips, and all taxes. ☎ 800/256–4211 ⊕ www.aloha-hawaiian. com ✉ From $1,995.

Globus. On its Grand Hawaii Vacation, Globus visits the main Hawaiian Islands, including the Big Island. Guests visit the Kona Coffee Living History Farm and the world's most active volcano, Kilauea. This very popular tour sells out quickly. Check online as tours to the Big Island frequently change, and some years only interisland cruises are available. ☎ 866/755–8581 ⊕ www.globusjourneys. com ✉ From $3,100.

Road Scholar. Focusing on travelers over 50, this nonprofit organization leads all-inclusive learning adventures, including cultural and educational tours of Hawaii; other tours are adventure-focused. Several multi-island tour packages include stays on the Big Island, where participants can explore such places as Hawaii Volcanoes National Park, Puuhonua O Honaunau National Historical Park, and the Cloud Forest Sanctuary above Kailua-Kona. ☎ 800/454–5766 ⊕ www. roadscholar.org ✉ From $2,899.

Trafalgar. Offering a wide range of Hawaii tour itineraries and pricing, Trafalgar is great for visitors who want to see a lot of Hawaii without having to arrange all the fly-drive-hotel details themselves. On most of its Big Island legs, the company takes you to Hawaii Volcanoes National Park, with stops along the way, and then gives you a free day to enjoy snorkeling, whale-watching, or manta ray dives. ☎ 866/809–8426 ⊕ www.trafalgar.com ✉ From $3,439.

YMT Vacations. Billing itself as the best choice in affordable travel, YMT offers a 13-day, four-island tour and a 12-day Hawaiian Islands cruise and tour. ☎ 877/322–6185 ⊕ www.ymtvacations. com ✉ From $1,999.

Adventure Study

A tour of Kilauea Volcano—the most active volcano on earth—is even better when led by an actual geologist, volcanologist, retired ranger, or even botanist.

Friends of Hawaii Volcanoes National Park. With tours tailored to small groups or individuals, the Friends of Hawaii Volcanoes National Park offers custom tours with specialist guides who help you make fascinating discoveries and learn details about such geologic features as lava tubes, vents, and fumaroles. Tours are tailored to your interest and group size and last four to eight hours. Another option is to join the Friends and participate in their regular programs. ☎ *808/985–7373* ⊕ *fhvnp.org* ✉ *From $325 for group of 1–6 people.*

Biking

If you're a bicycling enthusiast, you've got exciting options on the Big Island. ■ TIP→ **Most airlines accommodate bikes as luggage, provided they're dismantled and boxed.**

Bicycle Adventures. Take a seven-day Hawaii tour that includes biking, hiking, snorkeling, sailing, and whale-watching. Accommodations, meals, and park admissions are included. ☎ *800/443– 6060* ⊕ *www.bicycleadventures.com* ✉ *From $3,568.*

Bird-Watching

Because of its isolated location, nearly 2,500 miles from any major landmass, Hawaii's unique habitats have encouraged many unusual species of birds to evolve. Although many bird species have been lost due to hunting, introduced predators, or loss of habitat, some highly endangered birds still thrive, mostly in the Hakalau National Wildlife Refuge on the slopes of Maunakea, where their natural forest habitats have been replanted and protected. Birders from around the world come here and to other parts of the island to spot these amazing creatures—and you can, too, with the help of expert guides.

Hawaii Forest and Trail. This company offers two different bird-watching tours. The Endangered Native Habitat (Rainforest and Dryforest) Birding Adventure takes bird lovers to explore a cloud-misted rain forest on the slopes of Maunakea

as well as a dry-forest habitat on Mauna Loa. Expert guides help you search native forests for amakihi, iiwi, elepaio, *apapane*, and the endangered *akiapolaau.*

The Hakalau Forest tour offers outstanding opportunities to spot the rarest endemic birds, allowing exclusive access to the highly restricted Hakalau National Wildlife Refuge. You may even see such thrilling sights as the highly endangered, bright orange *akepa* juvenile being fed by its parents. Walking sticks, binoculars, rain ponchos, and meals are provided. ☎ *800/464–1993* ⊕ *www.hawaii-forest. com* ✉ *From $189.*

Victor Emanuel Nature Tours. The company has multiday trips that include the Big Island, led by well-known birding experts such as Brendan Mulrooney and Erik Bruhnke. Focusing on off-the-beaten path destinations and habitats, the tours offer birders the chance to spot such indigenous species as the amakihi, *apapane,* elepaio, and the comical scarlet iiwi, as well as endemic birds such as the omao, palila, and *akepa* honeycreepers. Tour prices include interisland flights and are offered in both spring and fall. ☎ *800/328–8368* ⊕ *www.ventbird.com* ✉ *From $4,895.*

Eco Tours

Sierra Club Outings. You'll stay at a grand historic home in Hilo while exploring the bounty of sights on land and underwater on the "Best of the Big Island" tour. With this company, tours include a service-project component, such as restoring critical bird habitats or beautifying gardens. Book early because most itineraries sell out fast. ☎ *415/977–5522* ⊕ *www.sierraclub. org/outings* ✉ *From $2,200.*

On the Calendar

February

Waimea Cherry Blossom Heritage Festival, first weekend in February. A celebration of Japanese culture takes places in conjunction with cherry blossom viewing in Waimea. See the Facebook page for information. ☎ *808/961–8706.*

March

Kona Brewers Festival, second weekend of March. A celebration of suds, hops, craft beers, and home brews is held on the grounds of the Courtyard King Kamehameha's Kona Beach Hotel in Kailua-Kona. ⊕ *www.konabrewersfestival.com* ☎ *808/987–9196.*

April

Merrie Monarch Festival, mid-April. The most prestigious hula competition in the world attracts hula dancers from around the globe at this weeklong event in Hilo. ⊕ *www.merriemonarch.com* ☎ *808/935–9168.*

May

Kau Coffee Festival, mid-May. While Kona coffee gets all the attention, this festival near Ka Lae (South Point) sets the record straight about the excellence of coffee grown in the Kau District. ⊕ *www.kaucof-feefestival.com.*

June

King Kamehameha Day Celebration Parade in Kailua-Kona, Saturday closest to June 11. Traditional Hawaiian equestrian units are the star attraction of this annual floral parade in Historic Kailua Village. ⊕ *www.konaparade.org.*

July

Parker Ranch Independence Day Rodeo, July 4. Witness Hawaiian *paniolos* (cowboys) in action at the rodeo grounds in Waimea. ⊕ *www.parkerranch.com* ☎ *808/885–7311.*

September

Big Island Slack Key Guitar Festival, late August. The free music festival at Court-yard King Kamehameha's Kona Beach Hotel features the island's top slack-key players. ⊕ *www.slackkeyfestival.com* ☎ *808/226–2697.*

October

Ironman World Championship, usually second Saturday in October. The Super Bowl of triathlons attracts tens of thousands of visitors to Kailua-Kona to watch the swim-bike-run competition that starts and ends near the pier. ⊕ *www.ironman.com/im-world-championship.*

November

Kona Coffee Cultural Festival, mid-November. Nearly 50 events over a 10-day period celebrate Kona's rich coffee heritage. ⊕ *www.konacoffeefest.com* ☎ *808/990–6511.*

December

Kailua-Kona Christmas Parade, first weekend in December. Holiday festivity is on display during this colorful, light-filled evening parade down Alii Drive in Historic Kailua Village. ⊕ *www.paradesinkona.com* ☎ *808/345–2108.*

Chapter 3

KAILUA-KONA AND THE KONA COAST

Updated by
Kristina Anderson

👁 Sights	🍴 Restaurants	🛏 Hotels	🛍 Shopping	🍸 Nightlife
★★★★★	★★★☆☆	★★★☆☆	★★★☆☆	★★☆☆☆

WELCOME TO KAILUA-KONA AND THE KONA COAST

TOP REASONS TO GO

★ **Hulihee Palace:** Now a museum, this lovely oceanfront palace dates to the 19th century.

★ **Kamakahonu and Ahuena Heiau:** This compound, a National Historic Landmark, served as the seat of government for King Kamehameha and housed his personal *heiau*, or temple.

★ **Kahaluu Beach Park:** If you are a snorkeling newbie, this pretty, accessible beach park is the perfect place to start.

★ **Kailua-Kona Village:** Once a sleepy fishing village, today Kailua-Kona hosts a lively array of restaurants, shops, and historic sites.

★ **Kealakekua Bay State Historical Park:** This stunning, pristine bay is blessed with the clearest water on the island.

★ **Puuhonua O Honaunau National Historical Park:** Step back into ancient Hawaii and visit an authentic "place of refuge," where transgressors of the *kapu* (law) were forgiven their sins or crimes.

With one of the island's two airports (Kona International Airport is 7 miles north of the town center, while the other airport is on the island's east side, in Hilo), Kailua-Kona is the closest thing the Big Island has to a "city" on the windward coast and is the location of most of the Big Island's major resorts. It's also where the first Christian missionaries landed in 1820 and changed life in the islands forever.

1 Kailua-Kona. Formerly a quaint fishing town, Kailua-Kona is now a lively tourist area dotted with historical sites such as Hulihee Palace and Ahuena Heiau, final home of King Kamehameha I (Kamehameha the Great). Development is centered along Alii Drive, which runs along the waterfront and where you'll find most of the area's condo complexes, restaurants, and shops. Many of the island's biggest resort hotels are here as well. Because of the concentration of establishments, this can be one of the most congested parts of the Big Island.

2 South Kona. The gateway to the hilly Kona coffee belt, South Kona is home to rural farming communities, jaw-dropping topography, and one of the state's most beautiful bays, Kealakekua Bay. The main settlement in South Kona is Captain Cook. The area has drawn local and transplated artists to the Big Island of Hawaii for decades, and many have settled in the small town of Holoaloa, just south of Kailua-Kona. Several coffee farms invite visitors to watch their harvesting and production processes as well as take (mostly free) guided and self-guided tours of the facilities. South Kona accommodations are mostly small hotels and guest houses.

3 North Kona. Some of the most stellar Big Island beaches and historical sites, including Kekaha Kai State Park and Kaloko-Honokohau National Historical Park, are in North Kona, which is largely undeveloped with the exception of the luxurious Four Seasons resort. While the area's expansive black lava plains are the dominant feature, beautiful white beaches can be found dotting the coastline a mere highway turnoff away.

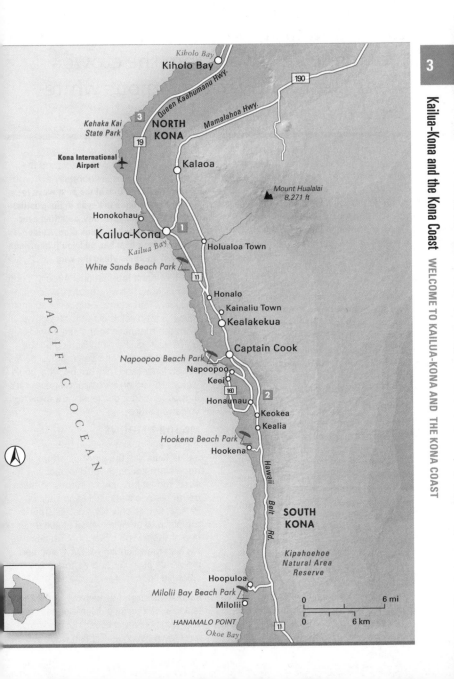

More laid-back than the tonier Kohala Coast, the Kona Coast and its largest town, Kailua-Kona, are great if you are looking to get away from the crowds along the island's more famous white-sand beaches.

Except for the rare deluge, the sun shines year-round. Mornings offer cooler weather, smaller crowds, and more birds singing in the banyan trees; you'll see tourists and locals out running on Alii Drive, the town's main drag, by about 5 am every day. Afternoons sometimes bring clouds and light rain, but evenings often clear up so you can enjoy cool drinks, brilliant sunsets, gentle trade winds, and lazy hours spent gazing out over the ocean. Though there are better beaches north of town on the Kohala Coast, Kailua-Kona is home to a few gems, including a fantastic snorkeling beach (Kahaluu) and a tranquil bay perfect for kids (Kamakahonu Beach, in front of the Courtyard King Kamehameha's Kona Beach Hotel).

The south Kona Coast is quiet and relatively rural. Much of the farmland is in leasehold status, which explains why this part of the Big Island has remained rather untouched by development. Tour one of the coffee farms to find out what the big deal is about Kona coffee, and enjoy a free sample while you're at it. A 20-minute drive off the highway from Captain Cook leads to beautiful Kealakekua Bay, where Captain James Cook arrived in 1778, dying here not long after. Hawaiian spinner dolphins frolic in the bay, now a Marine Life Conservation District, nestled alongside high green cliffs that jut dramatically out to sea. Snorkeling is superb here, so you may want to bring your gear

and spend an hour or so exploring the coral reefs. The bay is normally extremely calm. ■ TIP→ **One of the best ways to spend a morning is to kayak in the pristine waters of Kealakekua Bay, paddling over to see the spot where Cook died. Guided tours are your best bet, and you'll likely see plenty of dolphins along the way.**

North of Kona International Airport, along Mamalahoa Highway, brightly colored bougainvilleas stand out in relief against miles of jet-black lava fields stretching from the mountain to the sea. Sometimes visitors liken it to landing on the moon when they first see it. True, the dry barren landscape may not be what you'd expect to find on a tropical island, but it's a good reminder of the island's evolving volcanic nature.

MAJOR REGIONS

A lively and quaint seaside town, **Kailua-Kona** has the souvenir shops and open-air restaurants you'd expect in a small tourist hub, plus a surprising number of historic sites, including Hulihee Palace, Kona's only royal palace. This is the place to enjoy a mai tai at sunset at one of the town's oceanfront restaurants. It's also fun to cruise Alii Drive and people-watch as locals and visitors enjoy this splendid spot.

South Kona stretches halfway to the Big Island's southern tip. Mamalahoa Highway hugs splendid coastlines and small rural towns such as Captain Cook and

Honaunau, leaving busy streets behind. The winding upcountry road takes you straight to the heart of coffee country, where fertile plantations (some open for tours and tastings), simple houses, and jaw-dropping views offer a taste of what Hawaii was like before the resorts took over.

North Kona is rather barren, with vast lava fields that turn off onto some of the island's most beautiful beaches. It's also where you'll find the Four Seasons Resort Hualalai, one of the Big Island of Hawaii's ultra-luxurious resorts.

Planning

Planning Your Time

Half a day is plenty of time to explore Kailua-Kona, as most of the town's sights are in or near the downtown area. Still, if you add in a beach trip (Kahaluu Beach has some of the best and easiest snorkeling on the island), it's tempting to while away the day here. Another option is to extend your visit a day or two and take a short trip up a small hill to the artsy village of Holualoa or to the coffee farms in the mountains just above Kealakekua Bay, adding a visit down to the bay before you're through. Don't miss the evocative Puuhonua O Honaunau National Historical Park near the bay, which preserves an ancient temple complex and traditional place of refuge.

Getting Here and Around

AIR
The Big Island of Hawaii has two airports, with Ellison Onizuka Kona International Airport being the busiest, with the most direct flights from the mainland United States. It has staffed booths that provide visitor information.

The town closest to Kona International Airport (it's about 7 miles away), Kailua-Kona is a convenient home base from which to explore the island.

BUS
The Hele-On Bus (⊕ *www.heleonbus. org*) offers some service around the immediate Kailua-Kona area, but other routes run less frequently and aren't really useful or recommended for tourists with limited time. The fare is $2 per ride ($1 for students and seniors).

CAR
It's really essential to rent a car when you're coming to this part of the Big Island. There is no organized bus service beyond the immediate Kailua-Kona area, so you'll need transportation if you want to explore even a bit.

The easiest place to park your car in Kailua-Kona is at Courtyard King Kamehameha's Kona Beach Hotel, but you'll have to pay a daily parking fee. Some free parking is also available: when you enter Kailua via Palani Road, turn left onto Kuakini Highway, drive for a half block, and turn right into the small marked parking lot. Walk *makai* (toward the ocean) on Likana Lane a half block to Alii Drive, and you'll be in the heart of Kailua-Kona.

Hotels

Bustling Kailua-Kona offers tons of lodging options. In addition to hotels, oceanfront Alii Drive is lined with condos and vacation homes. All the conveniences are here, and there are several grocery stores and big-box retailers nearby for those who need to stock up on supplies. Kailua-Kona has a handful of beaches—Magic Sands, Kahaluu, and Kamakahonu (at the pier) among them. The downside to staying here is that you'll have to drive 30 to 45 minutes up the road to the Kohala Coast to visit Hawaii's signature, long, white-sand beaches. However, you'll also pay about half what you would at any of the major resorts, not to mention that Kailua-Kona offers a bit more local charm.

There are no resorts along the Kona Coast (other than the Four Seasons Resort Hualalai in North Kona), but there are plenty of fantastic bed-and-breakfasts and vacation rental homes at Kealakekua Bay and in the hills above. The towns of Captain Cook and Kainaliu offer excellent dining and shopping options, and several coffee farms are open for tours. You can get to Hawaii Volcanoes National Park in about 90 minutes, and you're also close to several less well-known but wonderful beaches, including Hookena Beach Park. Kailua-Kona is a 30-minute drive from Captain Cook, while the iconic, white-sand beaches of the Kohala Coast are an hour or more away.

Restaurants

While all the hotels in the area have an upscale restaurant or two, the majority of establishments in Kailua-Kona tend to be family owned and feature locally sourced seafood, meat, and produce. A handful of restaurants offer Hawaiian plate specialties, along with Japanese and Thai cuisine. If you want a mai tai at sunset, you've come to the right place. Just about every restaurant hosts a nightly happy hour. Prices are slightly lower than at the Kohala resorts, and Kailua-Kona eateries definitely offer greater choice and diversity, plus some amazing ocean-front views of crashing surf and sunsets.

Once you drive up the big hill heading south, dining choices are far fewer, but you will find excellent Japanese, American, and Chinese cuisine. There are also some farm-to-table options, cafés, delis, coffee shops, taco trucks, and fast food and veggie wrap places. Keep your eye out for the little local holes-in-the-wall that offer fantastic *laulau* (pork wrapped with steamed taro and banana leaves). Most restaurants upcountry close early, so keep that in mind if traveling after sunset.

HOTEL AND RESTAURANT PRICES

Hotel prices in the reviews are the lowest cost of a standard double room in high season. Restaurant prices in the reviews are the average cost of a main course at dinner, or if dinner is not served, at lunch. Restaurant and hotel reviews have been shortened. For full information, visit Fodors.com.

What it Costs in U.S. Dollars			
$	$$	$$$	$$$$
RESTAURANTS			
under $17	$17–$26	$27–$35	over $35
HOTELS			
under $180	$180–$260	$261–$340	over $340

Tours

Kona Historical Society

SELF-GUIDED | The society, based in Kealakekua, sells a 24-page *Historic Kailua Village Map* booklet ($15) with a map and more than 40 historical photos. You can take a self-guided walking tour to learn more about the village's fascinating past. Order the booklet online before you travel so you have the guidebook in hand for your tour. ⊠ *81-6551 Mamalahoa Hwy., Kealakekua* ☎ *808/323–3222* ⊕ *www.konahistorical.org.*

Kailua-Kona

Kailua-Kona is about 7 miles south of the Kona airport.

The largest town on the Kona Coast, lively Kailua-Kona offers plenty to accommodate the needs of locals and visitors, but it also has some signficant historic sites. Scattered among the shops, restaurants, and condo complexes of Alii Drive are Ahuena Heiau, a temple complex restored by King Kamehameha the

Great and the spot where he spent his last days (he died here in 1819); the last royal palace in the United States (Hulihee Palace); and a battleground dotted with the graves of ancient Hawaiians who fought for their way of life and lost. It was also here in Kailua-Kona that Kamehameha's successor, King Liholiho, broke with the ancient *kapu* (roughly translated as "forbidden," it was the name for the strict code of conduct that islanders were compelled to follow) system by publicly sitting and eating with women. The following year, on April 4, 1820, the first Christian missionaries came ashore here, changing life in the Islands forever.

GETTING HERE AND AROUND

Most first-time visitors to the island are startled by touching down on the seemingly endless black lava fields that makes up the airport area and immediate surroundings. However, just a 10-minute drive on Queen Kaahumanu Highway heading south takes you into the seaside town of Kailua-Kona and nearby retail centers. To get to town, take a right onto Palani Road, and a left on Kuakini, and find one of the free lots along Kuakini Highway. You can park and walk right to the village and the seawall. You can also get to the restaurant row area by taking Kuakini Highway and turning right into the Coconut Grove Marketplace's vast free lot. From there, you can reach oceanfront establishments such as Bongo Ben's, Humpy's Big Island Alehouse, and Island Lava Java. Alii Drive, the town's main street, runs north and south along the water and is popular for walking, with plenty of shops and restaurants. Sunsets here are spectacular.

◉ Sights

Courtyard King Kamehameha's Kona Beach Hotel

HOTEL—SIGHT | Even if you're not staying here, make time to stroll through the expansive lobby of this Kailua-Kona fixture to view impressive displays of Hawaiian artifacts, including feathered helmets, capes, ancient hula instruments, and battle weapons. Portraits of Hawaiian royalty adorn the walls. You'll also see mounted marlin from Hawaii International Billfish tournaments (from when Kailua Pier was still the weigh-in point). These are "granders," marlin weighing 1,000 pounds or more. One of the best collections of works by Hawaiian artist Herb Kane is on display in the breezeway. Activities in Hawaiian arts and crafts are conducted regularly by on-site cultural staff. ✉ 75-5660 Palani Rd., Kailua-Kona ☎ 808/329–2911, 800/367–2111 ⊕ www.konabeachhotel.com ◪ Full-day parking $15.

★ Holualoa

TOWN | Hugging the hillside along the Kona Coast, the artsy village of Holualoa is 3 miles up winding Hualalai Road from Kailua-Kona. Galleries here feature all types of artists—painters, woodworkers, jewelers, gourd makers, and potters—working in their studios in back and selling their wares up front. Look for frequent town-wide events such as art strolls and block parties. Then relax with a cup of coffee in one of the many cafés or stores. Formerly the exclusive domain of coffee plantations, Holualoa still boasts quite a few coffee farms offering free tours and inviting cups of Kona. ✉ Holualoa ⊕ www.holualoahawaii.com.

Holualoa Kona Coffee Company

FARM/RANCH | There is a lot going on at this truly all-organic coffee farm and processing facility, from growing the beans to milling and drying. The processing plant next door to the farm demonstrates how the beans are roasted and packaged. A flock of 50 geese welcomes visitors and "provides fertilizer" for the plantation at no charge. Holualoa also processes beans for 100 coffee farms in the area. ✉ 77-6261 Old Mamalahoa Hwy., Holualoa ☎ 808/322–9937, 800/334–0348 ⊕ konalea.com ◪ Free ☉ Closed weekends.

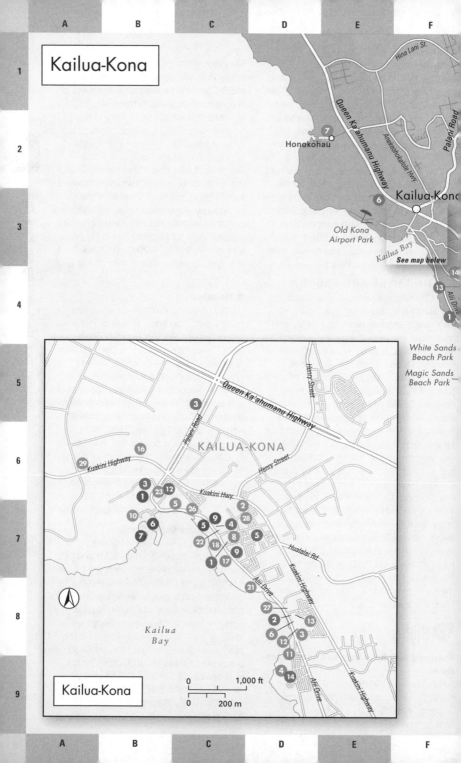

KEY

① Exploring Sights
① Restaurants
① Quick Bites
① Hotels

Sights ▼

1 Courtyard King Kamehameha's Kona Beach Hotel **B6**
2 Holualoa **G4**
3 Holualoa Kona Coffee Company **H5**
4 Hula Daddy Kona Coffee **G1**
5 Hulihee Palace **C7**
6 Kailua Pier **B7**
7 Kamakahonu and Ahuena Heiau **B7**
8 Kuamoo Battlefield and Lekeleke Burial Grounds **G7**
9 Mokuaikaua Church **C7**
10 St. Peter's by the Sea Chapel **G6**

Restaurants ▼

1 Bianelli's Gourmet Pizza and Pasta **G6**
2 Big Island Grill **C7**
3 Bongo Ben's Island Café **D8**
4 Don the Beachcomber at Royal Kona Resort **D9**
5 The Fish Hopper **C7**
6 Foster's Kitchen **D8**
7 Harbor House **E2**
8 Hayashi's You Make the Roll **C7**
9 Holuakoa Gardens and Cafe **H4**
10 Honu's on the Beach **B7**
11 Huggo's **D8**
12 Humpy's Big Island Alehouse **D8**
13 Island Lava Java **D8**
14 Jackie Rey's Ohana Grill **F4**
15 Kenichi Pacific **G6**
16 Kona Brewing Co. Pub and Brewery **B6**
17 Kona Inn Restaurant **C7**
18 Kona Taeng On Thai **C7**
19 La Bourgogne **G4**
20 Magics Beach Grill **G5**
21 Mi's Waterfront Bistro **D8**
22 Pancho and Lefty's Cantina **C7**
23 Quinn's Almost by the Sea **B6**
24 Rays On The Bay **G6**
25 Sam Choy's Kai Lanai **G6**
26 Sushi Cocoro and Udon Tuna-ichi **C7**
27 Thai Rin Restaurant and Bar **D8**
28 TK Noodle House **C7**
29 Umekes Fish Market Bar and Grill **A6**

Quick Bites ▼

1 Frenchman's Cafe **C7**
2 Kanaka Kava **D8**
3 Kona Coffee and Tea **C5**
4 Kope Lani **C7**
5 Los Habaneros **G6**
6 Ultimate Burger **E3**

Hotels ▼

1 Aston Kona by the Sea **F4**
2 Castle Kona Bali Kai **G4**
3 Courtyard King Kamehameha's Kona Beach Hotel **B6**
4 Hale Hualalai Bed and Breakfast **G1**
5 Holiday Inn Express and Suites Kailua-Kona **D7**
6 Holua Resort at Mauna Loa Village **G7**
7 Holualoa Inn **H4**
8 Kanaloa at Kona by Outrigger **G6**
9 Kona Bay Hotel **C7**
10 Kona Coast Resort **G6**
11 Kona Magic Sands **G5**
12 Kona Seaside Hotel **B6**
13 Kona Tiki Hotel **F4**
14 Royal Kona Resort **D9**
15 Sheraton Kona Resort and Spa at Keauhou Bay **G7**

Hula Daddy Kona Coffee

FARM/RANCH | On a walking tour of this working coffee farm (by advance reservation only), visitors can witness the workings of a small plantation, pick and pulp their own coffee beans, watch a roasting demonstration, and have a tasting. The gift shop carries whole beans and logo swag including bags, T-shirts, and mugs. Coffee brewing workshops and one-on-one tours with a master roaster are also offered. ✉ *74-4944 Mamalahoa Hwy., Holualoa* ☎ *808/327–9744, 888/553–2339* ⊕ *www.huladaddy.com* ✉ *From $15* ☉ *Closed weekends.*

★ Hulihee Palace

CASTLE/PALACE | On the National Register of Historic Places, this lovely two-story oceanfront home, surrounded by jewel-green grass and elegant coco palms and fronted by an elaborate wrought-iron gate, is one of only three royal palaces in America (the other two are in Honolulu). The royal residence was built by Governor John Adams Kuakini in 1838, a year after he completed Mokuaikaua Church. During the 1880s, it served as King David Kalakaua's summer palace.

Built of lava rock and coral lime mortar, it features vintage koa furniture, weaving, European crystal chandeliers, giant four-poster beds, royal portraits, tapa cloth, feather work, and Hawaiian quilts. After the overthrow of the Hawaiian monarchy in 1893, the property fell into disrepair. Set to be torn down for a hotel, it was rescued in 1920 by the Daughters of Hawaii, a nonprofit organization dedicated to preserving the culture and royal heritage of the Islands. The organization oversees and operates the site to this day. ✉ *75-5718 Alii Dr., Kailua-Kona* ☎ *808/329–1877* ⊕ *www.daughtersof-hawaii.org* ✉ *$8 self-guided tour, $10 guided.*

Kailua Pier

MARINA | Though most fishing boats use Honokohau Harbor in Kailua-Kona, this pier dating from 1918 is still a hub of ocean activity. Outrigger canoe teams practice and race, shuttles transport cruise ship passengers to and from town, and tour boats depart from these docks daily. Along the seawall, children and old-timers cast their lines. For youngsters, a bamboo pole and hook are easy to come by, and plenty of locals are willing to give pointers. September brings the world's largest long-distance canoe race, while in October, 1,700 elite athletes leave from the pier to swim 2.4 miles as part of the famous Ironman World Championship triathlon. ✉ *Alii Dr., Kailua-Kona* ✛ *Across from Courtyard King Kamehameha's Kona Beach Hotel* ✉ *Free.*

★ Kamakahonu and Ahuena Heiau

ARCHAEOLOGICAL SITE | In the early 1800s, King Kamehameha the Great built a large royal compound at Kamakahonu, the bay fronting what is now the Courtyard King Kamehameha's Kona Beach Hotel. Today it is one of the most revered and historically significant sites in all of Hawaii. Kamakahonu, meaning "eye of the turtle," was named for a prominent turtle-shaped rock there, covered in cement when the hotel and pier were built. The Ahuena Heiau, a stunning *heiau* (temple), was dedicated to Lono, the Hawaiian god of peace and prosperity. It was also used as a seat of government.

Today the compound features a scaled-down replica of the temple and is a National Historic Landmark. It sustained some damage in the 2011 tsunami and has been repaired. You can't go inside the *heiau*, but you can view it from the beach or directly next door at the hotel's luau grounds. ✉ *75-5660 Palani Rd., Kailua-Kona* ⊕ *www.nps.gov/places/kamakahonu.htm.*

Kuamoo Battlefield and Lekeleke Burial Grounds

ARCHAEOLOGICAL SITE | In 1819, an estimated 300 Hawaiians were killed on this vast lava field. Their burial mounds are still visible at the south end of Alii Drive (called

Mokuaikaua Church in Kailua-Kona, completed in 1837, was the first Christian church in the Hawaiian Islands.

the "End of the World" by locals). After the death of his father, King Kamehameha, the newly crowned King Liholiho ate at a table with women, breaking the ancient *kapu* (taboo) system. Chief Kekuaokalani, his cousin and co-heir, held radically different views about religious traditions and unsuccessfully challenged Liholiho's forces in battle here. ⊠ *Alii Dr., Kailua-Kona.*

★ Mokuaikaua Church
RELIGIOUS SITE | Site of the first Christian church in the Hawaiian Islands, this solid lava-rock structure, built in 1836, is mortared with burned lime, coral, and *kukui* (candlenut) oil and topped by an impressive steeple. The ceiling and interior were crafted of timbers harvested from a forest on Hualalai and held together with wooden pegs, not nails. Inside, behind a panel of gleaming koa wood, rests a model of the brig *Thaddeus* as well as a koa-wood table crafted by Henry Boshard, pastor for 43 years. The gift shop is open most mornings, and a talk is given by the church historian Sundays at noon.

You may also encounter Aloha Greeters within the sanctuary, who love to share the history of Mokuaikaua with visitors. The church still holds services and hosts community events, so please be respectful when entering the building. ⊠ *75-5713 Alii Dr., Kailua-Kona* ☎ *808/329–0655* ⊕ *www.mokuaikaua.org* ✉ *Free.*

St. Peter's by the Sea Chapel
RELIGIOUS SITE | This tiny oceanfront Roman Catholic chapel by Kahaluu Beach Park, with its crisp white-and-blue trim and old-fashioned steeple, sits next to the site of an ancient *heiau* (temple), now marked by a dry-stack rock wall. This is not the church's original location, however. In 1912, it was dismantled and carried here piece by piece from a site across from Magic Sands Beach. Due to past issues with vandalism, the church is locked at all times other than for mass on Saturday morning at 7:30. ⊠ *78-6684 Alii Dr., Kailua-Kona* ✛ *Just north of mile marker 5, by Kahaluu* ⊕ *stmichaelparish-kona.org.*

Beaches

Kahaluu Beach Park

BEACH—SIGHT | Shallow and easily accessible, this salt-and-pepper beach is one of the Big Island's most popular swimming and snorkeling sites, thanks to the fringing reef that helps keep the waters calm, visibility high, and reef life—especially *honu* (gree sea turtles) and colorful fish—plentiful. Because it is so protected, it's great for first-time snorkelers. Outside the reef, very strong rip currents can run, so caution is advised. Never hand-feed the unusually tame reef fish here; it upsets the balance of the reef. ■**TIP**➔ **Experienced surfers find good waves beyond the reef, and scuba divers like the shore dives—shallow ones inside the breakwater, deeper ones outside.** Snorkel equipment and boards are available for rent nearby, and surf schools operate here. Kahaluu was a favorite of the Hawaiian royal family. **Amenities:** food and drink; lifeguards; parking (no fee); showers; toilets. **Best for:** snorkeling; surfing; swimming. ✉ *78-6720 Alii Dr., Kailua-Kona* ✛ *5½ miles south of Kailua-Kona, across from Beach Villas* ☎ *808/961–8311* 🔳 *Free.*

Kamakahonu Beach

BEACH—SIGHT | **FAMILY** | This is where King Kamehameha spent his final days—the restored Ahuena Heiau sits on a platform across from the sand. Adjacent to Kailua Pier, the scenic crescent of white sand is one of the few beaches in downtown Kailua-Kona. The water here is almost always calm and the beach clean, making this a perfect spot for kids. For adults, it's a great place for swimming, stand-up paddleboarding (SUP), watching outrigger teams practice, or enjoying a lazy beach day. It can get crowded on weekends. Snorkeling can be good north of the beach, and snorkeling, SUP, and kayaking equipment can be rented nearby. There's lots of grass and shade, and free parking in county lots is a short stroll away. **Amenities:** food and drink; showers; toilets; water sports. **Best for:** snorkeling; swimming. ✉ *75-5660 Palani Rd., at Alii Dr., Kailua-Kona* 🔳 *Free.*

Magic Sands Beach Park (*White Sands Beach*)

BEACH—SIGHT | Towering coconut trees provide some shade and lend a touch of tropical beauty to this pretty little beach park (also called Laaloa), which may well be the Big Island's most intriguing stretch of sand. A migratory beach of sorts, it can disappear when waves wash away the small white-sand parcel (hence the name "Magic Sands"). Then suddenly, all the sand can reappear within days. You'll know you've found it when you see the body- and board surfers. It's often quite crowded, no matter what time of year. **Amenities:** lifeguards; parking (no fee); showers; toilets. **Best for:** sunset; surfing. ✉ *77-6470 Alii Dr., Kailua-Kona* ✛ *4½ miles south of Kailua-Kona* ☎ *808/961–8311* 🔳 *Free.*

Old Kona Airport Park

BEACH—SIGHT | **FAMILY** | Hugging the long shoreline adjacent to the runway that served Kona's airport until 1970, this beach is flat, generally clean, and dotted with rocks and coral pieces. Calm waters make for good snorkeling, and a few accessible small coves of white sand offer safe water entry and tide pools for children. Shady areas are good for picnics or admiring the Kona skyline, complete with a whale (in season) and a cruise ship or two. A well-tended community jogging trail and dog park opposite the runway are worth checking out. Just north, an offshore surf break known as Old A's is popular with local surfers. It's usually not crowded, but this area can get busy on weekends. **Amenities:** parking (no fee); showers; toilets. **Best for:** sunset; walking. ✉ *Kailua-Kona* ✛ *North end of Kuakini Hwy.* ☎ *808/961–8561* 🔳 *Free.*

🍴 Restaurants

Bianelli's Gourmet Pizza and Pasta
$ | **ITALIAN** | **FAMILY** | With indoor and outdoor seating, this easygoing Italian restaurant serves up gourmet pizzas and a tasty selection of pasta dishes, calzones, sandwiches, and salads. For a couple of bucks, order a slice of pizza and pair it with an island-fresh dinner salad. **Known for:** cozy dining room with quick service; patio seating inside upscale shopping center; pies you can take and bake at home. [$] *Average main: $14* ✉ *Keauhou Shopping Center, 78-6831 Alii Dr., Kailua-Kona* ☎ *808/322–0377* 🌐 *www.bianellis.com* 🕑 *Closed Sun. No lunch.*

Big Island Grill
$ | **HAWAIIAN** | **FAMILY** | A local-style Hawaiian restaurant, this place looks like an old coffee shop—it's large and nondescript inside, with booths, basic tables, and bingo-hall chairs. Local families love it for the huge portions of pork chops, *loco moco* (meat, rice, and eggs smothered in gravy), and an assortment of fish specialties at very reasonable prices. "Biggie's" also serves a decent breakfast. **Known for:** authentic local vibe; Sunday breakfast; popularity with large groups and families. [$] *Average main: $15* ✉ *75-5702 Kuakini Hwy., Kailua-Kona* ☎ *808/326–1153* 🕑 *No lunch or dinner Sun.*

★ **Bongo Ben's Island Café**
$ | **AMERICAN** | At the entry of this super-casual, oceanfront diner with views of Kailua Bay, menus printed on the giant bongos tell the story. Offering great deals on a plethora of breakfast, lunch, and dinner items, the open-air restaurant bakes its own breads, cinnamon rolls, desserts, pizza crust, and hamburger buns on-site. **Known for:** early opening hours for breakfast; prime rib night and other weekly specials; discounts on morning and happy hour cocktails. [$] *Average main: $15* ✉ *75-5819 Alii Dr., Kailua-Kona* ☎ *808/329–9203* 🌐 *www.bongobens.com.*

Don the Beachcomber at Royal Kona Resort
$$ | **HAWAIIAN** | The "original home of the mai tai," Don the Beachcomber features an open-air, retro, tiki-bar setting with the absolute best view of Kailua Bay in town. Service can be slow, but the coconut prawns are worth the wait, as is the New York steak paired with bacon-wrapped shrimp. **Known for:** slow-roasted prime rib; dining on the water's edge; Don's Mai Tai Bar with menu items and 10 types of mai tais. [$] *Average main: $25* ✉ *Royal Kona Resort, 75-5852 Alii Dr., Kailua-Kona* ☎ *808/329–3111* 🌐 *www.royalkona.com* 🕑 *No lunch. No dinner Sun.–Wed.*

The Fish Hopper
$$ | **SEAFOOD** | **FAMILY** | With a bayside view in the heart of Historic Kailua Village, the open-air Hawaii location of the popular Monterey, California, restaurant has an expansive menu for breakfast, lunch, and dinner. Inventive fresh-fish specials as well as simple fish-and-chips and clam chowder are what the original is known for. **Known for:** award-winning clam chowder; tropical oceanfront dining; signature Volcano flaming cocktail. [$] *Average main: $24* ✉ *75-5683 Alii Dr., Kailua-Kona* ☎ *808/326–2002* 🌐 *www.fishhopper.com.*

★ **Foster's Kitchen**
$$ | **AMERICAN** | Ocean breezes flow through this open-air, bayfront restaurant on Alii Drive, known for a quality menu infused with Cajun and island influences; almost all dishes are made to order and feature non-GMO, hormone-free, or USDA certified organic ingredients. A must-try is the seafood pesto puff pastry on the appetizer menu, and for dinner, the steak house pasta (creamy mushroom pasta topped with a New York strip steak) is a good bet. **Known for:** scratch-made food and cocktails; live entertainment nightly; two happy hours daily. [$] *Average main: $23* ✉ *75-5805 Alii Dr., Kailua-Kona* ☎ *808/326–1600* 🌐 *www.fosterskitchen.com.*

★ Harbor House

$ | AMERICAN | On the docks at Kona's sleepy harbor, this open-air restaurant is an authentic place to grab a beer and a bite after a long day fishing, beaching, or diving. The venue is nothing fancy, but Harbor House is one of the best spots in Kona for fresh-fish sandwiches, a variety of fried fish-and-chip combos, and even burgers. **Known for:** chilled schooners of Kona Brewing Co. lager; closing at 6:30 pm and 6 on Sunday; fun waterfront dining on the way to or from Kona International Airport. $ *Average main: $10* ✉ *Honokohau Harbor, 74-425 Kealakehe Pkwy., Suite 4, Kailua-Kona* ☎ *808/326–4166* ⊕ *harborhouserestaurantkona.com.*

★ Hayashi's You Make the Roll

$ | JAPANESE | Tiny and locally owned, this sushi shack in the heart of town has gained an incredible following and serves up custom-made rolls, filled with three or four ingredients of your choice. It's very popular and gets crazy crowded, so expect a long wait—but it's worth it. (Wait times can exceed an hour, but they let you know how long before you order.) Just chill and sit on the seawall while you wait. **Known for:** affordable, take-out sushi rolls; small, low-key location that includes outdoor patio seating; closing at 6 pm. $ *Average main: $7* ✉ *75-5725 Alii Dr., Suite D101, Kailua-Kona* ☎ *808/326–1322* ☾ *Closed Sun.*

Holuakoa Gardens and Cafe

$$ | AMERICAN | This respected slow-food restaurant features fine dining in a lush, open-air setting beneath the shade of an old monkeypod tree. The proprietors, top chefs from the Bay Area, strive to use all local and organic ingredients for such dinner entrées as handcrafted house gnocchi or Mediterranean seafood stew. **Known for:** farm-to-table cuisine; adjacent coffeehouse lounge; biodynamic and organic wines. $ *Average main: $25* ✉ *76-5900 Old Government Rd., Holualoa* ☎ *808/322–2233* ⊕ *www.holuakoagardens.com* ☾ *No dinner Sun.*

Honu's on the Beach

$$$ | HAWAIIAN | Featuring alfresco dining near the sand, this is one of the few truly beachfront restaurants in Historic Kailua Village and is part of Courtyard King Kamehameha's Kona Beach Hotel. The venue offers prime views of Kailua Pier and the historic grounds of Kamakahonu Bay, as well as a menu dominated by Hawaii regional cuisine, highlighted by Hawaii ranchers' "natural" New York steak, fresh catch of the day, and sushi. **Known for:** views of sacred temple; daily breakfast buffet; tiki torches and inviting firepits at night. $ *Average main: $28* ✉ *Courtyard King Kamehameha's Kona Beach Hotel, 75-5660 Palani Rd., Kailua-Kona* ☎ *808/329–2911* ⊕ *www. marriott.com* ☾ *No lunch.*

Huggo's

$$$$ | HAWAIIAN | A Kona icon since 1969, family-owned Huggo's is one of the few restaurants in town with prices and atmosphere comparable to the splurge restaurants at the Kohala Coast resorts. Dinner offerings sometimes fall short, considering the prices, but the *pupus* (appetizers) and small plates are usually a good bet. **Known for:** dining at the water's edge; landmark Kona restaurant; nightlife hot spot. $ *Average main: $36* ✉ *75-5828 Kahakai Rd., off Alii Dr., Kailua-Kona* ☎ *808/329–1493* ⊕ *www.huggos.com.*

Humpy's Big Island Alehouse

$ | AMERICAN | This place is usually packed for a reason: the more than 36 craft brews on tap, plus an upstairs and downstairs bar with plenty of outdoor seating. Take in the oceanfront view with amazing sunsets while chowing down on stone-baked pizza, fresh salads, fish-and-chips, fish tacos, burgers, stone-baked subs, and lots of appetizers. **Known for:** largest selection of craft beer on the island; great crab cakes; good nightlife (for Kona). $ *Average main: $15* ✉ *Coconut Grove MarketPlace, 75-5815 Alii Dr., Kailua-Kona* ☎ *808/324–2337* ⊕ *humpys-kona.com.*

Island Lava Java

$$ | **AMERICAN** | With cocktail bars both upstairs and downstairs, oceanfront Island Lava Java serves eggs Benedict for breakfast, fresh fish tacos for lunch, and pasta, steak, and seafood for dinner, plus towering, fresh bistro salads. There are also pizzas, sandwiches, and plenty of choices for both vegetarians and meat eaters. **Known for:** large portions using mostly local organic ingredients; bar with extensive cocktail menu; 100% Kona coffee. [$] *Average main: $20* ✉ *Coconut Grove MarketPlace, 75-5801 Alii Dr., Kailua-Kona* ☎ *808/327–2161* 🌐 *www.islandlavajava.com.*

★ Jackie Rey's Ohana Grill

$$ | **AMERICAN** | **FAMILY** | The brightly decorated, open-air restaurant is a favorite lunch and dinner destination of visitors and residents, thanks to generous portions and a nice variety of chef's specials, steaks, and seafood dishes. Meals pair well with selections from Jackie Rey's well-rounded wine list. **Known for:** strong local following; great-value lunch menu with ribs and fish-and-chips; $5 happy hour. [$] *Average main: $23* ✉ *Pottery Terrace, 75-5995 Kuakini Hwy., Kailua-Kona* ☎ *808/327–0209* 🌐 *www.jackiereys.com* ⏲ *No lunch weekends.*

Kenichi Pacific

$$$ | **JAPANESE** | With black-lacquer tables and lipstick-red banquettes, Kenichi offers a more sophisticated dining atmosphere than what's normally found in Kona. This is where residents go when they feel like splurging on top-notch sushi, steak, and Asian-fusion cuisine. **Known for:** upscale dining at much less than resort prices; happy hour discounts on sushi; cheaper lounge menu of small plates. [$] *Average main: $30* ✉ *Keauhou Shopping Center, 78-6831 Alii Dr., Suite D-125, Kailua-Kona* ☎ *808/322–6400* 🌐 *www.kenichirestaurants.com* ⏲ *No lunch.*

★ Kona Brewing Co. Pub and Brewery

$ | **AMERICAN** | **FAMILY** | An ultrapopular destination with an outdoor patio, Kona Brewing offers an excellent, varied menu, including famous brews, pulled-pork quesadillas, gourmet pizzas, and a killer spinach salad with Gorgonzola cheese and macadamia nuts. The sampler tray offers four of the 10 available microbrews. **Known for:** Longboard Lager and other famous brews made on-site; live music; money-saving beer sampler. [$] *Average main: $12* ✉ *74-5612 Pawai Pl., Kailua-Kona* ✣ *Off Kaiwi St. at end of Pawai Pl.* ☎ *808/329–2739* 🌐 *www.konabrewingco.com.*

Kona Inn Restaurant

$$ | **AMERICAN** | This vintage open-air restaurant at the historical Kona Inn Shopping Village offers a beautiful oceanfront setting on Kailua Bay. It's a great place to have a mai tai and some appetizers later in the day, or to enjoy a calamari sandwich, clam chowder, or salad at lunch. **Known for:** sunset-watching spot; nice bar and lounge at all times; inconsistent food at dinner. [$] *Average main: $20* ✉ *Kona Inn Shopping Village, 75-5744 Alii Dr., Kailua-Kona* ☎ *808/329–4455* 🌐 *www.windandsearestaurants.com.*

Kona Taeng On Thai

$ | **THAI** | A hidden gem, the open-air eatery is on the second floor of an oceanfront shopping center. Patrons can watch the scene below on bustling Alii Drive while enjoying freshly prepared Thai specialties, including plenty of vegetarian options and delicious Thai iced tea. **Known for:** uncrowded, spacious layout; open air on Alii Drive; large portions. [$] *Average main: $11* ✉ *Kona Inn Shopping Center, 75-5744 Alii Dr. , #208, 2nd fl., Kailua-Kona* ☎ *808/329–1994.*

La Bourgogne

$$$$ | **FRENCH** | A nondescript office building, just to the south of town, is home to this quiet, country-style bistro with dark-wood walls and private booths. The traditional French cuisine

might not impress visitors from France, but this popular local favorite offers such classics as escargots, beef with a Cabernet Sauvignon sauce, and rack of lamb with roasted garlic and rosemary; it's nice for a special occasion. **Known for:** reservations needed well ahead of time; great cassoulet; good wines by the glass. [$] *Average main: $44* ✉ *77-6400 Nalani St., Kailua-Kona* ☎ *808/329–6711* 🌐 *labourgognehawaii.com* 🕓 *Closed Sun. and Mon. No lunch.*

Magics Beach Grill

$$$ | **HAWAIIAN** | In a vintage building dating to 1965, Magics offers an exhilarating oceanfront location overlooking the famous Disappearing Sands Beach, also known as Magic Sands. From fried *ulu* (breadfruit) wedges in umami truffle oil aioli to griddled crab cakes and shoyu-and-coconut-braised pork belly, the eclectic menu features intriguing choices as well as family-friendly options. **Known for:** sunset beach views; spicy dragonfruit margarita; great happy hour 2–4 pm. [$] *Average main: $33* ✉ *77-6452 Alii Dr., Kailua-Kona* ☎ *808/ 662–4427* 🌐 *magicsbeachgrill.com.*

Mi's Waterfront Bistro

$$ | **ITALIAN** | Overlooking Kailua Bay in Waterfront Row, this steady presence in the Kona dining scene offers a reliable, consistent menu. The restaurant's husband-and-wife owners prepare homemade pastas and focaccia daily and also offer some delicious specials such as lasagna and risotto. **Known for:** waterfront views; herb-cheese ravioli; good desserts. [$] *Average main: $18* ✉ *75-5770 Alii Dr., Kailua-Kona* ☎ *808/323–3880* 🌐 *www.miswaterfrontbistro.com.*

Pancho and Lefty's Cantina

$ | **MEXICAN** | Across the street from the Kona Inn Shopping Village, in Kailua Village, this upstairs cantina is a nice perch for enjoying nachos and margaritas (try the hibiscus margarita) on a lazy afternoon, or to watch the passersby below on Alii Drive. The main entrées are mediocre, but the chips, salsa, and ceviche might just hit the spot. **Known for:** popular happy hour hangout; better for snacks than a full meal; homemade salsa. [$] *Average main: $15* ✉ *75-5719 Alii Dr., Kailua-Kona* ☎ *808/326–2171.*

★ **Quinn's Almost by the Sea**

$ | **AMERICAN** | **FAMILY** | With the bar in the front and the dining patio in the back, Quinn's may seem like a bit of a dive at first glance, but this venerable restaurant serves up the best darn cheeseburger and fries in town. The menu has many other tasty options, such as fish-and-chips and beef tenderloin tips. **Known for:** strong cocktails; comfort food like meatballs; old Kona vibe. [$] *Average main: $15* ✉ *75-5655 Palani Rd., Kailua-Kona* ☎ *808/329–3822* 🌐 *www.quinnsalmostbythesea.com.*

★ **Rays on the Bay**

$$ | **SOUTH PACIFIC** | The Sheraton Kona's signature restaurant overlooks Keauhou Bay, offering nighttime views of native manta rays that appear nightly beneath the balcony. The stellar dinner menu includes fresh-catch seafood, island-raised beef, and farm-fresh salads, plus tantalizing appetizers like kampachi (yellowtail) sashimi, pork pot stickers, and poke. **Known for:** spectacular bayfront location; late-night dining; live music nightly. [$] *Average main: $25* ✉ *Sheraton Kona Resort and Spa, 78-128 Ehukai St., Keauhou* ☎ *808/930–4949* 🌐 *www.raysonthebaykona.com* 🕓 *No lunch.*

Sam Choy's Kai Lanai

$$ | **HAWAIIAN** | **FAMILY** | Perched above a shopping center with a coastline view, celebrity chef Sam Choy's namesake restaurant includes a bar that looks like a charter-fishing boat and granite-topped tables with ocean views from every seat. Along with reasonably priced entrées, highlighted by Sam's trio of fish served with shiitake mushroom cream sauce, they also offer an ahi salad (served with deep-fried flour tortilla chips) for a refreshing choice. *Keiki* (kids') menus ccommodate families, and yes, the res- aurant can be noisy. **Known for:** limited arking for such a popular place; family riendly with a kid's menu; happy hour at he Short Bait Bar. [$] *Average main: $22* ✉ *Keauhou Shopping Center, 78-6831 Alii Dr., Suite 1000, Kailua-Kona* ☎ *808/333–3434* 🌐 *www.samchoyskailanai.com.*

hai Rin Restaurant and Bar

$ | **THAI** | This low-key oceanfront res- aurant on Alii Drive offers an excellent election of Thai food at decent prices. Everything is cooked to order, and he menu is brimming with choices, ncluding five curries, a green-papaya alad, and deep-fried fish. **Known for:** great views with both indoor and outdoor seating; appetizer platters for sharing; convenience to village shops. [$] *Average main: $18* ✉ *75-5799 Alii Dr., Kailua-Kona* ☎ *808/329–2929* 🌐 *kona123.com/thairin. html.*

TK Noodle House

$ | **ASIAN FUSION** | Former resort chef TK Keosavang serves up inventive Asian usion cuisine with the emphasis on noo- dles. Generous portions are beautifully plated, like the crispy pork belly sauté with Chinese greens and garlic sauce, and noodle soups and abundant salads don't disappoint. **Known for:** ample park- ng; seafood yentafo soup; shabu-shabu table option. [$] *Average main: $12* ✉ *75 Hanama Pl., Kailua-Kona* ✥ *Near Big Island Grill* ☎ *808/327–0070* 🌐 *www. cheftk.com.*

Sushi Cocoro and Udon Tuna-ichi

$ | **JAPANESE** | A tiny hidden gem behind Gertrude's Jazz Bar, this authentic little place offers excellent sushi at affordable prices. The Japanese-born chefs serve up such offerings as six-piece rolls for under $4. **Known for:** Red Hot Lava roll; inexpen- sive sushi combos for two; BYOB wel- come. [$] *Average main: $12* ✉ *75-5699 Alii Dr., Kailua-Kona* ☎ *808/331–0601* ⏲ *Closed Tues. and Wed.*

★ **Umekes Fish Market Bar and Grill**

$ | **HAWAIIAN** | **FAMILY** | Locals flock to this downtown Kailua-Kona restaurant for good reason: the poke is the most *onolicious* (superdelicious) in town, and the many other seafood offerings are just as stellar. Sandwiches, burgers, desserts, and salads round out the gourmet menu. **Known for:** daily specials using the freshest fish; locally sourced ingredients; authentic Kona experience. [$] *Average main: $12* ✉ *74-5563 Kaiwi St., Kailua-Kona* ✥ *Old Industrial Park at intersection of Kuakini across from West Hawaii Today* ☎ *808/238–0571* 🌐 *umekesrestaurants. com.*

Coffee and Quick Bites

Frenchman's Cafe

$ | **FRENCH** | A Parisian couple serves up authentic French crepes, omelets, galettes, and desserts at this hidden hideaway in Historic Kailua Village. For lunch, the croque monsieur is a good bet, while the list of savory or sweet crepes includes gluten-free options. **Known for:** friendly vibe; open early for breakfast; great croissants. [$] *Average main: $11* ✉ *Kona MarketPlace, 75-5729 Alii Dr., Kailua-Kona* ☎ *808/365–2671* ⏲ *Closed Sun. No dinner.*

Kanaka Kava

$ | **HAWAIIAN** | This is a popular local hangout, and not just because the kava drink makes you mellow. The Hawaiian proprietors also serve traditional Hawai- ian food, including fresh poke, bowls of pulled *kalua* (earth oven–baked) pork, healthy organic greens, *opihi* (limpets), and traditional Hawaiian *laulau* (pork or chicken wrapped in taro leaves and steamed). **Known for:** kava served in coconut cups; Hawaiian specialties like fresh fish and laulau; squid luau (the leaf from a taro plant). [$] *Average main: $12* ✉ *Coconut Grove Marketplace, 75-5803 Alii Dr., Space B6, Kailua-Kona* ☎ *808/327–1660.*

Kona Coffee and Tea

$ | CAFÉ | All of this family-owned coffee company's businesses—growing, roasting, brewing, and serving their authentic Kona coffee—operate within a 10-mile radius of the farm. At their homey little café, they offer a staggering array of coffee drinks, along with upscale deli items such as lox and a veggie focaccia sandwich; breakfast goodies include acai bowls. **Known for:** small-batch, estate-grown coffee; Kona coffee tastings every Wednesday; Hawaiian-made food treats for sale. $ *Average main: $8* ✉ *Kona Coast Shopping Center, 74-5588 Palani Rd., Kailua-Kona* ☎ *808/329–6577* ⊕ *www.konacoffeeandtea.com* ⊗ *No dinner.*

Kope Lani

$ | CAFÉ | Grab a tasty croissant sandwich or locally made ice cream and knock back some of Kona's best coffee at Kope Lani, directly across from Hulihee Palace. There's casual decor and limited indoor seating, but you will probably want to sit outside and watch passersby on Alii Drive. **Known for:** great downtown ambience; specialty ice creams, including tropical flavors; good coffee and espresso selections. $ *Average main: $6* ✉ *75-5719 Alii Dr., Kailua-Kona* ☎ *808/329–6152* ⊕ *www.kopelani.com* ⊗ *No dinner.*

Los Habaneros

$ | MEXICAN | FAMILY | Hidden in the corner of Keauhou Shopping Center adjacent to the movie theater, Los Habaneros serves up fast, albeit average, Mexican food for low prices. Favorites are usually combos, which can be anything from enchilada plates to homemade sopas and chiles rellenos. **Known for:** before- or after-beach stop; margaritas, tequila shots, and Mexican beer; take-out-quality Mexican food. $ *Average main: $7* ✉ *Keauhou Shopping Center, 78-631 Alii Dr., Kailua-Kona* ☎ *808/324–4688* ⊗ *Closed Sun.*

Ultimate Burger

$ | DINER | FAMILY | Located in the Office Max shopping complex in Kailua-Kona, this excellent burger joint may look like a chain, but it's an independent, locally owned and operated eatery that serves 100% organic, grass-fed Big Island beef on buns locally made. Be sure to order a side of seasoned Big Daddy fries served with house-made aioli dipping sauce. **Known for:** organic, hormone-free ingredients; supporting local farmers and ranchers; excellent French fries. $ *Average main: $8* ✉ *Kona Commons Shopping Center, 74-5450 Makala Blvd., Kailua-Kona* ☎ *808/329–2326* ⊕ *www.ultimateburger.net.*

🛏 Hotels

Aston Kona by the Sea

$$$$ | RENTAL | FAMILY | Complete modern kitchens, tiled lanai, and washer-dryer units are found in every suite of this comfortable oceanfront condo complex with a welcoming entry lobby and reception area that feels like a hotel. **Pros:** oceanfront location; lobby and activities desk; ocean-fed saltwater pool next to the property. **Cons:** no beach access (2 miles away); not walking distance to Kailua Village; individually owned units, so prices may vary. $ *Rooms from: $359* ✉ *75-6106 Alii Dr., Kailua-Kona* ☎ *808/327–2300, 877/997–6667* ⊕ *www. astonhotels.com* ⤵ *86 units* ⦿ *No meals.*

Castle Kona Bali Kai

$$ | RENTAL | FAMILY | These slightly older condominium units, spread out among three low-rises on the ocean side of Alii Drive, are situated at Kona's most popular surfing spot, Banyans, and also just a couple of minutes' drive from Kailua Village and within walking distance of popular Magic Sands Beach Park. **Pros:** close to town and beaches; convenience mart and beach-gear rental nearby; views of surfers on the water. **Cons:** mountain-view rooms close to noisy street; oceanfront rooms don't have a/c; older-looking concrete buildings. $ *Rooms from: $180* ✉ *76-6246 Alii Dr.,*

Kailua-Kona ☎ *808/329–9381, 800/535–0085* 🌐 *www.castleresorts.com* 🛏 *64 units* 🍴 *No meals.*

Courtyard King Kamehameha's Kona Beach Hotel

$$$ | **HOTEL** | **FAMILY** | Right in the heart of Historic Kailua Village, this landmark hotel right on the beach offers good vibrations and authentic local hospitality—all for less than the price of a Kohala Coast resort. **Pros:** central location; historical ambience; on-site restaurant and poolside bar. **Cons:** most rooms have partial ocean views; some rooms face the parking lot; pricey buffet. [$] *Rooms from: $335* ✉ *75-5660 Palani Rd., Kailua-Kona* ☎ *808/329–2911* 🌐 *marriott.com* 🛏 *452 rooms* 🍴 *No meals.*

Hale Hualalai Bed and Breakfast

$ | **B&B/INN** | In cool, upcountry Holualoa, Hale Hualalai offers two exceptionally large suites with exposed beams, whirlpool tubs, and private lanai, but perhaps most memorable is the food—owner Ricky Brewster was a chef at Four Seasons Hualalai Resort's Beach Tree restaurant. **Pros:** gourmet breakfasts; tastefully decorated house; whirlpool tubs. **Cons:** not for kids; not a central location; frequently booked. [$] *Rooms from: $161* ✉ *74-4968 Mamalahoa Hwy., Holualoa* ☎ *808/464–7074* 🌐 *www.hale-hualalai.com* 🛏 *2 suites* 🍴 *Free breakfast.*

Holiday Inn Express and Suites Kailua-Kona

$$ | **HOTEL** | **FAMILY** | While the location feels more parking lot than island paradise, this practical and comfortable hotel, which isn't far from the ocean, offers lots of pluses. **Pros:** convenient downtown location; 24-hour business center; free high-speed Wi-Fi. **Cons:** most rooms don't have views; no landscaping; parking lot views on lower level. [$] *Rooms from: $200* ✉ *75-146 Sarona Rd., Kailua-Kona* ☎ *808/329–2599* 🌐 *www.ihg.com* 🛏 *75 rooms* 🍴 *Free breakfast.*

★ **Holualoa Inn**

$$$$ | **B&B/INN** | Six spacious rooms and suites—plus two vintage, one-bedroom cottages perfect for honeymooners—are available at this 30-acre coffee-country estate, a few miles above Kailua Bay in the heart of the artists' village of Holualoa. **Pros:** within walking distance of art galleries and cafés; everything necessary for hosting a wedding or event; luxurious, Zen-like vibe. **Cons:** not kid friendly; non-heated swimming pool; no dinners. [$] *Rooms from: $440* ✉ *76-5932 Mamalahoa Hwy., Holualoa* ☎ *808/324–1121, 800/392–1812* 🌐 *www.holualoainn.com* 🛏 *8 rooms* 🍴 *Free breakfast.*

Holua Resort at Mauna Loa Village

$$$ | **RESORT** | Tucked away by Keauhou Bay amid a plethora of coconut trees, this well-maintained enclave of blue-roofed villas offers lots of amenities, including an 11-court tennis center (with a center court, pro shop, and lights), swimming pools, hot tubs, fitness center, manicured gardens, waterfalls, and covered parking. **Pros:** tennis center; upscale feeling; walking distance to major resort restaurants. **Cons:** no beach; partial ocean views; no on-site restaurant. [$] *Rooms from: $323* ✉ *78-7190 Kaleiopapa St., Kailua-Kona* ☎ *808/324–1550* 🌐 *www.shellhospitality.com* 🛏 *73 units* 🍴 *No meals.*

Kanaloa at Kona by Outrigger

$$ | **RENTAL** | The 18-acre grounds provide a peaceful and verdant background for this low-rise condominium complex bordering the Keauhou-Kona Country Club and within a five-minute drive of the nearest beaches (Kahaluu and Magic Sands). **Pros:** within walking distance of Keauhou Bay; three pools with hot tubs; shopping center and restaurants nearby. **Cons:** no restaurant on property; mandatory cleaning fee at check-in; a/c available only by paying a daily fee. [$] *Rooms from: $259* ✉ *78-261 Manukai St., Kailua-Kona* ☎ *808/322–9625, 808/322–7222, 800/688–7444* 🌐 *www.outrigger.com* 🛏 *63 units* 🍴 *No meals.*

Kona Bay Hotel

$ | HOTEL | Also known as Uncle Billy's, this old-fashioned lodge holds a prime spot in Kailua-Kona, directly across from the Kona Inn, and is an option if you need a budget-minded place with decent rooms—just ratchet down your expectations and don't expect new, perfect, or fancy here. **Pros:** walking distance to beach and restaurants; ocean views; no resort fees. **Cons:** very basic rooms; some cleanliness issues; yes, this is Kona, but the place is run down. $ *Rooms from: $171* ✉ *75-5739 Alii Dr., Kailua-Kona* ☎ *800/367–5102* ⊕ *unclebilly. com* ⤳ *141 rooms* ⦿ *No meals.*

Kona Coast Resort

$$ | RENTAL | FAMILY | Just below Keauhou Shopping Center, this resort offers furnished condos on 21 acres with pleasant ocean views and a host of on-site amenities, including two swimming pools, beach volleyball, a cocktail bar, barbecue grills, a hot tub, tennis courts, a fitness center, hula classes, equipment rentals, and children's activities. **Pros:** all rooms updated in 2018; good amenities for kids; away from the bustle of downtown Kailua-Kona. **Cons:** some units have parking lot views; not on the beach; time-share salespeople. $ *Rooms from: $220* ✉ *78-6842 Alii Dr., Keauhou* ☎ *808/324–1721* ⊕ *www.shellhospitality.com* ⤳ *268 units* ⦿ *No meals.*

Kona Magic Sands

$$ | RENTAL | Cradled between a lovely grass park and Magic Sands Beach Park, this condo complex is great for swimmers, surfers, and sunbathers. **Pros:** adjacent to popular Magic Sands Beach Park; affordable studio units; oceanfront view from all units. **Cons:** studios only; some units are dated; popular complex, but you have to book through a third-party site. $ *Rooms from: $180* ✉ *77-6452 Alii Dr., Kailua-Kona* ☎ *808/329–9393, 800/622–5348* ⤳ *15 units* ⦿ *No meals.*

Kona Seaside Hotel

$ | HOTEL | FAMILY | Located right in the heart of the action across the street from Kailua Pier in Kailua-Kona, Kona Seaside Hotel offers standard, relatively tasteful accommodations ideal for visitors on a budget. **Pros:** much more affordable than a resort; central location in heart of Kailua-Kona; lots of on-site amenities. **Cons:** limited parking; $12 daily fee for parking; slightly dated. $ *Rooms from: $139* ✉ *75-5646 Palani Rd., Kailua-Kona* ☎ *808/329–2455* ⊕ *www.konaseaside hotel.com* ⤳ *142 rooms* ⦿ *No meals.*

Kona Tiki Hotel

$ | HOTEL | This three-story walk-up budget hotel about a mile south of downtown Kailua Village, with modest, pleasantly decorated rooms—all of which have lanai right next to the ocean—is simply the best deal in town. **Pros:** friendly staff; oceanfront lanai on every room; free parking and continental breakfast. **Cons:** only one studio has a kitchen (others have fridges only); no TV in rooms; parking can be a challenge. $ *Rooms from: $169* ✉ *75-5968 Alii Dr., Kailua-Kona*

☎ 808/329–1425 ⊕ www.konatikihotel.
com ⤳ 16 rooms ⦿ Free breakfast.

Royal Kona Resort

$$ | RESORT | FAMILY | If you're on a budget, this is a great option—the location is central; the bar, lounge, pool, and restaurant are right on the water; and the rooms feature contemporary Hawaiian decor with Polynesian accents. **Pros:** convenient location; waterfront pool; restaurant and bar with great views. **Cons:** can be crowded; $18 per day parking fee; grounds have dated feel. $ Rooms from: $189 ⊠ 75-5852 Alii Dr., Kailua-Kona ☎ 808/329–3111, 800/222–5642 ⊕ www. royalkona.com ⤳ 430 rooms ⦿ No meals.

Sheraton Kona Resort and Spa at Keauhou Bay

$$$ | RESORT | FAMILY | What this big concrete structure lacks in intimacy, it makes up for with its beautifully manicured grounds, historical sense of place, stylish interiors, and stunning location on Keauhou Bay. Many rooms have great views of the bay and feel like they're right on the water, and each is decorated in a modern Polynesian style. **Pros:** cool pool; manta rays on view nightly; resort style at lower price. **Cons:** no beach; long walk from parking area; Wi-Fi can be spotty. $ Rooms from: $290 ⊠ 78-128 Ehukai St., Keauhou ☎ 808/930–4900 ⊕ marriott. com ⤳ 484 rooms ⦿ No meals.

🖢 Nightlife

BARS

The Mask-querade Bar

BARS/PUBS | Hidden away in an unassuming strip mall, this is one of the Big Island's most venerable gay bars. Drag shows, hot DJs, live music, karaoke, drink specials, fiestas, and Sunday barbecues are included in the roster of weekly events. All are welcome. ⊠ Kopiko Plaza, 75-5660 Kopiko St., Kailua-Kona ⤭ Below Longs Drugs ☎ 808/329–8558 ⊕ www. themask-queradebar.com.

Oceans Sports Bar and Grill

BARS/PUBS | A popular gathering place, this sports bar in the back of the Coconut Grove Marketplace has a pool table and an outdoor patio, along with dozens of TVs screening the big game (whatever it happens to be that day). It really gets hopping on the weekends and for karaoke on Tuesday and Thursday. There's good happy hour pricing and $3 Taco Tuesdays. ⊠ Coconut Grove Marketplace, 75-5811 Alii Dr., Kailua-Kona ☎ 808/327–9494.

★ Ola Brew

BARS/PUBS | An exciting start-up, this employee-owned brewing company offers an enticing and creative array of beers, ales, ciders, and hard seltzers. Ola Brew is committed to community investing with sponsorships and support of local farmers and merchants. Take a barstool at a picture window facing the main brewing operation and enjoy a fresh, on-tap draft and an appetizer. They sometimes host musicians or food trucks on the street out front or do trivia nights. The taproom menu features reasonably priced salads, flatbreads, and poke bowls. Brewery tours start daily at 1. ⊠ 74-5598 Luhia St., Kailua-Kona ☎ 808/339–3599 ⊕ www.olabrewco.com.

CLUBS

★ Gertrude's Jazz Bar

MUSIC CLUBS | You know you're in the right place when you climb the stairs to this little gem and notice that the steps are painted like piano keys. With a location in the heart of town, including a perfect view of Kailua Bay, this open-air club features an incredible variety of music (jazz, Latin, country, classical) and special events such as dance lessons, art nights, wine tastings, and themed dress-up parties. One of the owners is a renowned jazz musician and plays with his own group or with guest musicians. The tapas menu is straightforward and a tad overpriced. A small cover charge helps pay the musicians a living wage. ⊠ 75-5699

Alii Dr., Kailua-Kona ☎ *808/327–5299*
⊕ *gertrudesjazzbar.com.*

Huggo's on the Rocks

PIANO BARS/LOUNGES | Jazz, Island, and classic-rock bands perform here nightly, and outside you may see people dancing in the sand. The food can miss, but the location, on the waterfront by the Royal Kona Resort, doesn't get better. Happy hour is 3 to 6. ✉ *75-5824 Kahakai Rd., at Alii Dr., Kailua-Kona* ☎ *808/329–1493* ⊕ *www.huggosontherocks.com.*

Laverne's Sports Bar

DANCE CLUBS | On weekends, live concerts are on tap. Sometimes Hawaiian and island music headliners perform here, such as local recording artists Anuhea or Rebel Souljahz. Local musicians with followings also draw their "groupies." After 10, DJs spin tunes on the ocean-breeze-cooled dance floor. ✉ *Coconut Grove Marketplace, 75-5819 Alii Dr., Kailua-Kona* ☎ *808/331–2633* ⊕ *www.laverneskona.com.*

🎭 Performing Arts

FESTIVALS

★ King Kamehameha Day Celebration Parade

FESTIVALS | Each summer on the Saturday nearest to King Kamehameha Day (June 11), at least 100 regal riders on horseback parade through Historic Kailua Village, showing off the colorful flora and aloha spirit of Hawaii. The traditional royal *pau* riders (women dressed in long skirts) include a queen and princesses representing the major Hawaiian Islands. A cultural festival with live music and a *houlaulea* (local fundraiser) always follow on the historic grounds of Hulihee Palace, Hawaii Island's only royal palace. This spectacular free event is one of the highlights of summer. ✉ *Historic Kailua Village, Alii Dr., Kailua-Kona* ⊕ *www. konaparade.org.*

★ Kona Brewers Festival

FESTIVALS | At this lively annual celebration in early March by Kailua Pier, 70 types of ales and lagers by Hawaii and mainland craft brewers are showcased, along with culinary contributions by Hawaii Island chefs. There's also live "Blues and Brews" music, an art auction, a home brewers competition, a 5k run/walk, fashion shows, and a golf tournament. The multiday event is a community fundraiser and local favorite, but you must be 21 to attend. ■**TIP**➔ **Get tickets early online, as this event always sells out.** ✉ *Courtyard King Kamehameha's Kona Beach Hotel, 75-5660 Palani Rd., Kailua-Kona* ☎ *808/331–3033* ⊕ *www. konabrewersfestival.com.*

★ Kona Coffee Cultural Festival

FESTIVALS | Held over 10 days in early November, on the Kona side, the longest-running food festival in Hawaii celebrates world-renowned Kona coffee. The highly anticipated festival includes coffee contests, serious cupping (tasting) competitions, a lecture series, label contests, farm tours, and a colorful community parade featuring the newly crowned Miss Kona Coffee. During the Holualoa Village Coffee and Art Stroll, you can meet artists and sample estate coffees. ✉ *Kailua-Kona* ☎ *808/323–2006* ⊕ *www. konacoffeefest.com.*

FILM

Regal Keauhou Stadium 7 Cinemas

FILM | This is a splendid theater complex with several pre- or post-movie food options in the shopping center. ✉ *Keauhou Shopping Center, 78-6831 Alii Dr., Kailua-Kona* ☎ *808/324–0172* ⊕ *www. regmovies.com.*

Regal Makalapua Stadium 10 Cinemas

FILM | **FAMILY** | The 10-screen theater has stadium seating and digital surround sound. ✉ *74-5469 Kamakaeha Ave., Kailua-Kona* ☎ *808/327–0444* ⊕ *www. regmovies.com.*

LUAU AND POLYNESIAN REVUES

Haleo Luau at the Sheraton Kona Resort and Spa at Keauhou Bay

CULTURAL FESTIVALS | On the graceful grounds of the Sheraton Kona Resort and Spa at Keauhou Bay, this popular luau (Monday and Friday evening) takes you on a journey of song and dance, celebrating the historic Keauhou region, birthplace of King Kamehameha III. Before the show, you can participate in workshops on topics ranging from coconut-frond weaving to poi ball techniques. The excellent buffet is a feast of local favorites, including *kalua* (earth oven–baked) pig, poi, ahi poke, chicken long rice, fish, and mango chutney. Generous mai tai refills are a plus, and a highlight is the dramatic fire-knife dance finale. ⊠ *Sheraton Kona Resort and Spa at Keauhou Bay, 78-128 Ehukai St., Kailua-Kona* ☎ *808/930–4900* ⊕ *marriott.com* ⊠ *$109.*

Island Breeze Luau

CULTURAL FESTIVALS | With traditional dancing showcasing the interconnected Polynesian roots of Hawaii, Samoa, Tahiti, and New Zealand, the "We Are *Ohana* (family)" luau is not a hokey tourist-trap event. These performers take their art seriously, and it shows. The historic oceanfront location on the Courtyard King Kamehameha's Kona Beach Hotel's luau grounds, which is directly next to the king's former royal compound and Ahuena Heiau, adds to the authenticity. The bounty of food includes *kalua* (earth oven–baked) pig cooked in an underground *imu* (oven). The hotel validates parking. ⊠ *75-5660 Palani Rd., Kailua-Kona* ☎ *866/482–9775* ⊕ *www.island-breezeluau.com* ⊠ *$114.*

Voyagers of the Pacific

CULTURAL FESTIVALS | The Royal Kona Resort lights its torches for a spectacular show and oceanfront buffet four times a week (Monday–Wednesday and Friday). The entire Polynesian Triangle is represented through song and dance by seasoned professional performers who love sharing their dance traditions with visitors. Traditional luau fare is served along with succulent pork cooked in an authentic underground *imu* (oven), and an open bar offers mai tais and other tropical concoctions. An exciting Samoan fire-knife dancer caps off the show. It may just be the best luau deal in town. ⊠ *Royal Kona Resort, 75-5852 Alii Dr., Kailua-Kona* ☎ *808/329–3111* ⊕ *www. royalkona.com* ⊠ *$82.*

🛍 Shopping

ARTS AND CRAFTS

★ Hula Lamps of Hawaii

CRAFTS | Located near Costco in the Kaloko Light Industrial complex, this one-of-a-kind shop features the bronze creations of artist Charles Moore. Inspired by the vintage hula-girl lamps of the 1930s, Moore creates art pieces sought by visitors and residents alike. Mix and match with an array of hand-painted lampshades. ⊠ *73-5613 Olowalu St., Suite 2, Kailua-Kona* ✛ *Near Costco on upper road* ☎ *808/326–9583* ⊕ *www.hulalamps.com.*

Just Ukes

LOCAL SPECIALTIES | As the name suggests, this place is all about ukeleles—from music books to T-shirts and accessories like cases and bags. The independently owned shop carries a variety of ukuleles ranging from low-priced starter instruments to high-end models made of koa and mango. ⊠ *Kona Inn Shopping Village, 75-5744 Alii Dr., Kailua-Kona* ☎ *808/769–5101* ⊕ *justukes. com.*

★ Kimura's Lauhala Shop

CRAFTS | Originally a general store built in 1914, this shop features handmade products crafted by local lauhala weavers. Among the offerings are hats, baskets, containers, and mats, many of which are woven by the proprietors. Owner Alfreida Kimura-Fujita was born in the house behind the shop, and her daughter Renee is also an accomplished weaver. ✉ *77-996 Hualalai Rd., Holualoa* ☎ *808/324–0053.*

BOOKSTORES

Kona Stories

BOOKS/STATIONERY | With more than 10,000 titles, this bookstore also sells Hawaiiana, children's toys, and whimsical gifts. Special events, such as readings and book signings, are held weekly. ✉ *Keauhou Shopping Center, 78-6831 Alii Dr., Kailua-Kona* ✛ *Located in Keahou Shopping Center near KTA* ☎ *808/324–0350* ⊕ *www.konastories.com.*

CLOTHING AND SHOES

Honolua Surf Company

CLOTHING | Surfer chic, compliments of Roxy, Billabong, and the like, is for sale here for both men and women. This is a great place to shop for a bikini or board shorts, or to pick up a cool, retro-design T-shirt or Hawaii-style embroidered hoodie. Another location at the Waikoloa Kings' Shops on the Kohala Coast focuses on *wahine* (women's) apparel. ✉ *Kona Inn Shopping Village, 75-5744 Alii Dr., Kailua-Kona* ☎ *808/329–1001* ⊕ *www. honoluasurf.com.*

Mermaids Swimwear

CLOTHING | Local residents know that Mermaids is the best place in Kona to buy fashion-forward ladies' swimwear, sandals, hats, sunglasses, and other stylish beach accessories. The owner's husband, Tony, is a famous surfboard maker whose World Core surf shop is just around the corner. ✉ *Kona Inn Shopping Village, 75-5744 Alii Dr., Kailua-Kona* ☎ *808/329–6677.*

FOOD AND WINE

Kailua Candy Company

FOOD/CANDY | Since 1977, this chocolate company has been satisfying sweet tooths with decadent desserts and sinful bites of chocolate heaven. Many truffles and candies incorporate local ingredients (passion-fruit truffles and chocolate-covered mango—yum). Cheesecakes and mousse cakes melt in your mouth.

Of course, tasting is part of the fun. ■ **TIP→ Through a glass wall you can watch the chocolate artists at work Monday through Saturday from 9 to 5.** ✉ *Kaloko Light Industrial Park, 73-5612 Kauhola St. Kailua-Kona* ☎ *808/329–2522* ⊕ *www. kailuacandy.com.*

★ Kona Wine Market

WINE/SPIRITS | Near Costco, this longtime local wineshop carries both local and imported varietals (with more than 600 high-end wines), specialty liquors, 150 craft beers, gourmet foods, and even cigars. As a bonus, the market delivers wine and gift baskets to hotels and homes. ✉ *73-5613 Olowalu St., Kailua-Kona* ☎ *808/329–9400* ⊕ *www. konawinemarket.com.*

★ Mrs. Barry's Kona Cookies

FOOD/CANDY | Since 1980, Mrs. Barry and her family have been serving yummy home-baked cookies, including macadamia nut, white chocolate–macadamia nut, oatmeal raisin, and coffee crunch. Packaged in beautiful gift boxes or bags, the cookies make excellent gifts for family back home. Stop by on your way to Costco or the airport and pick up a bag or two or three. Ah heck, just ask Mrs. Barry to ship your stash instead. ✉ *73-5563 Maiau St., Kailua-Kona* ✛ *By Costco in the Kaloko Light Industrial Area* ☎ *808/329–6055* ⊕ *www.konacookies. com.*

★ Westside Wines

WINE/SPIRITS | Tucked away in a small downtown Kona retail center below Longs, this nifty gourmet wine and spirits shop offers restaurant-quality "wine list" wines at affordable prices. It's also the place to find large-format craft beers, French Champagne, single-malt Scotches, organic vodka, small-batch bourbon, rye whiskey, fresh bread, and artisan cheese from around the world. George Clooney's Casamigos tequila is the store's house tequila. A certified wine specialist, proprietor Alex Thropp was one of the state's top wholesale wine reps for decades. Wine tastings take place Friday and Saturday afternoons from 3 to 6. ⊠ *75-5660 Kopiko St., #4, Kailua-Kona ✛ Below Longs Drugs in Kopiko Plaza* ☏ *808/329–1777.*

GALLERIES

Holualoa Gallery

ART GALLERIES | One of several excellent galleries along the narrow highway in this historic artists' village, this shop carries stunning contemporary *raku* pottery, original paintings by co-owner Mary Lovein and other local artists, plus jewelry, silks, and other fine collectibles. Also on display are gallery co-owner Matt Lovein's famous Wish Keepers ceramic sculptures. ⊠ *76-5921 Mamalahoa Hwy., Holualoa* ☏ *808/322–8484* ⊕ *www.lovein. com.*

Kona Art Gallery

ART GALLERIES | Gary and Elizabeth Therault showcase a variety of local art here, including Gary's Big Island life photos and Elizabeth's hand-painted drums and rattles. The gallery owners also feature work from other artists, including Hawaiian *ipus* (gourds used as instruments in hula dancing), exotic wood items, paper sculptures, quilts, and jewelry. ⊠ *76-5938 Mamalahoa Hwy., Holualoa* ☏ *808/322–5125.*

HOUSEWARES

The Spoon Shop

HOUSEHOLD ITEMS/FURNITURE | Williams-Sonoma has nothing on this excellent gourmet kitchenware store that brims with every manner of accoutrement for the avid cook. There's a great selection of gourmet seasonings, olive oils (try the truffle-infused olive oil!), dressings, and condiments. If you're planning a party or reception during your stay in paradise, the Spoon Shop has items for every occasion. Cooking classes with guest chefs take place weekly in the store's high-end demo kitchen. ⊠ *73-4976 Kamanu St., #105, Kailua-Kona ✛ Near Home Depot in New Industrial*

Area ☏ *808/887–7666* ⊕ *www.thespoon-shopkona.com.*

MARKETS

Alii Gardens Marketplace

OUTDOOR/FLEA/GREEN MARKETS | The outdoor stalls at this mellow, park-like market, open daily except Monday, offer tropical flowers, produce, soaps, kettle corn, coffee, coconut postcards, cookies, jewelry, koa wood, clothing, antiques and collectibles, handmade lei, silk flowers, and kitschy crafts. The homemade barbecue is a real hit. A food kiosk also serves shave ice, fish tacos, coconut water, fresh-fruit smoothies, and hamburgers. Free parking and Wi-Fi are available. ⊠ *75-6129 Alii Dr., Kailua-Kona ✛ 1½ miles south of Kona Inn Shopping Village* ⊕ *alii-gardens-marketplace.business.site.*

Keauhou Farmers Market

OUTDOOR/FLEA/GREEN MARKETS | **FAMILY** | Held once a week in the parking lot at Keauhou Shopping Center, this cheerful market is the place to go on Saturday morning for live music, local produce (much of it organic), goat cheese, honey, island-raised meat, flowers, macadamia nuts, fresh-baked pastries, Kona coffee, and plenty of local color. ⊠ *Keauhou Shopping Center, 78-6831 Alii Dr., Kailua-Kona* ⊕ *www.keauhoufarmersmarket. com.*

Kona Inn Farmers' Market

OUTDOOR/FLEA/GREEN MARKETS | An awesome florist creates custom arrangements while you wait at this touristy farmers' market near the ocean. There are more than 40 vendors with lots of crafts for sale, as well as some of the best prices on fresh produce and orchids in Kona. The market is held in a parking lot at the corner of Hualalai Road and Alii Drive, Wednesday to Sunday 7 to 4. Parking is free. ⊠ *75-7544 Alii Dr., Kailua-Kona.*

SHOPPING CENTERS
Coconut Grove Marketplace

SHOPPING CENTERS/MALLS | The meandering oceanfront marketplace includes gift shops, cafés, restaurants (Outback Steakhouse, Humpy's Big Island Alehouse, Bongo Ben's, Lava Java, Foster's Kitchen, Fumi's Kitchen), sports bars, sushi, boutiques, Jack's Diving Locker, a running store, and several art galleries. At night, locals gather to watch outdoor sand volleyball games held in the courtyard or grab a beer and enjoy live music. This place is always hopping, and it has the biggest free parking lot in downtown Kailua-Kona. ⊠ *75-5795–75-5825 Alii Dr., Kailua-Kona* ⊕ *www.thecoconutgrovemarketplace.com.*

Crossroads Shopping Center

SHOPPING CENTERS/MALLS | The in-town shopping center includes a Safeway with an excellent deli section for on-the-go snacks, as well as a Walmart, where visitors can find affordable Hawaii souvenirs, including aloha wear, discounted Kona coffee, and macadamia nuts. For a quick meal, there's a Denny's, a Subway, and a Domino's, as well as a small sushi restaurant. The Laulima Food Patch offers fresh salads and local-style specialties. Sakura is known for Japanese and other Asian plates. ⊠ *75-1000 Henry St., Kailua-Kona* ☎ *808/329-4822.*

Kaloko Light Industrial Park

SHOPPING CENTERS/MALLS | Located south of the airport, this large retail complex includes Costco, the best place to stock up on food if you're staying at a vacation rental. Kona Wine Market and the Spoon Shop feature gourmet finds, and Mrs. Barry's Kona Cookies sells beautifully packaged, delicious "souvenirs." ⊠ *Off Hwy. 19 and Hina Lani St., near Kona airport, Kailua-Kona.*

Keauhou Shopping Center

SHOPPING CENTERS/MALLS | About 5 miles south of Kailua Village, this neighborhood shopping center includes KTA Superstore, Longs Drugs, Kona Stories bookstore, and a multiplex movie theater. Kenichi Pacific, an upscale sushi restaurant, and Peaberry & Galette, a café that serves excellent crepes, are favorite eateries, joined by Bianelli's Pizza and Sam Choy's Kai Lanai, which is perched above the center. You can also grab a quick bite at Los Habaneros, Subway, or L&L Hawaiian Barbecue. ⊠ *78-6831 Alii Dr., Kailua-Kona* ☎ *808/322-3000* ⊕ *www.keauhoushoppingcenter.com.*

Kona Commons

SHOPPING CENTERS/MALLS | This downtown center features a Ross Dress for Less (for suitcases, shoes, swimsuits, and aloha wear) and Hawaiian Island Creations (for a great selection of surf gear, clothing, and accessories). Food and drink options include fast-food standbys like Dairy Queen, Subway, and Panda Express, as well as Ultimate Burger, for local beef and delicious homemade fries, and Genki Sushi, where the goods are delivered via conveyer belt. ■TIP➔ **Across the street, Target has fresh-flower lei for a fraction of the cost of local florists.** ⊠ *75-5450 Makala Blvd., Kailua-Kona* ⊕ *www.konacommons.com.*

Kona Inn Shopping Village

SHOPPING CENTERS/MALLS | Originally a hotel, the Kona Inn was built in 1928 to woo a new wave of wealthy travelers. As newer condos and resorts opened along the Kona and Kohala Coasts, it was transformed into a low-rise, outdoor shopping village with clothing boutiques, spas, art galleries, gift shops, an ice cream shop, a crystal store, and island-style eateries. Broad lawns with coconut trees on the ocean side provide a lovely setting for an afternoon picnic. The open-air Kona Canoe Club restaurant is a favorite for burgers. The iconic Kona Inn is best for drinks and appetizers, rather than full dinners. ⊠ *75-5744 Alii Dr., Kailua-Kona.*

Kona Marketplace

SHOPPING CENTERS/MALLS | On the *mauka* (mountain) side of Alii Drive, near Hulihee Palace, this small retail enclave in

Historic Kailua Village includes galleries, T-shirt/souvenir shops, a tattoo parlor, Holy Donuts doughnut shop, Frenchman's Cafe, and Sam's Hideaway bar. Local favorite Hayashi's You Make the Roll offers shaded outdoor seating and affordable sushi to go. ⊠ *75-5744 Alii Dr., Kailua-Kona.*

Makalapua Center

SHOPPING CENTERS/MALLS | On the *mauka* (moutain) side of the highway above Kona's Old Industrial area, this shopping center attracts visitors with island-influenced clothing, jewelry, and housewares at the upscale Macy's, the best place in Kona to find aloha shirts. The center also has one of the island's largest movie theaters. ⊠ *Kamakaeha Ave. at Hwy. 19, Kailua-Kona.*

Activities

SPAS

A Ala Hawaii Oceanfront Massage and Spa

FITNESS/HEALTH CLUBS | With oceanfront views of Kailua Bay, this spa offers a full menu of massage treatments as well as scrubs, wraps, facials, and waxing. It's a convenient place to get pampered before hitting the village shops or restaurants. ⊠ *Kona Inn Shopping Village, 75-5744 Alii Dr., Suite 245, Kailua-Kona* ☎ *808/937–9707* ⊕ *www.oceanfrontmassage.com* ✉ *Massages from $85, facials from $79.*

The Lotus Center

FITNESS/HEALTH CLUBS | Tucked away on the first floor of the Royal Kona Resort, the Lotus Center provides a convenient option for massage treatments, facials, and waxing. There's also a chiropractor on the premises. Ocean-side massage is available on a private patio outside the treatment rooms. Alternative offerings include acupuncture, yoga, Reiki, crystal-energy sessions, and biofeedback.
■**TIP**➜ **Ask about discounted packages.**
⊠ *Royal Kona Resort, 75-5852 Alii Dr., Kailua-Kona* ☎ *808/334–0445* ⊕ *www.*

konaspa.com ✉ *Massages from $65, facials from $65.*

The Spa at Hualalai

FITNESS/HEALTH CLUBS | For the exclusive use of Four Seasons Resort guests and members, this spa features 28 massage treatment areas. Tropical breezes waft through 14 outdoor massage *hales* (huts), situated in beautiful garden settings. The therapists are top-notch, and a real effort is made to incorporate local traditions. Apothecary services allow you to customize your treatment with almost 40 ingredients like *kukui* (candlenut) nuts, Hawaiian salts, and coconut. Massage options range from traditional lomilomi to Thai. ⊠ *Four Seasons Resort Hualalai, 72-100 Kaupulehu Dr., Kailua-Kona* ☎ *808/325–8000* ⊕ *www.fourseasons.com/hualalai/spa* ✉ *Massages from $190, facials from $95.*

South Kona

Kealakekua is 14 miles south of Kailua-Kona.

Between its coffee plantations, artsy havens, and Kealakekua Bay—one of the most beautiful spots on the Big Island—South Kona has plenty of activities to occupy a day. Bring a swimsuit and snorkel gear, and hit Kealakekua Bay first thing in the morning. You'll beat the crowds, have a better chance of a dolphin sighting, and see more fish. After a morning of swimming or kayaking, head to one of the homey cafés in nearby Captain Cook to refuel.

The meandering road leading to Kealakekua Bay is home to a historic painted church, as well as coffee-tasting spots and several reasonably priced B&Bs with great views. The communities surrounding the bay (Kealakekua and Captain Cook) are brimming with local and transplanted artists. They're great places to shop for gifts or antiques, have some coffee, or take an afternoon stroll.

Several coffee farms around the Kona coffee-belt area welcome visitors to watch all or part of the coffee-production process, from harvest to packaging. Some tours are self-guided and most are free, with the exception of the Kona Coffee Living History Farm.

GETTING HERE AND AROUND
To get to Kealakekua Bay, follow the signs off Highway 11 and park at Napoopoo Beach. It's not much of a beach (it used to be before Hurricane Iniki washed it away in 1992), but it provides easy access into the water.

◉ Sights

★ Captain James Cook Monument
MEMORIAL | On February 14, 1779, famed English explorer Captain James Cook was killed here during an apparent misunderstanding with local residents. He had chosen Kealakekua Bay as a landing place in November 1778. Arriving during the celebration of Makahiki, the harvest season, Cook was welcomed at first. Some Hawaiians saw him as an incarnation of the god Lono. Cook's party sailed away in February 1779, but a freak storm forced his damaged ship back to Kealakekua Bay. Believing that no god could be thwarted by a mere rainstorm, the Hawaiians were not so welcoming this time. The theft of a longboat brought Cook and an armed party ashore to reclaim it. Shots were fired, daggers and spears were thrown, and Captain Cook fell, mortally wounded. A 27-foot-high obelisk marks the spot where he died. ✉ Captain Cook ⊕ dlnr.hawaii.gov/dsp/parks/hawaii.

Greenwell Farms
FARM/RANCH | FAMILY | The Greenwell family played a significant role in the cultivation of the first commercial coffee in the Kona area (as well as the first grocery store). Depending on the season, the 20-minute walking tour of this working farm takes in various stages

of coffee production, including a look at the 100-year-old coffee trees. No reservations are required. Sample a cup of their famous Kona coffee at the end; the gift shop stays open until 5. ✉ 81-6581 Mamalahoa Hwy., Kealakekua ✛ Ocean side, between mile markers 112 and 111 ☎ 808/323–2295 ⊕ www.greenwellfarms.com ☞ Free.

Hikiau Heiau
RELIGIOUS SITE | This stone platform was once an impressive temple dedicated to the god Lono. When Captain Cook arrived in 1778, ceremonies in his honor were held here. It's still considered a religious site, so visit with respect. ✉ Captain Cook ✛ Bottom of Napoopoo Rd. at bay ☞ Free.

H. N. Greenwell Store Museum
HISTORIC SITE | Established in 1850, the homestead of Henry N. Greenwell served as cattle ranch, sheep station, store, post office, and family home all in one. Now, all that remains is the 1875 stone structure, which is listed on the National Register of Historic Places. It houses a fascinating museum with exhibits on ranching and coffee farming. It's also headquarters for the **Kona Historical Society,** which archives and preserves the history of the Kona district. An interesting aside: today, direct descendants of Henry Greenwell operate a popular South Kona grocery store, Choicemart, bringing their ancestors' legacy full circle. ✉ 81-6551 Mamalahoa Hwy., mile marker 112, Kealakekua ☎ 808/323–3222 ⊕ www.konahistorical.org ☞ $5 🕐 Closed Wed. and Fri.–Sun.

Kainaliu Town
TOWN | This is the first town you encounter to the south heading upcountry from Kailua Town. In addition to a ribbon of funky old stores, clothing boutiques, coffee bars, and bistros, a handful of galleries and antiques shops have sprung up. Browse around the Blue Ginger Gallery, Oshima's Surf and Skate, Kiernan Music, and Kimura's, founded in 1927,

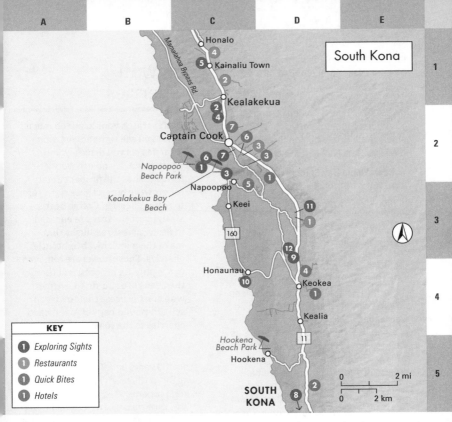

South Kona

Honalo
Kainaliu Town
Kealakekua
Captain Cook
Napoopoo Beach Park
Napoopoo
Kealakekua Bay Beach
Keei
160
Honaunau
Keokea
Kealia
Hookena Beach Park
Hookena
SOUTH KONA

Mamalahoa Bypass Rd

11

0   2 mi
0   2 km

KEY

1 Exploring Sights
1 Restaurants
1 Quick Bites
1 Hotels

Sights ▼

1 Captain James Cook
  Monument................**C2**
2 Greenwell Farms.........**C2**
3 Hikiau Heiau..............**C2**
4 H.N. Greenwell Store
  Museum **C2**
5 Kainaliu Town **C1**
6 Kealakekua Bay
  State Historical Park **C2**
7 Kona Coffee
  Living History Farm **C2**
8 Kona RainForest
  Farms....................**D5**
9 Lions Gate Farms **D3**
10 Puuhonua O Honaunau
  National
  Historical Park **C4**
11 Royal Kona
  Coffee Museum and
  Coffee Mill..............**D3**
12 St Benedict's
  Painted Church **D3**

Restaurants ▼

1 Kaaloa's Super J's
  Authentic
  Hawaiian Food **D3**
2 Keei Cafe at
  Hokukano.................**C1**
3 Manago Hotel
  Restaurant...............**C2**
4 Teshima's
  Restaurant...............**C1**

Quick Bites ▼

1 The Coffee Shack........**D2**

Hotels ▼

1 Aloha Guest House.....**D4**
2 Horizon Guest House...**D5**
3 Kaawa Loa
  Plantation.................**C2**
4 Kane Plantation
  Guesthouse..............**D4**
5 Luana Inn.................**C3**
6 Manago Hotel............**C2**
7 Mermaid Dreams
  Bed and Breakfast.......**C2**

to find fabrics and Japanese goods beyond tourist trinkets. Pop into a local café for everything from burgers to New York–style deli. Peek into the 1932-vintage Aloha Theatre, where a troupe of community-theater actors might be practicing a Broadway revue. ⊠ *Hwy. 11, mile markers 112–114, Kainaliu.*

★ **Kealakekua Bay State Historical Park**
NATIONAL/STATE PARK | One of the most beautiful spots in the state, this underwater marine reserve has dramatic cliffs that surround super-deep, crystal-clear, turquoise water chock-full of stunning coral pinnacles and tropical fish. The protected dolphins that frequent the sanctuary should not be disturbed, as they use the bay to escape predators and sleep. There's very little sand at west-facing **Napoopoo Beach,** but this is a nice easy place to enter the water and swim, as it's well protected from currents. At times, you may feel tiny jellyfish stings. There are no lifeguards, but there are bathrooms, a pavilion, shower, and (limited) parking. The **Captain James Cook Monument**, marking where the explorer died, is at the northern edge of the bay. Stay at least 300 feet from the shoreline along the cliffs, which have become unstable during recent earthquakes. A limited number of tour operators offer snorkeling and kayaking tours here, a good and very popular option. ⊠ *Beach Rd. off Government Rd. from Puuhonua Rd. (Hwy. 160), Captain Cook ⊕ dlnr.hawaii.gov/dsp/parks/hawaii ⊠ Free.*

★ **Kona Coffee Living History Farm**
HISTORIC SITE | On the National Register of Historic Places, this perfectly preserved farm was completely restored by the Kona Historical Society. It includes a 1913 farmhouse first homesteaded by the Uchida family and is surrounded by coffee trees, a Japanese bathhouse, a *kuriba* (coffee-processing mill), and a *hoshidana* (traditional drying platform). Caretakers still grow, harvest, roast, and sell the coffee exactly as they did more

Hawaii Cherries 🍴

Don't scratch your head too much when you see signs advertising "cherries" as you drive around South Kona. It's no use wondering if Hawaii has the proper climate for growing bings; these signs refer to coffee cherries. Coffee beans straight off the tree are encased in fleshy, sweet red husks that make them look like bright little cherries. These husks are removed in the pulping process, and then the beans are sun-dried. Farmers who don't process their own can sell 100-pound bags of just-picked cherries to the roasters.

than 100 years ago. The H. N. Greenwell Store Museum is located on the same property. ⊠ *82-6199 Mamalahoa Hwy., mile marker 110, Captain Cook ☎ 808/323–2006 ⊕ www.konahistorical.org ⊠ $15 ⊙ Closed weekends.*

Kona RainForest Farms
FARM/RANCH | This family's commitment to growing 100% organic coffee starts even before the plants are in the ground, with organic mulch and naturally developed fertilizers that they also sell throughout Hawaii. No pesticides or commercial fertilizers are used on the 80-acre farm. Because it's such a difficult and exacting process, only 2% of Kona coffee can claim to be 100% certified organic. The farm does private tours (with tastings) by appointment only and even offers a guesthouse should you wish to stay a little longer than a day. Plans are under way for building a visitor center in 2021 or 2022. Note that the property can only be accessed by four-wheel-drive vehicles. ⊠ *87-2854 Mamalahoa Hwy., Captain Cook ☎ 808/328–1941*

St. Benedict's Roman Catholic Church was painted by Father John Velge, the parish's priest in the early 20th century.

⊕ *organiccoffeehawaii.com* ⊠ *Free*
⊙ *Tours by appointment only.*

★ Lions Gate Farms

FARM/RANCH | For a century, three generations have grown coffee on this pretty farm with spectacular ocean views in the heart of Honaunau. The coffee is processed in a mill that dates to 1942. Tours given by the friendly proprietors proudly show visitors how coffee and macadamia nuts are cultivated and harvested. The farmers also sell packaged coffee, nuts, and jams and jellies from this year's harvest and are passionate about producing only the best estate-grown Kona coffee. ⊠ *84-5085 Mamalahoa Hwy., mile marker 105, Honaunau* ☎ *808/989–4883* ⊕ *www.coffeeofkona.com* ⊠ *Free.*

★ Puuhonua O Honaunau National Historical Park (*Place of Refuge*)

HISTORIC SITE | The 420-acre National Historical Park houses the best preserved *puuhonua* (place of refuge) in the state. Providing a safe haven for noncombatants, *kapu* (taboo) breakers, defeated warriors, and others, the *puuhonua* offered protection and redemption for anyone who could reach its boundaries, by land or sea. The oceanfront, 960-foot stone wall still stands and is one of the park's most prominent features. A number of ceremonial temples, including the restored **Hale o Keawe Heiau** (circa 1700), have served as royal burial chambers. An aura of ancient sacredness and serenity still imbues the place. ⊠ *Rte. 160, Honaunau* ⊹ *About 20 miles south of Kailua-Kona* ☎ *808/328–2288* ⊕ *www. nps.gov/puho* ⊠ *$20 per vehicle.*

Royal Kona Coffee Museum and Coffee Mill

FACTORY | Take an easy, self-guided tour by following the descriptive plaques located around the coffee mill. Then stop off at the small museum to see coffee-making relics, peruse the gift shop, and watch an informational film. Visitors are also invited to enjoy the beautiful views as well as stroll through a real lava tube on the property. ⊠ *83-5427 Mamalahoa Hwy., Captain Cook* ⊹ *Next to the tree house* ☎ *808/328–2511* ⊕ *www.*

Kona Coffee

The Kona coffee belt, some 16 miles long and about a mile wide, has been producing smooth, aromatic coffee for more than a century. The slopes of massive Mauna Loa at this elevation provide the ideal conditions for growing coffee: sunny mornings; cloudy, rainy afternoons; and rich, rocky, volcanic soil. More than 600 farms, most just 3 to 7 acres in size, grow the delicious—and luxurious, at generally more than $35 per pound—gourmet beans. Only coffee from the North and South Kona districts can be called Kona (labeling requirements are strict and fiercely defended), and Hawaii is the only state in the United States that produces commercially grown coffee.

In 1828, Reverend Samuel Ruggles, an American missionary, brought a cutting over from the Oahu farm of Chief Boki, Oahu's governor. That coffee plant was a strain of Ethiopian coffee called Arabica, which is still produced today, although a Guatemalan strain of Arabica introduced in the late 1800s is produced in far higher quantities.

In the early 1900s, the large Hawaiian coffee plantations subdivided their lots and began leasing parcels to local tenant farmers, a practice that continues. Many tenant farmers were Japanese families. In the 1930s, local schools switched summer vacation to "coffee vacation," August to November, so that children could help with the coffee harvest, a practice that held until 1969.

When coffee trees are flowering, the white blossoms are fondly known as "Kona snow." Once ripened, coffee is harvested as "cherries"—beans encased in a sweet, red shell. Kona coffee trees are handpicked several times each season to guarantee the ripest product. The cherries are shelled, their parchment layer sun-dried and removed, and the beans roasted to perfection. Today most farms—owned and operated by Japanese-American families, West Coast mainland transplants, and descendants of Portuguese and Chinese immigrants—control production from cultivation to cup.

royalkonacoffee.com ☒ Free ☉ Closed weekends.

St. Benedict's Painted Church
RELIGIOUS SITE | In the late 1800s, Belgian-born priest and self-taught artist Father John Velge painted the walls, columns, and ceiling of this Roman Catholic church with religious scenes in the style of Christian folk art found throughout the South Pacific. The tiny chapel evokes the European Gothic cathedral tradition and is listed on the Hawaii State Register of Historic Places and the National Register of Historic Places. Mass is offered Saturday and Sunday. ☒ 84-5140 Painted Church Rd., off Hwy. 160, Captain Cook ☎ 808/328–2227 ⊕ thepaintedchurchhawaii.org ☒ Free, donations welcome.

⛱ Beaches

Hookena Beach Park
BEACH—SIGHT | FAMILY | The 2½-mile road to this secluded little gem feels like you're venturing off the beaten path. The area is rich in history, with remnants of an old steamship pier testifying to its former role as a thriving port town, complete with (now gone) post office, church, and stores. Today, though much quieter, it's still an active Hawaiian fishing

Kealakekua Bay is generally considered the best snorkeling spot on the Big Island.

village, beloved by residents and tended to by a local nonprofit. It has a clean, soft mix of dark brown and gray sand and is backed by steep emerald embankments and a dramatic sloping *pali* (cliff) making for picturesque tropical vistas. The bay is usually calm, tranquil, and clear with small surf. The park partnership oversees beach concessions, camping permits, and security. You can rent equipment, beach chairs, and umbrellas. **Amenities:** food and drink; parking (no fee); showers; toilets; water sports. **Best for:** snorkeling; swimming. ⊠ *Hwy. 11 between mile markers 101 and 102, Captain Cook ⊹ 23 miles south of Kailua-Kona* ☎ *808/961–8311* ⊕ *www.hookena.org* ⊠ *Free.*

★ Kealakekua Bay Beach

BEACH—SIGHT | Gorgeous and undeveloped, this area offers extraordinary vistas and protected swimming. The shoreline is rocky, but the area is surrounded by high green cliffs, creating calm conditions for superb swimming, snorkeling, and diving (beware of jellyfish). Protected Hawaiian spinner dolphins come to

rest and escape predators during the day. Captain James Cook first landed in Hawaii here in 1778, but when he returned a year later, he was killed in a skirmish with Hawaiians, now marked by a monument on the north end of the bay. Rocky but walkable trails lead to Hikiau Heiau, a sacred place for the Hawaiian people. Please proceed respectfully and do not walk on it or enter it. Parking is very limited. ⚠ **Be aware of the off-limits area (in case of rockfalls) marked by orange buoys.** **Amenities:** parking (no fee); showers; toilets. **Best for:** snorkeling; swimming. ⊠ *Kealakekua Bay State Historical Park, Napoopoo Rd. off Hwy. 11, just south of mile marker 111, Kealakekua* ☎ *808/961–9544.*

🍴 Restaurants

★ Kaaloa's Super J's Authentic Hawaiian Food

$ | HAWAIIAN | It figures that the best *laulau* (pork or chicken wrapped in taro leaves and steamed) in West Hawaii can be found at a roadside hole-in-the-wall rather than at an expensive resort luau; in fact, this humble family-run eatery was featured on the Food Network's *The Best Thing I Ever Ate*. Plate lunches to go include tender chicken or pork *laulau*, steamed for up to 10 hours. **Known for:** tasty kalua pig and cabbage; friendly and welcoming proprietors; plate lunches with chicken or pork laulau. [$] *Average main: $9* ⊠ *83-5409 Mamalahoa Hwy., between mile markers 106 and 107, Honaunau* ☎ *808/328–9566* ⊗ *Closed Sun.*

Keei Cafe at Hokukano

$$ | ECLECTIC | This nicely appointed restaurant, just 15 minutes south of Kailua-Kona, serves delicious dinners with Brazilian, Asian, and European flavors highlighting fresh ingredients from local farmers. Favorites are the Brazilian seafood chowder or peanut-miso salad, followed by pasta primavera smothered with a basil-pesto sauce. **Known for:** most upscale restaurant in South Kona; live dinner music; cash-only place. [$] *Average main: $20* ⊠ *79-7511 Mamalahoa Hwy., Kealakekua* ✦ *½ mile south of Kainaliu* ☎ *808/322–9992* ⊕ *www.keeicafe.net* ▭ *No credit cards* ⊗ *Closed Sun. and Mon. No lunch.*

Manago Hotel Restaurant

$ | HAWAIIAN | FAMILY | The historic Manago Hotel is like a time warp, complete with a vintage neon sign, Formica tables, and old photos. T-shirts brag (and it's not false advertising) that the restaurant has the best grilled pork chops in the world, and the fresh fish is excellent as well, especially the ono and ahi. **Known for:** one of the only places in Kona serving opelu, a local fish; mains come with a variety of side dishes; local hospitality. [$] *Average main: $10* ⊠ *82-6155 Mamalahoa Hwy., Captain Cook* ☎ *808/323–2642* ⊕ *www.managohotel.com* ⊗ *Closed Mon.*

Teshima's Restaurant

$ | JAPANESE | FAMILY | It doesn't look like much, either inside or out, but Teshima's has been a *kamaaina* (local) favorite since 1929 for a reason. Locals gather at this small landmark restaurant whenever they're in the mood for fresh sashimi, puffy shrimp tempura, or *hekka* (beef and vegetables cooked in an iron pot). **Known for:** excellent tempura combos; long-standing family-owned establishment; authentic local flavor. [$] *Average main: $15* ⊠ *79-7251 Mamalahoa Hwy., Honalo* ☎ *808/322–9140* ⊕ *www.teshimarestaurant.com.*

☕ Coffee and Quick Bites

The Coffee Shack

$ | AMERICAN | Visitors enjoy stopping here before or after a morning of snorkeling at Kealakekua Bay, and for good reason: the views of the Honaunau Coast from this roadside restaurant are stunning. This place is best for breakfast or a quick bite, as overpriced lunch plates can miss; but if you're in the mood for a Hawaiian smoothie, iced honey-mocha latte, scone, or homemade luau bread, it's worth the stop. **Known for:** scenic views of South Kona coastline; house-baked bread; its own brand of Kona coffee. [$] *Average main: $12* ⊠ *83-5799 Mamalahoa Hwy., Captain Cook* ☎ *808/328–9555* ⊕ *www.coffeeshack.com* ⊗ *No dinner.*

🛏 Hotels

Aloha Guest House

$$ | B&B/INN | In the hills above Puuhonu O Honaunau National Historical Park, this guesthouse offers quiet elegance, complete privacy, and ocean views from every room. **Pros:** eco-conscious option; full breakfast; views of the South Kona coastline. **Cons:** remote location up a bumpy 1-mile dirt road; 40 minutes from downtown; four-wheel drive recommended. [$] *Rooms from: $236* ⊠ *Old Tobacco Rd. off Hwy. 11, near mile marker 104, Honaunau* ☎ *808/328–8955* ⊕ *www.alohaguesthouse.com* ⤳ *5 rooms* ⊗ *Free breakfast.*

Horizon Guest House

$$$ | B&B/INN | Surrounded by McCandeless Ranch on 40 acres in South Kona, this place may seem remote, but it's actually just a short drive from some of the best water attractions on the island, including Puuhonua O Honaunau, Kealakekua Bay, and Hookena Beach. **Pros:** private and quiet; heated pool with Jacuzzi; lovely ocean views. **Cons:** not on the beach; 40 minutes from Kailua-Kona; remote location. $ *Rooms from: $275* ⊠ *Mamalahoa Hwy., between mile markers 101 and 100, Captain Cook* ☎ *808/938–7822* ⊕ *www.horizonguesthouse.com* ⌁ *4 suites* ⦿ *Free breakfast.*

★ Kaawa Loa Plantation

$$ | B&B/INN | Proprietors Mike Martinage and Greg Nunn operate a grand yet reasonably priced B&B, on a 5-acre coffee farm above Kealakekua Bay, in a home that features a 2,000-square-foot wraparound veranda with excellent views of the bay and the entire Honaunau Coast. **Pros:** gracious and friendly hosts; excellent breakfast; Hawaiian steam room. **Cons:** not within walking distance of bay; some rooms share a bath; slightly steep turnoff. $ *Rooms from: $209* ⊠ *82-5990 Napoopoo Rd., Captain Cook* ☎ *808/323–2686* ⊕ *www.kaawaloaplantation.com* ⌁ *5 rooms* ⦿ *Free breakfast.*

Kane Plantation Guesthouse

$$$ | B&B/INN | The former home of late legendary artist Herb Kane, this luxury boutique guesthouse occupies a 16-acre avocado farm overlooking the South Kona coastline. **Pros:** sauna, hot tub, massage therapy room; upscale amenities; beautiful artwork. **Cons:** not on the beach; off the beaten track; 25 minutes to downtown. $ *Rooms from: $325* ⊠ *84-1120 Telephone Exchange Rd., off Hwy. 11, Honaunau* ⊹ *¼ mile past mile marker 105, south of Captain Cook* ☎ *808/328–2416* ⊕ *www.kaneplantationhawaii.com* ⌁ *3 suites* ⦿ *Free breakfast.*

Luana Inn

$$$$ | B&B/INN | This B&B, with its rare location within walking distance to splendid Kealakekua Bay, offers three high-luxury rooms with kitchenettes in the main house that share the pool patio area. **Pros:** renovated in 2019; Jacuzzi spa at sunset; tranquility and privacy. **Cons:** no breakfast; three-night minimum; as pricey as Kohala resorts. $ *Rooms from: $525* ⊠ *82-5856 Napoopoo Rd., Captain Cook* ☎ *808/731–6634* ⊕ *www.luanainn. com* ⌁ *5 units* ⦿ *No meals.*

Manago Hotel

$ | HOTEL | If you want to escape the touristy thing but still be close to the water and attractions like Kealakekua Bay and Puuhonua O Honaunau National Historical Park, this historical hotel is a good option. **Pros:** local color; rock-bottom prices; terrific on-site restaurant. **Cons:** not the best sound insulation between rooms; cheapest rooms share a community bath; some rooms have highway noise. $ *Rooms from: $75* ⊠ *81-6155 Mamalahoa Hwy., Captain Cook* ☎ *808/323–2642* ⊕ *www.managohotel. com* ⌁ *64 rooms* ⦿ *No meals.*

Mermaid Dreams Bed and Breakfast

$ | B&B/INN | "Aloha" is the operative word at this mermaid-themed B&B a 10-minute drive from Kealakekua Bay. A self-proclaimed mermaid herself, hostess/proprietor Heather Reynolds takes guests on morning mermaid swims in the bay, where they can learn to swim while wearing a tail (she even has mermaid tails for rent if you need one). **Pros:** gracious hosts; beautifully landscaped grounds; fireside lounge outside for evening cocktails. **Cons:** not on the beach; no children under age 13; two-night minimum stay. $ *Rooms from: $177* ⊠ *81-1031 Keopuka Mauka Rd., Kealakekua* ☎ *808/649–9911* ⊕ *www. mermaiddreamsbedandbreakfast.com* ⌁ *5 rooms* ⦿ *Free breakfast.*

Nightlife

★ Korner Pocket

BARS/PUBS | A favored haunt of the South Kona crowd, Korner Pocket is tucked in the back of an office plaza. But don't let that deter you. They serve fantastic, affordable food, ranging from scrumptious burgers to a killer prime rib. Popular local bands frequently perform, with no cover, and everyone gets up to dance. You can also play pool. It's the only place open late down south. ⊠ 81-970 Halekii St., Kealakekua ☎ 808/322–2994.

Shopping

CLOTHING

Paradise Found

CLOTHING | Carrying contemporary silk and rayon clothing for women, this venerable shop is in the up-country town of Kainaliu, near Aloha Theatre, but there's also a branch at Keauhou Shopping Center. ⊠ 79-7406 Mamalahoa Hwy., Kainaliu ☎ 808/322–2111 Kainaliu location, 808/324–1177 Keauhou location.

GALLERIES

Cliff Johns Gallery

ART GALLERIES | Though ownership has changed, this fine-art gallery still retains the name of local woodworker Cliff Johns, who had a knack for sourcing unique, handcrafted finds by Big Island artists. The gallery features wood sculptures, paintings, carvings, and other crafts different from the standard fare, not to mention jewelry and other finely crafted carvings and *netsuke* (small sculptures). ⊠ Mango Court, 79-7460 Mamalahoa Hwy., Kealakekua ✛ Next to Annie's Burgers ☎ 808/322–0044.

LOCAL SPECIALTIES

Mahina Mele Market

LOCAL SPECIALTIES | Small on space but huge on sustainable quality, this shop carries the owners' full line of proprietary organic skincare products created mostly of botanicals grown on their farm. The store also stocks the organic macadamia nuts and coffee grown on 60 acres the proprietors own and manage in South Kona. ⊠ Mango Court, 79-7460 Mamalahoa Hwy., Suite A-103, Kealakekua ☎ 808/217–7622.

MARKETS

Pure Kona Green Market

OUTDOOR/FLEA/GREEN MARKETS | **FAMILY** | A favorite in Captain Cook, this Sunday farmers' market runs from 9 to 2 and offers great hot breakfast and lunch items, produce from local farms, and artists selling their work. ⊠ Amy B. H. Greenwell Ethnobotanical Garden Grounds, 82-6160 Mamalahoa Hwy., Captain Cook.

Activities

SPAS

Kona Shiatsu Clinic

FITNESS/HEALTH CLUBS | Hidden away in a vintage bungalow near Manago Hotel, this peaceful little clinic offers deep-tissue shiatsu massage, Japanese style. A master of shiatsu since 1980, Tom Langenstein helps clients work out the kinks, relieve headaches, or recover from injuries. ⊠ 82-6161 Mamalahoa Hwy., Captain Cook ☎ 808/323–3111 ⊕ www.konashiatsu.com ▦ Massages from $40.

Mamalahoa Hot Tubs and Massage

FITNESS/HEALTH CLUBS | Tucked into a residential neighborhood above Kealakekua, this is a welcome alternative to the large Kohala Coast resort spas. It feels like a secret hideaway aglow with tiki torches, and Hawaiian lomilomi and hot-stone massages are offered at affordable prices. ■TIP→ **Soaking tubs, enclosed in their own thatched gazebos with roof portholes for stargazing, are great for a couple's soak.** ⊠ 81-1016 St. John's Rd., Kealakekua ☎ 808/323–2288 ⊕ www.mamalahoa-hot-tubs.com ▦ Massage from $190.

Kua Bay is protected from wind by the rocky shores that surround it.

North Kona

The North Kona district is characterized by vast lava fields, dotted with turnoff points to some of the most beautiful beaches in the world. Most of the lava flows here originate from the last eruptions of Hualalai, in 1800 and 1801, although some flows by the resorts hail from Mauna Loa. The stark black lavascapes contrast spectacularly with luminous azure waters framed by coco palms and white-sand beaches. Some of the turnoffs will take you to state parks with parking lots and bathrooms, while others are simply a park-on-the-highway-and-hike-in adventure.

GETTING HERE AND AROUND

Head north from Kona International Airport and follow Highway 19 along the coast. Take caution driving at night between the airport and where resorts begin on the Kohala Coast; it's extremely dark, and there are few road signs or traffic lights on this two-lane road. Wild donkeys may appear on the roadway without warning.

◉ Sights

Kaloko–Honokohau National Historical Park
NATIONAL/STATE PARK | FAMILY | The trails at this sheltered 1,160-acre coastal park near Honokohau Harbor, just north of Kailua-Kona, are popular with walkers and hikers. The free park is a good place to observe Hawaiian archaeological history and intact ruins, including a *heiau* (temple), house platforms, ancient fishponds, and numerous petroglyphs, along a boardwalk. The park's wetlands provide refuge to waterbirds, including the endemic Hawaiian stilt and coot. Two beaches here are good for swimming, sunbathing, and sea turtle spotting: **Aiopio,** a few yards north of the harbor, is a small and calm, protected swimming areas (good for kids), while **Honokohau Beach** is a ¾-mile stretch with ruins of ancient fishponds, also north of the harbor. Of the park's three entrances, the middle one leads to a visitor center

with helpful rangers and lots of information. Local docents with backgrounds in geology or other subjects give nature talks. To go directly to the beaches, take the harbor road north of the Gentry retail center, park in the gravel lot, and follow the signs. ⊠ *74-425 Kealakehe Pkwy., off Hwy. 19 near airport, Kailua-Kona* ☎ *808/329–6881* ⊕ *www.nps.gov/kaho* ✉ *Free.*

Mountain Thunder
FARM/RANCH | This coffee producer offers hourly "bean-to-cup" tours, including a tasting and access to the processing plant, which shows dry milling, sizing, coloring, sorting, and roasting. For $10, take the lava tube/nature walk in the cloud forest ecosystem. There's a small retail store where you can purchase coffee and souvenirs. Remember that afternoon rains are common at this elevation, so bring an umbrella and sturdy shoes. ⊠ *73-1944 Hao St., Kailua-Kona* ☎ *808/325–5566* ⊕ *www.mountainthunder.com* ✉ *Free.*

Natural Energy Lab of Hawaii Authority
COLLEGE | Just south of Kona International Airport, a large, mysterious group of buildings with a large photovoltaic (solar) panel installation resembles a top-secret military station, but it's actually the site of the Natural Energy Lab of Hawaii Authority, NELHA for short, and administered by the Friends of NELHA. Here, scientists, researchers, and entrepreneurs make use of a cold, deep-sea pipeline to develop and market everything from desalinated, mineral-rich drinking water and super-nutritious algae products to energy-efficient air-conditioning systems and environmentally friendly aquaculture techniques. Seahorses, abalone, *kampachi*, Dungeness crab, and Maine lobsters are also raised here. Start your visit at the gateway building and take the Seas the Day tour to learn about the Ocean Science and Technology Park, the Ocean Conservation tour, or the Sustainable Aquaculture tour. ⊠ *73-4485 Kahilihili St., Kailua-Kona* ☎ *808/329–8073* ⊕ *www.energyfuturehawaii.org* ✉ *$49* ☉ *Closed weekends.*

⚏ Beaches

Kekaha Kai State Park—Kua Bay Side
BEACH—SIGHT | On the northernmost stretch of the park's coastline, this lovely beach is on an absolutely beautiful bay. The water is crystal clear, deep aquamarine, and peaceful in summer, but the park's paved entrance, amenities, and parking lot make it very accessible and, as a result, often crowded. Fine white sand sits in stark contrast to old black lava flows, and there's little shade—bring umbrellas as it can get hot. Rocky shores on either side protect the beach from winds in the afternoon. Gates open daily from 8 to 7. ⚠ **In winter, surf can get very rough, and often the sand washes away. Amenities:** parking (no fee); showers; toilets. **Best for:** surfing; swimming. ⊠ *Hwy. 19, north of mile marker 88, Kailua-Kona* ⊹ *Across from Veterans Cemetery* ✉ *Free.*

★ Kekaha Kai State Park—Mahaiula Side
BEACH—SIGHT | It's slow going down a 1.8-mile, bumpy but paved road off Highway 19 to this beach park, but it's worth it. This state park encompasses three beaches: from south to north, **Mahaiula**, **Makalawena**, and **Kua Bay**, which has its own entrance. Mahaiula and Makalawena are beautiful, wide expanses of white-sand beach with dunes. Makalawena has great swimming and body boarding. (Note: Makalawena, sandwiched between the two state parks, is private property and falls under the jurisdiction of Kamehameha Schools Bishop Estates.) From Makalawena, a 4½-mile trail leads to Kua Bay. If you're game, work your way on foot to the top of Puu Kuili, a 342-foot-high cinder cone with a fantastic coastline view. However, be prepared for the heat and bring lots of water, as none is available. Gates at the highway entrance close promptly at 7, so you need

Sights

1 Kaloko-Honokohau National Historical Park **B4**

2 Mountain Thunder..... **C4**

3 Natural Energy Lab of Hawaii Authority.... **A3**

Restaurants

1 Beach Tree at the Four Seasons Resort Hualalai..... **B1**

2 Pine Tree Cafe **B4**

3 Ulu Ocean Grill and Sushi Lounge at the Four Seasons Resort Hualalai..... **B1**

Hotels

1 Four Seasons Resort Hualalai..... **B1**

2 Silver Oaks Guest Ranch....... **B4**

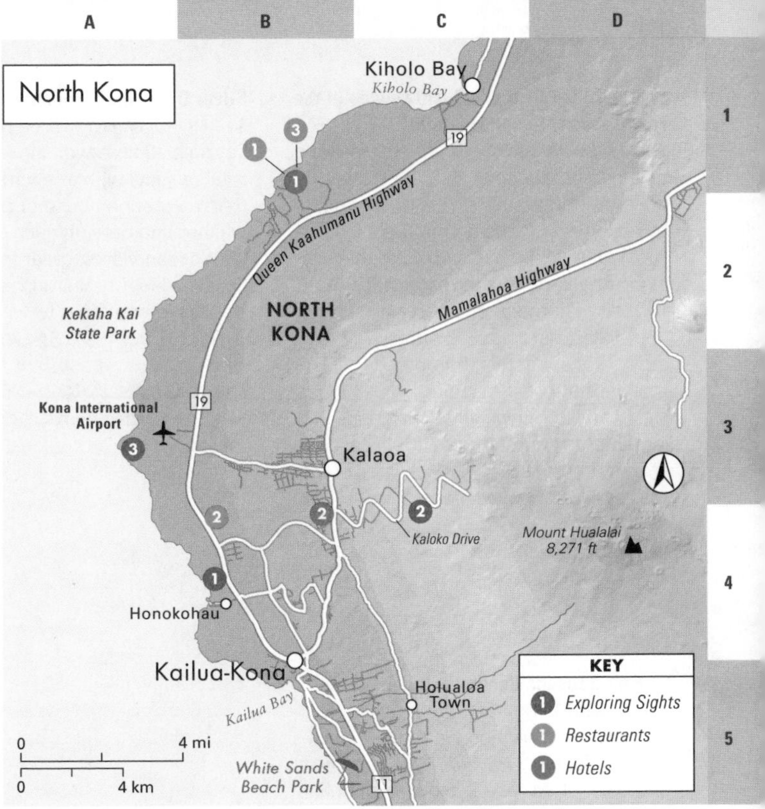

to leave the lot by 6:30. ⚠ **Watch out for rough surf and strong currents. Amenities:** toilets. **Best for:** swimming. ✉ *Hwy. 19, Kailua-Kona* ✣ *Turnoff is about 2 miles north of Kona International Airport* ☎ *808/327–4958, 808/974–6200* 🎟 *Free.*

🍴 Restaurants

Beach Tree at the Four Seasons Resort Hualalai

$$$ | MODERN ITALIAN | FAMILY | Beautifully designed, this venue provides a relaxed and elegant setting for alfresco dining near the sand, with its boardwalk-style deck, outdoor seating under the trellis, and enormous vaulted ceiling. The menu features brick-oven pizzas, gnocchi with Keahole lobster, seafood entrées, steak, and farm-fresh salads, and there's a kids' menu too. **Known for:** special Ohana Table four-course dinner; 60 wines by the glass; elegant resort atmosphere. [$] *Average main: $35* ✉ *Four Seasons Resort Hualalai, 72-100 Kaupulehu Dr., Kailua-Kona* ☎ *808/325–8000* 🌐 *www.fourseasons.com/hualalai.*

Pine Tree Cafe

$ | HAWAIIAN | FAMILY | Named for a popular nearby surf spot, the café offers local classics such as *loco moco* (meat, rice, and eggs smothered in gravy), alongside new inventions like crab curry bisque. The fresh-fish plate is decent, and all meals are served with fries or rice and macaroni salad. **Known for:** early-morning breakfast; fresh fish; popularity with locals. [$] *Average main: $12* ✉ *Kohanaiki Plaza, 73-4354 Mamalahoa Hwy. (Hwy. 11), Kailua-Kona* ☎ *808/327–1234.*

★ Ulu Ocean Grill and Sushi Lounge at the Four Seasons Resort Hualalai

$$$$ | **MODERN HAWAIIAN** | Casual elegance takes center stage at the resort's flagship oceanfront restaurant, one of the most upscale restaurants on the Big Island. Breakfast can be à la carte or buffet, but nighttime is when the magic happens, with diverse menu choices—roasted beet salad, flame-grilled prime New York steak, Kona lobster, shrimp pad Thai, and more—that make deciding what to order a challenge. **Known for:** sushi lounge; ingredients sourced from 160 local purveyors; impressive wine list. [$] *Average main: $45* ✉ *Four Seasons Resort Hualalai, 72-100 Kaupulehu Dr., Kailua-Kona* ☎ *808/325–8000* 🌐 *www.fourseasons.com* 🕒 *No lunch.*

Hotels

★ Four Seasons Resort Hualalai

$$$$ | **RESORT** | **FAMILY** | Beautiful views everywhere, polished wood floors, custom furnishings and linens in warm earth and cool white tones, and Hawaiian fine artwork make this oceanfront resort a peaceful retreat. **Pros:** beautiful location; gourmet restaurants; renowned service. **Cons:** not the best beach among the resorts; quite pricey; 20-minute drive to Kailua-Kona. [$] *Rooms from: $950* ✉ *72-100 Kaupulehu Dr., Kailua-Kona* ☎ *808/325–8000, 888/340–5662* 🌐 *www.fourseasons.com/hualalai* 🛏 *243 rooms* 🍴 *No meals.*

Silver Oaks Guest Ranch

$ | **RENTAL** | **FAMILY** | Three private cottages set on a 10-acre working ranch afford total privacy, with a few more amenities than a vacation house or condo. **Pros:** washer and dryer in each cottage; deck with ocean views; great for animal lovers. **Cons:** five-night minimum stay; rural country location not near town; dated decor. [$] *Rooms from: $175* ✉ *73-4570 Mamalahoa Hwy., just south of Kaloko Dr., Kailua-Kona* ☎ *808/325–2000* 🌐 *www.silveroaksranch.com* 🛏 *3 cottages* 🍴 *No meals.*

Chapter 4

THE KOHALA COAST AND WAIMEA

Updated by
Kristina Anderson

4

⊙ Sights	🍴 Restaurants	🛏 Hotels	🛍 Shopping	🍸 Nightlife
★★★★★	★★★★★	★★★★★	★★★★☆	★★☆☆☆

WELCOME TO
THE KOHALA COAST AND WAIMEA

TOP REASONS TO GO

★ **Hapuna Beach State Recreation Area:** With soft sand and clear blue water, Hapuna is a ½-mile strand of exquisite loveliness that often makes lists of the world's best beaches.

★ **Puukohala Heiau National Historic Site:** A massive temple structure dating to the 18th century, this was Kamehameha the Great's homage to the war god in order to unify the Hawaiian Islands.

★ **Parker Ranch:** The largest working cattle ranch in Hawaii features historic homes open to the public for tours.

★ **Kaunaoa Beach:** Framed by snow-topped mountains and coco palms, this magnificent crescent beach is recognizable on many a postcard of Hawaii.

★ **Anaehoomalu Bay:** This beautiful bay, ideal for swimming and snorkeling, is easily accessible and presents the perfect tropical beach setting.

The Kohala coast is where you'll find the majority of the Big Island's large, luxurious resorts, not to mention most of its gorgeous white-sand beaches (some off the beaten path and worth exploring), golf courses, and top-chef restaurants. It's not called the "Gold Coast" for nothing.

1 Waikoloa. Home to several major resorts, this region also boasts golf, lots of shopping (including two of the island's biggest shopping center), and excellent beaches. The resorts here offer all manner of activities.

2 Mauna Lani. Known as a five-star destination for its resorts, with lavish spas and championship golf courses, the area is home to historical sites such as petroglyph fields.

3 Mauna Kea and Hapuna. This area has two resorts and two truly spectacular beaches, including Kaunaoa Beach—a gorgeous, white-sand crescent fronting a peaceful, sheltered bay—and Hapuna Beach—considered by some to be the island's finest sunset-watching spots (a place to come to see the coveted "green flash").

4 Kawaihae. An important windwardside commercial hub, Kawaihae is not a manicured resort area, but several excellent eateries are a draw, and the working harbor is also the jumping off point for tourist boats on the weekends, not to mention commercial fishermen. The harbor has been important since the days of King Kamehameha, and it's the port where the first cattle came ashore in the 18th century.

5 Hawi and Kapaau. These onetime sugar towns on the far north end of the island thrived during the plantation days, and when the sugar business dried up, they turned to artists, who were keen to preserve the town's past. Today, artsy shops and lovingly restored buildings offer a dose of authentic old Hawaiian character.

6 Waimea. Unlike any other part of the Big Island, the rolling green hills and open pastureland lend a pastoral quality to this appealing upcountry town known for good dining. It was once dominated by the Parker family and their ranch, still one of the largest privately owned ranches in the United States.

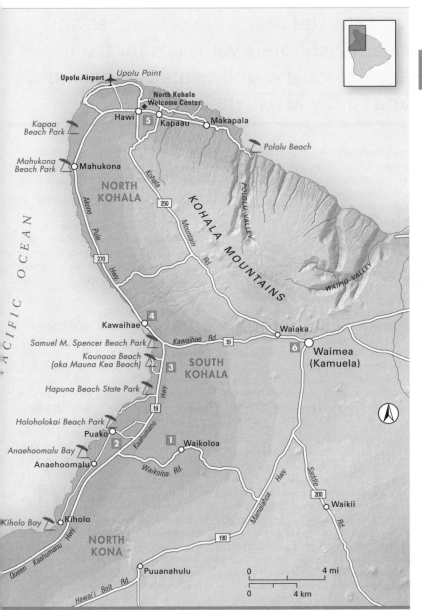

If you had only a weekend to spend on the Big Island, this is probably where you'd want to be. The Kohala Coast is a mix of the island's best beaches and swankiest hotels yet is not far from ancient valleys and temples, waterfalls, and funky artist enclaves.

The Kohala Coast is home to almost all of the Big Island's megaresorts. Dotting the coastline are manicured lawns and golf courses, restaurants, and destination spas. But the real attraction here is the area's glorious beaches. On a clear day, you can see Maui, and during the winter months, numerous glistening humpback whales cleave the waters just offshore. Many visitors to the Big Island check in here and rarely leave the area. If you're looking to be pampered and lounge on the beach or by the pool all day with an umbrella drink in hand, this is where you need to be. You can still see the rest of the island since most of the hiking and adventure-tour companies offer pickups at the Kohala Coast resorts, and many of the hotels have connections to car-rental agencies (though the number of cars is limited, and you will need to book ahead).

Rounding the northern tip of the island, the arid coast shifts rather suddenly to green villages and hillsides, leading to lush Pololu Valley in North Kohala, as the hot sunshine along the coast gives way to cooler temperatures. In this area are the quaint sugar-plantation towns turned artsy villages of Hawi and Kapaau. New galleries are interspersed with charming reminders of old Hawaii—wooden board-walks, quaint local storefronts, ice cream shops, delicious neighborhood restaurants, friendly locals, and a delightfully

slow pace. There's great shopping for everything from antiques and designer beachwear to authentic Hawaiian crafts.

A short drive from the resorts, Waimea's upcountry, pastoral countryside is sprinkled with well-tended, vintage homes with picket fences and flower beds. There's a gentle *paniolo* (Hawaiian cowboy) vibe thoughout the town, which boasts a number of excellent restaurants worth seeking out.

MAJOR REGIONS

Sometimes referred to as the "Gold Coast" of the Big Island, the stunning **Kohala Coast** pairs stark black lava fields with azure oceans and white-sand beaches. It's home to all the major resorts: Waikoloa, Mauna Lani, and Mauna Kea boast five-star resorts, spas, golf, and restaurants. Kawaihae, in contrast, is a small harbor town with some restaurants and amenities. In North Kohala, the tiny towns of Hawi and Kapaau round out the island's northern tip. Having survived the decline of the sugar business, today they evoke a low-key, artsy, historical vibe.

Situated at an elevation of 2,600 feet, cool **Waimea** has splendors that include mists, rainbows, sun, and verdant green hills. Ranchlands sprawl across the cool upland meadows of the area, known as cowboy country.

Planning

Planning Your Time

Two days is sufficient time for experiencing each unique side of Kohala—one day for the resort perks, including the beach, the spa, the golf, and the restaurants; one day for hiking and admiring the waterfalls and valleys of North Kohala, coupled with a wander around Hawi and Kapaau. In addition, don't miss a quick drive up to explore the rustic town of Waimea, with its restaurants, galleries, and bucolic scenery.

The best way to explore the valleys of North Kohala is with a hiking tour. Look for one that includes lunch, maybe a zipline, and a dip in one of the area's waterfall pools.

Getting Here and Around

AIR
The Kohala Coast and Waimea are most accessible from the Ellison Onizuka Kona International Airport. South Kohala is a roughly 30-minute drive from the airport, while it's double that to either Hawi or Waimea.

CAR
While some resort guests enjoy staying at a resort for their entire trip (shopping and restaurants are within walking distance), others appreciate having a rental car to sightsee and explore the island's wide diversity at their own pace. There are many rental options at the airport, but if you change your mind mid-trip and want to rent a car, the rental companies operate a satellite office from the Fairmont Orchid Hotel and one in Waikoloa Village.

Beaches

Most of the Big Island's white, sandy beaches are on the Kohala Coast, also called the "Gold Coast," which is home to the majority of the island's world-class resorts. Simply incomparable beauty, enchanting contrasts of pitch-black lava with light sands, groves of coconut trees, active reefs, and shimmering, clear water all combine to create the beaches that the world wants to visit. Hawaii's beaches are public property, and the resorts are required to provide public access, so don't be frightened off by a guard shack and a fancy sign. Most resorts do have public parking, although it's limited. Resort beaches aside, there are some real hidden gems, accessible only by boat, four-wheel drive, or a 15- to 20-minute hike. It's well worth the effort to get to at least one of these. ■TIP→ **The west side of the island tends to be calmer, but the surf still gets rough in winter.**

Hotels

If you are a resort kind of traveler, it doesn't get better than the famous Kohala Coast. Several resort properties offer options for most lifestyles, tastes, and budgets. All properties have daily resort fees except for the Mauna Kea Beach Hotel. Most resorts have adjacent condo complexes that offer short-term rentals, too. You may also find housing developments in Waikoloa and the Kawaihae area with vacation homes for rent, primarily through local property management companies. However, some owners handle rentals themselves, through websites like Vrbo and Airbnb. Short-term rental regulations here mean travelers need to check that the property they are considering is operating legally. Ask rental owners about operating permits, parking, taxes, and cleaning deposits. Nothing in this area will be far from beaches, restaurants, the airport, and good weather.

The rolling hills and emerald pastures of Waimea offer a sharp contrast to the hot, arid beachfront resorts. Just a 20-minute drive up a small hill takes you into this peaceful ranching enclave, with its charming residential areas and easy proximity to attractions along the Hamakua Coast and North Kohala. Bed-and-breakfasts and short-term rental options are great choices, as you can enjoy chilly evenings (lots of fireplaces up here) and then have your morning coffee with views of misty hills, sun, and rainbows.

Restaurants

The restaurants along the Kohala Coast range from fine-dining, oceanfront experiences to quick food court choices and beach shacks serving hot dogs and sandwiches. The resorts hire some of the best chefs in the world to design and prepare their cuisine, and the menu prices reflect that star quality. Hawaii regional cuisine, farm-to-table fare, and Asian fusion are popular resort cuisine styles. That said, some resort offerings are overpriced and will disappoint. However, you can find affordable local choices a short distance away in Kawaihae and Waimea.

HOTEL AND RESTAURANT PRICES

Hotel prices in the reviews are the lowest cost of a standard double room in high season. Restaurant prices in the reviews are the average cost of a main course at dinner, or if dinner is not served, at lunch. Restaurant and hotel reviews have been shortened. For full information, visit Fodors.com.

What it Costs in U.S. Dollars			
$	**$$**	**$$$**	**$$$$**
RESTAURANTS			
under $17	$17–$26	$27–$35	over $35
HOTELS			
under $180	$180–$260	$261–$340	over $340

Visitor Information

CONTACTS North Kohala Welcome Center. ⊠ *55-3393 Akoni Pule Hwy., Hawi ⊹ Just past the "Welcome to Kohala" sign* ☎ *808/889–5523* ⊕ *www.northkohala.org.*

Waikoloa

25 miles north of Ellison Onizuka Kona International Airport.

Waikoloa is a region known for its two large resort properties (one a bit outlandish), excellent golf, and eclectic shopping at both the Kings' Shops and Queens' MarketPlace. Sushi, local grills, food courts, and pricey restaurants all combine to give you abundant eating choices in Waikoloa. The natural gem here is the stunning, classically tropical Anaehoomalu Bay, once the site of royal fishponds and today an ideal spot to soak up some sun, explore along the trails, or try windsurfing. Waikoloa Village, a few miles inland and up the hill to the northeast, offers golf and rental condos for a fraction of the cost of the big resorts.

Beaches

★ Anaehoomalu Bay

BEACH—SIGHT | FAMILY | This gorgeous, expansive stretch of white sand, classically fringed with coco palms, fronts the Waikoloa Beach Marriott and is a perfect spot for swimming, windsurfing, snorkeling, and diving. Unlike some Kohala Coast beaches near hotel properties, this one is very accessible to the public and offers plenty of free parking. The bay is well protected, so even when surf is rough or the trade winds are blasting, it's fairly calm here. (Mornings are calmest.) Snorkel gear, kayaks, and body boards are available for rent at the north end. **TIP→ Locals will appreciate your efforts to use the proper name rather than simply its nickname, "A-Bay."**

Behind the beach are two ancient Hawaiian fishponds, **Kuualii** and **Kahapapa,** that once served ancient Hawaiian royalty. A walking trail follows the coastline to the Hilton Waikoloa Village next door, passing by tide pools, ponds, and a turtle sanctuary where sea turtles can often be spotted sunbathing on the sand. Footwear is recommended for the trail. **Amenities:** food and drink; parking (no fee); showers; toilets; water sports. **Best for:** snorkeling; sunset; swimming; walking. ✉ *69-275 Waikoloa Beach Dr., Waikoloa* ✣ *Just south of Waikoloa Beach Marriott; turn left at Kings' Shops* 🎫 *Free.*

Kiholo State Park Reserve
BEACH—SIGHT | One of the state park system's newest treasures, Kiholo Bay is still in the planning stage, so facilities are sparse (portable toilets, for example) and not yet complete. The brilliant turquoise waters of this stunning bay, set against stark black lava fields, are a cooling invitation on a warm Kohala day. The shore is rocky and the water's a bit cold and hazy due to freshwater springs, but there are tons of green sea turtles in residence year-round. The swimming and snorkeling are excellent when the tide is calm. Thanks to the eruptions of Mauna Loa, what was once the site of King Kamehameha's gigantic fishpond is now several freshwater ponds encircling the bay, with a picturesque lava-rock island in the middle. Bring plenty of drinking water. Gates are locked promptly at the times indicated; weekend camping is allowed with fee and permit. Community group Hui Aloha Kiholo helps the state manage the park. **Amenities:** parking (no fee); toilets. **Best for:** snorkeling; swimming; walking. ✉ *Hwy. 19 between mile markers 82 and 83, Waikoloa* ✣ *Just south of the lookout* ☎ *808/974–6200* 🌐 *dlnr.hawaii.gov/dsp/parks/hawaii/kiholo-state-park-reserve* 🎫 *Free.*

🍴 Restaurants

★ A-Bay's Island Grill
$ | MODERN HAWAIIAN | Beachy yet upscale, the restaurant has an in-house beer sommelier who advises on the perfect pairing with your food choice, which can range from fresh catch, steak, burgers, and sandwiches to crab cakes and escargots. This sports bar offers a 24-tap digital beer tower and 10 TV screens. **Known for:** fish tacos; one of the only restaurants on the Kohala Coast open until midnight; great tapas menu. [$] *Average main: $14* ✉ *Kings' Shops, 250 Waikoloa Beach Dr., Waikoloa* ☎ *808/209–8494* 🌐 *www.a-bays.com.*

Hawaii Calls Restaurant and Lounge at Waikoloa Beach Marriott Resort and Spa
$$$ | HAWAIIAN | FAMILY | The only full-service restaurant at the Waikoloa Beach Marriott offers a very farm-to-table, island-inspired menu. Photos of surf breaks from around the world adorn the walls of this spacious open-air restaurant, which has plenty of patio seating with sunset views. **Known for:** weekly special nights, including lobster night and prime rib and crab nights; good breakfast buffet; famous Kuu Alii mai tai. [$] *Average main: $29* ✉ *Waikoloa Beach Marriott Resort and Spa, 69-275 Waikoloa Beach Dr., Waikoloa* ☎ *808/886–6789* 🌐 *www.waikoloabeachmarriott.com.*

KPC (Kamuela Provision Company) at the Hilton Waikoloa Village
$$$$ | MODERN HAWAIIAN | The breezy lanai has the most spectacular view of the leeward coast of any restaurant on the

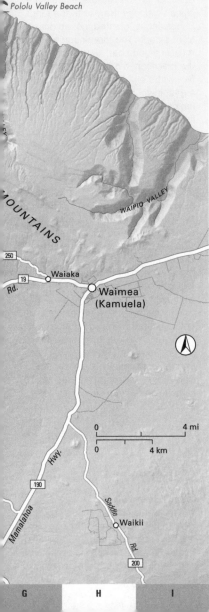

Kohala Coast

Pololu Valley Beach

MOUNTAINS

WAIPIO VALLEY

250

19

Waiaka

Rd.

**Waimea
(Kamuela)**

0   4 mi

0   4 km

190

Hwy.

Saddle

Mamalahoa

Waikii

Rd.

200

Sights ▼

1 Holoholokai Beach Park and Petroglyph Trail **D7**

2 Keokea Beach Park **F2**

3 King Kamehameha Statue **E2**

4 Lapakahi State Historical Park **C3**

5 Mookini Heiau........... **D1**

6 Puukohola Heiau National Historic Site.... **E6**

Restaurants ▼

1 A-Bay's Island Grill **D8**

2 Binchotan Bar and Grill............. **D7**

3 Blue Dragon Tavern and Cosmic Musiquarium............. **E5**

4 Brown's Beach House at the Fairmont Orchid Hawaii........... **D7**

5 CanoeHouse at the Mauna Lani, Auberge Resorts Collection **D7**

6 Hau Tree **E6**

7 Hawaii Calls Restaurant and Lounge at Waikoloa Beach Marriott Resort and Spa.......... **D8**

8 KPC (Kamuela Provision Company) at the Hilton Waikoloa Village.................... **D8**

9 Lava Lava Beach Club Restaurant.............. **D8**

10 Manta at the Mauna Kea Beach Hotel **E6**

11 Meridia.................... **E6**

12 Pueo's Osteria............ **F8**

13 Roy's Waikoloa Bar and Grill............. **D8**

14 Ruth's Chris Steakhouse Mauna Lani............. **D7**

15 Sansei Seafood Restaurant and Sushi Bar **D8**

16 Seafood Bar and Grill............. **E5**

17 Shiono at Mauna Lani............. **D7**

18 Sushi Rock............... **E1**

19 Tommy Bahama Restaurant and Bar..... **D7**

Quick Bites ▼

1 Anuenue Ice Cream and Shave Ice................ **E5**

2 Island Fish and Chips... **D8**

3 Kimo Bean Coffee Co... **D7**

4 Kohala Coffee Mill and Tropical Dreams **E2**

Hotels ▼

1 Aston Shores at Waikoloa................ **D8**

2 Fairmont Orchid Hawaii.................... **D7**

3 Fairway Villas Waikoloa by Outrigger **D8**

4 Hawaii Island Retreat at Ahu Pohaku Hoomaluhia............... **E1**

5 Hilton Waikoloa Village.................... **D8**

6 Kolea at Waikoloa Beach Resort............ **D8**

7 Lava Lava Beach Club Cottages **D8**

8 Mauna Kea Beach Hotel, Autograph Collection.... **E6**

9 Mauna Lani, Auberge Resorts Collection **D7**

10 Mauna Lani Point and the Islands at Mauna Lani............... **D7**

11 Puakea Ranch........... **D2**

12 Waikoloa Beach Marriott Resort and Spa.......... **D8**

13 The Westin Hapuna Beach Resort............ **E6**

Big Island, and it's the perfect accompaniment to the elegant yet down-to-earth Hawaii regional cuisine and specialty cocktails. Entrées are on the pricey side, but the ginger-steamed *monchong* (a deep-water Hawaiian fish) is a winner, and the Keahole lobster chowder does not disappoint. **Known for:** specialty cocktails, such as the Island Passion mango martini; the island's best sunset dinner spot; decadent Kona Coffee Mud Slide dessert. $ *Average main: $50* ⊠ *Hilton Waikoloa Village, 69-425 Waikoloa Beach Dr., Waikoloa* ☎ *808/886–1234* ⊕ *www. hiltonwaikoloavillage.com* ⊗ *No lunch.*

★ **Lava Lava Beach Club Restaurant**

$$$ | **HAWAIIAN** | **FAMILY** | Dig your toes into the sand and enjoy one of the most happening, entertaining, and memorable bar/restaurants on the Kohala Coast. There's something for everybody here, whether you want cocktails and *pupus* (appetizers) for sunset or a fine-dining experience; highlights include black Angus truffled New York steak and the chef's signature gazpacho topped with macadamia nut pesto. **Known for:** dining in the sand; great Parmesan lava tots and coconut shrimp; signature Sandy Toes cocktail. $ *Average main: $30* ⊠ *69-1081 Kuualii Pl., Waikoloa* ☎ *808/769–5282* ⊕ *lavalavabeachclub. com/bigisland.*

Pueo's Osteria

$$$ | **ITALIAN** | Hidden in a shopping center in residential Waikoloa Village, this late-night destination serves dinner from 5 until midnight (*pueo* means "owl" in Hawaiian, and refers to the restaurant's "night owl" concept). Renowned executive chef James Babian (Four Seasons Hualalai, Fairmont Orchid) serves up multiregional Italian offerings that combine farm-fresh ingredients with fine imported Italian products like prosciutto from Parma. **Known for:** Early Owl specials daily from 5 to 6 pm; late-night bar menu until 1 am; Tuscan-inspired dining room. $ *Average main: $27* ⊠ *Waikoloa Village Highlands Center, 68-1845 Waikoloa Rd., Waikoloa* ✛ *Near Subway* ☎ *808/339–7566* ⊕ *www.pueososteria. com* ⊗ *No lunch.*

Roy's Waikoloa Bar and Grill

$$$$ | **MODERN HAWAIIAN** | **FAMILY** | One of celebrity chef Roy Yamaguchi's Hawaii restaurants, this reliable, albeit pricey, place overlooks the lake at the Kings' Shops and is, granted, not an oceanfront setting. The three-course, prix-fixe meal is a good bet, as is blackened ahi; the macadamia nut–crusted Hawaiian fish with Kona lobster cream sauce is a melt-in-your-mouth encounter. **Known for:** great appetizers to share; extensive list of wines by the glass; outstanding kids' menu. $ *Average main: $40* ⊠ *Kings' Shops at Waikoloa Village, 69-250 Waikoloa Beach Dr., Waikoloa* ☎ *808/886–4321* ⊕ *www.roysrestaurant. com* ⊗ *No lunch.*

Sansei Seafood Restaurant and Sushi Bar

$$ | **JAPANESE** | **FAMILY** | Creative sushi and contemporary Asian cuisine take center stage at this entertaining restaurant at Queens' MarketPlace, where you can make a meal out of appetizers and sushi rolls or feast on great entrées from both land and sea. Though it has tried-and-true mainstays, the menu is consistently updated to include options such as Hawaiian *moi* (a local Hawaiian fish) sashimi rolls and Japanese yellowtail nori aioli poke. **Known for:** sushi bar specials; panko-encrusted ahi sashimi roll; karaoke on the weekends. $ *Average main: $20* ⊠ *Queens' MarketPlace, 201 Waikoloa Beach Dr., Suite 801, Waikoloa* ☎ *808/886–6286* ⊕ *www.sanseihawaii. com* ⊗ *No lunch.*

🍵 Coffee and Quick Bites

Island Fish and Chips

$ | **AMERICAN** | **FAMILY** | Hidden lakeside at the Kings' Shops, this little take-out place is a best-kept secret in the Waikoloa Beach Resort. The combo baskets brim with tempura fresh-catch fish, chicken,

Kohala Condo Comforts 🍴

Renting a resort condo is a great way to relax near the beach with many of the comforts of home. The upside is that you get all the pluses of being near a resort with all the privacy of your own place. Most condos have kitchens or a place to barbecue, so you'll want to stock up on groceries. The nearest full-service market is KTA Super Stores (✉ *68-3916 Paniolo Ave., Waikoloa Village* ☎ *808/883–1088*), no more than a half hour from the resorts.

Even closer are both the **Kings' Shops** (✉ *250 Waikoloa Beach Dr., Waikoloa* ☎ *808/886–8811*) and the **Queens' MarketPlace** (✉ *201 Waikoloa Beach Dr., Waikoloa* ☎ *808/886–8822*) in the Waikoloa Beach Resort. There is a small general store with a liquor department and several nice restaurants at the Kings' Shops. Across the street, Queens' MarketPlace also has a food court and sit-down restaurants, as well as a gourmet market where you can get pizza baked to order.

hrimp, and more. **Known for:** breakfast ptions such as loco moco (meat, rice, nd eggs smothered in gravy) laden with empura fish fillet; local ownership since 000; great fish-and-chips to go. [$] *Average main: $12* ✉ *Kings' Shops, 69-250 Vaikoloa Beach Dr., #D3, Waikoloa* ☎ *808/886–0005.*

Hotels

ston Shores at Waikoloa

$$ | **RENTAL** | **FAMILY** | Villas with terra-cot-a-tile roofs are set amid landscaped goons and waterfalls at the edge of he championship Waikoloa Village Golf ourse. **Pros:** good prices for the area; reat location; kid-friendly option with pool and in-room kitchens. **Cons:** no estaurants on-site; daily resort fee; older ecor in some rooms. [$] *Rooms from: 309* ✉ *69-1035 Keana Pl., Waikoloa* ☎ *808/886–5001, 800/922–7866* 🌐 *www.quaaston.com* 🛏 *120 suites* 🍴 *No meals.*

airway Villas Waikoloa by Outrigger

| **RENTAL** | **FAMILY** | These large and omfy town houses and condominiums re located just off the fairway of the Vaikoloa Beach Course and are a short walk from Anaehoomalu Bay. Designed in the style of plantation-era homes, these villas are decorated with rattan furniture and tropical themes and come complete with top-notch appliances in fully equipped kitchens. **Pros:** good location for beach, shopping, dining, and golf; infinity pool; well-equipped kitchens. **Cons:** no ocean views; lots of guest rules and regulations; expensive cleaning fees. [$] *Rooms from: $155* ✉ *Waikoloa Beach Resort, 69-200 Pohakulana Pl., Waikoloa* ☎ *808/886–0036* 🌐 *www.outrigger.com* 🛏 *70 units* 🍴 *No meals.*

Hilton Waikoloa Village

$$$$ | **RESORT** | **FAMILY** | Gondola trams glide by; pint-size guests zoom down the 175-foot waterslide; a bride poses on the grand staircase; a fire-bearing runner lights the torches along the seaside path at sunset—these are some typical scenes at this 62-acre megaresort. **Pros:** family-friendly saltwater lagoon; lots of restaurant and activity options, including two golf courses; close to retail shopping. **Cons:** gigantic and crowded; $45 per night resort fee; restaurants are pricey. [$] *Rooms from: $346* ✉ *69-425 Waikoloa Beach Dr., Waikoloa* ☎ *808/886–1234, 800/445–8667* 🌐 *www.*

hiltonwaikoloavillage.com ↪ 1,241 rooms ◉ No meals.

★ **Kolea at Waikoloa Beach Resort**

$$$$ | RENTAL | FAMILY | These modern, impeccably furnished condos offer far more high-end amenities than the average condo complex, including both an infinity pool and a sand-bottom children's pool at its oceanside Beach Club; a fitness center; and a hot tub. **Pros:** high design; close to beach and activities; resort amenities of nearby Hilton. **Cons:** pricey for not being directly on the beach; no on-property restaurants; limited view from some units. $ *Rooms from: $400* ✉ *Waikoloa Beach Resort, 69-1000 Kolea Kai Circle, Waikoloa* ☎ *808/987–4519* ⊕ *www.koleavacations.com* ↪ *53 units* ◉ *No meals.*

★ **Lava Lava Beach Club Cottages**

$$$$ | RENTAL | FAMILY | Spend the day swimming at the beach just steps away from your private lanai and fall asleep to the sound of the ocean at one of four artfully decorated, one-room cottages on the sandy beach at Anaehoomalu Bay. These cottages are among the few beachfront rentals you will find anywhere on the island. **Pros:** on the beach; fully air-conditioned; fun, Hawaii-themed decor. **Cons:** beach is public, so there may be people in front of cottage; quite expensive; often booked up. $ *Rooms from: $495* ✉ *69-1081 Kuualii Pl., Waikoloa* ☎ *808/769–5282* ⊕ *www.lavalavabeachclub.com* ↪ *4 cottages* ◉ *No meals.*

Waikoloa Beach Marriott Resort and Spa

$$$$ | RESORT | FAMILY | Encompassing 15 acres replete with ancient fishponds, historic trails, and petroglyph fields, the Marriott has rooms with sleek modern beds, bright white linens, Hawaiian art, and private lanai. **Pros:** more low-key than the Hilton Waikoloa; sunset luau Wednesday and Saturday; sand-bottom pool for kids. **Cons:** some rooms lack views; expensive daily parking charge; resort fee of $30 per day. $ *Rooms from: $400*

✉ *69-275 Waikoloa Beach Dr., Waikoloa* ☎ *808/886–6789, 800/228–9290* ⊕ *www.marriott.com* ↪ *297 rooms* ◉ *No meals.*

▣ Nightlife

BARS

Kona Tap Room

BARS/PUBS | A favorite after-work spot for employees from the surrounding hotels, this sports bar lounge in the Hilton Waikoloa Village offers friendly bartenders, free Wi-Fi, and pool tables. Enjoy tropical cocktails, craft beers, light fare, and live music from 8 to 10 nightly. ✉ *Hilton Waikoloa Village, 425 Waikoloa Beach Dr., Waikoloa* ☎ *808/886–1234* ⊕ *www.hiltonwaikoloavillage.com.*

▣ Performing Arts

LUAU AND POLYNESIAN REVUES

Legends of Hawaii Luau at Hilton Waikoloa Village

CULTURAL FESTIVALS | FAMILY | Presented outdoors at the Kamehameha Court, this show is aptly subtitled "Our Big Island Story." A delicious buffet offers Big Island–grown luau choices as well as more familiar fare and tropical drinks. Pay a small fee and upgrade to Alii seating for a front-row vantage; unlimited cocktails, beer, and wine; and your own buffet station. A children's station has kid favorites. Delicious desserts such as *haupia* (with coconut milk) cream puffs and Kona-coffee cheesecake top it all off. ✉ *Hilton Waikoloa Village, 69-425 Waikoloa Beach Dr., Waikoloa* ☎ *808/886–1234* ⊕ *www.hiltonwaikoloavillage.com/luau* ▣ *$142.*

Waikoloa Beach Marriott Resort and Spa Sunset Luau

CULTURAL FESTIVALS | Overlooking the white sands of Anaehoomalu Bay, this Polynesian luau includes a spectacular Samoan fire-dance performance as well as traditional music and dances from various Pacific Island cultures. Traditional dishes are served alongside more familiar Western fare, and there's also

Hawaiian Music on the Big Island

It's easy to forget that Hawaii has its own music until you step off a plane onto the Islands—and then there's no escaping it. It's a unique blend of the strings and percussion imported by early Portuguese settlers and the chants and rituals of the ancient Hawaiians, reflecting the unique mixed heritage of this special place. Hawaiian music today includes Island-born tunings of acoustic guitar—slack key and steel guitar—along with the ukulele and vocals.

This is one of the few folk music traditions in the United States that is fully embraced by the younger generation, with no prodding from their parents or grandparents. A good many radio stations on the Big Island play Hawaiian/"island"/reggae music, and concerts performed by Island favorites like Makana or L. T. Smooth are filled with fans of all ages.

The best introduction is one of the annual festivals: the free **Hawaiian Slack Key Guitar Festival** (Labor Day weekend), with a handful of greats performing at the Sheraton Kona Resort and Spa; the **Great Waikoloa Ukulele Festival** (March), which features prominent players and everything ukulele; and the **KWXX Hoolaulea** (September), a popular Island music jam with big names performing on four stages in downtown Hilo.

Or you can catch live performances most nights at a handful of local bars and clubs, including **Chillin' on the Bay, Huggo's on the Rocks, Lavern's,** and the **Kona Brewing Co.** in Kailua-Kona; **Korner Pocket** in Kealakekua; and **Cronies Bar and Grill** in Hilo.

n open bar. ⊠ *Waikoloa Beach Marriott Resort and Spa, 69-275 Waikoloa Beach Dr., Waikoloa* ☎ *808/886–8111* ⊕ *www. waikoloabeachresort.com* ☎ *$117.*

🛍 Shopping

ARTS AND CRAFTS

Hawaiian Quilt Collection

CRAFTS | The Hawaiian quilt is a work of art that is prized and passed down through generations. At this store, you'll find everything from hand-quilted purses and bags to wall hangings and blankets. More than likely, a friendly Hawaiian *tutu* (grandma) will be in the shop talking story. You can even get a take-home kit and sew your own Hawaiian quilt. ⊠ *Queens' MarketPlace, 69-201 Waikoloa Beach Dr., #305, Waikoloa* ☎ *808/886–0494* ⊕ *www. hawaiian-quilts.com.*

CLOTHING

Blue Ginger

CLOTHING | The Waikoloa branch of this fashion veteran offers really sweet matching aloha outfits for the entire family. There are also handbags, shoes, robes, jewelry, and lotions. ⊠ *Queens' MarketPlace, 69-201 Waikoloa Beach Dr., Waikoloa* ☎ *808/886–0022* ⊕ *www. blueginger.com.*

Reyn Spooner

CLOTHING | The dressy clothing here has been a tradition in Hawaii since 1959 and remains popular among locals and visitors alike. The store offers rayon, cotton, and silk aloha shirts for both men and boys, men's shorts, and some dresses for women and girls. Prices may be high, but you're buying the best. ⊠ *Queens' MarketPlace, 69-201 Waikoloa Beach Dr., Waikoloa* ☎ *808/886–1162* ⊕ *www. reynspooner.com.*

GALLERIES

★ Lava Light Galleries

ART GALLERIES | C.J. Kale is an accomplished, award-winning photographer famous for capturing extraordinary images of lava flowing through the curl of a wave. Not a believer in using photo manipulation or special effects, Kale produces work that is as authentic as it gets. He and gallery partners Linda and Don Hurlzeler showcase their fine images of the beauty of Hawaii and other scenic places around the world. ⊠ *Queens' MarketPlace, 69-201 Waikoloa Beach Dr., #F-13, Waikoloa* ☎ *808/756-0778* ⊕ *www.lavalightgalleries.com.*

JEWELRY AND ACCESSORIES

Island Pearls by Maui Divers

JEWELRY/ACCESSORIES | Among the fine jewelry at this boutique is a wide selection of high-end pearl jewelry, including Tahitian black pearls, South Sea white and golden pearls, and chocolate Tahitian pearls. Also here are freshwater pearls in the shell, black coral (the Hawaii state gemstone), and diamonds. Prices are high but so is the quality. ⊠ *Queens' MarketPlace, 69-201 Waikoloa Beach Dr., #J-11, Waikoloa* ☎ *808/886–4817* ⊕ *www.mauidivers.com.*

SHOPPING CENTERS

Kings' Shops at Waikoloa Beach Resort

SHOPPING CENTERS/MALLS | Stores here include Martin & MacArthur, featuring koa furniture and accessories, and Tori Richard, which offers upscale resort wear, as well as high-end chains Coach, Tiffany, and Michael Kors. Gourmet offerings include Roy's Waikoloa Bar and Grill, A-Bay's Island Grill, and Island Fish and Chips. Stock your hotel fridge with fresh local produce from the Kings' Shops Farmers Market, held Wednesday 8:30 to 2:30. ⊠ *Waikoloa Beach Resort, 250 Waikoloa Beach Dr., Waikoloa* ☎ *808/339–7145* ⊕ *www.kingsshops.com.*

Queens' MarketPlace

SHOPPING CENTERS/MALLS | The largest shopping complex on the Kohala Coast houses fashionable clothing stores, jewelry boutiques, galleries, gift shops, and restaurants, including Sansei Seafood Restaurant and Sushi Bar; Daylight Mind and Romano's Macaroni Grill. Island Gourmet Markets and Starbucks are also here, as is an affordable food court. Waikoloa Luxury Cinemas offers the ultimate movie experience and includes a restaurant called Bistro at the Cinemas. ⊠ *Waikoloa Beach Resort, 201 Waikoloa Beach Dr., Waikoloa* ☎ *808/886–8822* ⊕ *www.queensmarketplace.net.*

🏃 Activities

SPAS

Kohala Spa at the Hilton Waikoloa Village

FITNESS/HEALTH CLUBS | Naupaka (a flowering shrub) grows in abundance along the shores of Hawaii Island, and Kohala Spa pays it tribute with the 80-minute Signature Naupaka White Flower Ritual. The feast for the senses incorporates a foot massage with awa root and Hawaiian ginger, followed by warmed body compressions with healing herbs and a full-body massage, blending essential oils. Locker rooms are outfitted with a wealth of beauty and bath products, and the spa's retail facility offers signature Coco-Mango lotions, body washes, and shampoos. An open-air, seaside cabana provides a tropical spot for a massage overlooking the Pacific, while the fitness center has the latest machines and plentiful classes. ⊠ *Hilton Waikoloa Village, 69-425 Waikoloa Beach Dr., Waikoloa* ☎ *808/886–2828* ⊕ *www.kohalaspa.com* 🖾 *Massages from $170.*

Mandara Spa at the Waikoloa Beach Marriott Resort

FITNESS/HEALTH CLUBS | Overlooking the hotel's main pool and with a distant view of the ocean, Mandara offers a complete spa menu, with lomilomi massage, scrubs, wraps, and numerous facial options. Mandara, which operates spas all over the world, uses Elemis products and incorporates local ingredients (lime and ginger in the scrubs, warm coconut milk in the wraps). The facility, which fuses contemporary and traditional Asian motifs, is beautiful. A glam squad awaits you at the full-service salon. ✉ *Waikoloa Beach Marriott Resort and Spa, 69-275 Waikoloa Beach Dr., Waikoloa* ☎ *808/886–8191* 🌐 *www.mandaraspa.com* 🎟 *Massages from $140, facials from $145.*

Mauna Lani

8 miles north of Waikoloa.

Mauna Lani is known for its expensive resorts, but fortunately it's so much more. In addition to cooling trade winds, black lava landscapes, and turquoise seas, the region has numerous historical sites, including ancient fishponds, petroglyphs, and historical trails that invite lovers of history and culture to explore numerous spots along this coast.

👁 Sights

Holoholokai Beach Park and Petroglyph Trail

BEACH—SIGHT | While mostly rocky topography makes swimming and snorkeling a bit difficult here, this little park is still scenic and relaxing. Take the short trail over to the petroglyph trail; interpretive signs will guide you. There are showers, picnic tables, and restrooms. ✉ *Holoholokai Beach Park Rd., Mauna Lani* ✥ *Near the end of N. Kaniku Dr.* ☎ *808/657–3293* 🎟 *Free.*

🍴 Restaurants

Binchotan Bar and Grill

$$$ | **ASIAN FUSION** | In a sophisticated setting that includes open-air patio seating, this new restaurant offers the flavors of contemporary Asian cuisine, among them meats, prawns, peppers, and more grilled over an open flame in the traditional style. Blending locally sourced ingredients with Japanese and Hawaiian influences, Chef Justin Kalaluhi creates a menu that pays homage to multiple cultures. **Known for:** Robatayaki Experience (chef's selection of grilled items); okonomiyaki (savory Japanese-style pancakes) featuring Kona lobster and macadamia nut shrimp; shared plates. [$] *Average main: $28* ✉ *Fairmont Orchid Hawaii, 1 N. Kaniku Dr., Mauna Lani* ☎ *808/885–5778* 🌐 *www.fairmont.com* 🕐 *Closed Tues. and Wed. No lunch.*

Brown's Beach House at the Fairmont Orchid Hawaii

$$$$ | **MODERN HAWAIIAN** | Sitting right on the resort's sandy bay, Brown's Beach House offers beautiful sunset dining and innovative cuisine. Attention to detail is evident in the sophisticated menu, which may include crab-crusted Kona *kampachi* or other dishes with sea fish, roasted duck breast, or Kona coffee–crusted venison, as well as locally grown produce. **Known for:** Dungeness crab and lobster tail; tiki torches and live Hawaiian music beneath starry skies; vegetarian and gluten-free options. [$] *Average main: $40* ✉ *Fairmont Orchid Hawaii, 1 N. Kaniku Dr., Mauna Lani* ☎ *808/885–2000* 🌐 *www.fairmont.com* 🕐 *No lunch.*

★ **CanoeHouse at the Mauna Lani, Auberge Resorts Collection**

$$$$ | **MODERN HAWAIIAN** | One of the most romantic settings on the Kohala Coast, this landmark restaurant on the oceanfront showcases traditional Hawaiian flavors, artful presentations, and locally grown or raised products. The progressive menu spotlights standout entrées such as roasted beef tenderloin, lamb, fresh fish caught locally, shellfish, island-fresh greens, and local goat cheese. **Known for:** memorable sunsets with tiki torches; good choice of wines by the glass; customized dining program by the chef offered at the Captain's Table. [$] *Average main: $48* ✉ *Mauna Lani, Auberge Resorts Collection, 68-1400 Mauna*

Lani Dr., Mauna Lani ☎ *808/885–6622* 🌐 *www.maunalani.com* ⏲ *No lunch.*

Ruth's Chris Steakhouse Mauna Lani
$$$$ | **STEAKHOUSE** | The Big Island location of the popular upscale Louisiana steakhouse franchise serves the sizzling steaks (yes, they do sizzle on the plate) and heaping sides the restaurant is known for, in a sophisticated setting that includes a beautiful bar area with lounge seating. Lobster and chicken are also on the menu, and there *are* vegetarian options, but Ruth's Chris is a true steak house and is best suited to meat lovers. **Known for:** happy hour food specials and early-evening Prime Time specials; wine-maker dinners; muddled-cucumber margaritas. [$] *Average main: $40* ✉ *The Shops at Mauna Lani, 68-1330 Mauna Lani Dr., Mauna Lani* ☎ *808/887–0800* 🌐 *www.ruthschris.com* ⏲ *No lunch.*

Shiono at Mauna Lani
$$ | **JAPANESE** | With three locations and a fourth coming up, this very popular Japanese establishment does not disappoint. At this location especially, high-end fish and meats (some flown in daily from Japan) highlight an eclectic menu of handcrafted sushi, combination platters, and entrées. **Known for:** outstanding omakase (chef chooses the food) experience; fresh ingredients, both local and imported; fine collection of premium sakes. [$] *Average main: $25* ✉ *The Shops at Mauna Lani, 68-1330 Mauna Lani Dr., Suite 111 (2nd fl.), Mauna Lani* ☎ *808/881–1111* 🌐 *www.sushishiono.com/mauna-lani* ⏲ *No lunch.*

Tommy Bahama Restaurant and Bar
$$$$ | **MODERN HAWAIIAN** | **FAMILY** | This breezy, open-air restaurant, located upstairs at the Shops at Mauna Lani, offers an excellent roster of appetizers, including seared-scallop sliders and coconut-crusted crab cakes, as well as meat and fish mains and decadent desserts. The chef here has freedom to cook up his own daily specials, and the seared ahi is a standout. **Known for:** the chain's reliable cuisine and relaxed vibe; popular cocktail bar and lounge; house-baked breads and specialty butters. [$] *Average main: $38* ✉ *The Shops at Mauna Lani, 68-1330 Mauna Lani Dr., Suite 102, Mauna Lani* ☎ *808/881–8686* 🌐 *www.tommybahama.com.*

Coffee and Quick Bites

Kimo Bean Coffee Co
$ | **AMERICAN** | Kimo's is the perfect spot to grab coffee and breakfast in the morning or to try the pesto grilled cheese for a satisfying midday snack. The food menu is small but mighty and includes chicken quesadillas, homemade pastries, a specialty club sandwich, and smoothies. **Known for:** central location in the Shops at Mauna Lani; wonderful Hawaiian estate coffee; chocolate chip waffles. [$] *Average main: $5* ✉ *The Shops at Mauna Lani, 68-1330 Mauna Lani Dr., Suite 300, Mauna Lani* ☎ *808/885–2111* 🌐 *kimobean.com.*

Hotels

★ **Fairmont Orchid Hawaii**
$$$ | **RESORT** | **FAMILY** | This first-rate resort overflows with tropical gardens, cascading waterfalls, a sandy beach cove, beautiful wings with "open sesame" doors, a meandering pool, and renovated rooms with all the amenities. **Pros:** oceanfront location; excellent pool; aloha hospitality. **Cons:** central pool can get very crowded; 40-minute drive to Kailua-Kona; not the best beach among Kohala Coast resorts. [$] *Rooms from: $269* ✉ *1 N. Kaniku Dr., Mauna Lani* ☎ *808/885–2000, 800/845–9905* 🌐 *www.fairmont.com* 🛏 *540 rooms* 🍴 *No meals.*

★ **Mauna Lani, Auberge Resorts Collection**
$$$$ | **RESORT** | Popular with honeymooners and anniversary couples for decades, this elegant Kohala Coast classic is still one of the most beautiful resorts on

the island, highlighted by a breathtaking, open-air lobby with cathedral-like ceilings, Zen-like koi ponds, and illuminated sheets of cascading water. **Pros:** beautiful design; award-winning spa; many Hawaiian cultural programs. **Cons:** no luau; limited dining selection on-site; 26 miles from airport. $ *Rooms from: $579* ✉ *68-1400 Mauna Lani Dr., Mauna Lani* ☎ *808/885–6622, 808/657–3293* ⊕ *aubergeresorts.com/maunalani* ⤳ *338 rooms* ❍ *No meals.*

Mauna Lani Point and the Islands at Mauna Lani

$$$$ | RENTAL | Surrounded by the emerald greens of a world-class oceanside golf course, the private, independent, luxury condominiums at Islands at Mauna Lani offer spacious two-story suites, while Mauna Lani Point's villas are closer to the beach. **Pros:** friendly front desk; stellar views; extra-large units. **Cons:** quite pricey; individually owned units vary in decor and amenities; some units are a distance from the barbecue/pool area. $ *Rooms from: $665* ✉ *Mauna Lani Point, 68-1050 Mauna Lani Point Dr., Mauna Lani* ☎ *808/885–5022, 800/642–6284* ⊕ *www.classicresorts.com* ⤳ *66 units* ❍ *No meals.*

▼ Nightlife

BARS

Luana Lounge

BARS/PUBS | The contemporary lounge in the Fairmont Orchid has a large terrace and an impressive water view. Bartenders are skilled at mixology, and service is impeccable. The crowd is mellow, so it's a nice place for an early evening cocktail or after-dinner liqueur. Happy hour is from 5 to 6, and live music begins at sunset and continues until 9. ✉ *Fairmont Orchid Hawaii, 1 N. Kaniku Dr., Mauna Lani* ☎ *808/885–2000* ⊕ *www.fairmont.com.*

🎭 Performing Arts

LUAU AND POLYNESIAN REVUES

Hawaii Loa Luau

CULTURAL FESTIVALS | Slickly produced and well choreographed, this gorgeous show incorporates both traditional and contemporary music and dance, along with an array of beautiful costumes. It tells the tale of Hawaiiloa, the great navigator from Tahiti, and of the celestial object—*Hokulea,* "Star of Gladness"—that guided him to the islands later named Hawaii. Presented under the stars at the Fairmont Orchid Hawaii on Saturdays, the meal offers several stations with a variety of Hawaiian and Hawaii regional cuisine dishes, and there's a full bar for mai tais and other tropical libations. ✉ *Fairmont Orchid Hawaii, 1 N. Kaniku Dr., Mauna Lani* ☎ *808/885–2000, 808/326–4969* ⊕ *www.gatheringofthekings.com* ✆ *$131.*

MAGIC

★ Kona Kozy's Comedy and Magic Show

MAGIC | Paul "Kona Kozy" Kozak, a veteran Vegas and New York comedy club entertainer, brings a world-class magic show to the Kohala Coast. Every show is different but, guaranteed, each one is hilarious. Held within his fine-art tiki gallery, the shows will truly have you asking "How'd he do that?" for days afterward. Kozy knows his stuff: he once did a command performance for Prince Charles and Princess Diana. The show is for ages 18 and up. ✉ *The Shops at Mauna Lani, 68-1330 Mauna Lani Drive, Suite 106, Mauna Lani* ☎ *808/430–1957* ⊕ *konakozy.com.*

🛍 Shopping

SHOPPING CENTERS

The Shops at Mauna Lani

SHOPPING CENTERS/MALLS | The best part about this complex is its roster of restaurants, which includes coffee, smoothie, and sandwich shops, Tommy Bahama Restaurant and Bar, Ruth's Chris

Steakhouse, and Under the Bodhi Tree café (gourmet vegetarian options). You can find tropical apparel at Jams World, high-end housewares at Oasis Lifestyle, and original art at a number of galleries. ⊠ *68-1330 Mauna Lani Dr., Mauna Lani* ☎ *808/885–9501* ⊕ *www.shopsatmaunalani.com.*

Mauna Kea and Hapuna

6 miles north of Mauna Lani.

Every visitor to the Big Island should put Hapuna Beach State Recreation Area on an itinerary, especially if you're not staying at the Westin Hapuna Beach Resort, located beachfront. This glorious stretch of white-sand beauty will not fail to take your breath away, no matter what the season or time of day. Sheer enchantment also defines the luminous waters and curve of white sand at Kaunaoa, also called Mauna Kea Beach, but it's more difficult to access due to the Mauna Kea Beach Hotel's control of the parking area.

🏖 Beaches

★ **Hapuna Beach State Recreation Area**
BEACH—SIGHT | FAMILY | One of Hawaii's finest beaches, Hapuna is a ½-mile-long stretch of white perfection. The turquoise water is calm in summer, so it's good for kids, with just enough rolling waves to make bodysurfing and body boarding fun. Watch for the undertow; in winter it can be rough. There is excellent snorkeling around the jagged rocks that border the beach on either side, but high surf brings strong currents. Known for awesome sunsets, this is one of the best places on the island to see the "green flash" as the sun dips below a clear horizon.

The north end of the beach fronts the Westin Hapuna Beach Resort, which rents water-sports equipment and has a food concession with shaded picnic tables. There is ample parking, although the lot can fill up by midday and the beach can get crowded on holidays. Lifeguards, on duty during peak hours, cover the state park section, not areas north of the rocky cliff that juts out near the middle of the beach. **Amenities:** food and drink; lifeguards; parking (fee); showers; toilets; water sports. **Best for:** sunset; surfing; swimming; walking. ⊠ *Hwy. 19 near mile marker 69, Mauna Kea* ✛ *Just south of the Westin Hapuna Beach Resort* ☎ *808/961–9544* ⊕ *dlnr.hawaii.gov* 🎫 *$5 per vehicle.*

★ **Kaunaoa Beach** (*Mauna Kea Beach*)
BEACH—SIGHT | FAMILY | Hands down one of the most beautiful beaches on the island, if not the whole state, Kaunaoa features a long crescent of pure white sand framed by coco palms. The beach, which fronts the Mauna Kea Beach Hotel, slopes very gradually, and there's great snorkeling along the rocks. Classic Hawaii postcard views abound, especially in winter, when snow tops Maunakea to the east. When conditions permit, waves are good for body- and board surfing also. Currents can be strong in winter, so be careful. Get a cocktail at the beach cabana and enjoy the sunset. ■ **TIP→ Public parking is limited to a few spaces, so arrive before 10 am or after 4 pm. If the lot is full, head to nearby Hapuna Beach, where there's a huge parking lot ($5 per vehicle). Try this spot again another day—it's worth it! Amenities:** parking (no fee); showers; toilets; water sports. **Best for:** snorkeling; sunset; swimming; walking. ⊠ *62-100 Mauna Kea Beach Dr., Mauna Kea* ✛ *Entry through gate to Mauna Kea Beach Hotel.*

🍴 Restaurants

Hau Tree
$$$ | MODERN HAWAIIAN | Though it sits on a patio by the pool, this beachside restaurant and beach bar is not just for *pupus* (appetizers) and cocktails. The island-infused dinner menu features excellent entrées, such as the grass-fed

Hapuna Beach State Recreation area protects the island's largest white-sand beach. At the northern end sits the Westin Hapuna Beach Resort.

Kulana beef tenderloin brochettes, plus plentiful seafood dishes and greens from local farms. **Known for:** famous Fredrico cocktail; great sunset views; Saturday clambake. $ *Average main: $27 ⊠ Mauna Kea Beach Hotel, 62-100 Mauna Kea Beach Dr., Mauna Kea ☎ 808/882–5707 ⊕ www.maunakeabeachhotel.com.*

★ **Manta at the Mauna Kea Beach Hotel**
$$$$ | **MODERN HAWAIIAN** | Perched on the edge of a bluff overlooking the sparkling waters of Kaunaoa Beach, the resort's flagship restaurant is a compelling spot for a romantic meal at sunset, especially at one of the outside tables. The culinary team's take on Hawaii regional cuisine highlights locally sourced, sustainable fish, chicken, and beef. **Known for:** beachfront balcony dining; exhibition kitchen; Sunday brunch with prime rib, smoked salmon, and omelet station. $ *Average main: $40 ⊠ Mauna Kea Beach Hotel, 62-100 Mauna Kea Beach Dr., Mauna Kea ☎ 808/882–5707 ⊕ www.maunakeabeachhotel.com ⊗ No lunch.*

★ **Meridia**
$$$$ | **MEDITERRANEAN** | This open-air restaurant at the Westin Hapuna Beach Resort has high ceilings and a lanai that overlooks the pool and the sandy-white shores of Hapuna Beach. With a focus on the freshest seafood, the small-plate appetizers and main course options also showcase a bounty of Big Island ingredients infused with Mediterranean influences. **Known for:** friendly waitstaff; almond-crusted ahi; fantastic location (including for sunset viewing) with interesting architecture. $ *Average main: $43 ⊠ The Westin Hapuna Beach Resort, 62-100 Kaunaoa Dr., Mauna Kea ☎ 808/880–1111 ⊕ www.meridiarestaurant.net ⊗ No lunch.*

🛏 Hotels

Mauna Kea Beach Hotel, Autograph Collection

$$$$ | **RESORT** | The grande dame of the Kohala Coast has long been regarded as one of the state's premier vacation

resort hotels, and it borders one of the world's finest white-sand beaches, Kaunaoa. **Pros:** good dining options; premier tennis center; no resort fees. **Cons:** some oceanfront rooms are noisy; $30 daily valet parking fee; 27 miles from airport. $ *Rooms from: $629* ✉ *62-100 Mauna Kea Beach Dr., Mauna Kea* ☎ *808/882–7222, 866/977–4589* ⊕ *www.maunakeabeachhotel.com* ⇨ *252 rooms* ⊙ *No meals.*

The Westin Hapuna Beach Resort

$$$$ | RESORT | FAMILY | Slightly more affordable than its neighbor resorts and with direct access to the Big Island's largest white-sand beach, this massive hotel has enormous columns and a terraced, open-air lobby with rotunda ceiling, curved staircases, and skylights. **Pros:** extra-large rooms, all ocean-facing; direct access to one of island's best beaches; resort has 18-hole championship golf course. **Cons:** fitness center a five-minute walk from the hotel; $30 daily resort fee; 30 miles from Kailua-Kona. $ *Rooms from: $539* ✉ *62-100 Kaunaoa Dr., Mauna Kea* ☎ *808/880–1111, 866/774–6236* ⊕ *www.marriott.com* ⇨ *249 rooms* ⊙ *No meals.*

🎭 Performing Arts

LUAU AND POLYNESIAN REVUES

Mauna Kea Beach Hotel Clambake

CULTURAL FESTIVALS | The weekly clambake near the sand at Hau Tree beach restaurant features an extensive menu with oysters on the half shell, Manila clams, Dungeness crab legs, mussels, sashimi, and "all-you-can-eat" Keahole lobster. There's even prime rib and a dessert station. Live Hawaiian music is often accompanied by a graceful hula dancer. ✉ *Mauna Kea Beach Hotel, 62-100 Mauna Kea Beach Dr., Mauna Kea* ☎ *808/882–5707* ⊕ *maunakeabeachhotel.com* 🍴 *$122.*

★ Mauna Kea Beach Luau

CULTURAL FESTIVALS | FAMILY | On the oceanfront North Side Luau Grounds, you can indulge in the best of island cuisine—a traditional feast of *kalua* (earth oven–baked) pig roasted in an *imu* (oven), island fish, lomilomi salmon, and sashimi—while enjoying entertainment by renowned local performers. The luau, originally created in 1960 for *Newsweek* magazine and going strong ever since, includes an amazing fire-knife dance, spirited chanting, and very traditional hula. *Keiki* (children) can learn the *hukilau* (a traditional song and dance), and you can relax right on the beach, under the stars. If you choose one luau during your visit to the Big Island, this should be the one, and it's surprisingly affordable. ■ TIP→ **You can elect to see only the show for a reasonable fee.** ✉ *Mauna Kea Beach Hotel, Autograph Collection, 62-100 Mauna Kea Beach Dr., Mauna Kea* ☎ *808/882–5810, 808/882–7222* ⊕ *www.maunakeabeachhotel.com* 🍴 *$137; show only, $64.*

Kawaihae

6 miles north of Hapuna.

This no-frills industrial harbor, where in 1793 the first cattle landed in Hawaii, is a hub of commercial and community activity, including interisland transports. It's also where King Kamehameha and his men set out to conquer the neighboring islands. It's especially busy on weekends, when paddlers, surfers, tourist charters, and local fishing boats share the waters. Second in size only to Hilo Harbor, the port serves interisland cargo carriers and often shelters the *Makalii*, one of three traditional Hawaiian sailing canoes. Kawaihae Village has several restaurants with nice sunset views.

Sights

★ **Puukohola Heiau National Historic Site**

HISTORIC SITE | Quite simply, this is one of the most historic and commanding sites in all of Hawaii. It was here in 1810, on top of Puukohola (Hill of the Whale), that Kamehameha the Great built the war *heiau*, or temple, that would serve to unify the Hawaiian Islands, ending 500 years of almost continual warring chiefdoms. The oceanfront, fortresslike site is foreboding and impressive. A paved ½-mile, looped trail runs from the visitor center to the main temple sites. An even older temple, dedicated to the shark gods, lies submerged just offshore, where sharks can be spotted swimming, usually first thing in the morning. A museum displays ancient Hawaiian weapons, including clubs, spears, a replica of a bronze cannon that warriors dragged into battle on a Hawaiian sled, and three original paintings by artist Herb Kane. Rangers are available to answer questions, or you can take a free audio tour on your own smartphone. Plan about an hour to see everything. ✉ *62-3601 Kawaihae Rd., Kawaihae* ☎ *808/882–7218* 🌐 *www.nps.gov/puhe* 🎟 *Free.*

Beaches

Spencer Park at Ohaiula Beach

BEACH—SIGHT | **FAMILY** | This white-sand beach is popular with local families because of its reef-protected waters. ■ **TIP→ It's probably the safest beach in West Hawaii for young children.** It's also safe for swimming year-round, which makes it a reliable spot for a lazy day at the beach. There is a little shade, plus a volleyball court and pavilion, and the soft sand is perfect for sand castles. It does tend to get crowded with families and campers on weekends, but the beach is generally clean. Although you won't see a lot of fish if you're snorkeling here, in winter you can often catch sight of a breaching whale or two. The beach park lies just below Puukohola Heiau National Historic Park, site of the historic war temple built by King Kamehameha the Great in 1810 after uniting the Islands. **Amenities:** lifeguards (weekends and holidays only); parking (no fee); showers; toilets. **Best for:** sunset; swimming. ✉ *Hwy. 270, Kawaihae* ↔ *Toward Kawaihae Harbor, just after road forks from Hwy. 19* ☎ *808/961–8311.*

Restaurants

★ **Blue Dragon Tavern and Cosmic Musiquarium**

$ | **MODERN HAWAIIAN** | Across from the harbor in Kawaihae, you can dine and dance under the stars and palms at this wildly popular outdoor tavern, whose focus is to build a local community gathering spot to support bands, musicians, and farmers. The grog offerings are super fun, with inventive cocktails such as the Wizard's Elixir and the Dragon's Tale: no watered-down drinks here. **Known for:** showcase for local performers; open-air dancing under trade winds and swaying palms; early take-out breakfasts. [$] *Average main: $13* ✉ *61-3616 Kawaihae Rd., Kawaihae* ☎ *808/882–7771* 🌐 *www.bluedragontavern.com* 🕒 *Closed Mon. and Tues. No lunch.*

★ **Seafood Bar and Grill**

$$ | **SEAFOOD** | Upstairs in a historical building, this seafood tiki bar has been a hot spot for years, serving up a dynamite and well-priced bar menu with tasty *pupus* (appetizers), signature seafood dishes such as the coconut shrimp or poke burger, and even a prime rib special on Tuesdays. Don't let the funky appearance deter you; this place is frequented by legacy celebrities whose names you know or whose records you've bought. **Known for:** funky tiki theme; seafood quesadilla; two nightly happy hours. [$] *Average main: $23* ✉ *61-3642 Kawaihae Harbor (Hwy. 270), Kawaihae* ☎ *808/880–9393* 🌐 *www.seafoodbarandgrill.com.*

Hawaii Beach Safety

Hawaii's world-renowned, beautiful beaches can be extremely dangerous at times due to large swells and strong currents—so much so that the state rates wave hazards using three signs: a yellow square (caution), a red stop sign (high hazard), and a black diamond (extreme hazard). Signs are posted and updated three times daily or as conditions change.

Never swim alone or dive into unknown water or shallow breaking waves. If you're unable to swim out of a rip current by swimming sideways, tread water and wave your arms in the air to signal for help.

Even in calm conditions, this is still the ocean, and there are other dangerous things in the water to be aware of, including razor-sharp coral, jellyfish, eels, and sharks, to name a few.

Signs are posted along beaches when jellyfish are present. Box jellyfish swarm Hawaii's leeward shores 9 to 10 days after a full moon. Portuguese man-of-wars are usually found when winds blow from the ocean onto land. Reactions to a sting range from usually mild (burning sensation, redness, welts) to severe (breathing difficulties). Rinse the affected area with rubbing alcohol and apply ice. Seek first aid if you experience a severe reaction.

The chances of a shark bite in Hawaiian waters are very low; sharks attack swimmers or surfers three or four times per year. Of the 40 species of sharks found near Hawaii, tiger sharked (recognized by their blunt snouts and verticle bars on their sides) are considered the most dangerous because of their size and indiscriminate feeding behavior.

To reduce your shark-attack risk, avoid swimming at dawn, dusk, and night, when some shark species may move inshore to feed. Steer clear of murky waters, harbor entrances, areas near stream mouths (especially after heavy rains), channels, or steep drop-offs.

The website 🌐 *oceansafety.soest.hawaii.edu* provides beach hazard maps for the main islands, as well as current weather and surf advisories, listings of closed beaches.

Coffee and Quick Bites

Anuenue Ice Cream and Shave Ice
$ | **HAWAIIAN** | Shave ice and ice cream in every imaginable flavor can be found at the ideal spot, close to the resort coast beaches. Prepare to wait in line for 15–20 minutes as you ponder your options, but don't fret: it's worth it. **Known for:** lilikoi shave ice; Kona fudge ice cream; long waits. [$] *Average main: $6* ✉ *Kawaihae Harbor Shopping Center, 61-3665 Akoni Pule Hwy., Kawaihae* ☎ *808/882–1109.*

Nightlife

BARS

★ **Blue Dragon Tavern and Cosmic Musiquarium**
MUSIC CLUBS | Five nights a week, you can dance under the stars and swaying coconut trees at West Hawaii's premier nightlife spot. Recently renovated and reimagined, the open-air Musiquarium is now a sustainable initiative by a local 1HeartHub, which unites businesses with social purpose. By supporting local farmers, artists, and musicians, they also help sustain the broader community. Live music includes jazz, R&B, soft rock, and

classic Hawaiian and island-style tunes. Tavern-style pub fare and drinks are on tap if you need a break from dancing. ☎ 61-3616 Kawaihae Rd., Kawaihae ✦ Across from harbor ☎ 808/882–7771 ⊕ www.bluedragonrestaurant.com.

🛍 Shopping

GALLERIES

Harbor Gallery

ART GALLERIES | Since 1990, this gallery has been enticing visitors with a vast collection of paintings and sculptures by more than 200 Big Island artists. There are also antique maps and prints, wooden bowls, paddles, koa furniture, jewelry, and glasswork. The shop hosts two annual wood shows. ⊠ Kawaihae Harbor Shopping Center, 61-3665 Akoni Pule Hwy., Kawaihae ☎ 808/882–1510 ⊕ www.harborgallery.biz.

SHOPPING CENTERS

Kawaihae Harbor Shopping Center

SHOPPING CENTERS/MALLS | This almost-oceanfront shopping plaza houses the exquisite Harbor Gallery, which represents many Big Island artists. Try the Big Island–made ice cream and shave ice (the best in North Hawaii) at local favorite Anuenue. Also here are Mountain Gold Jewelers and Kohala Divers. ⊠ 61-3665 Akoni Pule Hwy., Kawaihae.

Hawi and Kapaau

8 miles north of Kawaihae.

Near the birthplace of King Kamehameha, these North Kohala towns thrived during the plantation days, once bustling with hotels, saloons, and theaters—even a railroad. They took a hit when "Big Sugar" left the island, but both towns are blossoming once again, thanks to strong local communities, tourism, athletic events, and an influx of artists keen on honoring the towns' past. They are full of lovingly restored vintage buildings

housing fun and funky shops and galleries, as well as eateries worth a stop for a quick bite. Hawi is internationally known as the turnaround point for the cycling portion of the Ironman triathlon event.

◉ Sights

Keokea Beach Park

NATIONAL/STATE PARK | A renovated pavilion (it was damaged in a 2006 quake) welcomes visitors to this 7-acre beach park fronting the rugged shore in North Kohala. This is a popular local spot for picnics, fishing, and surfing. ⚠ **Enjoy the scenery, but don't try to swim here—the water is very rough. Be careful on the hairpin curve going down.** ⊠ Hwy. 270, Kapaau ✦ On the way to Pololu Valley, near mile marker 27 🆓 Free.

King Kamehameha Statue

PUBLIC ART | A statue of Kamehameha the Great, the legendary king who united the Hawaiian Islands, stands watch over his descendants in North Kohala. The 8½-foot-tall figure bears the king's sacred feather *kihei*, *mahiole*, and *kaei* (cape, helmet, and sash). It's actually the original of the statue fronting the Judiciary Building on King Street in Honolulu. Cast in Florence in 1880, it was lost at sea. A replica was commissioned and shipped to Honolulu, but the original statue was found later in a Falklands Island junkyard. It now stands in front of the old Kohala Courthouse in Kapaau, next to the highway on the way toward Pololu Valley. Every year on King Kamehameha Day (June 11), Kohala residents honor their most famous son with a celebration that involves a parade and draping the statue in dozens of handmade floral lei. ⊠ 54-3900 Kapaau Rd., Kapaau.

Lapakahi State Historical Park

HISTORIC SITE | A self-guided, 1-mile walking tour leads through the ruins of the once-prosperous fishing village Koaie, which dates as far back as the 15th century. Displays illustrate early Hawaiian fishing and farming techniques, salt gathering, games, and legends. Because the shoreline near the state park is an officially designated Marine Life Conservation District (and part of the site itself is considered sacred), swimming, swim gear, and sunscreen are not allowed in the water. Portable restrooms are available but not drinking water. ⚠ **Gates close promptly at 4 pm, and they mean business!** ✉ *Hwy. 270 at mile marker 14, between Kawaihae and Mahukona, Kapaau* ☎ *808/327–4958* ⊕ *www.hawaiistateparks.org* 💲 *Free.*

Mookini Heiau

ARCHAEOLOGICAL SITE | This isolated National Historic Landmark within Kohala Historical Sites State Monument is so impressive in size and atmosphere that it's guaranteed to give you what locals call "chicken skin" (goose bumps). Dating as early as AD 480, the parallelogram-shape structure is a stunning example of a *luakini heiau*, used for ritualized human sacrifice to the Hawaiian war god Ku. The place feels haunted, and even more so if you are the only visitor and the skies are dark and foreboding. Visit with utmost care and respect. Nearby is Kapakai Royal Housing Complex, the birthplace of Kamehameha the Great. Although it is now under the care of the National Park Service, the site is still watched over by family descendants. ⚠ **Don't drive out here if it's been raining; even with a four-wheel drive, you could easily get stuck.** ✉ *Coral Reef Pl./Upolu Point Rd., off Upolu Airport Rd. and Hwy. 270 (Akoni Pule Hwy.), Hawi* ✛ *Turn at sign for Upolu Airport, near Hawi, and hike or drive 1½ miles southwest* ☎ *808/961–9540* ⊕ *www.nps.gov* 💲 *Free* ⊙ *Closed Wed.*

Beaches

Mahukona Beach Park

BEACH—SIGHT | Snorkelers and divers make exciting discoveries in the clear waters of this park. Long ago, when

sugar was the economic staple of Kohala this harbor was busy with boats waiting for overseas shipments. Now it's a great swimming hole and an underwater museum of sorts. Remnants of shipping machinery, train wheels and parts, and what looks like an old boat are easily visible in the clear water. There's no actual beach here, but a ladder off the old dock makes getting in the water easy. ⚠ **It's best to venture out only on tranquil days, when the water is calm; conditions can get windy and the ocean choppy.** A popular place for locals, Mahukona is busy on weekends. A camping area on the south side of the park has picnic tables and an old covered pavilion. A trail also leads to nearby Lapakahi State Park, about a ½-mile hike. **Amenities:** showers; toilets. **Best for:** snorkeling; swimming. ✉ *Hwy. 270 between mile markers 14 and 15, Hawi* ✛ *About 7 miles south of Hawi* ☎ *808/961–8311.*

Pololu Valley Beach

BEACH—SIGHT | On the North Kohala peninsula, this is one of the Big Island's most scenic beaches. After about 8 miles of lush, winding road past Hawi Town, Highway 270 ends at the overlook of Pololu Valley. Snap a few photos of the stunning view, then take the 15-minute hike down (allow twice as long to go back up) to the beach. The trail is steep and rocky; it can also be muddy and slippery, so watch your step. The beach itself is a wide expanse of fine gray sand with piles of large, round boulders and driftwood. It'surrounded by sheer green cliffs and backed by high dunes and ironwood trees. A gurgling stream leads to the beach from the back of the valley. ⚠ **This is not a safe swimming beach even though locals do swim, body board, and surf here. Dangerous rip currents and usually rough surf pose a real hazard.** Because this is a remote, isolated area far from emergency help, extreme caution is advised. **Amenities:** none. **Best for:** solitude. ✉ *Hwy 270 at end of road, Kapaau.*

Pololu Valley Beach is one of the island's most beautiful, but you may want to enjoy it from the lookout at the top; it's a steep, 15-minute climb down to reach the light gray sand.

Restaurants

★ Sushi Rock

$$$ | **JAPANESE** | Located in historic Hawi Town, Sushi Rock isn't big on size—its narrow dining room is brightly painted and casually decorated with Hawaiian and Japanese knickknacks—but discerning locals and *akamai* (in-the-know) visitors come here for some of the island's best sushi. The restaurant prides itself on using local ingredients like grass-fed beef tenderloin, goat cheese, macadamia nuts, and mango in the Islands-inspired sushi rolls. **Known for:** well-priced trios with beef, poke, and other choices; cone sushi; extensive salad menu. $ *Average main: $33* ⊠ *55-3435 Akoni Pule Hwy., Hawi* ☎ *808/889–5900* ⊕ *sushirockrestaurant.net.*

Coffee and Quick Bites

Kohala Coffee Mill and Tropical Dreams

$ | **CAFÉ** | If you're looking for something sweet—or savory—this busy café in downtown Hawi serves great local coffee, breakfast (bagels, espresso machine–steamed eggs), and lunch (hot dogs, burgers, chili, salads, vegan soup) until 6. Sit outside and watch the world go by as you enjoy locally made ice cream that is *ono* (delicious), as well as other sweet treat specialties. **Known for:** great ice cream; sometimes crowded; outstanding coffee. $ *Average main: $4* ⊠ *55-3412 Akoni Pule Hwy., Hawi* ☎ *808/889–5577* ⊗ *No dinner.*

Hotels

★ Hawaii Island Retreat at Ahu Pohaku Hoomaluhia

$$$$ | **B&B/INN** | Here, above the sea cliffs in North Kohala's Hawi, sustainability meets luxury without sacrificing comfort: the resort generates its own solar and wind-turbine power, harnesses its own water, and grows much of its own food. **Pros:** stunning location; emphasis on organic food; affordable yurts are one lodging option. **Cons:** somewhat isolated and not within walking distance

of restaurants; yurts don't have in-unit showers; four-night minimum. $ *Rooms from: $425* ✉ *250 Maluhia Rd., Kapaau* ⚓ *Off Hwy. 270 in Hawi* ☎ *808/889–6336* ⊕ *www.hawaiiislandretreat.com* ⤴ *20 rooms* ❤️ *Free breakfast.*

★ Puakea Ranch

$$$ | RENTAL | FAMILY | Four beautifully restored ranch houses and bungalows occupy this historic country estate in Hawi, where guests enjoy their own private swimming pools, horseback riding, round-the-clock concierge availability, and plenty of fresh fruit from the orchards. **Pros:** charmingly decorated; beautiful bathrooms; private swimming pools. **Cons:** 15 minutes to the beach; spotty cell-phone coverage; sometimes windy. $ *Rooms from: $289* ✉ *56-2864 Akoni Pule Hwy., Hawi* ☎ *808/315–0805* ⊕ *www.puakearanch.com* ⤴ *4 houses* ❤️ *No meals.*

🛍️ Shopping

ARTS AND CRAFTS

Bamboo Gallery

CRAFTS | The real draw of the Bamboo Restaurant is its art gallery, which seduces with elegant koa-wood furniture and an array of gift items, such as hand-sewn crafts, boxes, jewelry, and even aloha shirts. ✉ *Bamboo Restaurant and Gallery, 55-3415 Akoni Pule Hwy., Hawi* ☎ *808/889–1441* ⊕ *www.bamboorestauranthawaii.com.*

Elements Jewelry and Fine Crafts

CRAFTS | The beautiful little shop carries lots of original handmade jewelry made by local artists as well as carefully chosen gifts, including unusual ceramics, paintings, prints, glass items, baskets, fabrics, bags, and toys. ✉ *55-3413 Akoni Pule Hwy., Hawi* ⚓ *Next to Bamboo Restaurant* ☎ *808/889–0760* ⊕ *www.elementsjewelryandcrafts.com.*

CLOTHING

As Hawi Turns

CLOTHING | This landmark North Kohala shop, housed in the 1932 Toyama Building, stocks sophisticated offerings in resort wear with items made of hand-painted silk in tropical designs by local artists. There are plentiful vintage treasures, jewelry, gifts, hats, bags, and toys, plus handmade ukuleles by local luthier David Gomes. ✉ *55-3412 Akoni Pule Hwy., Hawi* ☎ *808/889–5023.*

GALLERIES

Ackerman Fine Art Gallery

ART GALLERIES | Kapaau-based, this multiple-gallery/café is truly a family affair. Local artist Gary Ackerman's wife, Yesan, runs Ackerman Fine Art Gallery, featuring Gary's original oil paintings, fused glass art, and glass sculpture, plus works from other local artists. Down the street, Gary's daughter, Alyssa, and her husband, Ronnie, run Ackerman Gift Gallery, which showcases fine art, photography, and gifts, and their own King's View Cafe located across from the historic King Kamehameha statue. ✉ *54-3878 Akoni Pule Hwy., Kapaau* ☎ *808/889–5138 Ackerman Fine Art Gallery* ⊕ *www.ackermangalleries.com.*

Rankin Gallery

ART GALLERIES | Watercolorist and oil painter Patrick Louis Rankin showcases his own work at his shop in a restored plantation store next to the bright-green Chinese community and social hall, on the way to Pololu Valley. The building sits right at a curve in the road, at the first gulch past Kapaau. ✉ *53-4380 Akoni Pule Hwy., Kapaau* ☎ *808/889–6849* ⊕ *www.patricklouisrankin.net.*

Wishard Gallery

ART GALLERIES | A Big Island–born artist whose verdant landscapes, sea views, and *paniolo* (cowboy)-themed paintings have become iconic throughout the Islands, Harry Wishard showcases his original oils at this gallery, along with works by other renowned local artists like Kathy Long, Edward Kayton, and Lynn Capell. ⌧ *55-498 Hawi Rd., Hawi* ☎ *808/731-6556* ⊕ *www.wishardgallery. com.*

LOCAL SPECIALTIES

Hawaii Cigar and Ukulele

MUSIC STORES | It may seem like an odd combination to offer, but this funky little shop knows how to do both right. Handcrafted instruments start at just $100 and are made by local master luthiers David Gomes and Mark Evans. One lesson is included with your purchase, and they also have a great selection of other stringed instruments and accessories. Cigar lovers can sit in the lounge and enjoy a custom, hand-rolled Nicaraguan cigar for just $10. Or you can partake of the CBD option if cigars aren't your thing, then browse the cool selection of Hawaiiana in the gift shop before you leave. ⌧ *55-3419 Akoni Pule Hwy., Hawi* ☎ *808/889–1282.*

🏃 Activities

SPAS

Hawaii Island Retreat Maluhia Spa

FITNESS/HEALTH CLUBS | Remote and elegant, this sanctuary in North Kohala offers three artfully appointed indoor treatment rooms and two outdoor massage platforms that overlook the valley. The spa is first-rate, with handcrafted wooden lockers, rain-style showerheads, and a signature line of lotions and scrubs made locally. The owners also create their own scrubs and wraps from ingredients grown on the property. Massage options include lomilomi, Thai, and deep tissue. ⌧ *250 Maluhia Rd., Kapaau* ☎ *808/889–6336* ⊕ *www.hawaiiislandretreat.com* 🍴 *Massages from $130, facials from $70.*

Waimea

Waimea is 40 miles northeast of Kailua-Kona and 10 miles east of the Kohala Coast.

Thirty minutes over the mountain from Kohala, Waimea (sometimes called "Kamuela" to distinguish it from the similarly named places on Kauai and Oahu) offers a completely different experience than the rest of the island. Rolling green hills, large open pastures, light rain, cool evening breezes and morning mists, along with abundant cattle, horses, and regular rodeos, are just a few of the surprises you'll stumble upon here in *paniolo* (cowboy) country. Parker Ranch, one of the largest privately held cattle ranches in the United States, surrounds this attractive little town.

Waimea is also where some of the island's top Hawaii regional cuisine chefs practice their art using local ingredients, which makes it an ideal place to find yourself at dinnertime. In keeping with the recent restaurant trend toward featuring local farm-to-table ingredients, a handful of Waimea farms and ranches supply most of the restaurants on the island, and many sell to the public as well. With its galleries, coffee shops, brewpubs, restaurants, beautiful countryside, and *paniolo* culture, Waimea is well worth a stop if you're heading to Hilo or Maunakea. ■**TIP→ The short highway, or mountain road, that connects Waimea to North Kohala (Highway 250) affords some of our favorite Big Island views.**

GETTING HERE AND AROUND

From the Kohala Coast, it's a reasonable drive to Waimea. From the Mauna Kea and Hapuna resorts, it's about 12 miles; from the Waikoloa resorts, it's about 19 miles via Waikoloa Road. You can see most of what Waimea has to offer in one day, but if you're heading up to Maunakea for stargazing—which you should—it could easily be stretched

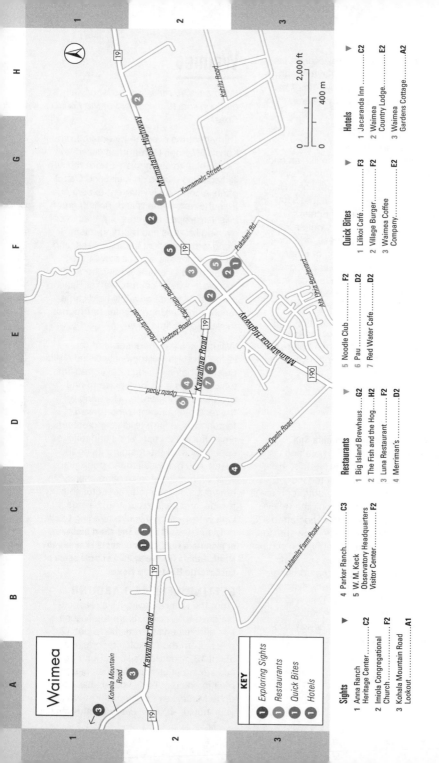

Waimea

KEY

- ▶ *Exploring Sights*
- ❶ *Restaurants*
- ❶ *Quick Bites*
- ❶ *Hotels*

Sights ▶
1 Anna Ranch Heritage Center............**C2**
2 Imiola Congregational Church............**F2**
3 Kohala Mountain Road Lookout............**A1**
4 Parker Ranch............**C3**
5 W. M. Keck Observatory Headquarters Visitor Center............**F2**

Restaurants ▶
1 Big Island Brewhaus....**G2**
2 The Fish and the Hog....**H2**
3 Luna Restaurant.........**F2**
4 Merriman's.................**D2**
5 Noodle Club...............**F2**
6 Pau...........................**D2**
7 Red Water Cafe............**D2**

Quick Bites ▶
1 Liliko¡ Café..................**F3**
2 Village Burger..............**F2**
3 Waimea Coffee Company..................**E2**

Hotels ▶
1 Jacaranda Inn...............**C2**
2 Waimea Country Lodge...........**E2**
3 Waimea Gardens Cottage.........**A2**

2,000 ft

0 ___ 400 m

to two. If you stay in Waimea overnight (there are many B&B options), spend the afternoon browsing through town or touring some of the area's ranches and historic sites. Then indulge in a gourmet dinner before heading up the Daniel K. Inouye Highway, also known as the Saddle Road, for world-renowned stargazing on Maunakea. Just gas up and bring water, snacks, and warm clothes with you (there are plenty of gas stations, cafés, and shops in Waimea).

◉ Sights

★ Anna Ranch Heritage Center

FARM/RANCH | This stunning heritage property, on the National and State Registers of Historic Places, belonged to the "first lady" of Hawaii ranching, Anna Lindsey Perry-Fiske. Here is a rare opportunity to see a fully restored cattle ranch compound and learn about the life of this fascinating woman, who butchered cattle by day and threw lavish parties by night. Wander the picturesque grounds and gardens on a self-guided walk, watch a master saddle maker and an ironsmith in action, and take a guided tour (by appointment only) of the historic house, where Anna's furniture, gowns, and elaborate *pau* (parade riding) costumes are on display. The knowledgeable staff shares anecdotes about Anna's life. (Some staff and visitors have even reported strange goings-on in the main house, suggesting that Anna herself may still be "around.") ⊠ *65-1480 Kawaihae Rd., Waimea (Hawaii County)* ☎ *808/885–4426* ⊕ *www.annaranch.org* ⊠ *Grounds and Discovery Trail free, historic home tours $10* ☉ *Closed Sat.–Mon.*

Imiola Congregational Church

RELIGIOUS SITE | Highlights of this church, which was established in 1832 and rebuilt in 1857, are a gleaming, restored koa interior and unusual wooden calabashes hanging from the ceiling. Be careful not to walk in while a service is in progress, as the front entry is behind the

Waimea or Kamuela? ◉

Both, actually. Everyone knows it as Waimea, but the sign on the post office says Kamuela, which is Hawaiian for "Samuel," referring to Samuel Parker, the son of the founder of Parker Ranch. That designation is used to avoid confusion with communities named Waimea on the islands of Kauai and Oahu. But the official name of the town is Waimea.

pulpit. ⊠ *65-1084 Mamalahoa Hwy., on "Church Row," Waimea (Hawaii County)* ☎ *808/885–4987* ⊕ *www.imiolachurch. com* ⊠ *Free.*

Kohala Mountain Road Lookout

VIEWPOINT | The road between North Kohala and Waimea is one of the most scenic drives in Hawaii, passing Parker Ranch, open pastures, rolling hills, and tree-lined mountains. There are a few places to pull over and take in the view; the lookout at mile marker 8 provides a splendid vista of the Kohala Coast and Kawaihae Harbor far below. On clear days, you can see well beyond the resorts to Maui, while at other times an eerie mist drifts over the view. ⊠ *Kohala Mountain Rd. (Hwy. 250), Waimea (Hawaii County).*

★ Parker Ranch

FARM/RANCH | An enormous cattle ranch exceeding 130,000 acres and regularly running tens of thousands of head of cattle, Parker Ranch is an impressive and compelling backdrop for the scenic town of Waimea. It was established in 1847 by a sailor from Massachusetts, John Palmer Parker, who was permitted by the Hawaiian ruler King Kamehameha I to cull vast herds of out-of-control cattle; thus, the ranch was born. The ranch later grew into the empire it is today, and the foundation started by Parker's descendants supports the community in healthcare and education. In addition to taking self-guided tours of two of the ranch's historic homes—Hale Mana and Puuopelu—free of charge, you can also visit Parker Ranch Center (a shopping and restaurant center) to peruse gift items in the Parker Ranch Store. ⊠ *Parker Ranch Headquarters, 66-1304 Mamalahoa Hwy., Waimea (Hawaii County)* ☎ *808/885–7311* ⊕ *parkerranch.com* ⊠ *Free* ⊗ *Closed weekends.*

W. M. Keck Observatory Headquarters Visitor Center

OBSERVATORY | Although the twin, 10-meter optical/infrared telescopes (among the largest and most scientifically productive in the world) are at the summit of Maunakea, the headquarters and visitor center of the observatory are in downtown Waimea and make a great stop if you want to learn more about the telescopes without making the long journey up the mountain. Top global astronomy teams have used the scopes to make astounding discoveries, thanks in part to their location atop the mountain, far above the turbulence of the atmosphere. Docents at the visitor center offer personalized tours weekdays from 10 am to 2 pm, showing you models of the telescopes and the observatory, as well as one of the original instruments. You can also peruse the exhibits and interpretive infographics at your own pace. About six times per year, highly renowned speakers, including Nobel Prize laureates, give free astronomy talks to the public. ⊠ *65-1120 Mamalahoa Hwy., Waimea (Hawaii County)* ✛ *Across from hospital* ☎ *808/885–7887* ⊕ *www.keckobservatory.org* ⊠ *Free* ⊗ *Closed weekends.*

🍴 Restaurants

★ Big Island Brewhaus

$ | AMERICAN | A hands-down island favorite, this casual brewpub from owner and veteran brewmaster Tom Kerns churns out premium ales, lagers, and specialty beers from his on-site brewery in Waimea. With a focus on fresh ingredients, the brewpub's menu includes outstanding burgers, grilled steak, poke, fish tacos, burritos, rellenos, and quesadillas fresh to order. **Known for:** coconut-infused White Mountain porter; affordable sampler with six beer choices; amazing grass-fed burgers. $ *Average main: $12* ⊠ *64-1066A Mamalahoa Hwy., Waimea (Hawaii County)* ☎ *808/887–1717* ⊕ *www.bigislandbrewhaus.com.*

The Fish and the Hog

$ | ECLECTIC | This casual little restaurant along the highway serves up generous sandwiches, salads, and melt-in-your-mouth barbecue items. Because the owners are fisherpeople, the poke and nightly fish specials showcase fish caught from their boat. **Known for:** enormous, puffy, onion rings; kiawe-smoked pulled pork, ribs, pork ribs, and brisket; yummy banana cream pie. $ *Average main: $15* ⊠ *64-957 Mamalahoa Hwy. (Hwy. 11), Waimea (Hawaii County)* ☎ *808/885–6268* ⊕ *fishandthehog.com.*

★ Luna Restaurant

$ | ITALIAN | FAMILY | Tucked away in a strip mall near KTA at Waimea Center, this unassuming little restaurant with low-key decor makes some of the best pizza on the Big Island. Pastas and salads, Italian specialties like caprese, and the Hamakua mushroom risotto incorporate island-fresh ingredients. **Known for:** gourmet toppings, including house-made Italian sausage and grilled chicken; friendly proprietor; pork belly with caramelized onion, pineapple, and mozzarella. $ *Average main: $12* ⊠ *Waimea (KTA) Center, 65-1158 Mamalahoa Hwy., Waimea (Hawaii County)* ☎ *808/887–1313*

www.lunawaimea.com ⊙ *Closed Mon.
and Tues.*

Merriman's
$$$ | MODERN HAWAIIAN | The signature restaurant of Peter Merriman, one of the pioneers of Hawaii Regional Cuisine, is the home of the original wok-charred ahi: it's seared on the outside, leaving sashimi on the inside. Although lunch prices are reasonable, dinner is "resort pricey," so prepare to splurge. **Known for:** grilled-to-order New York steak; locally raised Kahua Ranch braised lamb; chocolate oblivion torte. $ *Average main: $45 ⊠ Opelo Plaza, 65-1227 Opelo Rd., Waimea (Hawaii County)* ☎ *808/885–5822* ⊕ *www.merrimanshawaii.com.*

Noodle Club
| JAPANESE FUSION | FAMILY | Star Wars toys and action figures line the shelves of Noodle Club, a fun destination with serious food in Parker Ranch Center. Veteran resort chef Edwin Goto simmers his broths for up to 36 hours to create the noodle, or saimin, dishes such as the savory Bowl of Seoul or the All Things Pork Ramen. **Known for:** homemade pork, beef, and vegetable broths; bao buns with Hamakua Alii mushrooms; delicous desserts, including dairy-free chocolate mousse. $ *Average main: $14 ⊠ Parker Ranch Center, 67-1185 Mamalahoa Hwy., #A106, Waimea (Hawaii County)* ☎ *808/885–8825* ⊕ *www.noodleclub-waimea.com* ⊙ *Closed Mon.*

Pau
$ | ITALIAN | FAMILY | Its name is Hawaiian for "done," perhaps an allusion to how eagerly the pizzas are gobbled up at this eatery with cool artwork and a relaxed vibe. On offer is a wide selection of appetizers, salads, sandwiches, pastas, and pizzas loaded with lots of local fresh ingredients. **Known for:** build-your-own pizza option; superfood salad with quinoa and brown rice; triple slice lunch special. $ *Average main: $12 ⊠ 65-1227 Opelo Rd., Waimea (Hawaii County)* ⊕ *Near*

Merriman's ☎ *808/885–6325* ⊕ *www. paupizza.com.*

Red Water Cafe
$$$$ | ECLECTIC | FAMILY | Chef David Abraham serves Hawaiian café food with a twist and a side of aloha. There's a full sushi menu as well; the Fuji roll is prepared tempura style, and sashimi is served with organic greens. **Known for:** worthy saketini (sake martini); Kansas City rib-eye steak, Berkshire pork chops, and short ribs; good kids' menu. $ *Average main: $36 ⊠ 65-1299 Kawaihae Rd., Waimea (Hawaii County)* ☎ *808/885–9299* ⊕ *www.redwatercafe. com* ⊙ *No lunch.*

☕ Coffee and Quick Bites

Lilikoi Café
$ | EUROPEAN | FAMILY | Locals love this gem of a café, tucked away in the back of the Parker Ranch Center, in part because it's hard to find and they want to keep its delicious breakfast crepes, freshly made soups, and croissants Waimea's little secret. It's just as good for lunch: owner and chef John Lorda creates an impressive selection of salad choices daily, including chicken curry, beet, fava bean, chicken pesto, and Mediterranean pasta. **Known for:** handpainted murals; Israeli couscous with tomato, red onion, and cranberry; creative sandwiches and hot lunch entrées. $ *Average main: $9 ⊠ Parker Ranch Center, 67-1185 Mamalahoa Hwy. (Hwy. 11), Waimea (Hawaii County)* ☎ *808/887–1400* ⊙ *Closed Sun. No dinner.*

Village Burger
$ | AMERICAN | FAMILY | At this little eatery that brings a whole new meaning to gourmet hamburgers, locally raised, grass-fed, hormone-free beef is ground fresh, hand-shaped daily on-site, and grilled to perfection right before your eyes. Top your burger (be it ahi, veal, Kahua Ranch Wagyu beef, Hamakua mushroom, or Waipio taro) with

Big Island Farm Tours

As local ingredients continue to play a prominent role on Big Island menus, chefs and farmers are working together to support a burgeoning agritourism industry in Hawaii. Several local farms make specialty items that cater to the island's gourmet restaurants. The **Hawaii Island Goat Dairy** (🌐 *www.hawaiiislandgoatdairy.com*) on the Hamakua Coast produces specialty cheese; **Big Island Bees** (🌐 *www.bigislandbees.com*) boasts its own beekeeping museum and tasting room above Kealakekua Bay; and **Hamakua Mushrooms** (🌐 *www.fungaljungle.com*) has turned harvested koa forests into a safe haven for gourmet mushrooms. Many farms—like **Greenwell Farms** (🌐 *www.mountainthunder.com*), which produces 100% organic Kona coffee, and **Hawaiian Vanilla Company** (🌐 *www.hawaiianvanilla.com*), which is cultivating vanilla from orchids on the Hamakua Coast—are open to the public and offer free tours.

everything from local avocados, baby greens, and chipotle goat cheese to tomato marmalade. **Known for:** delicious brioche buns baked fresh in nearby Hawi; lots of toppings for burgers; ice cream for milkshakes made fresh in Waimea. [$] *Average main: $10* ✉ *Parker Ranch Center, 67-1185 Mamalahoa Hwy. (Hwy. 11), Waimea (Hawaii County)* ☎ *808/885–7319* 🌐 *www.villageburgerwaimea.com.*

Waimea Coffee Company

$ | **CAFÉ** | This is a good stop for a steaming latte and a warm pastry, a cup of hot soup, or a freshly made salad. The small lanai offers enjoyable views of Waimea's compact rolling hills dappled with rain, fog, and sunlight. **Known for:** delicious specialty coffee drinks; convenient to Waimea shopping; limited seating. [$] *Average main: $4* ✉ *Parker Square, 65-1279 Kawaihae Rd., Waimea (Hawaii County)* ☎ *808/885–8915* 🌐 *www.waimeacoffeecompany.com* ⏲ *No dinner.*

Hotels

Though it seems a world away, Waimea is only about a 15- to 20-minute drive from the Kohala Coast resorts, which places it considerably closer to the island's best beaches than Kailua-Kona. Yet few visitors think to book lodging in this pleasant upcountry ranching community, where you can enjoy cool mornings and evenings after a day spent basking in the sun. To the delight of residents and visitors, there are some very good restaurants. Sightseeing is easy from here, too: Maunakea is a short drive away, and Hilo and Kailua-Kona are about an hour away. There aren't as many condos and hotels here, but there are some surprisingly good B&B and cottage options—as well as some great deals, especially considering their vantage point. Many have spectacular views of Maunakea, the ocean, and the beautiful green hills of Waimea.

Jacaranda Inn

$$ | **B&B/INN** | While the historical Jacaranda Inn may not always live up to its potential, this sprawling estate, built in 1897 and once the home of the manager of Parker Ranch, provides a unique lodging option for visitors who appreciate history. **Pros:** historical charm; hot tubs in most rooms; walking distance to Waimea restaurants. **Cons:** service not always reliable; no Wi-Fi or TV on property; can be rainy and windy. [$] *Rooms from:*

199 ✉ 65-1444 Kawaihae Rd., Waimea (Hawaii County) ☎ 808/557–5068 🌐 www.jacarandainn.com 🛏 9 rooms 🍴 No meals.

Waimea Country Lodge

$ | **HOTEL** | In the heart of cowboy country, this quaint ranch house–style lodge offers views of the green, rolling slopes of Waimea and distant view of Maunakea. **Pros:** beautiful views; kitchenettes in some rooms; free coffee in morning. **Cons:** not near the beach; no pool; no on-site restaurant. [$] *Rooms from: $109* ✉ *65-1210 Lindsey Rd., Waimea (Hawaii County)* ☎ *808/885–4100, 800/367–5004* 🌐 *www.waimeacountrylodge.com* 🛏 *22 rooms* 🍴 *No meals.*

Waimea Gardens Cottage

$$ | **RENTAL** | Surprisingly luxe yet cozy and quaint, the three charming country cottages and one suite at this historical Hawaiian homestead are surrounded by flowering private gardens and a backyard stream. **Pros:** charming, self-contained units; manicured gardens; cascading stream. **Cons:** 50% deposit within two weeks of booking and payment in full six weeks before arrival; only personal or bank checks accepted; 3-night minimum stay. [$] *Rooms from: $205* ✉ *Waimea (Hawaii County)* ✣ *Located off Kawaihae Rd., 2 miles from Waimea Town* ☎ *808/885–8550* 🌐 *www.waimeagardens.com* 💳 *No credit cards* 🛏 *4 units* 🍴 *Free breakfast.*

Shopping

FOOD AND WINE

Crackseed, Etc.

FOOD/CANDY | As local as it gets, this little shop is a classic Big Island tradition. Look for preserved Hawaiian-style seeds, *li hing mui* (sweet and sour plums), Japanese snacks such as *arare* (small crackers), and handmade candies, in addition to authentic Hawaiian souvenirs. ✉ *65-1290 Kawaihae Rd, Waimea (Hawaii County)* ☎ *808/885–6966.*

Kamuela Liquor Store

WINE/SPIRITS | From the outside it doesn't look like much, but this store sells the best selection of premium spirits, wines, and gourmet items on the island. Alvin, the owner, is a collector of fine wines, as evidenced by his multiple cellars. Wine tastings take place Friday afternoon from 3 to 6 and Saturday at noon. ✉ *64-1010 Mamalahoa Hwy., Waimea (Hawaii County)* ☎ *808/885–4674.*

★ **Waimea General Store**

HOUSEHOLD ITEMS/FURNITURE | Since 1970, this Waimea landmark at Parker Square has been a favorite of locals and visitors alike. Although specialty kitchenware takes center stage, the shop brims with local gourmet items, books, kimonos, and Hawaiian gifts and souvenirs. ✉ *Parker Square, 65-1279 Kawaihae Rd., Suite 112, Waimea (Hawaii County)* ☎ *808/885–4479* 🌐 *www.waimeageneralstore.com.*

GALLERIES

Firehouse Gallery

ART GALLERIES | Local Big Island artwork is featured in Waimea's original firehouse building at the intersection of Lindsey Road and Mamalahoa Highway. Supporting the Waimea Arts Council, the gallery is home to annual juried shows as well as solo and group exhibitions by its many award-winning multimedia artists and artisans. Call to check if it's open, as hours aren't always regular. ✉ *67-1201 Mamalahoa Hwy., Waimea (Hawaii County)* ✣ *Across from Waimea Chevron* ☎ *808/887–1052* 🌐 *www.waimeaartscouncil.org.*

★ **Gallery of Great Things**

ART GALLERIES | You might lose yourself exploring the trove of fine art and collectibles in every price range at this gallery, which represents hundreds of local artists and has a low-key, unhurried atmosphere. The "things" include hand-stitched quilts, ceramic sculptures, vintage kimonos, original paintings, koa-wood bowls and furniture, etched glassware, Niihau shell lei, and feather art by local artist Beth McCormick. ⊠ *Parker Square, 65-1279 Kawaihae Rd., Waimea (Hawaii County)* ☎ *808/885–7706* ⊕ *www.gallery-ofgreatthingshawaii.com.*

SHOPPING CENTERS
Parker Ranch Center
SHOPPING CENTERS/MALLS | With a snazzy ranch-style motif, this shopping hub includes a supermarket, some great local eateries (Village Burger, Noodle Club, and Lilikoi Café), a coffee shop, a natural foods store, galleries, and clothing boutiques. The Parker Ranch Store and Parker Ranch Visitors Center and Museum are also here. ⊠ *67-1185 Mamalahoa Hwy. (Hwy. 11), Waimea (Hawaii County)* ⊕ *parkerranchcenter.com.*

Activities

SPAS
Auberge Spa at Mauna Lani Resort
FITNESS/HEALTH CLUBS | Available only to hotel guests, this is a one-of-a-kind experience with a mix of traditional standbys (lomilomi massage, moisturizing facials) and innovative treatments influenced by ancient traditions and incorporating local products. Deep tissue, Swedish, and the Mailani scalp and foot massage round out the offerings. The hibiscus and papaya body exfoliation will leave your skin glowing. ⊠ *Mauna Lani Resort, Auberge Collection, 68-1365 Pauoa Rd., Waimea (Hawaii County)* ☎ *808/885–6622* ⊕ *www.aubergeresorts.com* ⊠ *Massage from $195, facials from $195.*

Hapuna Spa by Mandara
FITNESS/HEALTH CLUBS | At this resort spa, luxury awaits visitors who select from a menu of body treatments and massages, the most popular being the traditional Hawaiian lomilomi massage. An outdoor, covered treatment lanai is the spot for couples to enjoy fresh tropical breezes and ocean sounds. ⊠ *The Westin Hapuna Beach Resort, 62-100 Kaunaoa Dr., Waimea (Hawaii*

County) ☎ *808/880–3335* ⊕ *marriott.com* ⊠ *Massages from $180.*

Mauna Kea Spa by Mandara
FITNESS/HEALTH CLUBS | Mandara blends European methods and indigenous treatments to create the ultimate spa experience. Though this facility is on the smaller side, the excellent treatments are up to the international company's exacting standards. Try the Mandara Signature Facial or the coconut poultice massage, which uses heated, scented herbs to relax muscles and release tension. Traditional Hawaiian lomilomi is also available. ⊠ *Mauna Kea Beach Hotel, Autograph Collection, 62-100 Mauna Kea Beach Dr., Waimea (Hawaii County)* ☎ *808/882–5630* ⊕ *www.mandaraspa.com* ⊠ *Massages from $150, facials from $150.*

★ Spa Without Walls at the Fairmont Orchid Hawaii
FITNESS/HEALTH CLUBS | The spa ranks among the best massage facilities on the island, partially due to the superlative setting—private massage areas are situated amid the waterfalls, freshwater pools, and meandering gardens, as well as right on the beach. ■**TIP→ The Fairmont Orchid is one of the few resorts on the island to offer beachside massage.** Splurge on the 110-minute Alii Experience, with hot coconut-oil treatments, lomilomi, and hot-stone massage. Combine it with a fragrant herbal wrap or a coffee-and-vanilla scrub. Where else can you relax to the sounds of cascading waterfalls while watching tropical yellow tang swim beneath you through windows in the floor? ⊠ *Fairmont Orchid Hawaii, 1 N. Kaniku Dr., Waimea (Hawaii County)* ☎ *808/887–7540* ⊕ *www.fairmont.com/orchid-hawaii/spa* ⊠ *Massages from $159, facials from $99.*

THE HAMAKUA COAST

WITH MAUNAKEA

Updated by
Kristina Anderson

⊙ **Sights**
★★★★★

🍴 **Restaurants**
★★★☆☆

🛏 **Hotels**
★★☆☆☆

🛍 **Shopping**
★☆☆☆☆

🍸 **Nightlife**
★☆☆☆☆

WELCOME TO
THE HAMAKUA COAST

TOP REASONS TO GO

★ **Waipio Valley:** This stunning "amphitheater" valley, surrounded by sheer cliffs and plunging waterfalls, and edged with an expansive black-sand beach, is one of Hawaii's most dramatic gems.

★ **Akaka Falls State Park:** An easy, ½-mile loop trail takes you to these gorgeous falls that plunge 420 feet into cascading pools.

★ **Honokaa:** Remnants of its sugar-plantation past dot this little town, with its historic buildings, small shops, and cafés.

★ **Kalopa State Recreation Area:** The park's 2,000-foot elevation gives visitors a break from the heat to enjoy native forests and birds.

★ **Honomu:** Quaint and tiny, the town is a fun place to poke through or grab a bite after you've visited Akaka Falls.

★ **Maunakea:** Located in the middle of the island, this 13,796-foot peak rises above 40 percent of the earth's atmosphere, making it the best place in the world for astronomy.

Though Highway 19 is the fastest route through the area, any turnoff along this coast could lead to an incredible view, so take your time and go exploring up and down the side roads, being mindful of private property.

If you're driving from Kailua-Kona rather than around the northern tip of the island, cut across on the Mamalahoa Highway (Highway 190) to Waimea, and then catch Highway 19 to the coast. It takes a little longer but is worth it. If you've stopped to explore the quiet little villages with vintage buildings, wooden boardwalks, and dogs dozing in backyards, or if you've spent several hours in Waipio Valley, night will undoubtedly be falling. Don't worry: you can stop in Honokaa if you are heading toward Hilo.

The trip to Hilo via Highway 19 takes only about an hour. Or you can head the other direction and stop for dinner in Waimea before reaching the Kohala Coast (another 25 to 45 minutes).

Although you shouldn't have any trouble exploring the Hamakua Coast in a day, a handful of romantic bed-and-breakfasts are available if you do want to spend more time.

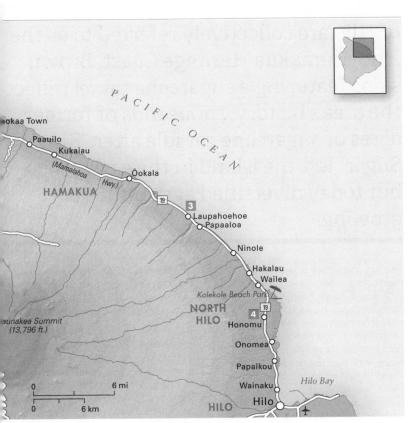

PACIFIC OCEAN

okaa Town
Paauilo
Kukaiau
(Mamalahoa Hwy.)
Ookala
HAMAKUA
19
3 Laupahoehoe
Papaaloa
Ninole
Hakalau
Wailea
Kolekole Beach Park
aunakea Summit
(13,796 ft.)
NORTH HILO
4 19
Honomu
Onomea
Papaikou
Hilo Bay
Wainaku
0   6 mi
0   6 km
HILO   Hilo

1 Waipio Valley. The "Valley of the Kings," an emerald-green valley surrounded by steep cliff faces, is a must-see.

2 Honokaa. A sleepy little town with a spark of the past, Honokaa offers little boutiques and a handful of restaurants.

3 Laupahoehoe. Laupahoehoe Point marks the spot where 24 people died during a tsunami in 1946. This area has a beach park (no swimming) and a museum.

4 Honomu. Sweet and small, this town borders the Akaka Falls area and has some cafés, ice cream shops, and antiques stores.

5 Maunakea. The nearly 14,000-foot Maunakea volcano, home to 11 observatories, is the best place in the world to view the heavens.

The spectacular waterfalls, mysterious jungles, emerald fields, and stunning ocean vistas along Highway 19 northwest of Hilo are collectively referred to as the Hilo–Hamakua Heritage Coast. Brown signs featuring a sugarcane tassel reflect the area's history: thousands of former acres of sugarcane sat idle after "King Sugar" left the island in the early 1990s, but today diversified agriculture is growing.

This is a great place to wander off the main road and see "real" Hawaii—untouched valleys, overgrown banyan trees, tiny coastal villages, and little plantation towns such as Honomu, Laupahoehoe, and Honokaa. Some small communities are still hanging on quite nicely, well after the demise of the big sugar plantations that first engendered them. They have homey cafés, gift shops, galleries, and a way of life from a time gone by. And today, plenty of farmers use premium agricultural lands serviced by the network of former cane roads and the restored and repaired Hamakua Ditch, growing crops such as Hamakua mushrooms, sweet potatoes, tomatoes, vanilla, coffee, and lettuce.

The dramatic Akaka Falls is only one of hundreds of waterfalls here, many of which tumble into a series of cascading pools. The falls may expand or retract depending on inclement weather. The pristine Waipio Valley was once a favorite getaway spot for Hawaiian royalty. The isolated valley floor has maintained the ways of old Hawaii, with taro patches, wild horses, and a handful of homes. The view from the lookout is breathtaking.

Before you head out to the coast, consider taking a side trip to Maunakea, the tallest peak in the Hawaiian Islands, and home to 11 powerful telescopes, co-managed by a consortium of nations, universities, and researchers. You can go with a licensed guide to the summit (recommended) or just drive up to the visitor center at 9,200 feet to peruse exhibits and check out the stars above for yourself.

MAJOR REGIONS

Offering a look at a Hawaii far different from big resorts, the **Hamakua Coast** has waterfalls, dramatic cliffs, ocean views, ancient hidden valleys, rain forests, sleepy small towns, and the stunning Waipio Valley.

From the coast, you can head inland and up to **Maunakea** for what's considered the world's best stargazing; multiple observatories are perched on top of the mountain. The safest, easiest way to get to the top is to book a tour with a licensed guide.

Planning

Getting Here and Around

AIR
Most visitors to the Hamakua Coast fly into Ellison Onizuka Kona International Airport on the west side, which is about 1 hour, 15 minutes, away.

CAR
A car is by far the best and most efficient way to see this coastline. You will want the freedom to leisurely stop off at various lookouts to take in the scenery or pause in a little town to grab a snack or lunch.

Beaches

Beaches along the Hamakua Coast are extremely limited. This is the windward side of the island, where the coast tends to be rocky and rugged and the surf violent. And that's on a calm day. However, you can wade, swim, or body board at Waipio Beach if conditions are good. Never venture out too far and keep in mind there are no lifeguards, as this is a remote area. Be careful crossing the river mouth, as waters can rise quickly and leave you stranded. For the novice, Waipio is probably best as a toe-dipping place rather than a swimming one. The beach parks beneath the Hakalau Bridge are currently closed due to lead contamination from paint flaking off the old bridge. Laupahoehoe is best for surf-watching; not even locals venture in.

Hotels

The stretch of coastline between Waimea and Hilo is an ideal spot for those seeking peace, tranquility, and beautiful views, which makes it a favorite with honeymooners avoiding the big resorts. Several über-romantic B&Bs dot the coast, each with its own personality and views. The beaches are an hour's drive away or more, so most visitors spend a few nights here and a few closer to the beaches on the west side. Vacation homes or home shares provide an extra level of comfort for couples, groups, or families. Honokaa Town is a charming area with a couple of restaurants, shops, banks, and convenience stores.

Restaurants

While there aren't a lot of dining choices along the Hamakua Coast, the few options available are surprisingly good. One of the standout stops is Tex Drive-In, with a full menu of local favorites, burgers, vegetarian burritos, pizza, and their famous *malasadas* (the Portuguese donuts that are popular in Hawaii). At Cafe il Mondo, the specialty is homemade Italian, and a tiny vegetarian place, the Sea Dandelion, serves up outstanding taro patty burgers and salads. If you plan on dinner, just know the area generally closes down at 8 pm.

HOTEL AND RESTAURANT PRICES
Hotel and restaurant reviews have been shortened; For full information, see Fodors.com. Hotel prices in the reviews are the lowest cost of a standard double room in high season. Restaurant prices in the reviews are the average cost of a main course at dinner, or if dinner is not served, at lunch.

What it Costs in U.S. Dollars			
$	**$$**	**$$$**	**$$$$**
RESTAURANTS			
under $17	$17–$26	$27–$35	over $35
HOTELS			
under $180	$180–$260	$261–$340	over $340

Tours

A guided tour from a locally owned and operated company is one of the best (and easiest) ways to see Waipio Valley. You can walk down and up the steep, narrow road yourself, but you need to be in good shape and you may not see as much. And as locals say, it's 15 minutes to walk down but about 45 minutes to walk back up. The cost for a tour depends on both the company and the transport mode.

Waipio Naalapa Stables

GUIDED TOURS | Friendly horses and friendly guides take guests on tours of the valley floor. The 2½-hour tours run Monday through Saturday (the valley rests on Sunday), with check-in times of 9 and 12:30. Riders meet at Waipio Valley Artworks, near the lookout, where they are transported to the valley floor in a four-wheel-drive van. ⊠ *Waipio Valley Artworks Bldg., 48-5416 Kukuihaele Rd., Kukuihaele* ☎ *808/775–0419* ⊕ *www. naalapastables.com* ⊠ *From $110.*

Waipio on Horseback

GUIDED TOURS | This outfit offers guided, 2½-hour horseback-riding tours on the Waipio Valley floor. Riders experience lush tropical foliage, curving rivers (Waipio means "curved water" in Hawaiian), flowering trees, a scenic beach, tranquil streams, and 3,000-foot-tall cliff walls. Local *paniolo* (cowboy) guides share the history, culture, and mythology of this magical valley and also give you a sneak peek into a traditional family farm where the owners tend Hawaiian staples such as taro. You'll also get to see the stunning Naalapa Falls. ⊠ *Hwy. 240 at mile marker 7.5, Honokaa* ✛ *Northwest of Honokaa* ☎ *808/775–7291, 877/775–7291* ⊕ *www. waipioonhorseback.com* ⊠ *From $105.*

Waipio Valley Shuttle

GUIDED TOURS | Not up for hiking in and out of the valley on foot? These informative, 1½- to 2-hour, four-wheel-drive tours do the driving for you, exploring the valley with lots of stops Monday through Saturday. The windows on the van are removed, allowing guests to snap unobstructed photos. You have the option to stay at the beach for two to four hours and come back up with the next tour. ⊠ *48-5416 Kukuihaele Rd., Kukuihaele* ☎ *808/775–7121* ⊕ *www.waipiovalley-shuttle.com* ⊠ *From $65.*

Waipio Valley

24 miles east and then north of Waimea.

Bounded by 3,000-foot cliffs, the "Valley of the Kings" was once a favorite retreat of Hawaiian royalty. Waterfalls drop thousands of feet feet from the North Kohala watershed to the Waipio Valley floor. The lush valley is breathtaking in every way and from every vantage: tropical foliage, abundant flowers, wild horses, misty pastures, curving rivers, and stands of ironwood trees combine with a wide, gray, boulder-strewn shore to make it one of the most picturesque spots in all of Hawaii. Though almost completely off the grid today, Waipio was once a center of Hawaiian life; somewhere between 4,000 and 20,000 people made it their home between the 13th and 17th centuries. In addition, it is a highly historic and culturally significant area, as it housed *heiau* (temples) and *puuhonua* (places of refuge) in addition to royal residences. King Kamehameha the Great launched a great naval battle from here, which marked the start of his unification (some would say conquest) and reign of the

Did You Know?

The dramatic Akaka Falls is only one of hundreds of waterfalls on the Hamakua Coast. Many falls tumble into pristine pools, so bring your camera for some incredible shots.

Did You Know?

At the mouth of the Waipio Valley, the Waipio River meets the ocean. The lush valley used to be a favorite getaway spot for Hawaiian royalty.

Hawaiian Islands. To preserve this pristine part of the island, commercial-transportation permits are limited—only a few outfitters offer organized valley floor trips.

A treacherous paved road leads down from the Waipio Valley Lookout, but no car-rental companies on the island allow their cars to be driven down. You can walk it, and you should if you can. The distance is actually less than a mile from the lookout point—just keep in mind that the climb back gains 1,000 feet in elevation and is highly strenuous, so bring water and a walking stick. Area landowners do not look kindly on public trespassing to access Hiilawe Falls at the back of the valley, so stick to the front by the beach. Hike all the way to the end of the beach for a glorious vantage point. Swimming, surfing, and picnics are all popular activities here, conditions permitting. You can also take the King's Trail from the end of the beach to access another waterfall not far down the trail. (Waterfalls can come and go depending on the level of recent rains.) If you do visit here, respect this area, as it is considered highly sacred to Hawaiians and is still home to several hundred full-time residents who cultivate taro on family farms.

GETTING HERE AND AROUND
After driving through the tiny hamlet of Kukuihaele on Highway 240, continue west for just under a mile to the Waipio Valley Lookout. There's plenty of free parking at the lookout. Please don't be tempted to take your rental car down the steep road. It's dangerous and will void your rental contract.

Sights

★ Waipio Valley Lookout
VIEWPOINT | If you are looking for an easily accessible access point to see the beauty of the Waipio Valley, this is it, offering a stunning view of the valley and the high cliffs that surround it. Not surprising, it's

a very popular spot, but there's plenty of parking to handle the cars on most days; the park at the top is maintained by Hawaii County. A treacherous paved roads leads down (Big Island car-rental companies don't usually allow their cars to be driven down because it's so steep, but you can walk down if you wish, though it's 1,000 feet back up). Your best bet to reach the valley floor is with a guided four-wheel-drive tour. ✉ *Hwy. 240, 8 miles west of Honokaa, Kukuihaele.*

🛍 Shopping

GALLERIES
Waipio Valley Artworks
ART GALLERIES | In this quaint gallery in a vintage home, you can find finely crafted wooden bowls, koa furniture, paintings, and jewelry—all made by local artists. There's also a great little café where you can pick up a sandwich or homemade ice cream before descending into Waipio Valley. ✉ *48-5416 Kukuihaele Rd., Kukuihaele* ☎ *808/775–0958* ⊕ *www. waipiovalleyartworks.com.*

Honokaa

8 miles east of Waipio Valley Lookout, 15 miles northeast of Waimea.

This quaint, cliff-top village fronting the ocean was built in the 1920s and 1930s by Japanese and Chinese workers who quit the nearby plantations to start businesses that supported the sugar economy. The intact historical character of the buildings, bucolic setting, and friendliness of the merchants provide a nice reason to stop and stroll. Cool antiques shops, a few interesting galleries, funky gift shops, and good cafés abound. There's even a vintage theater that often showcases first-rate entertainment. Most restaurants close by 8.

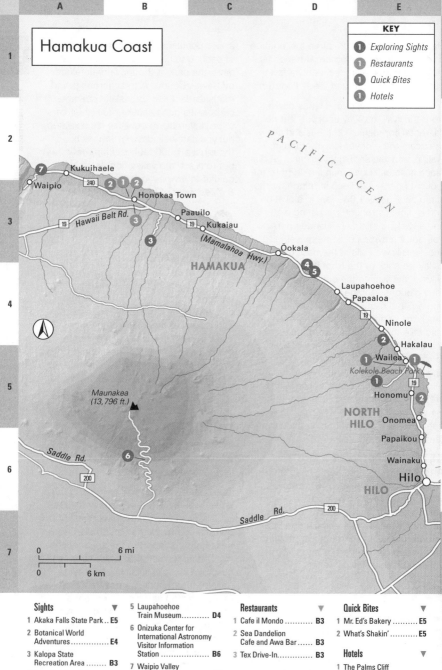

Hamakua Coast

KEY

- ① *Exploring Sights*
- ① *Restaurants*
- ① *Quick Bites*
- ① *Hotels*

PACIFIC OCEAN

⑦ Kukuihaele
Waipio
240 ② ① ②
Honokaa Town
Paauilo
③ 19 Kukaiau
Hawaii Belt Rd. 19
(Mamalahoa Hwy.)
Ōokala
③
HAMAKUA
④
⑤
Laupahoehoe
Papaaloa
19
Ninole
② Hakalau
① Wailea ①
Kolekole Beach Park
① 19
Honomu
②
NORTH HILO Onomea
Papaikou
Maunakea
(13,796 ft.)
Wainaku
Saddle Rd.
⑥ **Hilo**
200 **HILO**
Saddle Rd. 200

0 ——— 6 mi
0 ——— 6 km

Sights ▼

1 Akaka Falls State Park .. **E5**
2 Botanical World
Adventures **E4**
3 Kalopa State
Recreation Area **B3**
4 Laupahoehoe Point
Beach Park **D4**

5 Laupahoehoe
Train Museum **D4**
6 Onizuka Center for
International Astronomy
Visitor Information
Station **B6**
7 Waipio Valley
Lookout **A2**

Restaurants ▼

1 Cafe il Mondo **B3**
2 Sea Dandelion
Cafe and Awa Bar **B3**
3 Tex Drive-In. **B3**

Quick Bites ▼

1 Mr. Ed's Bakery **E5**
2 What's Shakin' **E5**

Hotels ▼

1 The Palms Cliff
House Inn **E5**
2 Waipio Wayside
B&B **B3**

GETTING HERE AND AROUND

If you're traveling from Waimea, you will not need to make any turns; just follow Highway 19 as it veers right. Keep driving until you reach the town of Honokaa on the *makai* (ocean side) of the highway. Coming from Hilo, turn right into the town after mile marker 53.

Sights

★ Kalopa State Recreation Area

NATIONAL/STATE PARK | **FAMILY** | North of the old plantation town of Paauilo, at a cool elevation of 2,000 feet, lies this sweet 100-acre state park. There's a lush forested area with picnic tables and restrooms, and an easy ¾-mile loop trail with additional paths in the adjacent forest reserve. Small signs identify some of the plants, including the gothic-looking native ohia and the rare loulu palm. It's chilly and damp here, making it a good escape from the heat at sea level. Three campground areas with full-service kitchens, as well as four cabins, can be reserved online. ✉ *44-3375 Kalopa Mauka Rd., Honokaa* ✥ *12 miles north of Laupahoehoe and 3 miles inland off Hwy. 19* ☎ *808/775–8852* 🌐 *hawaiistateparks.org* 🎟 *Free.*

Restaurants

★ Cafe il Mondo

$ | **ITALIAN** | Unquestionably the fanciest spot in Honokaa, this cozy Italian bistro known for its pizza and more feels like you've taken a step into Florence. Wood details, a full bar, travertine finishes, antique furnishings, pendant lighting, and a fantastic stone pizza oven combine to create a thoroughly welcoming ambience. **Known for:** variety of homemade calzones; pasta primavera; Paauilo penne. [$] *Average main: $11* ✉ *3580 Mamane St., Honokaa* ☎ *808/775–7711.*

★ Sea Dandelion Cafe and Awa Bar

$ | **VEGETARIAN** | A hip hole-in-the-wall with a hippie vibe, this tiny vegetarian café is a real winner with residents and visitors alike. They serve the Beyond Burger (which you cannot tell from Big Island grass-fed beef) on gluten-free buns, a probiotic poi bowl, Big Island Booch kombucha, and more; takeout is available, too. **Known for:** veggie poke salad; local fruit smoothies; cash-only location. [$] *Average main: $8* ✉ *45-3590 Mamane St., Honokaa* ☎ *802/765–0292* 💳 *No credit cards.*

★ Tex Drive-In

$ | **DINER** | A local institution, this casual place is famous for its *malasadas,* the puffy, doughy, deep-fried Portuguese doughnuts without a hole, best eaten hot; there are also cream-filled versions, including vanilla, chocolate, and coconut. For more than a snack, go for the Hawaiian burger, with a fat, juicy slice of sweet pineapple on top, the overstuffed burrito, or some decent homemade pizza. **Known for:** the island's best malasadas; food cooked to order; long waits. [$] *Average main: $6* ✉ *45-690 Pakalana St., at Hwy. 19, Honokaa* ☎ *808/775–0598* 🌐 *www.texdriveinhawaii.com.*

Hotels

Waipio Wayside B&B

$ | **B&B/INN** | Nestled amid the avocado, mango, coffee, and kukui trees of a historical plantation estate (circa 1932), this serene home provides a retreat close to the Waipio Valley. **Pros:** close to Waipio; gracious owner; full breakfast served in the dining room. **Cons:** remote location; close quarters; no lunch or dinner on property. [$] *Rooms from: $130* ✉ *42-4226 Waipio Rd. (Hwy. 240), Honokaa* ☎ *808/775–0275* 🌐 *www.waipiowayside.com* 🛏 *5 rooms* 🍴 *Free breakfast.*

🎬 Performing Arts

FILM

Honokaa People's Theatre

FILM | Screening art films during the week and more mainstream releases on weekends, this is the largest cinema on the Big Island, featuring a 50-foot screen as well as a huge stage and dance floor. Hula competitions, big-name concert performers, and other special events are also held at this gorgeous and beloved vintage theater. ■ TIP→ **Park properly, as police offers eagerly write tickets while theatergoers are watching the show.** ☒ 45-3574 Mamane St., Honokaa ☎ 808/775–0000 ⊕ honokaapeople.com.

Laupahoehoe

19 miles east of Honokaa.

After the devastating events of 1946, in which a tsunami raged ashore and 24 people were killed, the once-thriving railway town of Laupahoehoe was relocated to higher ground. Now all that's there is a small museum, convenience store, and beach park. It's a quick turn off the highway and well worth it to see the memorial to the schoolteachers and children who died here.

👁 Sights

Laupahoehoe Point Beach Park

NATIONAL/STATE PARK | Here the surf pounds the jagged black rocks at the base of a stunning point. There's a savage beauty to the place. But be advised: this is not a safe place for swimming, so bring only cameras and picnics, not swimsuits. Still vivid in the minds of longtime area residents is the 1946 tragedy in which 21 schoolchildren and three teachers were swept out to sea by a tsunami. ☒ Hwy. 19, Laupahoehoe ⊕ Makai (ocean) side, north of Laupahoehoe ☎ 808/961–8311 ☒ Free.

Laupahoehoe Train Museum

MUSEUM | FAMILY | Behind a stone loading platform of the once-famous Hawaii Consolidated Railway, constructed about 1900, the former manager's house is a poignant reminder of the era when sugar was the local cash crop. Today this museum displays artifacts from the sugar plantation era, the 1946 tsunami, local railway history, and the rich culture of the Hamakua Coast. The museum's Wye railyard has a vintage switch engine, large standard-gauge caboose, and narrow-gauge explosives boxcar. The trains even run a few yards along the restored tracks on special occasions. Call before coming: hours may vary according to docent availabilty. ☒ 36-2377 Mamalahoa Hwy., Laupahoehoe ☎ 808/962–6300 ⊕ www.thetrainmuseum.com ☒ $6 ⊙ Closed Mon.–Wed. (except by appointment).

Honomu

12 miles southeast of Laupahoehoe.

Bordering Akaka Falls State Park, this tiny town did not die when sugar did. Its sugar-plantation past is reflected in its wooden boardwalks and metal-roofed buildings. It's fun to browse through old, dusty shops filled with little treasures such as antique bottles. But you can also check out homemade baked goods, have an espresso, or browse the local art at one of the fine galleries.

GETTING HERE AND AROUND

On your way to Akaka Falls from Highway 19, you will pass through the quaint town of Honomu, which is about 5 miles from the park.

👁 Sights

★ Akaka Falls State Park

BODY OF WATER | A paved, 10-minute loop trail (approximately ½ mile) takes you to the best spots to see the spectacular cascades of Akaka. The majestic upper Akaka Falls drops more than 442 feet, tumbling far below into a pool drained by Kolekole Stream amid a profusion of fragrant white, yellow, and red torch ginger and other tropical foliage. Another 400-foot falls is on the lower end of the trail. Restroom facilities are available but no drinking water. The park is 4 miles inland, and vehicle parking closes at 6. **■ TIP→ A series of steps along parts of the trail may prove challenging for some visitors.** ✉ *875 Akaka Falls Rd., Honomu* ✥ *At the end of Akaka Falls Rd. (Hwy. 220)* ☎ *808/974–6200* 🌐 *dlnr.hawaii.gov/dsp/parks/hawaii/akaka-falls-state-park/* 🎟 *$5 per vehicle.*

Botanical World Adventures

GARDEN | **FAMILY** | Just off the highway, this garden park on more than 300 acres of former sugarcane land has wide views of the countryside and the ocean, and is the place to see the beautiful Kamaee waterfalls. You can also follow a walking trail with old-growth tropical gardens including orchids, palm trees, ginger, hibiscus, and heliconia; visit the 10-acre arboretum, which includes a maze made of orange shrubs; explore the river walk; ride the zipline; and take the only off-road Segway adventure on the island. Admission into the gardens (not including zipline and Segway) is good for seven days, and admission to the two adventures gives you a free pass to the gardens for seven days. If you skip the zipline, you can see it all in a few hours. This place is 3 miles northeast of Honomu. ✉ *31-240 Old Mamalahoa Hwy., Hakalau* ✥ *Just past mile marker 16 from Hilo, on mountain side* ☎ *808/963–5427* 🌐 *www.botanicalworld.com* 🎟 *Garden $15, zipline $177, Segway from $99.*

Coffee and Quick Bites

Mr. Ed's Bakery

$ | **BAKERY** | There's been a bakery in this building since 1912, when the previous owner served up cookies and treats to the kids of plantation workers. Dean and June Edmoundson took over the spot in 1990 and have been treating visitors and residents to delectable goodies, including guava bear claws, *paniolo* (cowboy) cookies, homemade preserves, ice cream, and shave ice. **Known for:** fresh-baked pastries and desserts every morning; to-go food such as hot dogs and manapua (pork in a steamed bun); proximity to Akaka Falls State Park. [$] *Average main: $4* ✉ *28-1672 Old Mamalahoa Hwy., Honomu* ☎ *808/960–5000* 🕓 *Closed Sun. No dinner.*

What's Shakin'

$ | **VEGETARIAN** | A cute vintage shack, painted a cheery yellow, is the home of the best smoothies and shakes on the Hamakua Coast. Order at the counter and take away, or sit awhile under the canopy while you indulge in a Mango Tango, Lava Java, Bananarama, or any of about 15 selections of creative smoothies; you can pair it with tasty turkey, fish, or chicken roll-ups and other wraps. **Known for:** healthy vegetarian and vegan wraps; smoothies made from fruit grown on location; one of the few places to stop on the way to Honokaa. [$] *Average main: $10* ✉ *27-999 Old Mamalahoa Hwy., Pepeekeo* ☎ *808/964–3080* 🌐 *whatsshakinbigisland.com* 🕓 *No dinner.*

Hotels

The Palms Cliff House Inn

$$$ | **B&B/INN** | About 15 minutes north of downtown Hilo and a few minutes from Akaka Falls, this handsome Victorian-style mansion is perched on the sea cliffs 100 feet above the crashing surf of the tropical coast. **Pros:** stunning oceanfront views; coffee and fresh fruit plate with breakfast every morning; all rooms have private outdoor entrances. **Cons:** no pool; remote location means driving 13 miles to Hilo for dinner; 50% booking deposit required. $ *Rooms from: $299* ✉ *28-3514 Mamalahoa Hwy., Honomu* ☎ *808/963–6076* ⊕ *www.palmscliff-house.com* ➲ *8 rooms* ⦿ *Free breakfast.*

🛍 Shopping

ANTIQUES AND COLLECTIBLES
Glass from the Past
ANTIQUES/COLLECTIBLES | A fun place to shop for a quirky gift or just to poke around before or after a visit to Akaka Falls, the store is chock-full of old Hawaiian bottles, antiques, vintage clothing, Japanese collectibles, and interesting ephemera. There's often even a "free" table out front to add to the discovery. ✉ *28-1672 Old Mamalahoa Hwy., Honomu* ☎ *808/963–6449.*

GALLERIES
Woodshop Gallery
ART GALLERIES | Run by local artists Peter and Jeanette McLaren, this Honomu gallery showcases their woodwork and photography collections along with beautiful ceramics, photography, glass, and paintings from other Big Island artists. The historical building still has a working soda fountain dating from 1935. ✉ *28-1690 Old Government Rd., Honomu* ☎ *808/963–6363* ⊕ *www.woodshopgallery.com.*

Maunakea

Maunakea's summit is 18 miles southeast of Waimea and 34 miles northwest of Hilo.

Maunakea ("white mountain") offers the antithesis of the typical tropical island experience. Freezing temperatures and arctic conditions are common at the summit, and snow can fall year-round. You can even snowboard or ski up here. Seriously.

But just because you can doesn't mean you'll want to. You should be in very good shape and a close-to-expert boarder or skier to get down the slopes near the summit and then up again in the thin air with no lifts. During the winter months, lack of snow is usually not a problem.

Winter sports, however, are the least of the reasons that most people visit this starkly beautiful mountain, a dormant volcano. From its base below the ocean's surface to its summit, Maunakea is the tallest island mountain on the planet. It's also home to little Lake Waiau, one of the highest natural lakes in the world, though lately, the word "pond" is closer to the truth.

Maunakea's summit—at 13,796 feet—is the world's best place for viewing the night sky. For this reason, the summit is home to the largest and most productive astronomical observatories in the world—and $1 billion (with a "B") worth of equipment. Research teams from 11 different countries operate 11 telescopes on Maunakea, several of which are record holders: the world's largest optical-infrared telescopes (the dual Keck telescopes), the world's largest dedicated infrared telescope (UKIRT), and the largest submillimeter telescope (the JCMT). The still-larger Thirty Meter Telescope (TMT) had been cleared for construction and was slated to open its record-breaking eye to the heavens until it got delayed by protests in 2019.

Maunakea is tall, but there are higher mountains in the world, so what makes this spot so superb for astronomy? It has more to do with atmosphere than with elevation. A tropical-inversion-cloud layer below the summit keeps moisture from the ocean and other atmospheric pollutants down at the lower elevations. As a result, the air around the Maunakea summit is extremely dry, which helps in the measurement of infrared and submillimeter radiation from stars, planets, and the like. There are also rarely clouds up here; the annual number of clear nights here blows every other place out of the water. And, because the mountain is far away from any interfering artificial lights (not a total coincidence—in addition to the fact that the nearest town is nearly 30 miles away, there's an official ordinance limiting certain kinds of streetlights on the island), skies are dark for the astronomers' research. To quote the staff at the observatory, astronomers here are able to "observe the faintest galaxies that lie at the very edge of the observable universe."

Teams from various nations and universities around the world must submit proposals years in advance to get the chance to use the telescopes on Maunakea. They have made major astronomical discoveries, including several about the nature of black holes, new satellites around Jupiter and Saturn, new Trojans (asteroids that orbit, similar to moons) around Neptune, new moons and rings around Uranus, and new moons around Pluto. Their studies of galaxies are changing the way scientists think about time and the evolution of the universe.

What does all this mean for you? A visit to Maunakea is a chance to see more stars than you've likely ever seen before and an opportunity to learn more about mind-boggling scientific discoveries in the very spot where these discoveries are being made. Only the astronomers, though, are allowed to use the telescopes and other equipment, but the scenery is available to all. (You must leave the summit before dark for your safety.) For you space geeks, a trip to Maunakea may just be the highlight of your trip. We recommend you go with a licensed summit tour company that takes care of the details for you. All take you to the summit for sunset and then present a star talk at about 11,000 feet, where the elevation is more comfortable.

If you're in Hilo, be sure to visit the Imiola Astronomy Center, which is near the University of Hawaii at Hilo. It offers presentations and planetarium films about the mountain and the science being conducted there, as well as exhibits describing the deep knowledge of the heavens possessed by the ancient Hawaiians. You can also visit the W. M. Keck Observatory Headquarters Visitor Center in Waimea to learn about the important work astronomers are conducting on the summit.

GETTING HERE AND AROUND

The summit of Maunakea isn't terribly far, but the drive takes about 90 minutes from Hilo and an hour from Waimea thanks to the steep road. Between the ride there, sunset on the summit, and stargazing, allot at least five hours for a Maunakea visit.

To reach the summit, you must take Saddle Road (Highway 200, now known as the Daniel K. Inouye Highway), which has been rerouted and is a beautiful shortcut across the middle of the island. At mile marker 28, John A. Burns Way, the access road to the visitor center (9,200 feet), is fine, but the road from there to the summit is a lot more precarious because it's unpaved washboard and very steep. Only four-wheel-drive vehicles with low range should attempt this journey. Two-wheel-drive cars are unsafe, especially in winter conditions. Unsuitable cars may experience engine failure as a result of the low oxygen levels. Legislation is pending regarding a total ban of anything but four-wheel-drive vehicles on the summit. And if you're driving back down in the dark, slow and cautious is the name of the game. ⚠ **Most rental car companies will not permit you to drive to the summit of Maunakea. Driving there without permission will void your contract and leave you responsible for damages. This happens more often than you'd think.**

If you haven't rented a four-wheel-drive vehicle from Harper or Big Island Jeep Rentals—the only rental companies

The world's largest optical and infrared telescopes are located at the Keck Observatory on Maunakea's summit.

that allow their vehicles on the summit—and don't want to deal with driving to the summit, or don't want to wait in line to use the handful of telescopes at the visitor center, the best thing to do is book a commercial tour. Operators provide transportation to and from the summit along with expert guides; some also provide parkas, gloves, telescopes, dinner, hot beverages, and snacks. All give their own star talks a few thousand feet below the summit. Companies that offer summit tours are headquartered in both Hilo and Kona.

Also remember that Maunakea's extreme altitude can cause altitude sickness, leading to disorientation, headaches, and light-headedness. Keeping hydrated is crucial. Scuba divers must wait at least 24 hours before traveling to the summit. Children under 16, pregnant women, and those with heart, respiratory, or weight problems should not go higher than the visitor center. While you can park at the visitor center and hike to the summit if you are in good shape, the trip takes

approximately seven hours one way, and no camping is allowed. That means you must leave in the predawn hours to be back before dark; a permit is also required for this hike.

The last potential obstacle to visiting the summit: it's cold—as in freezing—usually with significant wind chill, ice, and snow. Winds have been clocked exceeding 135 miles per hour. Be advised this is a wilderness area and there are no services or rangers, except in an absolute emeergency.

TOURS

Arnott's Lodge and Hiking Adventures
SPECIAL-INTEREST | This outfitter takes you to the summit for sunset and then stops along the way down the mountain, where guides give visual lectures (dependent on clear skies) using lasers. They focus on major celestial objects and Polynesian navigational stars. The excursion departs from Hilo and includes parkas and hot beverages. Pickup is available from Hilo hotels. The company also

Mauna Loa

Mauna Loa is the world's largest active volcano, and it makes up more than 50% of the Big Island of Hawaii. The volcano is so massive and heavy that it creates a depression in the sea floor (actually part of the Pacific tectonic plate) of 5 miles. In fact, if measured from its base on the ocean floor, Mauna Loa would dwarf Everest. It's been erupting for nearly 700,000 years and shows no signs of stopping, although it's currently in a long "quiet" period. Yet it remains fairly enigmatic to visitors (and locals) and is not often visited. On the rare days when the summit is visible from the southeast highway, the view does not appear very commanding. Indeed, you might drive right on by and either not notice that you are seeing the world's largest active volcano—or simply think it's just a rather large hill.

Looks can be deceiving. Mauna Loa is one of 16 "Decade Volcanoes," so designated by the International Association of Volcanology and Chemistry of Earth's Interior. These volcanoes are particularly dangerous to populated areas. Needless to say, the volcano looms large both in the history and daily life of the Hawaiian Islands.

Visiting Mauna Loa

Although equal in height and superlative in mass to Maunakea, nearby twin peak Mauna Loa is often forgotten in the typical visitor's itinerary. There are several reasons for this. For one thing, it's a very long drive on a single-lane road to reach the summit. A paved, 17½-mile road, accessed from mile marker 28 on the Daniel K. Inouye Highway (Highway 200, also called the Saddle Road), takes you to the 11,150-foot summit Mauna Loa Observatory, where the road ends. It's then a steep, rugged 6.4-mile hike to the summit, a trek recommended only for the fit, the well-prepared, and the adventurous. There is a cabin at the summit caldera, called Mokuaweoaweo Caldera (13,250 feet), and you may sleep there if you obtain a permit (available from the Kilauea Visitor Center at Hawaii Volcanoes National Park). The other way to access the summit is even more difficult and takes a minimum of three to four days. It's a 19½-mile journey where you will ascend in altitude by some 6,600 feet to reach the crater. Most hikers stop to acclimatize properly and camp in one of two basic cabins. You need a backcountry wilderness permit for this hike. But there are no services whatsoever in this subfreezing wilderness environment. It was from this vantage that several campers were awakened with the shock of their lives in 1984, when the summit erupted and sent lava flows within 6 miles of Hilo.

offers a traveler's lodge and a number of volcano park and Puna eruption site adventure hikes. ✉ 98 Apapane Rd., Hilo ☎ 808/339–0921 ⊕ www.arnottslodge. com 🛏 From $199.

★ Hawaii Forest and Trail

SPECIAL-INTEREST | The ultra-comfortable, highly educational Summit and Stars tour packs a lot of fun into a few hours.

Guides are knowledgeable about astronomy and Hawaii's geologic and cultural history, and the small group size (max of 14) encourages camaraderie. Included in the tour are dinner at an old ranching station, catered by a favorite local restaurant; sunset on the summit; and a fantastic private star show midmountain. The company's powerful 11-inch Celestron

Schmidt-Cassegrain telescope reveals many interesting celestial objects, including seasonal stars, galaxies, and nebulas. Everything from water bottles, parkas, and gloves to hot chocolate and brownies is included.

The company's Maunakea Sunrise tour begins in the wee hours before the sun comes up and includes a hike among the endangered silverswords as well as breakfast at the visitor center. And of course, the main event—a spectacular sunrise on the summit. The company also offers a daytime version of the summit tour. ⊠ *73-5593 Olowalu St., Kailua-Kona* ☎ *808/331–8505, 800/464–1993* ⊕ *www. hawaii-forest.com* ⊠ *From $225.*

Mauna Kea Summit Adventures

SPECIAL-INTEREST | As the first company to specialize in tours to the mountain, Mauna Kea Summit Adventures is a small outfit that focuses on stars. Cushy vans with panoramic windows journey first to the visitor center, where participants enjoy a hearty lasagna dinner on the lanai and acclimatize for 45 minutes before donning hooded arctic-style parkas and ski gloves for the sunset trip to the 14,000-foot summit. With the help of knowledgeable guides, stargazing through a powerful Celestron telescope happens midmountain, where the elevation is more comfortable and skies are just as clear. The tour includes dinner, hot cocoa and biscotti, and west-side pickup; it runs 364 days a year, weather permitting. ■TIP➜ **Book at least one month prior, as these tours sell out fast.** ⊠ *Kailua-Kona* ☎ *808/322–2366, 888/322–2366* ⊕ *www. maunakea.com* ⊠ *From $259.*

◉ Sights

Onizuka Center for International Astronomy Visitor Information Station

INFO CENTER | At 9,200 feet, this excellent amateur observation site has a handful of telescopes and a knowledgeable staff. Open daily from 9 am to 6 pm, the center is currently not offering stargazing activities at night, but this could change in the future. It's a good place to stop to acclimatize yourself to the altitude if you're heading for the summit. Fortunately, it's a pleasure to do so. Sip hot chocolate and peruse the gift shop and exhibits about ancient Hawaiian celestial navigation, the mountain's significance as a quarry for the best basalt in the Hawaiian Islands, and Maunakea as a revered spiritual destination. You'll also learn about modern astronomy and ongoing projects at the summit. Nights are clear 90% of the year, so the chances are good of seeing some amazing sights in the sky. ■TIP➜ **Keep in mind that no summit telescope facilities are open to the public, so this is a great way to get the sense of the observatory work without going all the way to the top.** ⊠ *Maunakea* ☎ *808/934–4550 visitor center, 808/935–6268 current road conditions* ⊕ *www.ifa.hawaii.edu/info/vis* ⊠ *Free, donations welcome.*

HILO

Updated by
Karen Anderson

⊙ Sights	🍴 Restaurants	🛏 Hotels	🛍 Shopping	🍸 Nightlife
★★★★☆	★★★★☆	★★★☆☆	★★★☆☆	★☆☆☆☆

WELCOME TO HILO

TOP REASONS TO GO

★ **Rainbow Falls and Boiling Pots:** The iconic Rainbow Falls puts on quite a show just above downtown Hilo, especially after heavy rains. Not far from Rainbow Falls, waterfalls spill into the natural cauldrons called Boiling Pots.

★ **Liliuokalani Gardens:** Ornamental Japanese gardens unveil arched bridges and meandering pathways in historic downtown Hilo by the bay.

★ **Shopping and Dining:** Shops, restaurants, and museums occupy historic buildings along the Hilo bayfront.

★ **Hilo Farmers Market:** An open-air market downtown features 200 vendors and is best visited on Saturday and Wednesday; a smaller market takes place on other days.

★ **Imiloa Astronomy Center:** Located above the campus of the University of Hawaii at Hilo, this planetarium and museum features daily presentations about the skies above Hawaii.

1 Downtown. Cooled by sea breezes from scenic Hilo Bay, the downtown area brims with shops, parks, and historic buildings. Side streets lead to fascinating museums, a landmark theater, and tempting eateries. All the best downtown destinations are within easy walking distance.

2 Liliuokalani Gardens and Reeds Bay. The hotel district of Hilo wraps around tree-lined Banyan Drive and is within walking distance of serene Liliuokalani Gardens and Reeds Bay. The gardens have meticulously manicured Japanese landscaping surrounded by sprawling banyan trees. Visitors can stroll across arched footbridges and venture into pagodas overlooking the bay.

3 Greater Hilo. Popular visitor destinations extend beyond downtown Hilo in every direction. You can learn about Hawaiian coffee and macadamia nuts at sites in the area, or stop by the Imiloa Astronomy Center at the University of Hawaii at Hilo campus to learn about Hawaii's starry skies. There's even a free zoo with more than 80 species of animals. Eight miles north of Hio is the thrilling Hawaii Tropical Botanical Garden.

Daniel K. Inouye Hwy.

200

Waiakea Forest Reserve

Stainback Highway

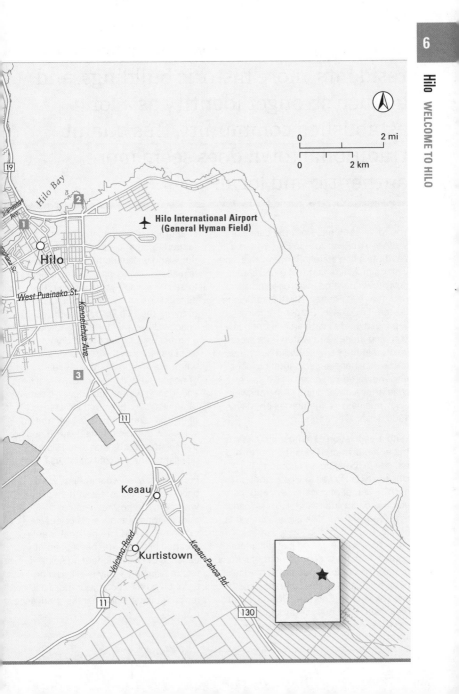

0   2 mi

0   2 km

19

Hilo Bay

2

Hilo International Airport
(General Hyman Field)

1

Hilo

West Puainako St.

Kanoelehua Ave.

3

11

Keaau

Volcano Road

Keaau-Pahoa Rd.

Kurtistown

11

130

In comparison to Kailua-Kona, Hilo is often deemed "the old Hawaii." With significantly fewer visitors than residents, more historic buildings, and a much stronger identity as a long-established community, this quaint, traditional town does seem more authentic and local.

The town stretches from the banks of the Wailuku River to Hilo Bay, where a few hotels line stately Banyan Drive. The vintage buildings that make up Hilo's downtown have been spruced up as part of a revitalization effort. Nearby, the 30-acre Liliuokalani Gardens, a formal Japanese garden with arched bridges, stepping-stones and waterways, were created in the early 1900s to honor the area's Japanese sugar plantation laborers. The garden also became a safety zone after a devastating tsunami swept away businesses and homes on May 22, 1960, killing 61 people.

With a population of almost 50,000 in the entire district, Hilo is the fourth-largest city in the state and home to the University of Hawaii at Hilo. Although it is the center of government and commerce for the island, Hilo is clearly a residential town. Mansions with yards of lush tropical foliage share streets with older, single-walled plantation-era houses with rusty corrugated roofs. It's a friendly community, populated primarily by descendants of the contract laborers—Japanese, Chinese, Filipino, Puerto Rican, and Portuguese—brought in to work the sugarcane fields during the 1800s.

One of the main reasons visitors have tended to steer clear of the east side of the island is its weather. With an average rainfall of 130 inches per year, it's easy to see why Hilo's yards are so green and its buildings so weatherworn. Outside of town, the Hilo District boasts scenic beach valleys, rain forests, and waterfalls, a terrain unlike the hot and dry white-sand beaches of the Kohala Coast. But when the sun does shine—usually part of nearly every day—the town sparkles, and, during winter, the snow glistens on Maunakea, 25 miles in the distance. Best of all is when the mists fall and the sun shines at the same time, leaving behind the colorful arches that earn Hilo its nickname: the City of Rainbows.

For a week every year in April, Hilo becomes the epicenter of the hula world when the Merrie Monarch Festival attracts tens of thousands of people to the renowned international event, steeped in traditions that represent the essence of Hilo's pioneering spirit. If you're planning a stay in Hilo during this time, be sure to book your room and car rentals at least eight months in advance.

Planning

Planning Your Time

Hilo is a great base for exploring the eastern and southern parts of the island, including Hawaii Volcanoes National Park; just be sure to bring an umbrella for—sporadic and sometimes torrential—showers. If you're passing through town or making a day-trip from either side of the island, you can focus your itinerary on the downtown area's museums, shops, and historical buildings. Street parking is relatively easy to find, and downtown is best experienced on foot. To experience all of what Hilo and the surrounding areas have to offer, book a two- or three-night stay. This will give you time to explore the sights in "Hawaii time," from gardens and natural sights to the Imiloa Astronomy Center. Early mornings in Hilo give you the best chance to enjoy sunny, blue skies before the afternoon clouds. If you're planning to visit in early April, keep in mind that the week-long Merrie Monarch Festival will make finding accommodations a challenge.

There are plenty of gas stations and restaurants in the area. Hilo is a good spot to load up on food and supplies—just south of downtown there are several large budget retailers. If you're here on Wednesday or Sunday, be sure to stop by the expansive Hilo Farmers Market to peruse stalls and stalls of produce, flowers, baked goods, coffee, honey, and more.

Getting Here and Around

AIR

Hilo International Airport is one of the island's two international airports, although flights to and from Kailua-Kona are more frequent. Still, this is the best airport to fly into if your main goal is to visit Hilo and Hawaii Volcanoes National Park.

AIRPORT Hilo International Airport (ITO). ✉ 2450 Kekuanaoa St., Hilo ☎ 808/961–9300 ⊕ www.airports.hawaii.gov/ito.

AIRPORT TRANSFERS

The Hilo airport is a five-minute drive from the hotels. There are no hotel shuttles to and from the airport. Take a taxi, Uber, or Lyft. You can also catch a Hele-On bus from the airport once every hour.

BUS

The Hele-On (⊕ www.heleonbus.org) public bus offers intra-Hilo transit service throughout town, but buses don't operate at night. For ultra-budget travelers, the Hele-On Bus is a cost-effective way to visit Hawaii Volcanoes National Park or Pahoa Town without having to rent a car. The cost is $2.

CAR

Bottom line, you must have a car to get around in Hilo. The rental car companies at the Hilo airport include Hertz, Alamo, Advantage, Budget, Dollar, and National. Off-site rental car companies in Hilo include Harper (⊕ www.harpershawaii.com) and Enterprise. Daily rates average $90 a day, not including taxes and fees. Reserve early, as fleets in Hilo are not as large as on the Kona side. If you're coming during the Merrie Monarch Festival, rental cars will be in short supply.

TAXI

A couple of taxi companies in Hilo provide relatively affordable rates. There are 17 taxi companies that service Hilo airport. Approximate cost to Hilo from the airport is $12, and to Banyan Drive hotels $10–$11. A taxi from Hilo to Volcano would cost around $70. There are rideshare (Uber and Lyft) services in Hilo, but wait times can be long.

CONTACTS AA Marshall's Taxi. ☎ 808/936–2654 ⊕ www.taxihilo.com. **Da Best Taxi Service.** ☎ 808/557–7059 ⊕ www.besttaxihilo.com.

Beaches

Hilo isn't exactly known for tropical white-sand beaches, but there are a few nice ones in the area that offer good swimming and snorkeling opportunities, and some are surrounded by lush rain forest.

Hotels

Hilo has a few decent hotels and one higher-end resort hotel. Bed-and-breakfasts occupy lovely historical homes and offer breakfasts that sometimes include ingredients from backyard gardens. Hawaii Volcanoes National Park is only a 40-minute drive, as are the sights of the Lower Puna region.

Hotel reviews have been shortened. For full information, visit Fodors.com.

Restaurants

The restaurant scene in Hilo is both eclectic and off the beaten path. As the saying goes, you can't judge a book by its cover; in this case some of the great culinary discoveries in Hilo are at seemingly hole-in-the-wall places. Some of the best eateries serve local-style specialties such as *laulau* (pulled pork and fish—usually salt cod—wrapped in taro leaves) *loco moco* (meat, rice, and eggs smothered in gravy), and mochi-covered strawberries, and Hilo restaurants also have immediate access to fresh-off-the-boat seafood.

Restaurant reviews have been shortened. For full information, visit Fodors. com.

What It Costs in U.S. Dollars			
$	$$	$$$	$$$$
RESTAURANTS			
under $17	$17–$26	$27–$35	over $35
HOTELS			
under $180	$180–$260	$261–$340	over $340

Downtown

Visitors to downtown Hilo might wonder why the bayfront shops and businesses are located such a distance from the actual bayfront. That's because the devastating tsunamis of 1946 and 1960 decimated the populated shoreline areas of Hilo's former downtown center. Still, local flavor abounds downtown, where vintage homes are the norm and businesses occupy older buildings, some historic. The Hilo Farmers Market, in full swing on Wednesday and Saturday, is a must-see here.

GETTING HERE AND AROUND
Driving around downtown Hilo can be confusing, even for longtime residents. The many one-way streets crisscross one another and meander in directions that can take you astray. The best thing to do is turn on your GPS app and hope that it can pronounce Hawaiian street names enough to be deciphered.

◉ Sights

Haili Congressional Church
RELIGIOUS SITE | Constructed in 1859 by New England missionaries, this church is known for its services in Hawaiian and for the choir, which sings hymns in Hawaiian. In 1902, Hawaiian musical legends Harry K. Naope Sr. and Albert Nahalea Sr. began the choral traditions still practiced by their descendants. The church, with its iconic yellow spire,

has an interesting history of being destroyed and rebuilt. ⊠ *211 Haili St., Hilo* ☎ *808/935–4847* ⊕ *www.hailichurch. org* ⊠ *Free, donations welcome.*

Kalakaua Park

CITY PARK | King Kalakaua (1836–1891), who revived the hula, was the inspiration for Hilo's Merrie Monarch Festival. A bronze statue, erected in 1988, depicts the king with a taro leaf in his left hand to signify the Hawaiian people's bond with the land. The park, a central town square, is surrounded by civic buildings and a war memorial, and also has a huge spreading banyan tree and small fishponds (but no picnic or recreation facilities). According to local tradition, families of military personnel often leave leftover floral displays and funeral wreaths along the fishpond walkway as a way of honoring and celebrating their loved ones. ⊠ *Kalakaua and Kinoole Sts., Hilo.*

Keawe Street

NEIGHBORHOOD | Buildings here have been restored to their original 1920s and '30s vintage plantation styles. Although most shopping is along Kamehameha Avenue, the ambience on Keawe Street offers a nostalgic sampling of Hilo as it might have been decades ago. Downtown Hilo won a major paint retailer's contest, so many of the buildings, which had a rain-worn, weathered look, are spruced up. ⊠ *Hilo.*

Lyman Museum and Mission House

MUSEUM | Built in 1839 by a missionary couple from New England, Sarah and David Lyman, the beautifully restored Lyman Mission House is the oldest wood-frame building on the island. On display are household utensils, artifacts, tools, and furniture used by the family, giving visitors a peek into the day-to-day lives of Hawaii's first missionaries. The Lymans hosted such literary dignitaries as Isabella Bird and Mark Twain here. The home is on the State and National Registers of Historic Places. Docent-guided tours are offered. An adjacent museum houses wonderful exhibits on volcanoes, island formation, island habitats and wildlife, marine shells, and minerals and gemstones. It also showcases native Hawaiian culture and immigrant ethnic groups. On permanent exhibit is a life-size replica of a traditional 1930s Korean home. The gift shop sells great Hawaiian-made items. ⊠ *276 Haili St., Hilo* ☎ *808/935–5021* ⊕ *www.lymanmuseum. org* ⊠ *$10* ⊘ *Closed Sun.*

Mokupapapa Discovery Center for Hawaii's Remote Coral Reefs

ZOO | FAMILY | This is a great place to learn about the stunning Papahanaumokuakea Marine National Monument, which encompasses nearly 140,000 square miles in the northwestern Hawaiian Islands and is the only mixed UNESCO World Heritage Site (meaning one that has both natural and cultural significance) in the United States. Giant murals, 3-D maps, and hands-on interactive kiosks depict the monument's extensive wildlife, including millions of birds and more than 7,000 marine species, many of which are found only in the Hawaiian archipelago. Knowledgeable staff and volunteers are on hand to answer questions. A 3,500-gallon aquarium and short films give insight into the unique features of the monument, as well as threats to its survival. Located in the refurbished F. Koehnen Building, the center is worth a stop just to get an up-close look at its huge stuffed albatross with wings outstretched or the monk seal exhibit. The price is right, too. ⊠ *F. Koehnen Bldg., 76 Kamehameha Ave., Hilo* ☎ *808/933–8180* ⊕ *www.papahanaumokuakea.gov/education/center.html* ⊠ *Free* ⊘ *Closed Sun. and Mon.*

Naha and Pinao stones

LOCAL INTEREST | These two huge, oblong stones are legendary. The Pinao stone is purportedly an entrance pillar of an ancient temple built near the Wailuku River. King Kamehameha I is said to have moved the 5,000-pound Naha

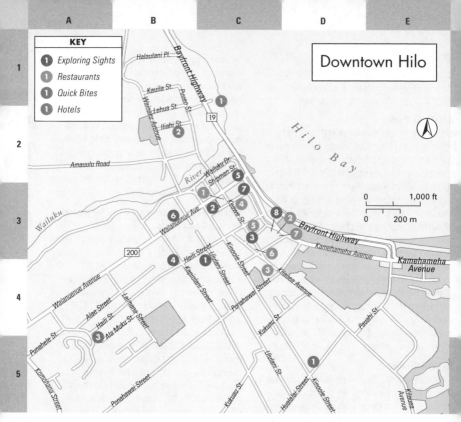

Downtown Hilo

A Walking Tour of Hilo

Put on some comfortable shoes, because all of the best downtown destinations are within easy walking distance of each other. Start your excursion in front of the public library, on Waianuenue Avenue, four blocks from Kamehameha Avenue. Here, you'll find the massive Naha and Pinao stones, which legend says King Kamehameha I was able to move as a teenager, thus foretelling that someday he would be a powerful king. Cross the road to walk southeast along Kapiolani Street, and turn right on Haili Street to visit the historic Lyman Museum and Mission House. Back on Haili Street, follow this busy road toward the ocean; on your right you'll pass Haili Church.

Soon you'll reach Keawe Street with its vintage, early-1900s shop fronts.

Stop at the Big Island Visitors Bureau on the right-hand corner for maps and brochures before taking a left. You'll bump into Kalakaua Street; for a quick respite turn left and rest on the benches in Kalakaua Park.

Continue *makai* (toward the ocean) on Kalakaua Street to visit the Pacific Tsunami Museum on the corner of Kalakaua and Kamehameha Avenues. Nearby, on the corner of Kamehameha and Waianuenue Avenues you'll find the free Mokupapapa Discovery Center for Hawaii's Remote Coral Reefs. After heading three blocks east along the picturesque bayfront, you'll come across the S. Hata Building, which has interesting shops and restaurants. You can't miss the Hilo Farmers Market, bustling with vendors and customers.

stone when he was still in his teens. Legend decreed that he who did so would become king of all the islands. The stones are in front of the Hilo Public Library. ⊠ *300 Waianuenue Ave., Hilo.*

Pacific Tsunami Museum

MUSEUM | FAMILY | A small but informative museum in a vintage First Hawaiian Bank building designed by a famous Hawaii architect provides tsunami education and scientific information. It may seem odd that downtown Hilo businesses tend to be far from the scenic bayfront, but tsunamis have killed more people in Hawaii than any other natural event, especially in Hilo. Visitors can peruse the poignant history of these devastating disasters, with accounts taken from tsunami survivors from Hawaii and worldwide. Exhibits include a wave machine and interactive tsunami warning center simulation as well as films and pictographs detailing recent tsunamis in Japan, Alaska, and

Indonesia. A safety-wall exhibit demonstrates how to be prepared and what steps to take during an evacuation. ⊠ *130 Kamehameha Ave., Hilo* ☎ *808/935–0926* ⊕ *www.tsunami.org* ⊠ *$8* ⊗ *Closed Sun. and Mon.*

S. Hata Building

STORE/MALL | Built as a general store in 1912 by Japanese immigrant and businessman Sadanosuke Hata and his family, this structure now houses galleries, a restaurant, and other small shops. When first built, it was one of the only buildings in Hawaii constructed out of concrete. During World War II, Hata family members were interned because of their heritage, and the building was confiscated by the U.S. government. When the war was over, a daughter repurchased it for $100,000. A beautiful example of Renaissance revival architecture, it won an award from the state for the authenticity of its restoration. The building is very close to the Hilo Farmers Market. ✉ *308 Kamehameha Ave., at Mamo St., Hilo.*

🍴 Restaurants

★ Bears' Coffee

$ | **DINER** | **FAMILY** | A fixture downtown since the late 1980s, this favorite, cozy breakfast spot is much loved for its fresh-fruit waffles and tasty morning coffee. For lunch the little diner serves up huge deli sandwiches and decent entrée-size salads, plus specials like hearty meat loaf, roasted chicken, and pot roast. **Known for:** reliable breakfasts; bear wallpaper and decor; specialty coffee such as the iced toddy cold brew. [$] *Average main: $10* ✉ *106 Keawe St., Hilo* ☎ *808/935–0708* 🕒 *No dinner.*

Café Pesto

$$ | **ITALIAN** | Located in a beautiful high-ceiling venue in the historical S. Hata building, Café Pesto offers creative pizzas with ingredients such as fresh Hamakua mushrooms, artichokes, and Gorgonzola. **Known for:** use of local farm produce; wood-fired pizza; happy hour from 2 pm. [$] *Average main: $20* ✉ *308 Kamehameha Ave., Hilo* ☎ *808/969–6640* 🌐 *www.cafepesto.com.*

Lucy's Taqueria

$ | **MEXICAN** | This little Mexican restaurant boasts a big menu brimming with consistently good traditional taqueria fare. The bar serves beer on tap and Mexican imports. **Known for:** all-day Mexican breakfast; affordable takeout within walking distance of downtown; local produce. [$] *Average main: $10* ✉ *194 Kilauea Ave., Hilo* ☎ *808/315–8246* 🌐 *lucystaqueria.com* 🕒 *Closed Tues.*

Moon and Turtle

$$$ | **INTERNATIONAL** | This sophisticated, intimate restaurant in a bayfront building offers a classy selection of international fare with the focus on locally sourced meats, produce, and seafood. The menu changes daily (see the Facebook page), but mushroom pappardelle is a highlight, along with seafood chowder, spicy *kajiki* (marlin) tartare, and crispy whole-fried *moi* (Pacific threadfin). **Known for:** smoky ahi sashimi; lychee martinis infused with Hawaiian influences; high prices for Hilo. [$] *Average main: $30* ✉ *51 Kalakaua St., Hilo* ☎ *808/961–0599* 🕒 *Closed Sun. and Mon.*

Ocean Sushi

$ | **JAPANESE** | **FAMILY** | What this casual restaurant lacks in ambience, it certainly makes up for in quality and value. We're talking about light and crispy tempura; tender, moist teriyaki chicken; and about 25 specialty sushi rolls, all at unbeatable prices. **Known for:** bento plates; hospital roll with shrimp tempura, cream cheese, and spicy ahi; good kids' menu. [$] *Average main: $12* ✉ *235 Keawe St., Hilo* ☎ *808/961–6625* 🕒 *Closed Sun.*

Pineapples

$ | **AMERICAN** | **FAMILY** | If you expect that a restaurant named Pineapples would serve tropical beverages in hollowed-out pineapples, you'd be exactly correct. Always packed, this open-air bistro looks like a tourist trap, but there is a fine-dining component to the menu, which includes fresh catch, *kalbi* ribs (grilled, Korean-style), teriyaki flank steak, burgers, wraps, and sandwiches. **Known for:** surprisingly inventive island cuisine; great pineapple salsa; live entertainment nightly. [$] *Average main: $14* ✉ *332 Keawe St, Hilo* ☎ *808/238–5324* 🕒 *Closed Mon.*

Reuben's Mexican Restaurant

$ | **MEXICAN** | **FAMILY** | It's not the best Mexican food you've ever had, but if you're jonesing for some carne asada or chicken flautas, Reuben's has you pretty well covered. You can make a meal out of the warm chips and salsa alone. **Known for:** reasonable prices; generous portions; house-made margarita mix with flavors such as lilikoi (passion fruit), guava, and mango. [$] *Average main: $10* ✉ *336 Kamehameha Ave., Hilo* ☎ *808/961–2552.*

Coffee and Quick Bites

K's Drive-In

$ | **HAWAIIAN** | Unassuming from the outside, this small, local-style plate-lunch eatery serves up top-quality genuine Hawaiian specialties in Hilo. All the staples are here, from *kalua* (earth oven–baked) pig to shoyu chicken and pork adobo, so order at the takeout window and grab a seat at one of the picnic tables outside. **Known for:** wide variety of loco moco (meat, rice, and eggs smothered in gravy); extremely affordable prices; favorite among locals. [$] *Average main: $8* ✉ *194 Hualalai St., Hilo* ☎ *808/935–5573* 🌐 *www.ksdrivein.com.*

Hotels

The Bay House Bed and Breakfast

$$ | **B&B/INN** | Overlooking Hilo Bay and just steps away from the Singing Bridge near Hilo's historical downtown area, this small, quiet B&B is vibrantly decorated, with Hawaiian-quilted beds and private lanai in each of the three rooms. **Pros:** oceanfront lanai in each room; cliffside hot tub; Hilo Bay views. **Cons:** only two people per room; occasional street noise; no twin beds. [$] *Rooms from: $189* ✉ *42 Pukihae St., Hilo* ☎ *888/235–8195, 808/961–6311* 🌐 *www.bayhousehawaii.com* 🛏 *3 rooms* 🍴 *Free breakfast.*

Dolphin Bay Hotel

$ | **HOTEL** | **FAMILY** | Units in this circa-1950s motor lodge are modest but charming, as well as clean and inexpensive; a glowing lava flow sign marks the office and bespeaks owner John Alexander's passion for the volcano. **Pros:** great value; full kitchens in all units; helpful and pleasant staff. **Cons:** no pool; no phones in the rooms; dated decor. [$] *Rooms from: $129* ✉ *333 Iliahi St., Hilo* ☎ *808/935–1466* 🌐 *www.dolphinbayhotel.com* 🛏 *18 rooms* 🍴 *No meals.*

Hilo Honu Inn

$ | **B&B/INN** | A charming old Craftsman home lovingly restored by a friendly and hospitable couple from North Carolina, the Hilo Honu offers quite a bit of variety in room decor. **Pros:** spectacular Hilo Bay views; historical setting; within walking distance of Hilo bayfront. **Cons:** no toddlers in the upstairs suite; not on the beach; a/c in only two of the three rooms. [$] *Rooms from: $150* ✉ *465 Haili St., Hilo* ☎ *808/935–4325* 🌐 *www.hilohonu.com* 🛏 *3 rooms* 🍴 *Free breakfast.*

Nightlife

BARS

Cronies Bar and Grill

BARS/PUBS | A sports bar by night and a good hamburger joint by day, Cronies is a local favorite. When the lights go down, the bar gets packed. ✉ *11 Waianuenue Ave., Hilo* ☎ *808/935–5158* 🌐 *www.cronieshawaii.com.*

Performing Arts

FESTIVALS

KWXX Hoolaulea

MUSIC FESTIVALS | For more than two decades, a local radio station has sponsored the largest free concert on the island. This famous *hoolaulea* (party) takes place mid-September in downtown Hilo, attracting a bounty of Big Island musical talent featuring Hawaiian, reggae, and island music styles. Some big names play here on four different stages, and there is dancing in the streets along the bayfront, rain or shine. ✉ *257 Kamehameha Ave., Hilo* ☎ *808/935–5461* 🌐 *www.kwxx.com.*

★ **Merrie Monarch Festival**

CULTURAL FESTIVALS | The mother of all Hawaii festivals, the world-class Merrie Monarch celebrates all things hula for one fantastic week every April in Hilo with competitions, activities, parades, and more. The esteemed event honors the legacy of King David Kalakaua, the man responsible for reviving fading

Hawaiian cultural traditions including hula. The three-day hula competition is staged at the Edith Kanakaole Multi-Purpose Stadium during the first week following Easter Sunday. Hula *halau* (studios) worldwide come to perform both *kahiko* (ancient) and *auana* (modern) dance styles, both solo and in groups.
■ TIP→ **You should reserve accommodations and rental cars up to a year in advance. Ticket requests must be mailed and postmarked after December 1 of the preceding year.** ⊠ *Edith Kanakaole Multi-Purpose Stadium, 350 Kalanikoa St., Hilo* ☎ *808/935–9168* ⊕ *www.merriemonarch.com.*

FILM
★ Palace Theater
FILM | This historic theater dating from the silent-movie era (1925) survived Hilo's many tsunamis and has been beautifully restored through community support. Today, it showcases everything from film festivals and old movies to musical productions and holiday concerts. There are even $10 jazz nights in the lobby and performances by big-name artists. It's open during the day, so you can have a peek through the curtains at the lovely vintage details and feel like you stepped back in time. ⊠ *38 Haili St., Hilo* ☎ *808/934–7010* ⊕ *www.hilopalace.com.*

🛍 Shopping

CLOTHING AND SHOES
Sig Zane Designs
CLOTHING | The acclaimed boutique sells distinctive island wearables with bold colors and motifs designed by the legendary Sig Zane, known for his artwork honoring native flora and fauna. All apparel is handcrafted in Hawaii, and is often worn by local celebrities and businesspeople. ⊠ *122 Kamehameha Ave., Hilo* ☎ *808/935–7077* ⊕ *www.sigzane.com.*

FOOD
★ Sugar Coast Candy
FOOD/CANDY | Located on the bayfront in downtown Hilo, this beautifully decorated candy boutique is a blast from the past, featuring an amazing array of nostalgic candies, artisan chocolates, and wooden barrels overflowing with saltwater taffy and other delights. ⊠ *274 Kamehameha Ave., Hilo* ☎ *808/935–6960.*

Two Ladies Kitchen
FOOD/CANDY | This hole-in-the-wall confections shop has made a name for itself thanks to its pillowy mochi. The proprietors are best known for their huge ripe strawberries wrapped in a white mochi covering, which won't last as long as a box of chocolates—most mochi items are good for only two or three days. To guarantee you get your fill, call and place your order ahead of time. ⊠ *274 Kilauea Ave., Hilo* ☎ *808/961–4766.*

GIFTS AND SOUVENIRS
Most Irresistible Shop in Hilo
GIFTS/SOUVENIRS | This place lives up to its name by stocking unique gifts from around the Pacific, be it pure Hawaiian ohia lehua honey, Kau coffee, aloha wear, or tinkling wind chimes. ⊠ *256 Kamehameha Ave., Hilo* ☎ *808/935–9644.*

HOME DECOR
Dragon Mama
HOUSEHOLD ITEMS/FURNITURE | Step into this hip downtown Hilo spot to find authentic Japanese fabrics, futons, and gifts along with an elegant selection of clothing, sleepwear, and tea-service accoutrements. Handmade comforters, pillows, and futon pads are sewn of natural fibers on-site. ⊠ *266 Kamehameha Ave., Hilo* ☎ *808/934–9081* ⊕ *www.dragonmama.com.*

MARKETS
★ Hilo Farmers Market
OUTDOOR/FLEA/GREEN MARKETS | The 200 vendors here—stretching a couple of blocks at the bayfront—sell a profusion of tropical flowers, locally grown

Liliuokalani Gardens, the largest ornamental Japanese garden outside of Japan, was built in 1917 to honor the island's first Japanese immigrants.

produce, aromatic honey, tangy goat cheese, hot breakfast and lunch items, and fresh baked specialties at extraordinary prices. This colorful, open-air market—the largest and most popular on the island—opens for business Wednesday and Saturday from 6 am to 4 pm. A smaller version on the other days features more than 30 vendors. ⊠ *Kamehameha Ave. and Mamo St., Hilo* ☎ *808/933–1000* ⊕ *www.hilofarmersmarket.com.*

🏃 Activities

SPAS

Spa Vive

FITNESS/HEALTH CLUBS | Located in historic downtown Hilo, this no-frills day spa and salon features six massage treatment rooms and aesthetician services. Body scrubs and waxings are also available upon request. ⊠ *224 Kamehameha Ave., Hilo* ☎ *808/930–3830* ⊕ *www.spavive. com* ✉ *Massages from $49, facials from $69.*

Liliuokalani Gardens and Reeds Bay

The hotel district near Banyan Drive is within walking distance of nearby scenic Liliuokalani Gardens. To its east, Reeds Bay is small and idyllic, surrounded by a tiny sand beach and some parks with picnic tables. There's a lot of local activity here, including kayaking, fishing, swimming, and stand-up paddleboarding. Several bayside restaurants are within walking distance of the hotels, some with spectacular bayfront views.

GETTING AROUND

Located along Banyan Drive and Lihiwai Street, this beautiful Japanese garden is within easy walking distance of the Banyan Drive hotels and Reeds Bay. You can stroll the meandering pathways in the garden and explore the parks on nearby Reeds Bay.

Sights

Banyan Drive

NEIGHBORHOOD | More than 50 enormous banyan trees with aerial roots dangling from their limbs were planted along the road, mostly during the 1930s but also after World War II, by visiting celebrities. Names such as Amelia Earhart and Franklin Delano Roosevelt can be seen on plaques affixed to the trees. A scenic loop beginning at the Grand Naniloa Hotel Hilo (93 Banyan Drive) makes a nice walk, especially in the evening when thousands of mynah birds roost. ✉ *Hilo.*

Liliuokalani Gardens

GARDEN | Designed to honor Hawaii's first Japanese immigrants and named after Hawaii's last reigning monarch, Liliuokalani Gardens' 30 acres of fish-filled ponds, stone lanterns, half-moon bridges, elegant pagodas, and a ceremonial teahouse make it a favorite Sunday destination. You'll see weddings, picnics, and families as you stroll. The surrounding area, once a busy residential neighborhood on Waiakea peninsula, was destroyed by a 1960 tsunami that caused widespread devastation and killed 61 people. ✉ *Banyan Dr., at Lihiwai St., Hilo* 🎟 *Free.*

Moku Ola (*Coconut Island*)

ISLAND | **FAMILY** | Also known as Coconut Island, this small island sits just offshore from Liliuokalani Gardens. Accessible via a footbridge, it was considered a place of healing in ancient times. Today it's a nicely manicured spot where children play in the tide pools and fisherfolk try their luck. ✉ *Banyan Dr., Hilo.*

Wailoa Center

MUSEUM | In Wailoa State Recreation Area, a beautiful park setting near downtown Hilo, this circular exhibition center mounts monthly shows featuring impressive work from local artists. Pieces range from photography, pottery, contemporary painting, quilts, glassworks, multimedia, and woodworking to musical instruments and artwork depicting Hawaii's native species. A visitor information center is also here. ✉ *200 Piopio St., off Kamehameha Ave., Hilo* ☎ *808/933–0416* 🌐 *www.wailoacenter.com* 🎟 *Free* 🕒 *Closed weekends.*

Beaches

Reeds Bay Beach Park

BEACH—SIGHT | Safe swimming, proximity to downtown Hilo, and a freshwater-fed swimming hole called the Ice Pond that flows into the backwaters of Hilo Bay are the enticements of this cove. No, there really isn't ice in the swimming hole; it just feels that way on a hot, sultry day. The large pond, between Hilo Seaside Hotel and the Ponds Hilo Restaurant, is a favorite of local kids, who enjoy jumping into and frolicking in the chilly fresh- and saltwater mix. The water is usually calm. **Amenities:** parking (no fee); showers. **Best for:** swimming. ✉ *277 Kalanianaole Ave., Hilo.*

Restaurants

Happy Valley Seafood Restaurant

$ | **CHINESE** | Don't let the name fool you: though Hilo's best Chinese restaurant does specialize in seafood, it also offers many other Cantonese treats, including salt-and-pepper pork, Mongolian lamb, and vegetarian specialties like garlic eggplant and crispy green beans. The food is good, portions are large, and the price is right, but don't come here expecting any ambience—this is a funky, cheap Chinese restaurant, with a few random pieces of artwork tacked up here and there. **Known for:** authentic Cantonese Chinese food; salt-and-pepper prawns; good soups. [$] *Average main: $12* ✉ *1263 Kilauea Ave., Suite 320, Hilo* ☎ *808/933–1083.*

★ Hilo Bay Cafe

$$ | **AMERICAN** | Overlooking Hilo Bay from its towering perch on the waterfront, this popular, upscale restaurant

has a sophisticated second-floor dining room that looks like it's straight out of Manhattan. A sushi bar complements the excellent selection of fresh fish, pork, beef, and vegan options. **Known for:** excellent bayside views; Blue Bay burger with shoestring fries; most upscale restaurant in Hilo. $ *Average main: $22* ⊠ *123 Lihiwai St., Hilo* ☎ *808/935–4939* ⊕ *www. hilobaycafe.com* ☉ *Closed Sun.*

★ Ken's House of Pancakes

$ | **DINER** | **FAMILY** | For years, this 24-hour diner near Banyan Drive between the airport and the hotels has been a gathering place for Hilo residents and visitors. Breakfast is the main attraction: Ken's serves 11 types of pancakes, plus all kinds of fruit waffles (banana, peach) and popular omelets, like the Da Bradda, teeming with meats. **Known for:** local landmark with old-fashioned vibe; extensive menu of Hawaiian and diner fare; weekly special nights like Sunday spaghetti and Tuesday tacos. $ *Average main: $15* ⊠ *1730 Kamehameha Ave., Hilo* ☎ *808/935–8711* ⊕ *www.ken-shouseofpancakes.com.*

Ponds Hilo

$$ | **HAWAIIAN** | **FAMILY** | Perched on the waterfront overlooking a serene and scenic pond, this restaurant has the look and feel of an old-fashioned, harborside steak house and bar. The menu features a good range of burgers and salads, steak, and seafood. **Known for:** Thursday lobster night; excellent fish and chips; popular Sunday brunch. $ *Average main: $20* ⊠ *135 Kalanianaole Ave., Hilo* ☎ *808/934–7663* ⊕ *www.pondshilo.com.*

★ Sombat's Fresh Thai Cuisine

$$ | **THAI** | There's a reason why locals flock to this hideaway for the best Thai cuisine in Hilo. Fresh local ingredients highlight proprietor Sombat Saenguthai's menu (many of the herbs come from her own garden) to create authentic and tasty Thai treats like coconut curries, fresh basil rolls, eggplant stir-fry, and green papaya salad. **Known for:** famous

pad Thai sauce available for purchase; friendly service; single owner and chef. $ *Average main: $17* ⊠ *Waiakea Kai Plaza, 88 Kanoelehue Ave., Hilo* ⊹ *Close to Ken's House of Pancakes* ☎ *808/969–9336* ⊕ *www.sombats.com* ☉ *Closed Sun. No lunch.*

☕ Coffee and Quick Bites

Cafe 100

$ | **HAWAIIAN** | **FAMILY** | Established in 1948, this family-owned restaurant is famous for its tasty *loco moco* (meat, rice, and eggs smothered in gravy), prepared in more than three dozen ways (with different meats, chicken, vegetables, and fish), and its low-priced breakfast and lunch specials. The word "restaurant," or even "café," is used loosely—you order at a window and eat on one of the outdoor benches provided—but you come here for the food, prices, and authentic, old-Hilo experience. **Known for:** local flavor; the Super Loco Moco; generous portions. $ *Average main: $6* ⊠ *969 Kilauea Ave., Hilo* ☎ *808/935–8683* ⊕ *www.cafe100. com* ☉ *Closed Sun.*

Verna's Drive-In

$ | **HAWAIIAN** | Verna's is tried and true among locals, who come for the juicy homemade burgers and filling plate lunches, and the price is right with a burger combo that includes fries and a drink. If you're hungry for more, try the traditional Hawaiian plate with either *laulau*, beef stew, chicken long rice, or lomilomi salmon. **Known for:** local grindz 24/7 with outdoor seating; smoked meat plate lunch; superlow prices. $ *Average main: $6* ⊠ *1765 Kamehameha Ave., Hilo* ☎ *808/935–2776.*

🛏 Hotels

Grand Naniloa Hotel Hilo–a DoubleTree by Hilton

$ | **HOTEL** | **FAMILY** | Hilo isn't known for its fancy resort hotels, but the Grand Naniloa, built in 1939, attempts to

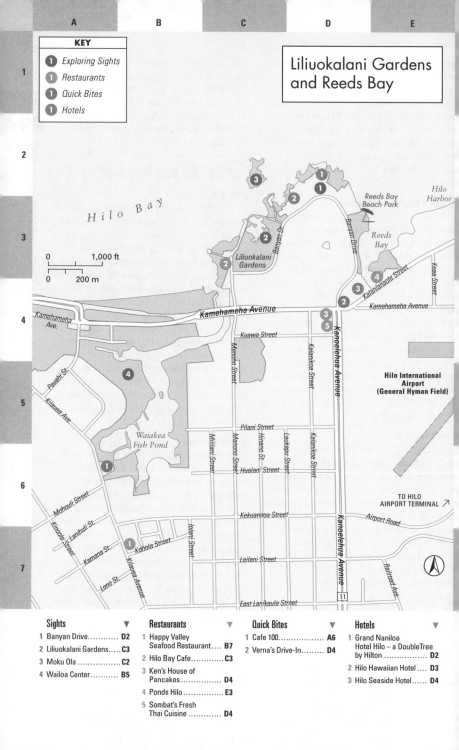

Liliuokalani Gardens and Reeds Bay

KEY
- 1 Exploring Sights
- 1 Restaurants
- 1 Quick Bites
- 1 Hotels

Hilo Bay

Hilo Harbor

Reeds Bay Beach Park

Reeds Bay

Liliuokalani Gardens

0 ——— 1,000 ft
0 ——— 200 m

Kamehameha Avenue

Kamehameha Ave.

Kamehameha Avenue

Banyan Dr.

Banyan Drive

Kanoelehua Avenue

Kanoelehua Avenue

Katanianaole Street

Keaa Street

Kuawa Street

Manono Street

Kalanikoa Street

Hilo International Airport
(General Hyman Field)

Waiakea Fish Pond

Peuahi St.

Kilauea Ave.

Mililani Street

Manono Street

Hinano St.

Laukapu Street

Kalanikoa Street

Pilani Street

Hualani Street

Kekuanaoa Street

Airport Road

TO HILO
AIRPORT TERMINAL ↗

Mohouli Street

Kinoole Street

Lanihuli St.

Kamana St.

Kilauea Avenue

Iolani Street

Kohola Street

Leilani Street

Long St.

East Lanikaula Street

Railroad Ave.

11

Sights ▼	Restaurants ▼	Quick Bites ▼	Hotels ▼
1 Banyan Drive............ **D2**	1 Happy Valley Seafood Restaurant.... **B7**	1 Cafe 100................. **A6**	1 Grand Naniloa Hotel Hilo – a DoubleTree by Hilton **D2**
2 Liliuokalani Gardens..... **C3**	2 Hilo Bay Cafe............ **C3**	2 Verna's Drive-In.......... **D4**	2 Hilo Hawaiian Hotel **D3**
3 Moku Ola **C2**	3 Ken's House of Pancakes................ **D4**		3 Hilo Seaside Hotel...... **D4**
4 Wailoa Center........... **B5**	4 Ponds Hilo **E3**		
	5 Sombat's Fresh Thai Cuisine **D4**		

emedy that situation in grand fashion, paying homage to hula, Hawaiian culture, and Big Island adventures. **Pros:** walking distance to botanical park and Coconut Island; rental kayaks, bikes, and SUPs; free golf at adjacent 9-hole course and driving range. **Cons:** some rooms don't have ocean views; limited parking spaces; small swimming pool. $ *Rooms from: $149* ⌂ *93 Banyan Dr., Hilo* ☎ *808/969–3333* ⊕ *www.grandnaniloahi-lo.com* ➫ *388 rooms* ⊚ *No meals.*

Hilo Hawaiian Hotel
$ | HOTEL | FAMILY | This landmark hotel has large bayfront rooms offering spectacular views of Maunakea and Coconut Island on Hilo Bay. Street-side rooms overlook the golf course, and the hotel is within walking distance to the botanical park. **Pros:** Hilo Bay views; private lanai in most rooms; free parking. **Cons:** pricey breakfast buffet; older hotel; lacks amenities. $ *Rooms from: $129* ⌂ *71 Banyan Dr., Hilo* ☎ *808/935–9361, 800/367–5004 from mainland, 800/272–5275 interisland* ⊕ *www.castleresorts.com* ➫ *286 rooms* ⊚ *No meals.*

Hilo Seaside Hotel
$ | HOTEL | Ten minutes from the airport, this local-flavor destination is a friendly, laid-back, and otherwise peaceful place, with tropical rooms that have private lanai. **Pros:** private lanai; friendly staff; budget friendly with frequent specials. **Cons:** not walking distance to historic bayfront; hotel is a little dated; no restaurant. $ *Rooms from: $99* ⌂ *126 Banyan Way, Hilo* ☎ *808/935–0821, 800/560–5557* ⊕ *www.hiloseasidehotel.com* ➫ *133 rooms* ⊚ *No meals.*

⊕ Shopping

BOOKSTORES
★ Basically Books
BOOKS/STATIONERY | The legendary shop stocks one of Hawaii's largest selections of maps, including topographical and relief maps, and Hilo's largest selection

of Hawaiian music (feel free to ask for advice about your selection). Of course, it also has a wealth of books about Hawaii, including great choices for children. If you're in need of an umbrella on a rainy Hilo day, this bookstore has plenty of them. ⌂ *1672 Kamehameha Ave., Hilo* ✛ *Near Ken's House of Pancakes* ☎ *808/961–0144* ⊕ *www.basicallybooks. com.*

Greater Hilo

Sights beyond the downtown area spread out in every direction and are often interspersed in between residential neighborhoods and industrial parks. Be sure to check out Panaewa Rainforest Zoo with its Hawaiian animals and hundreds of species of tropical plants. Above the University of Hilo campus, the Imiloa Astronomy Center has a planetarium and gift shop. For other things to do, Big Island Candies is a must-visit destination for world-class confections. Heading toward Hamakua, there are beaches, surf spots, a botanical garden, small towns, and the famed Akaka Falls (at the beginning of the Hamakua coast).

GETTTING HERE AND AROUND
You need a car to explore the spread-out sights in this area, but drive carefully. Some roads around Hilo are treacherous, riddled with potholes, unexpected turns, fast traffic, one-way streets, and confusing intersections. Take extra precautions at night, and always make sure you know where you're going before you get in your car. Don't get discouraged if you get temporarily lost. Getting disoriented when driving in Hilo happens to the best of Big Island residents.

⊙ Sights

Boiling Pots
BODY OF WATER | Four separate streams fall into a series of circular pools here, forming the Peepee Falls. The resulting

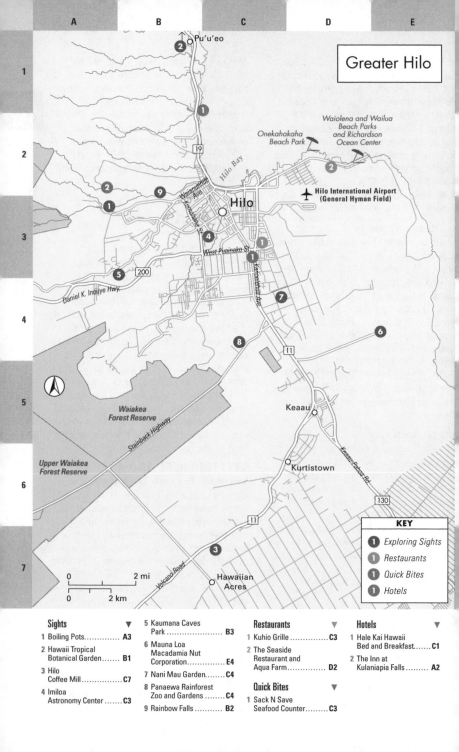

Greater Hilo

	A	B	C	D	E

Pu'u'eo

Waiolena and Wailua
Beach Parks
and Richardson
Ocean Center

Onekahakaha
Beach Park

Hilo Bay

Hilo

Hilo International Airport
(General Hyman Field)

Waianuenue Ave.

Kamehameha St.

West Puainako St.

Kamehameha Ave.

Daniel K. Inouye Hwy.

Keaau

Waiakea
Forest Reserve

Stainback Highway

Upper Waiakea
Forest Reserve

Kurtistown

Keaau-Pahoa Rd.

Volcano Road

**Hawaiian
Acres**

0   2 mi
0   2 km

KEY

1 *Exploring Sights*
1 *Restaurants*
1 *Quick Bites*
1 *Hotels*

Sights ▾

1 Boiling Pots.............. **A3**

2 Hawaii Tropical
Botanical Garden....... **B1**

3 Hilo
Coffee Mill.............. **C7**

4 Imiloa
Astronomy Center....... **C3**

5 Kaumana Caves
Park **B3**

6 Mauna Loa
Macadamia Nut
Corporation.............. **E4**

7 Nani Mau Garden........ **C4**

8 Panaewa Rainforest
Zoo and Gardens **C4**

9 Rainbow Falls **B2**

Restaurants ▾

1 Kuhio Grille **C3**

2 The Seaside
Restaurant and
Aqua Farm............... **D2**

Quick Bites ▾

1 Sack N Save
Seafood Counter......... **C3**

Hotels ▾

1 Hale Kai Hawaii
Bed and Breakfast....... **C1**

2 The Inn at
Kulaniapia Falls **A2**

turbulent action—best seen after a good rain—has earned this scenic stretch of the Wailuku River the nickname Boiling Pots. There's no swimming allowed at Peepee Falls or anywhere in the Wailuku River, due to extremely dangerous currents and undertows. The falls are 3 miles northwest of Hilo off Waianuenue Avenue; keep to the right when the road splits and look for the sign. The gate opens at 7 am and closes at 6 pm. △ **You may be tempted, as you watch others ignore the signs and climb over guardrails, to jump in, but resist. Swimming is expressly prohibited and unsafe, and people have died here.** You may want to combine a drive to this site with a visit to Rainbow Falls, a bit closer to downtown. ⊠ *Wailuku River State Park, Off Waianuenue Ave., Hilo* ⊕ *dlnr.hawaii.gov/dsp/parks/hawaii/wailuku-river-state-park* ⊠ *Free.*

Hawaii Tropical Botanical Garden

GARDEN | Stunning coastline views appear around each curve of the 4-mile scenic jungle drive that accesses this privately owned nature preserve next to Onomea Bay. Paved pathways in the 17-acre botanical garden lead past ponds, waterfalls, and more than 2,000 species of plants and flowers, including palms, bromeliads, ginger, heliconia, orchids, and ornamentals. The garden is well worth a stop, and your entry fee helps the nonprofit preserve plants, seeds, and rain forests for future generations. Trails can get slippery when it's raining. ⊠ *27-717 Old Mamalahoa Hwy., Papaikou* ⊹ *8 miles north of downtown Hilo* ☎ *808/964–5233* ⊕ *www.htbg.com* ⊠ *$25.*

Hilo Coffee Mill

FACTORY | With all the buzz about Kona coffee, it's easy to forget that estate-grown coffee is produced throughout the rest of the island. The Hilo Coffee Mill, located on 24 acres in lush Mountain View, is a pleasant reminder of that. In addition to farming its own coffee on-site, the mill has partnered with several small coffee

farmers in East Hawaii in an effort to put the region on the world's coffee map. You can sample their efforts, tour the mill, and watch the roasters in action. They host a farmers' market every Saturday from 9 to 2. ⊠ *17-995 Volcano Rd. (Hwy. 11), between mile markers 12 and 13, Mountain View* ☎ *808/968–1333* ⊕ *www.hilocoffeemill.com* ⊠ *Free* ⊗ *Closed Sun. and Mon.*

★ Imiloa Astronomy Center

OBSERVATORY | Part Hawaiian cultural center, part astronomy museum, this center provides an educational and cultural complement to the research being conducted atop 14,000-foot Maunakea. Although visitors are welcome at Maunakea, its primary function is as a research facility—not observatory, museum, or education center. Those roles have been taken on by Imiloa in a big way. With its interactive exhibits, full-dome planetarium shows, and regularly scheduled talks and events, the center is a must-see for anyone interested in the stars, the planets, or Hawaiian culture and history. Five minutes from downtown Hilo, near the University of Hawaii at Hilo, the center also provides an important link between the scientific research being conducted at Maunakea and its history as a sacred mountain for the Hawaiian people. Admission includes one planetarium show and an all-day pass to the exhibit hall, which features more than 100 interactive displays. The lunch buffet at the adjoining Sky Garden Restaurant is popular and affordable. ⊠ *University of Hawaii at Hilo Science and Technology Park, 600 Imiloa Pl., off Nowelo and Komohana, Hilo* ☎ *808/969–9700* ⊕ *www.imiloahawaii.org* ⊠ *$17.50* ⊗ *Closed Mon.*

Kaumana Caves Park

CAVE | Thanks to Hilo's abundant rainfall, this lava tube is lush with plant life. Concrete stairs lead down to the 2½-mile-long tube. There are no lighted areas and the ground is uneven and damp, so wear sturdy shoes, bring a flashlight, and explore as far as you dare to go. There are restrooms and a covered picnic table at the cave, and parking across the street. ⚠ **Heed all warning signs when entering the caves.** ✉ *1492 Kaumana Dr., Hilo* 💲 *Free.*

Mauna Loa Macadamia Nut Corporation

FACTORY | Acres of macadamia nut trees lead to a giant roasting facility and processing plant with viewing windows and self-guided tours. You can even watch demonstrations showing how they coat nuts and shortbread cookies with milk chocolate to create their famous products. There are free samples and plenty of gift boxes with mac nuts in every conceivable form of presentation for sale in the visitor center. There is no factory processing on weekends or holidays. Children can burn off extra energy on a nature trail. ✉ *16-701 Macadamia Rd., off Hwy. 11, Hilo* ✛ *5 miles south of Hilo* 📞 *808/966–8618, 888/628–6256* ⊕ *www. maunaloa.com.*

Nani Mau Garden

GARDEN | The name means "forever beautiful" in Hawaiian, and that's a good description of this 2-acre botanical garden (part of an event venue) filled with several varieties of fruit trees, rare palms, and hundreds of varieties of ginger, orchids, anthuriums, and other exotic plants. It was originally planted by a Japanese immigrant. Take a stroll and stay for an affordable lunch. ■**TIP**➔ **The restaurant offers a daily buffet lunch plus garden admission package.** ✉ *421 Makalika St., off Hwy. 11, Hilo* 📞 *808/959–3500* ⊕ *www.nanimaugardens.com* 💲 *$10* 🕙 *Closed weekends.*

★ Panaewa Rainforest Zoo and Gardens

ZOO | **FAMILY** | Billed as "the only natural tropical rain forest zoo in the United States," this sweet zoo features native Hawaiian species such as the state bird, the nene goose, and the *io* (hawk), as well as lots of other rare birds, monkeys, sloths, and lemurs. Two Bengal

tigers are also part of the collection. The white-faced whistling tree ducks are a highlight. There's a petting zoo on Saturdays from 1:30 to 2:30. It's a joy to stroll the grounds, which are landscaped with hundreds of species of lush and unusual tropical plants. To get here, turn left on Mamaki off Highway 11; it's just past the "Kulani 19, Stainback Hwy." sign. ✉ *800 Stainback Hwy., Hilo* 📞 *808/959–7224* 💲 *Free, donations encouraged.*

Rainbow Falls

BODY OF WATER | After a hard rain, these impressive falls thunder into the Wailuku River gorge, often creating magical rainbows in the mist. Rainbow Falls, sometimes known as the "Hilo Town Falls," are located just above downtown Hilo. Take Waianuenue Avenue west for a mile; when the road forks, stay right and look for the Hawaiian warrior sign. They remain open during daylight hours. If you're visiting the falls, you can also drive to the Boiling Pots, also inside the park but a bit farther from downtown. At this site, four streams fall into a series of turbulent pools. ✉ *Wailuku River State Park, Rainbow Dr., Hilo* ⊕ *dlnr.hawaii.gov/dsp/parks/hawaii* 💲 *Free.*

⚓ Beaches

Honolii Beach Park

BEACH—SIGHT | One of the most consistent places on the east side to catch a wave, Honolii is popular with the local surf crowd. The beach is a mix of black sand, coral, and sea glass, with plenty of rocks. A shady grassy area is great for picnics while you watch the surfers. ⚠ **The presence of surfers is not an indication that an area is safe for swimmers. Winter surf is very rough.** A pond just to the north is good for swimming, but it's deep and there is a drop-off. There's limited parking on the narrow roadside. Walk down the stairs and veer left over the rocks. **Amenities:** lifeguards; toilets. **Best for:** surfing. ✉ *Hwy. 19, Hilo* ✛ *1½ miles north of Hilo* 📞 *808/961–8311.*

Onekahakaha Beach Park

BEACH—SIGHT | **FAMILY** | Shallow, rock-wall-enclosed tide pools and an adjacent grassy picnic area make this park a favorite among Hilo families with small children. The protected pools are great places to look for Hawaiian marine life like sea urchins and anemones. There isn't much white sand, but access to the water is easy. The water is usually rough beyond the line of large boulders protecting the inner tide pools, so be careful if the surf is high. This beach gets crowded on weekends. **Amenities:** lifeguards (weekends, holidays, and summer only); parking (no fee); showers; toilets. **Best for:** swimming. ✉ *Onekahakaha Rd. and Kalanianaole Ave., via Kanoelehua St., Hilo* ✥ *3 miles east of Hilo* ☎ *808/961–8311.*

Waiolena and Wailua Beach Parks and Richardson Ocean Center

BEACH—SIGHT | **FAMILY** | Just east of Hilo, almost at the end of the road, three adjacent parks make up one beautiful spot with a series of bays, protected inlets, lagoons, and pretty parks. This is one of the best snorkeling sites on this side of the island, as rocky outcrops provide shelter for schools of reef fish and sea turtles. Resist the urge to get too close to turtles or disturb them; they are protected from harassment by federal and state law. Local kids use the small black-sand pocket beach for body boarding. The shaded grassy areas are great for picnics. Be warned: this place is very crowded on weekends. **Amenities:** lifeguards (weekends, holidays, and summer only); parking (no fee); showers; toilets. **Best for:** snorkeling; walking. ✉ *2349 Kalanianaole Ave., Hilo* ✥ *4 miles east of Hilo* ☎ *808/961–8311.*

🍴 Restaurants

Kuhio Grille

$ | **HAWAIIAN** | There's no atmosphere to speak of at this diner, and water is served in unbreakable plastic tumblers, but if you're searching for local fare—that undefinable fusion of ethnic cuisines—this is the place. Choose from *grindz* that include *loco moco* (meat, rice, and eggs smothered in gravy), oxtail soup, plate lunches, pork chops, steaks, saimin, stir-fry, and daily specials. **Known for:** authentic Hawaiian experience; good plate lunches; award-winning 1-pound laulau. [$] *Average main: $12* ✉ *Prince Kuhio Plaza, 111 E. Puainako St., at Hwy. 11, Hilo* ✥ *Near Macy's* ☎ *808/959–2336* 🌐 *www.kuhiogrill.com.*

The Seaside Restaurant and Aqua Farm

$$ | **SEAFOOD** | **FAMILY** | Owned and operated by the Nakagawi family since the early 1920s, this landmark restaurant features three separate dining rooms that overlook a 30-acre natural brackish fishpond, making this one of the most interesting places to eat in Hilo. Along wth *paniolo* (cowboy) prime rib, New York steak, and shrimp scampi, the menu highlights *aholehole* (Hawaiian flagtail) raised in the pond. **Known for:** authentic local experience; ocean and pond views at sunset; fried aholehole (young Hawaiian flagtail). [$] *Average main: $23* ✉ *1790 Kalanianaole Ave., Hilo* ☎ *808/935–8825* 🌐 *www.seasiderestauranthilo.com* ⏲ *Closed Mon. No lunch.*

☕ Coffee and Quick Bites

Sack N Save Seafood Counter

$ | **HAWAIIAN** | **FAMILY** | It may sound strange, but the takeout seafood counter tucked in the back of this grocery store serves some of the finest poke in Hilo. For $10 a bowl, you get enough seafood on a steaming pile of rice to feed two people. **Known for:** variety of fresh, Hawaiian-style poke offerings; house-made sauces; affordable grab-and-go lunch spot. [$] *Average main: $10* ✉ *Puainako Center, 2100 Kanoelehua Ave., Suite 101, Hilo* ☎ *808/959–5831* 🌐 *www.foodland.com/stores/sack-n-save-puainako.*

Hotels

Hale Kai Hawaii Bed and Breakfast
$$ | **B&B/INN** | On a bluff above Honolii surf beach, this modern 5,400-square-foot home is 2 miles from downtown Hilo and features four rooms—each with patio, deluxe bedding, and grand ocean views within earshot of the surf. **Pros:** delicious hot breakfast; panoramic views of Hilo Bay; smoke-free property. **Cons:** no kids under 13; just outside walking distance to downtown Hilo; occasional coqui frog noise. [$] *Rooms from: $187* ✉ *111 Honolii Pl., Hilo* ☎ *808/935–6330* 🌐 *www.halekaihawaii.com* 🛏 *4 rooms* 🍴 *Free breakfast.*

The Inn at Kulaniapia Falls
$$ | **B&B/INN** | Overlooking downtown Hilo and the ocean beyond, this inn sits next to a 120-foot waterfall that tumbles into a 300-foot-wide natural pond—ripe for swimming, conditions permitting. **Pros:** waterfalls on property; delicious full breakfast; eco-friendly option. **Cons:** isolated location away from Hilo sights; dark road challenging to navigate at night; no air-conditioning. [$] *Rooms from: $199* ✉ *100 Kulaniapia Dr., Hilo* ☎ *808/935–6789* 🌐 *www.waterfall.net* 🛏 *11 rooms* 🍴 *Free breakfast.*

Shopping

FOOD

★ Big Island Candies
FOOD/CANDY | A local legend in the cookie- and chocolate-making business, Big Island Candies is a must-see for connoisseurs of fine chocolates. The packaging is first-rate, which makes these world-class confections the ideal gift or souvenir. Enjoy a free cookie sample and a cup of Kona coffee as you watch through a window as sweets are being made. The store has a long list of interesting and tasty products, but it is best known for its chocolate-dipped shortbread cookies. The classy showroom is festive during holidays. ✉ *585 Hinano St., Hilo* ☎ *808/935–8890* 🌐 *www.bigislandcandies.com.*

SHOPPING CENTERS

Hilo Shopping Center
SHOPPING CENTERS/MALLS | Among this shopping plaza's 40 shops are a day spa, a pharmacy, Diva's Boutique, and popular Lanky's Pastries and Island Naturals Market and Deli, plus Sunlight Cafe and Restaurant Miwa, a Japanese restaurant. There's plenty of free parking. Across the street, the Kilauea Market has a wide variety of hard-to-find Asian cooking ingredients. ✉ *1261 Kilauea Ave., Hilo.*

Prince Kuhio Plaza
SHOPPING CENTERS/MALLS | The Big Island's most comprehensive mall has indoor shopping, entertainment (a multiplex), and dining, including KFC, Hot Dog on a Stick, Cinnabon, Genki Sushi, IHOP, and Maui Tacos. The kids might like the arcade (near the food court), while you enjoy the stores, anchored by Macy's and Old Navy. ✉ *111 E. Puainako St., Hilo* ☎ *808/959–3555* 🌐 *www.princekuhioplaza.com.*

Chapter 7

HAWAII VOLCANOES NATIONAL PARK, PUNA, AND KAU

7

Updated by
Karen Anderson

◉ Sights	🍴 Restaurants	🛏 Hotels	⬤ Shopping	▼ Nightlife
★★★★★	★★★☆☆	★★★★☆	★★☆☆☆	★☆☆☆☆

WELCOME TO HAWAII VOLCANOES NATIONAL PARK, PUNA, AND KAU

TOP REASONS TO GO

★ **Thurston Lava Tube:** This 600-foot-long underground cavern is traversed by foot.

★ **Halemaumau Crater:** Home to Hawaii's fire goddess, Pele, the awesome summit crater is the park's star attraction.

★ **Chain of Craters Road:** The spectacular 18.8-mile road winds through historic eruptions sites all the way down to the coast.

★ **Kilauea Iki Trail:** A switchback trail descends into fascinating Kilauea Iki Crater, which last erupted in 1959.

★ **Punaluu Black Sand Beach:** If you're driving from Ka Lae (South Point) to Volcano, this is a must for swimming, picnicking, and turtle viewing.

★ **South Point:** Known as Ka Lae, this is the southernmost place in the United States, where a famous green-sand beach beckons.

★ **Pahoa:** This small town in Lower Puna features shops, cafés, and a lava museum that documents life in a lava zone.

Hawaii Volcanoes National Park is a prime draw for tourists to the Big Island of Hawaii. From charming Volcano Village to the park itself to the wider Puna region, there's an interesting sight around every corner. Most visitors will visit, but they may do so only for a day. Those who have the time and interest should base themselves on the east side of the island for a day or three, allowing enough time to explore some of the less-visited sights beyond the national park.

1 Volcano Village. The artsy small town that surrounds the park has galleries, restaurants, shops, vacation accommodations, a golf course, and a winery.

2 Summit Area. Volcano House hotel, the Kilauea Visitor Center, Volcano Art Center Gallery, and intriguing steam vents and sulfur banks are all located at the park's summit.

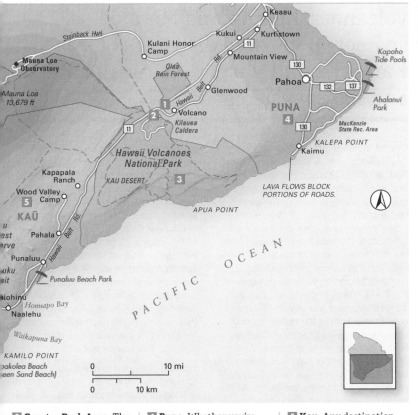

3 Greater Park Area. The park's fascinating geology extends all the way to the ocean, taking in enormous pit craters, historic eruption sites, cinder cones, and more, as well as hiking trails and a coastal sea arch.

4 Puna. Whether you're headed to Hawaii Volcanoes National Park from the east side or the west, Highway 11/Hawaii Belt Road is the road you'll take to get you there. If you're going to Lower Puna, the Keaau–Pahoa Road intersection will lead to Highway 130 and the town of Pahoa 11 miles farther down the road. For extra adventure, take Highway 130 all the way to Kalapana.

5 Kau. Any destination in the Kau District is easily accessed from Highway 11, also known as Hawaii Belt Road. The 12-mile road to South Point is easily accessed from the highway.

Dynamic, dramatic, and diverse, Hawaii Volcanoes National Park encompasses 333,308 acres across two active shield volcanoes: Kilauea and Mauna Loa. The sparsely populated districts of Puna and Kau surround the park to the northeast and southwest, respectively.

One of the state's most popular visitor destinations, Hawaii Volcanoes National Park, a UNESCO World Heritage Site and International Biosphere Reserve, beckons visitors to explore the sacred home of the fire goddess Pele, whose active presence shapes the primordial landscape. The area has recovered from the damaging events of the 2018 Kilauea eruption that rocked the region for months, beginning with the collapse of the Puu Oo Vent in the Lower East Rift Zone. The famed lava lake at Halemaumau Crater, known for its nighttime glow, is no more, having drained completely from view after sending hot liquid magma through underground lava channels to Lower Puna, where lava flows destroyed more than 700 homes and farms. At the summit, hundreds of earthquakes per day rocked the area for several months as Halemaumau Crater increased in volume to nearly 14 times its original size. The seismic events at the summit caused permanent damage to the Jaggar Museum and the Hawaii Volcano Observatory facility that overlooked the crater; both are closed.

Today the park has returned to normal, and visitors can explore most of the sights and trails that were open to the public prior to the eruption. Although the dramatic changes to Halemaumau Crater are evident to anyone who visited the park before the eruption, many of the park's favorite attractions have survived, including Thurston Lava Tube, Devastation Trail, and Kilauea Iki Trail. The park now has no active surface lava flows or eruptions, nor is any activity expected in the near future. Still, there are plenty of activities such as hiking, biking, and picnicking. And with attractions from incomparable scenic vistas to fascinating geological features including wide expanses of *aa* (rough) and *pahoehoe* (smooth) lava, Hawaii Volcanoes National Park is a must-see destination, whether for a half-day trek or a week-long deep dive into this unique place.

Located just outside of Hawaii Volcanoes National Park, the artsy, forested enclave of Volcano Village features fine-art galleries, glass-blowing studios, cozy cafés, restaurants, boutiques, and a Sunday farmers' market with breakfast items as well as crafts. The plentiful accommodations here include inns, bed-and-breakfasts, vacation cottages, and cabins. When staying in Volcano Village, you can partake in wine tastings and tours at a local winery, play golf at an 18-hole course, go bird-watching, or ride a bike along quiet, flat streets through rain forest neighborhoods. Nearby but inside the park, the Kilauea Military Camp has an arcade, bowling alley, a general store, and the Lava Lounge cocktail bar, all open to the public. And of course, you can just take in the starry nighttime sky or the ever-changing daytime skies with their random rain showers, rainbows, rolling clouds, and crystal-clear skies.

The districts of Kau and Puna lie adjacent to each other and are big and sparse, requiring lots of drive time to get to places of the most interest. The area is known for its wide-open spaces, vast desert regions, rugged coastline, dense macadamia groves, and windswept ranchlands.

With Kilauea Volcano looming directly upslope on the flank of Kilauea, Pahoa Town was threatened by lava in 2014 and 2018 but survived. The dramatic Kilauea eruption in 2018 sent molten lava throughout the region below Pahoa, decimating hundreds of homes as well as farmlands and agricultural operations. Tragically, unrelenting flows from the infamous Fissure 8 vent destroyed some of Lower Puna's most treasured destinations including Green Lake, Kapoho Tidepools, Kapoho Bay, and the famed warm ponds of Ahalanui. The beloved seaside residential communities of Kapoho Vacationland and Hawaiian Beach Lots were wiped off the face of the map by widespread, towering lava flows that completely transformed the coastline. A popular surf spot and fishing area, Pohoiki was transformed into a new black-sand beach that now surrounds the old boat ramp. Closer to Pahoa Town, the enormous subdivision of Lelani Estates became ground zero for dozens of fissure eruptions that took out hundreds of homes and changed residents' lives forever. Despite the natural disaster in the area, there is still much to experience in Lower Puna, including cafés, restaurants, boutique shops, artisan markets, festivals, and yoga retreats. Add Lava Tree State Monument and Kalapana to your itinerary.

MAJOR REGIONS

Located outside the park, the quiet, residential enclave of **Volcano Village** offers gas, food, lodging, shops, and recreational opportunities. This art-loving small town has attracted artists of all kinds, and their works are on display in local galleries.

The **Summit Area** of Kilauea Volcano encompasses the visitor center, Volcano House hotel, Volcano Art Center Gallery, Kilauea Military Camp, and a host of geological sights highlighted by the massive Kilauea Caldera.

Beyond the summit, the **Greater Park Area** spans vast open spaces, miles of lava flows, lush rain forests, and coastal regions. A drive along Chain of Craters Road takes you past trailheads and geological wonders to the coast and memorable, wide-open ocean views.

Puna and **Kau** are vast areas along the southern part of the island. The Puna district is divided into a lower and an upper region. Most of Upper Puna comprises portions of Hawaii Volcanoes National Park and the neighboring enclave of Volcano Village. Closer to sea level, Lower Puna includes the towns of Keaau, Mountain View, Kurtistown, and Pahoa, as well as the coastal community of Kalapana. Stretching from Ocean View on the southwest side of the Big Island, the Kau District continues all the way to South Point, Naalehu, and Pahala and to Hawaii Volcanoes National Park.

Planning

Getting Here and Around

The 27-mile drive on Highway 19 from Hilo to Volcano (all through Upper Puna) takes about 40 minutes. From Kailua-Kona, the drive requires traversing Saddle Road to Hilo and then heading up to Volcano; the one-way drive takes

In recent years, Kilauea's lava flows (now ceased) have produced some of the newest land on the face of the earth.

approximately 2½ hours. The park itself is easy to drive around, as there are only two main roads: Chain of Craters Road and Crater Rim Drive. Because of recent events at Kilauea Caldera, part of Crater Rim Drive remains closed to the public.

AIR

If your primary goal for visiting the Big Island is to visit Hawaii Volcanoes National Park, then fly into Hilo if you can. It's a long drive from Kona International Airport (about 2½ hours) to Volcano.

BUS

Five public Hele-On buses (⊕ www.heleonbus.org) travel from Volcano to downtown Hilo and back on weekdays and Saturday. Stops include Volcano Village and the Kilauea Visitor Center inside the park. The last bus leaves the park's visitor center at 5:50 pm. Once you're in the park, though, you'll be limited to sights within walking distance of the Kilauea Visitor Center. You can bring a bike with you on the bus, though; biking is a great way to see the park when it's

not raining. Transportation to Kau is even more limited. Only one bus departs each morning from Ocean View, traveling all the way to Hilo Town and returning to Ocean View in the evening.

CAR

You'll need a car to explore this vast region, but there's no need to rent a four-wheel drive. There are two main roads inside the park: Crater Rim Drive, which is at the summit, and Chain of Craters Road, which leads all the way down to the coast. It's easy to plan a driving itinerary within the park's boundaries.

Speed limits in the park are enforced for a reason. Not only is the region highly visited, the park strives to maintain visitor safety for all, as well as provide protection for the endangered Hawaiian nene goose that roams the area.

The roads connecting Pahoa to Kapoho and the Kalapana Coast form a loop that's about 25 miles long; driving times are from two to three hours, depending on the number of stops you make and the length of time at each stop. There are restaurants, stores, and gas stations in Pahoa, but services elsewhere in the region are spotty. Long stretches of the road may be completely isolated at any given point; this can be a little scary at night but beautiful and tranquil during the day.

The drive from Kailua-Kona to South Point is a long one (roughly two hours); from Volcano it's approximately 45 minutes. You can fill up on gas and groceries in Ocean View, or you can eat, fuel up, and get picnic fixings in nearby Naalehu. Weather tends to be warm, dry, and windy.

Hotels

If you visit Hawaii Volcanoes National Park—and you should—spend one night in Volcano Village at least. This allows you time to explore additional hiking trails and park attractions, as well as to see the village with its art galleries, cafés, restaurants, and shops. There are plenty of places to stay in the area, and many are both charming and reasonably priced. The park has one hotel, the famous Volcano House. (Kilauea Military Camp inside the park offers lodging in 90 vintage cottages only for military members/veterans and their families.) Volcano Village has just enough dining and art destinations to satisfy you for a day or two.

Puna is a world apart—thick rain forests, rugged shorelines, and homes that are decidedly off the beaten track. There are, however, a handful of well-priced vacation homes and bed-and-breakfasts. It's not your typical vacation spot: there are a few black-sand beaches (some of them clothing-optional), few dining or entertainment options, and quite a few, er, interesting locals. That said, for those who want to have a unique experience, get away from everything, and don't mind the sound of the chirping coqui

frogs at night, this is the place to do it. The Kilauea eruption of 2018 has made some parts of Puna inaccessible.

Far from the major South Kohala resorts, Kau is a good place for those looking to get away from it all. You won't find a lot in terms of amenities, but there are several nice options including vacation rental cottages, a B&B inn, and a condo resort complex with golf course. The main visitor attraction is the beautiful Punaluu Black Sand Beach, home of the endangered hawksbill turtle.

Restaurants

Inside the park, a restaurant and lounge (The Rim) inside Volcano House serves breakfast, lunch, and dinner overlooking the summit from the rim of Kilauea Caldera. There are also casual public eateries at Kilauea Military Camp within the park. You'll find a handful of dining options, several general stores, and a gas station in Volcano Village. If you can't find what you're looking for, Hilo is about a 35-minute drive away, and the Keaau grocery store and fast-food joints are 25 minutes away.

The best restaurants in the Puna District are located in Volcano Village and Pahoa. Dining in Kau is sporadic, with a handful of diners scattered throughout the region.

HOTEL AND RESTAURANT PRICES

Hotel prices in the reviews are the lowest cost of a standard double room in high season. Restaurant prices in the reviews are the average cost of a main course at dinner, or if dinner is not served, at lunch. Hotel and restaurant reviews have been shortened. For full information, see Fodors.com.

What it Costs in U. S. Dollars			
$	$$	$$$	$$$$
RESTAURANTS			
under $17	$17–$26	$27–$35	over $35
HOTELS			
under $180	$180–$260	$261–$340	over $340

Safety

When visiting Hawaii Volcanoes National Park, don't venture off marked trails or into closed areas, and don't get near open steam vents, ground cracks, or steep cliffsides. Many hikes in the park are on rugged, open lava fields where winds, rain, and searing sun can happen at a moment's notice. Wear plenty of sunscreen and a hat or hooded, light jacket and close-toed shoes; always carry plenty of water with you. Volcanic fumes can be hazardous. Heed any air-quality warnings that are posted at the Kilauea Visitor Center and throughout the park. Down along the coast, strong winds and high surf are possible.

Compared to big-city living, it's pretty tame, but there is a bit of a "locals-only" vibe in parts of Puna, and some areas suffer crime and drug problems. Don't wander around alone at night or get lost on backcountry roads.

Tours

Volcano Art Center

SPECIAL-INTEREST | Volcano Art Center offers a free Monday morning forest tour where visitors can learn about rare native Hawaiian rain forests. These hour-long walks take place on easily traversed gravel trails, rain or shine. No reservations are required, but they are recommended for groups of five or more. The center offers additional customized rain forest tours, as well as forest restoration

activities. ☎ 866/967–8222 for administration, 808/967–7565 for gallery ⊕ www.volcanoartcenter.org ⌲ From $10.

Visitor Information

The park is open 24/7. When you arrive at the park entrance during normal visiting hours, you'll receive a complimentary, detailed map and brochure about the park. The park entrance fee (good for seven days) is $30 per vehicle, $15 per pedestrian, and $25 per motorcycle. Inside the Kilauea Vistor Center, trail guide booklets written by park geologists are available for less than $3 each. Operated by Hawaii Pacific Parks, the park store features educational materials, apparel, gifts, books, and art. A small theater plays educational films about the history of the park, and park rangers are available to answer questions. There is always an itinerary of ranger-led activities. ■TIP→ **Purchase the Hawaii Tri-park Annual Pass for $55, which allows full access to Hawaii Volcanoes National Park and Puuhonua O Honaunau National Historical Park on the Big Island, and Haleakala National Park on Maui.**

Volcano Village

Located right outside the park boundary and surrounded by rain forest, Volcano Village is a residential neighborhood that offers vacation rental accommodations, B&B inns, a gas station, a post office, an art school, galleries, shops, a general store, and a fun Sunday farmers' market. The immediate area also has a country club and golf course, along with the popular Volcano Winery. Next door to the winery, the Keauhou Bird Conservation Center is not open to the public, but if you listen closely, you may be able to hear the call of the highly endangered *alala* (Hawaiian raven), which is being bred in captivity at the center.

Sights

Volcano Farmers' Market

MARKET | Local produce, flowers, crafts, and food products, including fresh-baked breads, pastries, coffee, pancakes, fresh coconuts with straws, and homemade Thai specialties are available every Sunday morning from 6 to 10 at one of the better farmers' markets on the island. It's best to get there early, before 7, as vendors tend to sell out of the best stuff quickly. There's also a great bookstore (paperbacks 50¢, hardbacks $1, and magazines 10¢) and a thrift store with clothes and knickknacks. The market is held in the covered Cooper Center, so it's safe from the rain. ✉ *Cooper Center, 19-4030 Wright Rd., Volcano* ☎ *808/936–9705* 🌐 *www.thecoopercenter.org* 🕒 *Closed Mon.–Sat.*

Volcano Garden Arts

MUSEUM | Located on beautifully landscaped grounds dotted with intriguing sculptures, this delightful gallery and garden lend credence to Volcano's reputation as an artists' haven. The charming complex includes an eclectic gallery representing more than 100 artists, an excellent organic café housed in redwood buildings built in 1908, and a cute, one-bedroom artist's cottage, available for rent. If you're lucky, you'll get to meet the eccentric owner/"caretaker" of this enclave, the multitalented Ira Ono, known for his whimsical art, recycled trash creations, and friendly personality. ✉ *19-3834 Old Volcano Rd., Volcano* ☎ *808/985–8979* 🌐 *www.volcanogardenarts.com* 🎟 *Free* 🕒 *Garden closed Sun. and Mon.*

Volcano Winery

WINERY/DISTILLERY | Not all volcanic soils are ideal for the cultivation of grapes, but this winery grows its own grapes and produces some interesting vintages. The Macadamia Nut Honey wine is a nutty, very sweet after-dinner drink. The Infusion pairs estate-grown black tea with South Kona's fermented macadamia nut honey for a smooth concoction perfect for brunch through early evening. Though this isn't Napa Valley, the vintners take their wine seriously, and the staff is friendly and knowledgeable. Wine tasting is available; you can also get wine and cheese to eat in the picnic area, and a gift store has a selection of local crafts. ✉ *35 Pii Mauna Dr., Volcano* ✥ *Past entrance to Hawaii Volcanoes National Park, by golf course* ☎ *808/967–7772* 🌐 *www.volcanowinery.com.*

Restaurants

Kilauea Lodge Restaurant

$$$ | **HAWAIIAN** | The koa-wood tables and intimate lighting are in keeping with the ambience of this cozy lodge in the heart of Volcano Village, built in 1937 as a YMCA camp and still retaining the Fireplace of Friendship, embedded with coins and plaques from around the world. The fare ranges from grass-fed Big Island beef burgers and Niihau lamb burgers to a chicken pasta, catch of the day, and farm-fresh salads. **Known for:** gourmet burgers; fine dining with prices to match; popular Sunday brunch. [$] *Average main: $30* ✉ *19-3948 Old Volcano Rd., Volcano* ☎ *808/967–7366* 🌐 *www.kilauealodge.com.*

Lava Rock Cafe

$ | **DINER** | **FAMILY** | This is an affordable place to grab a sandwich or a coffee and check your email (Wi-Fi is free with purchase of a meal) before heading to Hawaii Volcanoes National Park. The homey, sit-down diner caters to families, serving up heaping plates of pancakes and French toast for breakfast; on the lunch menu, burgers range from bacon-cheese to turkey and *paniolo* (cowboy) burgers made with Hawaii grass-fed beef. **Known for:** roadhouse atmosphere; live music in evenings; diner-style comfort food. [$] *Average main: $10* ✉ *19-3972 Old Volcano Hwy., Volcano* ✥ *Next to Kilauea General Store* ☎ *808/967–8526* 🕒 *No dinner Sun. and Mon.*

Continued on page 208

HAWAII VOLCANOES NATIONAL PARK

Exploring the surface of the world's most active volcano—from the moonscape craters at the summit to the red-hot lava flows on the coast to the kipuka, pockets of vegetation miraculously left untouched—is the ultimate ecotour and one of Hawaii's must-dos.

The park sprawls over 520 square miles and encompasses Kilauea and Mauna Loa, two of the five volcanoes that formed the Big Island nearly half a million years ago. Kilauea, youngest and most rambunctious of the Hawaiian volcanoes, erupted at its summit from the 19th century through 1982. Since then, the top of the volcano had been more or less quiet, frequently shrouded in mist; an eruption in the Halemaumau Crater in 2008 ended this period of relative inactivity.

Kilauea's eastern side sprang to life on January 3, 1983, shooting molten lava four stories high. This eruption has been ongoing, and lava flows are generally steady and slow, appearing and disappearing from view. Over 500 acres have been added to Hawaii's eastern coast since the activity began, and scientists say this eruptive phase is not likely to end anytime soon. However, the famed lava lake at Halemaumau Crater has drained, so for now, there's no flowing lava to see anywhere in the park.

The damaging events of 2018 have now subsided, and you can see the effects of creation elemental—when molten lava meets the ocean, cools, and solidifies into brand-new stretches of coastline. Although you can no longer view flowing lava, you can hike 150 miles of trails and camp amid wide expanses of aa (rough) and pahoehoe (smooth) lava. There's nothing quite like it.

🏠 P.O. Box 52, Hawaii Volcanoes National Park, HI 96718

☎ 808/985–6000

⊕ www.nps.gov/havo

💵 $30 per vehicle; $15 for pedestrians and bicyclists. Ask about passes. Admission is good for seven consecutive days.

🕐 The park is open daily, 24 hours. Kilauea Visitor Center: 9 am–5 pm. Volcano Art Center Gallery: 9–5.

(top) Kilauea Iki Trail
(left) Fuming rim of Puu Oo, source of the current eruption

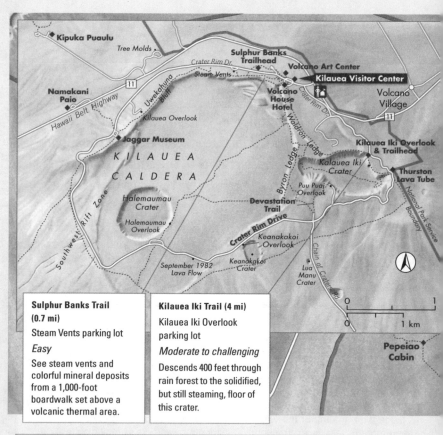

Sulphur Banks Trail (0.7 mi)

Steam Vents parking lot

Easy

See steam vents and colorful mineral deposits from a 1,000-foot boardwalk set above a volcanic thermal area.

Kilauea Iki Trail (4 mi)

Kilauea Iki Overlook parking lot

Moderate to challenging

Descends 400 feet through rain forest to the solidified, but still steaming, floor of this crater.

SEEING THE SUMMIT

The best way to explore the summit of Kilauea is to cruise along Crater Rim Drive to Kilauea Overlook. From Kilauea Overlook you can see all of Kilauea Caldera and Halemaumau Crater, an awesome depression in Kilauea Caldera measuring 3,000 feet across and nearly 300 feet deep. It's a huge and breathtaking view with pluming steam vents. At this writing, there are no active lava flows in the park after the lava lake in Halemaumau Crater drained suddenly and quickly after seismic events in 2018.

Regrettably, the events of 2018 damaged the Thomas A. Jaggar Museum beyond repair, and it is now permanently closed. You can visit the nearby Kilauea Military Camp, with its recreational activities and general store, and the park's star attractions, the Thurston Lava Tube, which you can walk through.

Other Highlights along Crater Rim Drive include sulfur and steam vents, fractures, and gullies along Kilauea's flanks. Kilauea Iki Crater, on the way down to Chain of Crater's Road, is smaller, but just as fascinating when seen from Puu Pai Overlook.

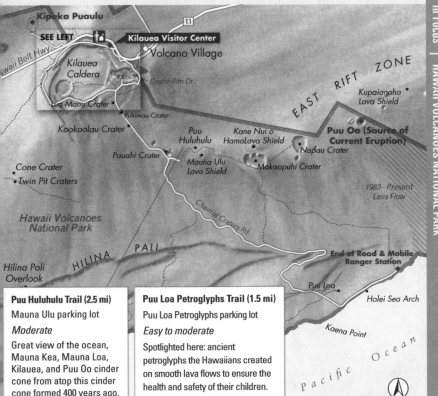

Puu Huluhulu Trail (2.5 mi)

Mauna Ulu parking lot

Moderate

Great view of the ocean, Mauna Kea, Mauna Loa, Kilauea, and Puu Oo cinder cone from atop this cinder cone formed 400 years ago.

Puu Loa Petroglyphs Trail (1.5 mi)

Puu Loa Petroglyphs parking lot

Easy to moderate

Spotlighted here: ancient petroglyphs the Hawaiians created on smooth lava flows to ensure the health and safety of their children.

SEEING LAVA

Lava flows have never been guaranteed, and at this writing there is no flowing lava in the park. But you can still see steam vents and sulfur banks, as well as the effects of millennia of past lava flows.

There are three guarantees about lava flows in HVNP. First: They constantly change. Second: Because of that, you can't predict when and where you'll be able to see them. Third: New land formed when lava meets the sea is highly unstable and can collapse at any time. Never go into areas that have been closed.

■TIP→ Even without flowing lava, Chain of Craters Road is a magnificent drive, and the park's best hiking trails how now reopened fully.

PLANNING YOUR TRIP TO HVNP

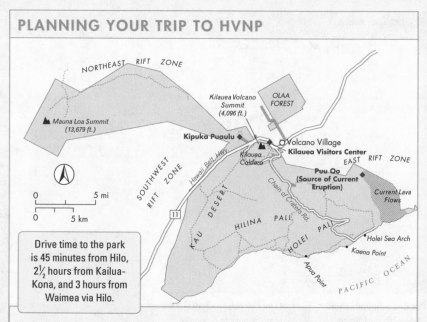

NORTHEAST RIFT ZONE

▲ Mauna Loa Summit
(13,679 ft.)

Kilauea Volcano
Summit
(4,096 ft.)

OLAA
FOREST

Kipuka Puaulu ◆

Volcano Village
Kilauea Visitors Center

Kilauea
Caldera

SOUTHWEST RIFT ZONE

EAST RIFT ZONE

**Puu Oo
(Source of Current
Eruption)**

Current Lava
Flows

Hawaii Belt Hwy.

0   5 mi

0   5 km

11

KAU DESERT

HILINA PALI

HOLEI PALI

Chain of Craters Rd.

Holei Sea Arch

Kaena Point

Apua Point

PACIFIC OCEAN

Drive time to the park
is 45 minutes from Hilo,
2½ hours from Kailua-
Kona, and 3 hours from
Waimea via Hilo.

Lava entering the ocean

WHERE TO START

Begin your visit at the Visitor Center,
where you'll find maps, books, and DVDs;
information on trails, ranger-led walks,
and special events; and current weather,
road, and lava-viewing conditions. Free
volcano-related film showings, lectures,
and other presentations are regularly
scheduled.

WEATHER

Weather conditions fluctuate daily,
sometimes hourly. It can be rainy and
chilly even during the summer; the
temperature usually is 14° cooler at the
4,000-foot-high summit of Kilauea than
at sea level.

Expect hot, dry, and windy coastal conditions at the end of Chain of Craters
Road. Bring rain gear, and wear layered
clothing, sturdy shoes, sunglasses, a
hat, and sunscreen.

Photographer on lava table filming lava flow into ocean

FOOD

It's a good idea to bring your own favorite snacks and beverages; stock up on provisions in Volcano Village, 1½ miles away. Kilauea Military Camp, near the summit, has a general store as well as casual dining options, and all are open to the public.

PARK PROGRAMS

Rangers lead daily walks at 10:30 and 1:30 into different areas; check with the Visitor Center for details as times and destinations depend on weather conditions and eruptions.

Over 60 companies hold permits to lead hikes at HVNP. Good choices are Hawaii Forest & Trail (www.hawaii-forest.com), Hawaiian Walkways (www.hawaiianwalkways.com), and Native Guide Hawaii (www.nativeguidehawaii.com).

CAUTION

"Vog" (volcanic smog) can cause headaches; breathing difficulties; lethargy; irritations of the skin, eyes, nose, and throat; and other health problems. Pregnant women, young children, and people with asthma and heart conditions are most susceptible, and should avoid areas such as Halemaumau Crater where fumes are thick.

Wear long pants and boots or closed-toe shoes with good tread for hikes on lava. Stay on marked trails and step carefully. Lava is composed of 50% silica (glass) and can cause serious injury if you fall.

Carry at least 2 quarts of water on hikes. Temperatures near lava flows can rise above 100°F, and dehydration, heat exhaustion, and sunstroke are common consequences of extended exposure to intense sunlight and high temperatures.

Remember that these are active volcanoes, and eruptions can cause parts of the park to close at any time. Check the park's website or call ahead for last-minute updates before your visit.

Volcanologists inspecting a vent in the East Rift Zone

Sights

1 Volcano Farmers' Market...... **C3**

2 Volcano Garden Arts.......... **C2**

3 Volcano Winery...... **A4**

Restaurants

1 Kilauea Lodge Restaurant.. **C3**

2 Lava Rock Cafe **B3**

3 Thai Thai Bistro and Bar **B3**

Hotels

1 Chalet Kilauea Rainforest Hotel......... **B1**

2 Hale Ohia Cottages.... **C4**

3 Kilauea Lodge........ **C3**

4 Volcano Mist Cottage...... **D4**

5 Volcano Teapot Cottage...... **B3**

6 Volcano Village Lodge........ **C1**

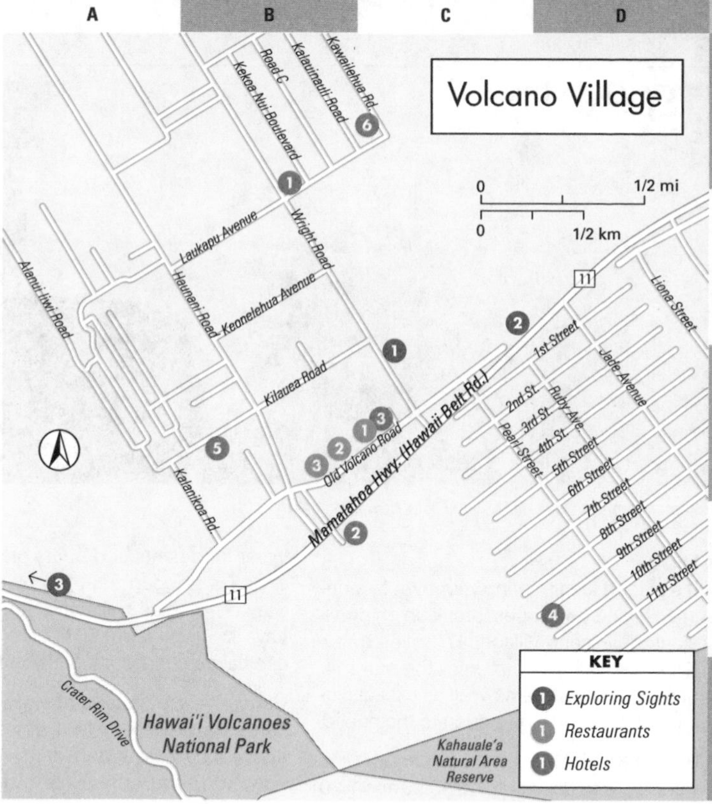

A
B
C
D
Volcano Village
0
1/2 mi
0
1/2 km
Kawailehua Rd.
Kalanianauli Road
Road C
Kekoa Nui Boulevard
Laukapu Avenue
Wright Road
Alanui Iiwi Road
Heunani Road
Keonelehua Avenue
Kilauea Road
Old Volcano Road
Mamalahoa Hwy. (Hawaii Belt Rd.)
Kalanikoa Rd.
11
1st Street
2nd St.
3rd St.
4th St.
Ruby Ave.
Pearl Street
5th Street
6th Street
7th Street
8th Street
9th Street
10th Street
11th Street
Jade Avenue
Liona Street
Crater Rim Drive
Hawai'i Volcanoes National Park
Kahauale'a Natural Area Reserve
KEY
Exploring Sights
Restaurants
Hotels

Thai Thai Bistro and Bar

$$ | **THAI** | **FAMILY** | The food is authentic and the prices are reasonable at this little Volcano Village find with Thai art and silk wall hangings in the pleasant dining room. A steaming-hot plate of curry is the perfect antidote to a chilly day at the volcano, and the chicken satay is excellent—the peanut dipping sauce a good blend of sweet and spicy. **Known for:** reliable Thai cuisine with plenty of spice; full bar; quick but friendly service. [$] *Average main: $20* ✉ *19-4084 Old Volcano Rd., Volcano* ☎ *808/967–7969* 🌐 *www.lavalodge.com.*

Hotels

Chalet Kilauea Rainforest Hotel

$ | **B&B/INN** | **FAMILY** | Quirky yet upscale, this accommodation features four artistically distinctive rooms that unveil beautiful views of the rain forest from a great location five minutes from Hawaii Volcanoes National Park. **Pros:** unique decor; friendly front desk; hot tub on property. **Cons:** space heaters; not close to the beach; can get cold at night. [$] *Rooms from: $169* ✉ *19-4178 Wright Rd., Volcano* ☎ *808/967–7786, 800/937–7786* 🌐 *www.volcano-hawaii.com* 🛏 *4 rooms* 🍴 *No meals.*

Hale Ohia Cottages

$ | **B&B/INN** | **FAMILY** | A stately and comfortable Queen Anne–style mansion, Hale Ohia was built in the 1930s as a summer home for a wealthy Scotsman (the property is listed on the State Historic Register). **Pros:** unique architecture; free Wi-Fi and parking; private location. **Cons:** no TVs; simple breakfast offerings; 30 minutes from downtown Hilo via car. [$] *Rooms from: $149* ✉ *11-3968 Hale*

Ohia Rd., Volcano ☎ *808/967–7986, 800/455–3803* 🌐 *www.haleohia.com* 🛏 *15 rooms* 🍴 *Free breakfast.*

Kilauea Lodge

$$ | HOTEL | A mile from the entrance of Hawaii Volcanoes National Park, this lodge was initially built as a YMCA camp in the 1930s; now it is a pleasant inn, tastefully furnished with European antiques, photographs, and authentic Hawaiian quilts. **Pros:** great restaurant; close to volcano; fireplaces in each room. **Cons:** no TV or phone in lodge rooms; 45 minutes to downtown Hilo; few shopping options nearby. [$] *Rooms from: $229* ✉ *19-3948 Old Volcano Rd., Volcano* ✥ *1 mile northeast of national park* ☎ *808/967–7366* 🌐 *www.kilauealodge.com* 🛏 *12 rooms* 🍴 *Free breakfast.*

Volcano Mist Cottage

$$$ | RENTAL | Both rustic and Zen, this magical cottage in the rain forest features cathedral ceilings, spruce walls, cork flooring, and amenities not usually found at Volcano vacation rentals, like bathrobes, a Bose home theater system, and Trek mountain bikes. **Pros:** isolated and private cottage; outdoor Jacuzzi tub; upscale amenities. **Cons:** not large enough for families; 45 minutes from downtown Hilo; limited shopping options nearby. [$] *Rooms from: $300* ✉ *11-3932 9th St., Volcano* ☎ *808/895–8359* 🌐 *www.volcanomistcottage.com* 🛏 *1 cottage* 🍴 *Free breakfast.*

Volcano Teapot Cottage

$$$$ | RENTAL | A near-perfect spot for couples seeking a romantic getaway in Volcano Village, this historical 1912 two-bedroom cottage evokes a vintage country feeling in keeping with the summer homes of the era. **Pros:** near town restaurants; fireplace and hot tub; laundry facilities. **Cons:** not quite large enough to accommodate four people—three people max; can get cold at night; more expensive option for this area. [$] *Rooms from: $350* ✉ *19-4041 Kilauea Rd., Volcano* ☎ *808/937–4976* 🌐 *www.volcanoteapot.com* 🛏 *1 cottage* 🍴 *Free breakfast.*

★ **Volcano Village Lodge**

$$$ | B&B/INN | Hospitality abounds at this luxurious B&B in a secluded rain forest, where the separate suites (connected by paths) offer amenities including fine furnishings, dining niches, jetted bathtubs, heated blankets, and private forest entrances. **Pros:** secluded and quiet; hospitable staff; outdoor hot tub on property. **Cons:** need an umbrella to get to the suite from the car; far from Hilo town; no restaurants within walking distance. [$] *Rooms from: $280* ✉ *19-4183 Kawailehua Rd., Volcano* ☎ *808/985–9500* 🌐 *www.volcanovillagelodge.com* 🛏 *5 suites* 🍴 *Free breakfast.*

Shopping

ARTS AND CRAFTS

★ **Kilauea Kreations**

CRAFTS | Beautiful hand-stitched Hawaiian quilts grace the walls here, quilting kits and books are plentiful, and the vast inventory of tropical fabrics is amazing. The friendly proprietors also offer fine art, photography, cards, and cool souvenirs you won't find anywhere else. A second location, Kilauea Kreations II in downtown Hilo, features a larger store and collection of fabrics as well as classroom space. ✉ *19-3972 Volcano Rd., Volcano* ✥ *Next to Lava Rock Cafe* ☎ *808/967–8090, 808/961–1100 Kilauea Kreations II* 🌐 *www.kilaueakreations.com.*

2400 Fahrenheit

CERAMICS/GLASSWARE | At the end of Old Volcano Road near Volcano Village, this small gallery and studio has hand-blown glass inspired by the eruption of Kilauea and the colors of the tropics. You can see the artists in action Thursday through Monday from 10 to 4, and Tuesday and Wednesday by appointment. ✉ *Old Volcano Rd. off Hwy. 11 between mile markers 23 and 24, Volcano* ☎ *808/985–8667* 🌐 *www.2400f.com.*

⚡ Activities

SPAS

Hale Hoola Spa in Volcano

FITNESS/HEALTH CLUBS | For those staying in Volcano, this spa offers a sweet alternative to the big resorts. Hale Hoola's menu features a bounty of local ingredients and traditional Hawaiian treatments, including *lomi hula*, which is lomilomi massage choreographed to hula music, and *laau hamo*, which blends lomilomi with traditional Hawaiian and Asian healing herbs and plant extracts. *Popo kapai* is a divine blend of hot-stone massage and *laau hamo*, incorporating lomilomi with warm compresses filled with healing herbs. Facials and body scrubs use traditional ginger, coconut, and macadamia nuts but also some surprises, including taro, vanilla, and volcanic clay. Rejuvenation packages include a full-body scrub, massage, facial, and hot steam. Couples are welcome. ■ **TIP→ Treatments are by appointment only.** ⊠ *Mauna Loa Estates, 11-3913 7th St., Volcano* ☎ *808/756–2421* ⊕ *www. halehoola.net* ⊠ *Massages from $85, facials from $85.*

Summit Area

In the heart of Hawaii Volcanoes National Park, a primeval landscape unfolds at the summit of Kilauea Volcano, where steam rises continuously from cracks in the earth and volcanic gases create malodorous sulfur banks. Here, Halemaumau Crater has doubled in diameter from the seismic events of the 2018 Kilauea eruption. In addition to the many geological sights, the summit area of the park includes Kilauea Visitor Center, Volcano Art Center Gallery, and Volcano House, a landmark hotel perched above the rim of the massive Kilauea Caldera. This is a good area to begin your visit to the park.

⊙ Sights

Devastation Trail

TRAIL | A paved pathway takes visitors across a barren lavascape strewn with chunky cinders that descended from towering lava fountains during the 1959 eruption of nearby Kilauea Iki Crater. The easy 1-mile (round-trip) hike ends at the edge of the Kilauea Iki Crater. This must-see view of the crater could yield such memorable sights as white-tailed tropic birds gliding in the breeze or a rainbow stretching above the crater's rim after a sunlit rain shower. ⊠ *Hawaii Volcanoes National Park* ⊹ *4 miles from visitor center at intersection of Crater Rim Dr. and Chain of Craters Rd.* ☎ *808/ 985–6101* ⊕ *www.nps.gov/havo.*

★ Halemaumau Crater

VOLCANO | For native Hawaiians, Halemaumau Crater is the sacred home of Pele, the fire goddess; for scientists at the Hawaiian Volcano Observatory, this mighty pit crater within the massive Kilauea Caldera is an ever-changing force to be reckoned with. Prior to Kilauea's 2018 eruption, Halemaumau's visible lava lake awed visitors for 10 years. Then Puu Oo Vent, which had been erupting in the East Rift Zone for 35 years, collapsed in April 2018. As lava from the distant vent drained away, so did the lava lake at Halemaumau Crater. A relentless series of seismic events at the summit followed, doubling the diameter of Halemaumau Crater and deepening it by 1,300 feet. To the surprise of scientists, a water pond has appeared at the bottom of the crater and continues to grow. Although the lookout point at the Jaggar Museum has permanently closed due to earthquake damage, there are still several places in the park to view the magnificent crater, including at the Steaming Bluff Overlook and at Volcano House hotel. ⊠ *Crater Rim Dr., Hawaii Volcanoes National Park* ☎ *808/985–6101* ⊕ *www.nps.gov/havo.*

★ Kilauea Iki Trail

TRAIL | The stunning 4-mile loop hike descends 400 feet into a massive crater via a forested nature trail. As part of this, you hike across the crater floor, walking on a solidified lava lake. Still steaming in places, the crater is dotted with baby ohia trees emerging from the cracks. Venture across the crater floor to the Puu Puai cinder cone that was formed by spatter from a towering lava fountain during the 1959 Kilauea Iki eruption. There are three different trailheads for Kilauea Iki; the main one, which takes two or three hours, begins at the Kilauea Iki Overlook parking lot off Crater Rim Drive. You can also access the crater from Devastation Trail or Puu Puai on the other side. ■TIP→ **Bring water, snacks, a hat, sunscreen, and hooded rain gear, as weather can change at a moment's notice.** ✉ *Crater Rim Dr., Hawaii Volcanoes National Park* ✛ *2 miles from visitor center* ☎ *808/ 985–6101* ⊕ *www.nps.gov/havo.*

Kilauea Military Camp

COMMERCIAL CENTER | **FAMILY** | Located inside the park, Kilauea Military Camp offers visitor accommodations to members of the military and their families but also has places open to the public, including an arcade, bowling alley, diner, buffet, general store, and gas station. In addition, the Lava Lounge cocktail bar features live music on weekends. ✉ *99-252 Crater Rim Dr., Hawaii Volcanoes National Park* ☎ *808/967–8333* ⊕ *www.kilaueamilitarycamp.com.*

Kilauea Visitor Center

INFO CENTER | Rangers and volunteers greet people and answer all questions at this visitor center, located just beyond the park entrance. There are lots of educational murals and displays, maps, and guidebooks. Also check out the daily itinerary of ranger-led activities and plan to sign up for some. The gift shop operated by the Hawaii Pacific Park Association stocks plenty of excellent art, books, apparel, and more. A small theater plays documentaries about the park. ✉ *1 Crater Rim Dr., Hawaii Volcanoes National Park* ☎ *808/985–6000* ⊕ *www.nps.gov/havo.*

Steam Vents and Sulfur Banks

VOLCANO | A short walk from the Kilauea Visitor Center leads to the smelly yet fascinating sulfur banks, where gases composed of hydrogen sulfide produce a smell akin to rotten eggs. Most of the rocks surrounding the vents have been dyed yellow due to constant gas exposure. Throughout the surrounding landscape, dozens of active steam vents emit white, billowing vapors that originate from groundwater heated by volcanic rocks. Located on the caldera's edge, Steaming Bluff is a short walk from a nearby parking area. ■TIP→ **The best steam vents are across the road from the main steam vent parking area; they vary in size and are scattered alongside the dirt trails.** ✉ *Crater Rim Dr., Hawaii Volcanoes National Park* ✛ *Within walking distance of Kilauea Visitor Center* ☎ *808/ 985–6101* ⊕ *www.nps.gov/havo.*

Thurston Lava Tube (Nahuku)

NATURE SITE | One of the star attractions in the park, the Thurston Lava Tube (named "Nahuku" in Hawaiian) spans 600 feet underground. The massive cave-like tube, discovered in 1913, was formed by hot molten lava traveling through the channel. To reach the entrance of the tube, visitors descend a series of stairs surrounded by lush foliage and the sounds of native birds. The Kilauea eruption of 2018 resulted in an almost two-year closure of the Thurston Lava Tube as engineers surveyed for potential structural damage. Long-term safety monitoring of the cave resulted in an "all clear" from engineers and specialists in March 2020. During the closure, the drainage system was improved to reduce standing water on the cave's floor, and electrical lines were replaced. Visitors should not touch the walls or delicate tree root systems that grow down through the ceiling.

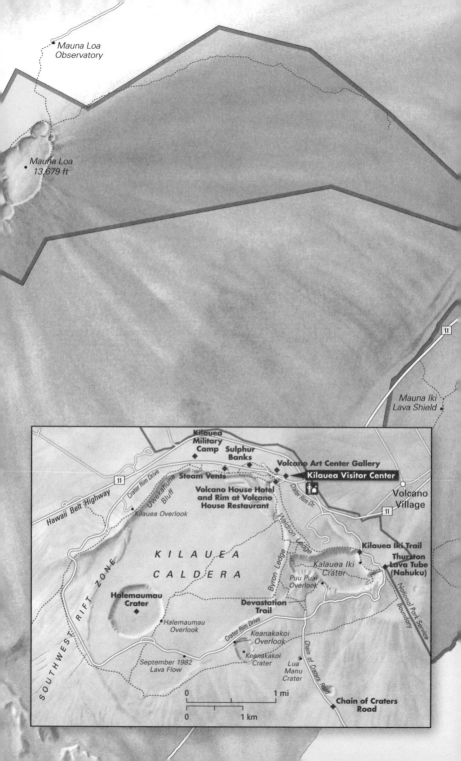

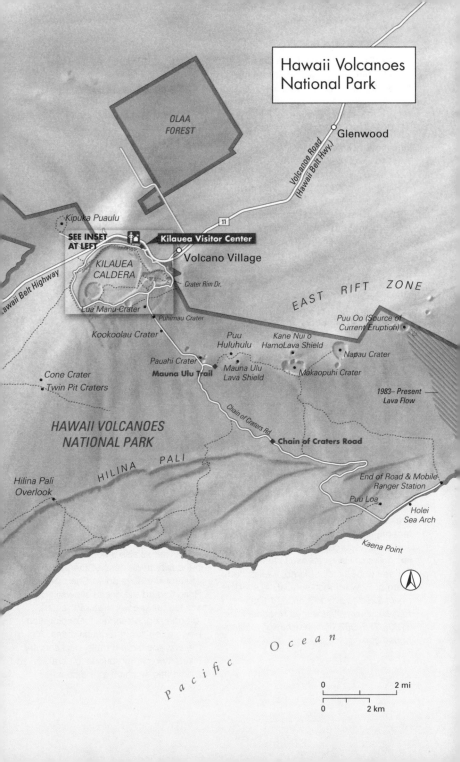

■ TIP→ Parking is limited near the tube; if the lot is full, you can park at the Kilauea Iki Overlook parking lot a ½ mile away. ✉ *Crater Rim Dr., Hawaii Volcanoes National Park* ✣ *1½ miles from the park entrance* ☎ *808/985–6101* 🌐 *www.nps.gov/havo.*

Volcano Art Center Gallery

MUSEUM | Occupying a portion of the original Volcano House hotel built in 1877, this mesmerizing art gallery, within walking distance of the hotel across the way, has showcased works by local artists since 1974. From stained and hand-blown glass to wood crafts, paintings, sculptures, original block prints, jewelry, photographs, and more, the gallery features fine art (for sale) that depicts indigenous and cultural themes of Hawaii Island. In addition, live hula shows in the ancient style are often featured on the lawn that fronts the gallery. ✉ *Crater Rim Dr., Hawaii Volcanoes National Park* ✣ *Within walking distance of Kilauea Visitor Center* ☎ *808/967–8222* 🌐 *www.volcanoart-center.org.*

🍴 Restaurants

The Rim at Volcano House

$$ | HAWAIIAN | FAMILY | This fine-dining restaurant overlooks the rim of Kilauea Caldera and the expansive Halemaumau Crater. Featuring two bars (one of which is adjacent to a lounge) and live entertainment nightly, the restaurant highlights island-inspired cuisine and locally sourced ingredients. **Known for:** views of Halemaumau Crater; Hilo coffee–rubbed rack of lamb; well-priced Taste of Hawaii lunch special. [$] *Average main: $25* ✉ *Volcano House, 1 Crater Rim Dr., Hawaii Volcanoes National Park* ☎ *808/756–9625* 🌐 *www.hawaiivolcano-house.com.*

🛏 Hotels

★ Volcano House

$$$ | HOTEL | Hawaii's oldest hotel—and the only one in Hawaii Volcanoes National Park—is committed to sustainable practices and promoting local Hawaiian culture and history through its locally sourced restaurants, artisan-crafted decor, and eco-focused guest programs. **Pros:** unbeatable location; views of crater; sense of place and history. **Cons:** basic facilities; books up quickly; some rooms have parking lot views. [$] *Rooms from: $285* ✉ *1 Crater Rim Dr., Hawaii Volcanoes National Park* ☎ *808/756–9625* 🌐 *www.hawaiivolcanohouse.com* 🛏 *33 rooms* 🍴 *No meals.*

🛍 Shopping

In addition to lodging (for miliary families only) and some recreational activities, Kilauea Military Camp has a general store and a gas station, making it the best place in the park to stop if you need supplies.

Greater Park Area

Spanning landscapes from sea level to the summits of two of the most active volcanoes in the world, Hawaii Volcanoes National Park boasts a diverse landscape with rain forests, rugged coastlines, surreal lava fields, and sacred cultural sites. There's also a sense of peace and tranquility here, despite the upheavals of nature. A drive down Chain of Craters Road toward the ocean allows you to access the greater area of the park, affording opportunities for exploration beyond the summit destinations. Along the way are birding trails, backcountry hikes, two campgrounds, pit craters, and a dramatic sea arch at the coast.

⊙ Sights

★ Chain of Craters Road

SCENIC DRIVE | The coastal region of Hawaii Volcanoes National Park is accessed via scenic Chain of Craters Road, which descends 18.8 miles to sea level. You could drive it without stopping, but it's well worth spending a few hours or a day exploring the various stops and trails. Winding past ancient craters and modern eruption sites, this scenic road was realigned in 1979 after parts of it were buried by the Mauna Ulu eruption.

Marked stops along the way include Lua Manu Crater, Hilina Pali Road, Pauahi Crater, the Mauna Ulu eruption site, Kealakomo Lookout, and Puu Loa Petroglyphs. As you approach the coast, panoramic ocean vistas prevail. The last marked stop features views of the striking natural Holei Sea Arch from an overlook. In recent years, many former sights along the coast have been covered in lava, including a black-sand beach and the old campground. ⊠ *Hawaii Volcanoes National Park* ☎ *808/ 985–6101* ⊕ *www. nps.gov/havo.*

★ Mauna Ulu Trail

TRAIL | The Mauna Ulu lava flow presents an incredible variety of geological attractions within a moderate, 2½-mile round-trip hike. The diverse lava landscape was created during the spectacular 1969–74 Mauna Ulu flow, which featured enormous "lavafalls" the size of Niagara Falls. Visitors can see everything from lava tree molds and fissure vents to cinder cones and portions of the old highway still exposed under the flow. Hawaiian nene geese roam the area, feeding on ripe ohelo berries.

Hike to the top of a small hill that survived the flow for an incredible view of the Puu Oo Vent in the distance. On clear days, you can see Mauna Loa, Maunakea, and the Pacific Ocean from atop this hill, known as Puu Huluhulu. ■TIP→ **Purchase** the Mauna Ulu trail booklet at the Kilauea Visitor Center for under $3. This excellent resource includes descriptions of trailside attractions, trail maps, history, eyewitness accounts, and photographs. ⊠ *Chain of Craters Rd., Hawaii Volcanoes National Park* ✛ *7 miles from Kilauea Visitor Center* ☎ *808/985–6101* ⊕ *www.nps.gov/havo.*

Puna

Puna is about 6 miles south of Hilo.

The Puna District is wild in every sense of the word. The jagged black coastline is changing all the time; the albizzia trees grow out of control, forming canopies over the few paved roads; the residential areas are remote; and the people—well, there's something about living in an area that could be destroyed by lava at any moment (as Kalapana was in 1990, or Kapoho in 1960, or parts of Pahoa Town in 2014, or Kapoho Vacationland in 2018) that makes the norms of modern society seem silly. Vets, surfers, hippies, yoga teachers, and other free spirits abound. And also a few ruffians. So it is that Puna has its well-deserved reputation as an "outlaw" region of the Big Island.

That said, it's well worth a detour, especially if you're near this part of the island anyway. Some mighty fine people-watching opportunities exist in Pahoa, a funky little town that the "Punatics" call home.

This is also farm country for an array of agricultural products. Local farmers grow everything from orchids and anthuriums to papayas, bananas, and macadamia nuts. Several of the island's larger, rural, residential subdivisions are nestled between Keaau and Pahoa, including Hawaiian Paradise Park, Orchidland Estates, Hawaiian Acres, and Hawaiian Beaches.

When dusk falls here, the air fills with the high-pitched symphony of thousands of coqui frogs. Though they look cute and seem harmless, the invasive frogs are considered pests by local residents weary of their shrieking, all-night calls.

GETTING HERE AND AROUND

The sprawling Puna District stretches northeast down to the coast. If you're staying in Hilo for the night, driving around Lower Puna is a great way to spend a morning.

◉ Sights

Lava Tree State Monument

NATIONAL/STATE PARK | Tree molds that rise like blackened smokestacks formed here in 1790, when a lava flow swept through the ohia forest. Some reach as high as 12 feet. A meandering trail provides closeup looks at some of Hawaii's tropical plants and trees. There are restrooms and a couple of picnic pavilions and tables. In 2018, the park narrowly avoided getting swallowed by lava flows that came within a couple hundred feet of the park. ⚠ **Mosquitoes live here in abundance, so come prepared.** ⊠ *Hwy. 132, Pahoa* ☎ *808/974–6200* 🎟 *Free.*

MacKenzie State Recreation Area

NATIONAL/STATE PARK | This park was one of the few coastal parks in the Puna region spared in the 2018 Kilauea eruption. Overlooking rocky shoreline cliffs in a breezy ironwood grove are a pavilion, picnic tables, and restrooms—but no drinking water. The park is significant for the restored section of the old King's Highway trail system, which circled the coast in the era before Hawaii was discovered by the Western world. In those days, regional chiefs used the trails to connect coastal villages, collect taxes, and maintain control over people. Views take in the rugged coast, rocky beach, and coastal dry forest. There's good shore fishing here, so you might see some locals with a line or two in the water. ⊠ *Hwy. 137, Pahoa* ⊕ *dlnr.hawaii. gov/dsp/parks/hawaii* 🎟 *Free.*

Pahoa Town

TOWN | This eclectic little town is reminiscent of the Wild West, with its wooden boardwalks and vintage buildings—not to mention a reputation as a pot growers' haven. Founded originally to serve the sugar plantation community, Pahoa today is a free-spirited throwback to the 1960s and '70s. You'll see plenty of hippies, vets, survivalists, woofers (workers on organic farms), yoga students, and other colorful characters pursuing alternative lifestyles. Secondhand stores, tie-dye/ hemp clothing boutiques, smoke shops, and art/antiques galleries add to the "trippy" experience. In 2014, lava flows from Kilauea almost intruded into the town, almost overrunning the transfer station and cemetery and destroying a couple of buildings. Residents began saying goodbye to their town and packed up as smoke from the flows billowed in the near distance and the flows glowed after dark. Then it all abruptly stopped within 500 yards of Pahoa Village Road, once again ensuring the town's status as a survivor—until 2018 when Pahoa became command central for disaster assistance, civil defense, and media reporters covering the nearby dramatic eruption of Kilauea in real time. Pahoa's funky main street—with buildings dating to 1910—boasts a handful of excellent, local-style eateries. (In 2017, a fire swept through parts of the boardwalk and buildings, which are still being rebuilt.) To get here, turn southeast onto Highway 130 at Keaau, and drive 11 miles and follow signs to the Village. ⊠ *Pahoa.*

Star of the Sea Painted Church

RELIGIOUS SITE | This historic church, now a community center, was moved to its present location in 1990 just ahead of the advancing lava flow that destroyed the Kalapana area. Dating from the

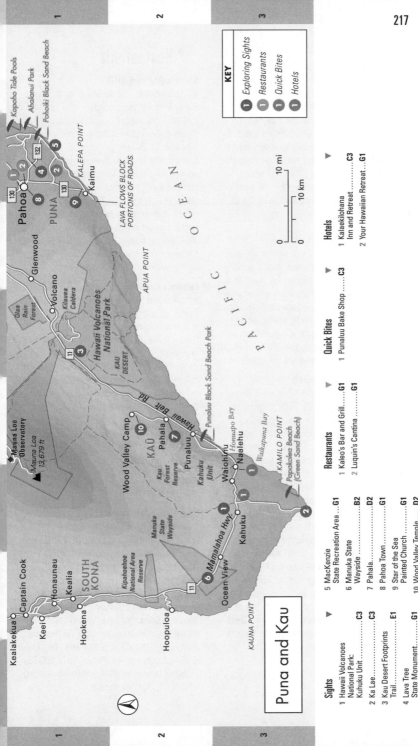

Puna and Kau

KEY
1 Exploring Sights
1 Restaurants
1 Quick Bites
1 Hotels

LAVA FLOWS BLOCK PORTIONS OF ROADS.

0   10 mi
0   10 km

Sights ▶

1 Hawaii Volcanoes
National Park:
Kuhuku Unit...............**C3**
2 Ka Lae......................**C3**
3 Kau Desert Footprints
Trail.........................**E1**
4 Lava Tree
State Monument........**G1**

5 MacKenzie
State Recreation Area...**G1**
6 Manuka State
Wayside.....................**B2**
7 Pahala.......................**D2**
8 Pahoa Town................**G1**
9 Star of the Sea
Painted Church...........**G1**
10 Wood Valley Temple.....**D2**

Restaurants ▶
1 Kaleo's Bar and Grill......**G1**
2 Luquin's Cantina **G1**

Quick Bites ▶
1 Punaluu Bake Shop **C3**

Hotels ▶
1 Kalaekilohana
Inn and Retreat............**C3**
2 Your Hawaiian Retreat....**G1**

1930s, the church was built by a Belgian Catholic missionary priest, Father Evarist Gielen, who also painted the detailed scenes on the church's interior. Though similar in style, the Star of the Sea and St. Benedict's were painted by two different Belgian priests. Star of the Sea also boasts several lovely stained-glass windows and is on the National Register of Historic Places. ✉ *12-4815 Pahoa Kalapana Rd., Kalapana* ✣ *1 mile north of Kalapana* 🎟 *Free, donations welcome.*

Beaches

Puna's few beaches have some unusual attributes—swaths of new black sand, volcano-heated springs, and a coastline that is beyond dramatic, with sheer walls of lava rock dropping into an electric-blue ocean surging with white water and ringed with coco palms. Ongoing eruptions of Kilauea have made parts of Puna inaccessible and closed some roads.

Pohoiki Black Sand Beach

BEACH—SIGHT | Located right next to Isaac Hale Beach is Madame Pele's newest creation, Pohoiki Black Sand Beach, which is open to the public daily from 7 am to 6 pm. The beach was formed when lava from the Lower Puna eruption of 2018 was pulverized as it flowed into the ocean, adding newly created— albeit very rough—sand that washed up on the shore and cut off access to the boat ramp. Although there is a portable restroom, there is no running water in the area. This is not a good swimming beach since the water can be rough and dangerous. To get there, take Highway 137 from Kalapana to an unpaved access route that cuts straight through the new lava flow of 2018. **Amenities:** none. **Best for:** walking. ✉ *Kalapana Kapoho Beach Rd., Pahoa.*

Restaurants

Kaleo's Bar and Grill

$ | **AMERICAN** | Pahoa Town isn't necessarily known for gourmet dining choices, but Kaleo's is pretty sophisticated for a small-town restaurant and remains a local favorite with very good food. Hawaiian-inspired fare blends the gamut of island ethnic influences with such choices as tempura ahi rolls, grilled burgers, and banana spring rolls. **Known for:** sophisticated menu; nightly entertainment; kalua (baked in an earth oven) pork wontons. [$] *Average main: $15* ✉ *15-2969 Pahoa Village Rd., Pahoa* ☎ *808/965–5600* 🌐 *www.kaleoshawaii.com.*

Luquin's Cantina

$ | **MEXICAN** | Long an island favorite for tasty, albeit greasy, Mexican grub, this landmark is making a comeback in the funky town of Pahoa after a tragic fire burned the original restaurant to the ground in 2017. Tacos are great (go for crispy), especially when stuffed with grilled, seasoned local fish on occasion. **Known for:** longtime Pahoa restaurant; affordable fare; delicious huevos rancheros. [$] *Average main: $9* ✉ *15-1448 Kahakai Blvd., Pahoa* ☎ *808/965–9990* 🌐 *www.luquins.com.*

Hotels

Your Hawaiian Retreat

$ | **RENTAL** | A collection of three little rentals deep in the heart of Puna and well off the beaten path comprise this exotic destination on an organic farm. **Pros:** affordable whole house rental options; breakfast items stocked for Mango and Avocado House; Ohana House good for groups. **Cons:** remote; not on the beach; three-night minimum stay. [$] *Rooms from: $100* ✉ *13-809 Kamaili Rd., Pahoa* ✣ *6 miles south of Pahoa* ☎ *808/965–7088* 🌐 *www.yourhawaiianretreat.org* 🛏 *3 units* 🍴 *No meals.*

Kau

South Point is 50 miles south of Kailua-Kona.

Perhaps the most desolate region of the island, Kau is nevertheless home to some spectacular sights. Mark Twain wrote some of his finest prose here, where macadamia nut farms, remote green-sand beaches, and tiny communities offer rugged, largely undiscovered beauty. The drive from Kailua-Kona to windswept South Point winds away from the ocean through a surreal moonscape of lava plains and patches of scrub forest. Coming from Volcano, as you near South Point, the barren lavascape gives way to lush vistas from the ocean to the hills.

At the end of the 12-mile, two-lane road to South Point, you can park and hike about an hour to Papakolea (Green Sands Beach). Back on the highway, the coast passes verdant cattle pastures, sheer cliffs, and the village of Naalehu on the way to the black-sand beach of Punaluu, a common nesting place of the Hawaiian hawksbill turtle.

GETTING HERE AND AROUND

Kau is usually combined with a quick trip to Hawaii Volcanoes National Park from Kona. This is probably cramming too much into one day, however. Visiting the volcano fills up at least a day (two is better), and the sights of this southern end of the island are worth more than a cursory glance.

Instead, make Green Sands Beach or Punaluu a full beach day, and see some of the other sights on the way there or back. Bring sturdy shoes, water, and a sun hat if Green Sands Beach is your choice (reaching the beach requires a hike). You can pay some enterprising locals $5 a head to give you a ride in their pickups to the beach. And be careful in the surf here. Don't go in unless you're used to ocean waves. There are no lifeguards at this remote beach. It's

decidedly calmer and you can sometimes snorkel at Punaluu, but use caution at these and all Hawaii beaches.

◉ Sights

Hawaii Volcanoes National Park: Kahuku Unit

NATIONAL/STATE PARK | Located off Highway 11 at mile marker 70.5, the Kahuku section of the park takes visitors over many trails through ancient lava flows and native forests. Endangered plants and animals are on display in this beautiful but isolated region of Hawaii Volcanoes National Park, encompassing more than 116,000 acres of protected parklands. Guided hikes with knowledgeable rangers are a regularly scheduled highlight. ⊠ *Hwy. 11 at mile marker 70.5, Kahuku* ☎ *808/985–6101* ⊕ *www.nps. gov/havo/index.htm* ⊠ *$30 per car, $15 for pedestrian* ☉ *Closed Mon. and Tues.*

Ka Lae (*South Point*)

NATIONAL/STATE PARK | It's thought that the first Polynesians came ashore at this southernmost point of land in the United States, also a National Historic Landmark. Old canoe-mooring holes, visible today, were carved through the rocks, possibly by settlers from Tahiti as early as AD 750. To get here, drive 12 miles down the turnoff road, past rows of giant electricity-producing windmills powered by the nearly constant winds sweeping across this coastal plain. Bear left when the road forks, and park in the lot at the end. Walk past the boat hoists toward the little lighthouse. South Point is just past the lighthouse at the southernmost cliff. You may see brave locals jumping off the cliffs and then climbing up rusty old ladders, but swimming here is not recommended. Don't leave anything of value in your car. The area is isolated and without services. Green Sands Beach is a 40-minute hike down the coast. ⊠ *South Point Rd. off Mamalahoa Hwy., near mile marker 70, Naalehu* ⊠ *Free.*

Kau Desert Footprints Trail

TRAIL | A short little hike, 1.6 miles round-trip, to see faded footprints, cast in mud formed by hardened ash. ⊠ *Naalehu* ⊹ *Take Hwy. 11 approximately 15 minutes west of the park entrance, between mile markers 38 and 39* ⛳ *Free.*

Manuka State Wayside

NATIONAL/STATE PARK | FAMILY | This lowland forest preserve spreads across several relatively recent lava flows. A semirugged trail follows a 2-mile loop past a pit crater, winding around interesting trees such as hau and *kukui* (candlenut). It's a nice spot to get out of the car and stretch your legs—you can wander through the well-maintained arboretum, snap a few photos of the eerie forest, and let the kids scramble around trees so large they can't get their arms around them. The pathways can get muddy and rough, so bring appropriate shoes if you plan to hike. Large populations of the Hawaiian hoary bat inhabit the area, which, in totality, encompasses 25,000 of forest reserve. Restrooms, picnic areas, and camping sites (by permit) are available. ⊠ *Hwy. 11, north of mile marker 81, Pahala* ☎ *808/974–6200* ⊕ *dlnr.hawaii. gov/dsp/parks/hawaii* ⛳ *Free.*

Pahala

TOWN | About 16 miles east of Naalehu, beyond Punaluu Beach Park, Highway 11 passes directly by this little town. You'll miss it if you blink. Pahala, once a booming sugar plantation company town, is sleepy today but still inhabited by retired cane workers and their descendants. There is a Longs Pharmacy, a gas station, and a small supermarket, but not much else in terms of conveniences. Beyond the town past a wide, paved cane road, is Wood Valley, once a prosperous community, now just a peaceful area heavily scented by eucalyptus trees, coffee blossoms, and night-blooming jasmine and often laden in mist. ⊠ *Pahala.*

Wood Valley Temple (*Nechung Temple*)

RELIGIOUS SITE | Behind the remote town of Pahala, this serene and beautiful Tibetan Buddhist temple, established in 1973, has hosted more than 50 well-known lamas, including the Dalai Lama on two occasions. Known as *Nechung Dorje Drayang Ling*, or "Immutable Island of Melodious Sound," this peaceful place welcomes all creeds. You can visit and meditate, leave an offering, walk the lush gardens shared by strutting peacocks, browse the gift shop, or stay in the temple's guesthouse, available for peaceful, nondenominational retreats taught by masters. ⊠ *96-2285 Wood Valley Rd., Pahala* ☎ *808/928–8539* ⊕ *www. nechung.org* ⛳ *$5.*

🏖 Beaches

You shouldn't expect to find sparkling white-sand beaches on the rugged and rocky coasts of Kau, and you won't. What you will find is something a bit rarer and well worth the visit: black- and green-sand beaches. And there's the chance to see the endangered hawksbill or Hawaiian green sea turtles close up.

Papakolea Beach (*Green Sands Beach*)

BEACH—SIGHT | Tired of the same old gold-, white-, or black-sand beach? Then how about a green-sand beach? You'll need good hiking shoes or sneakers to get to this olive-green crescent, one of the most unusual beaches on the island. It lies at the base of Puu O Mahana, at Mahana Bay, where a cinder cone formed during an early eruption of Mauna Loa. The greenish tint is caused by an accumulation of olivine crystals that form in volcanic eruptions. The dry, barren landscape is totally surreal but stunning, as aquamarine waters lap on green sand against reddish cliffs. ⚠ **The surf is often rough and swimming can be hazardous due to strong currents, so caution is advised**. Drive down to South Point; at the end of the 12-mile paved road, take the road to the left and park at the end.

To reach the beach, follow the 2¼-mile coastal trail, which ends in a steep and dangerous descent down the cliffside on an unimproved trail. The hike takes about two hours each way and it can get hot and windy, so bring lots of drinking water. Four-wheel-drive vehicles are no longer permitted on the trail. **Amenities:** none. **Best for:** solitude; walking. ✉ *Hwy. 11, Naalehu ✥ 2½ miles northeast of South Point.*

★ **Punaluu Black Sand Beach Park**
BEACH—SIGHT | A must-do on a south–southeast–bound trip to the volcano, this easily accessible black-sand beach is backed by low dunes, brackish ponds, and tall coco palms. The shoreline is jagged, reefed, and rocky. Most days, large groups of sea turtles nap on the sand—a stunning sight. Resist the urge to get too close or disturb them; they're protected by federal and state law, and fines for harassment can be hefty. Removing black sand is also prohibited. ⚠ **Extremely strong rip currents prevail, so only experienced ocean swimmers should consider getting in the water here.** A popular stop for locals and tour buses alike, this beach park can get very busy, especially on weekends (the north parking lot is usually quieter). Shade from palm trees provides an escape from the sun, and at the northern end of the beach, near the boat ramp, lie the ruins of Kaneeleele Heiau, an old Hawaiian temple. The area was a sugar port until the 1946 tsunami destroyed the buildings. Developers tried to bring a huge resort experience here in the early 1990s, but that has mostly failed. **Amenities:** parking (no fee); showers; toilets. **Best for:** walking. ✉ *Hwy. 11, between mile markers 55 and 56, Naalehu ✥ 27 miles south of Hawaii Volcanoes National Park* ☎ *808/961–8311.*

Coffee and Quick Bites

Punaluu Bake Shop
$ | **CAFÉ** | Billed as the southernmost bakery in the United States, it's a good spot to grab a snack, and the heavenly smell alone is worth the stop. Local-style plate lunches and sandwiches on the bakeshop's famous sweetbread buns go well with Kau coffee. **Known for:** plate lunches and sandwiches; goods all baked on-site; lilikoi-glazed malasada (Portuguese doughnuts). [$] *Average main: $8* ✉ *5642 Mamalahoa Hwy., Naalehu* ☎ *808/929–7343* 🌐 *www.bakeshophawaii.com.*

Hotels

Kalaekilohana Inn and Retreat
$$$$ | **B&B/INN** | You wouldn't really expect to find a top-notch B&B in Kau, but just up the road from South Point, this grand residence offers large private suites with locally harvested hardwood floors, private lanai with ocean and mountain views, and big, comfy beds with high-thread-count sheets and fluffy down comforters. **Pros:** luxurious beds; beautiful decor reminscent of old Hawaii; delicious complimentary breakfast. **Cons:** not for children under 12; no pool; very limited nearby shopping. [$] *Rooms from: $349* ✉ *94-2152 South Point Rd., Naalehu* ☎ *808/939–8052* 🌐 *www.kau-hawaii.com* 🛏 *4 suites* 🍴 *Free breakfast.*

Chapter 8

ACTIVITIES AND TOURS

Updated by
Kristina Anderson

With the Big Island's predictably mild year-round climate, it's no wonder you'll find an emphasis on outdoor activities. After all, this is the home of the annual Ironman World Championship triathlon. Whether you're an avid hiker or a beginning bicyclist, a casual golfer or a tennis buff, you'll find plenty of activities to lure you away from your resort or condo.

You can explore by bike, helicopter, ATV, zipline, or horse, or you can put on your hiking boots and use your own horsepower. No matter how you get around, you'll be treated to breathtaking backdrops along the Big Island's 266-mile coastline and within its 4,028 square miles (and still growing!). Aerial tours take in the latest eruption activity and lava flows, as well as the island's gorgeous tropical valleys, gulches, and coastal plains. Trips into the backcountry wilderness explore the rain forest, private ranchlands, and coffee farms, while sleepy sugar plantation villages offer a glimpse of Hawaii's bygone days.

Golfers will find acclaimed championship golf courses at the Kohala Coast resorts—Mauna Kea Beach Hotel, Autograph Collection; the Westin Hapuna Beach Resort; Mauna Lani, Auberge Resorts Collection; and Waikoloa Beach Resort, among others. During the winter, if snow conditions allow, you can even go skiing on top of Maunakea (elevation: 13,796 feet). It's a skiing experience unlike any other.

The ancient Hawaiians, who took much of their daily sustenance from the ocean, also enjoyed playing in the water, so it's no wonder that visitors want to get out onto the water as well. In fact, surfing was the sport of kings. Though it's easy to be lulled into whiling away the day baking in the sun on a white-, gold-, black-, or green-sand beach, getting into or onto the water is a highlight of most trips.

All of the Hawaiian Islands are surrounded by the Pacific Ocean, and blessed with a temperate latitude, making them some of the world's greatest natural playgrounds. But certain experiences are even better on the Big Island: nighttime diving trips to see manta rays; deep-sea fishing in Kona's fabled waters, where dozens of Pacific blue marlin of 1,000 pounds or more have been caught; and kayaking in pristine bays, to name a few.

From almost any point on the Big Island, the ocean is nearby. Whether it's body boarding and snorkeling or kayaking and surfing, there is a water sport for everyone. For most activities, you can rent gear and go it alone. Or book a group excursion with an experienced guide, who offers convenience and security, as well as special insights into Hawaiian marine life and culture. Want to try surfing? Contrary to what you may have heard, there *are* waves on the Big Island. You can take lessons from pros who promise to have you standing the first day out.

The Kona and Kohala Coasts of West Hawaii boast the largest number of ocean sports outfitters and tour operators. They operate from the small-boat harbors and piers in Kailua-Kona, Keauhou, Kawaihae, and at the Kohala Coast resorts. There are also several outfitters in the East Hawaii and Hilo areas.

As a general rule, the waves are gentler here than on the other Islands, but there are a few things to be aware of. First, don't turn your back on the ocean. It's unlikely, but if conditions are right, a wave could come along and push you face-first into the sand or drag you out to sea. Second, when the Big Island does experience high surf, dangerous conditions prevail and can change rapidly. Watch the ocean for a few minutes before going out to scan for waves, which arrive in sets. If it looks rough, don't chance it. Third, realize that ultimately you must keep yourself safe. We strongly encourage you to obey lifeguards and high surf advisories, and heed the advice of outfitters from whom you rent equipment, and even from locals on shore. It could save your trip or even your life.

Aerial Tours

There's nothing quite like the aerial view of a waterfall crashing down a couple of thousand feet into cascading pools, or watching lava flow to the ocean as exploding clouds of steam billow into the air. You can get this bird's-eye view from a helicopter or a fixed-wing small plane. All operators pay strict attention to safety. So how to get the best experience for your money? ■ TIP→ **Before you choose a company, be a savvy traveler and ask the right questions. What kind of aircraft do they fly? What is their safety record?**

Big Island Air Tours
FLYING/SKYDIVING/SOARING | This small company, in business since the 1980s, offers fixed-wing tours of the island, including a circle island tour, Kilauea sunset tour, or Maui–Big Island tour. It also features charters between all the major islands. This is a good alternative to the pricier helicopter tours. ☎ *808/329–4868* ⊕ *www.bigislandair.com* ✉ *From $297.*

Blue Hawaiian Helicopters
FLYING/SKYDIVING/SOARING | Hawaii Island's premier aerial tour is on Blue Hawaiian's roomy Eco-Star helicopters—so smooth and quiet you hardly realize you're taking off. There are no worries about what seat you get because each has great views. Pilots are also State of Hawaii–certified tour guides, so they are knowledgeable and experienced but not overly chatty. In the breathtaking Waimanu Valley, the helicopter hovers amazingly close to 2,600-foot cliffs and cascading waterfalls. The two-hour Big Island Spectacular also takes in the incredible landscapes of Hawaii Volcanoes National Park, as well as the stunning valleys; you can even choose an optional waterfall landing as part of it. Most tours leave from Blue Hawaiian's Waikoloa heliport, but the 50-minute Circle of Fire tour, the 15-minute Hilo Holoholo tour, and the fun Craters and Coffee tour all depart from Hilo. ✉ *Waikoloa Heliport, Hwy. 19, Waikoloa* ☎ *808/961–5600* ⊕ *www.bluehawaiian. com* ✉ *From $99 (15-minute tour).*

★ Paradise Helicopters
FLYING/SKYDIVING/SOARING | Even when the volcano is not actively flowing, there's still plenty to see from the air, with great options from this locally owned and operated company. Opt

for the Doors-Off Kohala Valleys and Waterfalls tour departing from the Waimea-Kohala Airport, which takes you soaring deep into the heart of the spectacular Kohala Valleys to view 2,500-foot waterfalls and sheer cliff walls. Or take the Doors-Off Lava and Rainforests Adventure, departing from Hilo, to see Hilo's rain forests and Rainbow Falls, as well as Puna's 2018 eruption site. You'll marvel at the incredible 8-mile river of frozen lava stretching from Fissure 8 to the Pacific Ocean; the newest black-sand beaches on earth; and the spectacular craters of Kilauea Volcano. Pilots, many of whom have military backgrounds, are fun and knowledgeable. ■ TIP➔ **The only helicopter company in Hawaii certified by the Hawaii Ecotour Association, Paradise offers you the option to offset your tour's carbon footprint by having a tree planted in Hawaii for each ride you take.** ☎ 808/969–7392, 866/876–7422 ⊕ www.paradisecopters.com ✉ From $274.

Safari Helicopters
FLYING/SKYDIVING/SOARING | Departing from the Hilo airport, Safari offers a 45-minute tour of the East Rift Zone or a 55-minute tour that includes Hawaii Volcanoes National Park plus the waterfalls. ■ TIP➔ **Book online for substantial discounts.** ✉ Hilo International Airport, 2350 Kekuanaoa St., Hilo ☎ 808/969–1259 ⊕ www.safarihelicopters.com ✉ From $189.

ATV Tours

A fun way to experience the Big Island's rugged coastline and wild ranchlands is through an off-road adventure—a real backcountry experience. At higher elevations, the weather gets nippy and rainy, but views can be awesome. Protective gear is provided, and everyone gets a mini driving lesson. Generally, you must be 16 or older to ride your own ATV; some outfitters allow children seven and older as passengers.

ATV Outfitters Hawaii
FOUR-WHEELING | These trips take in the scenic beauty of the rugged North Kohala Coast, traveling along coastal cliffs and the Kohala Ditch Trail into the forest in search of waterfalls, along 22 miles of trails. ATV Outfitters also offers double-seater ATVs for parents traveling with children or adults who don't feel comfortable operating their own vehicle. Knowledgeable guides stop at various points of interest and share the fascinating history of the region. The company also offers a Waterfall and Rainforest tour and a Deluxe Ocean and Waterfall adventure. ✉ 53-324 Lighthouse Rd., Kapaau ☎ 808/889–6000, 888/288–7288 ⊕ www.atvoutfittershawaii.com ✉ From $179.

Hawea Waipio Valley Adventures
TOUR—SPORTS | FAMILY | The owner-operators of this company are fifth-generation taro farmers and caretakers of the land who are passionate about sharing their love for Waipio Valley. They meet you in Honokaa and shuttle you to the valley floor, accommodating between three and six passengers (but can fit more with advance notice). This guided ATV tour of their 100-acre taro farm focuses on offering a historical, educational, and cultural experience. They will take you to the loi kalo (taro patch) to harvest and plant kalo, and give you a sample of their fresh poi. Allow three hours from start to finish. ■ TIP➔ **Check online for military discount code.** ✉ 45-3390 Mamane St., Honokaa ☎ 808/657–5227 ⊕ haweawaipiovalleyadventure.com ✉ $169.

Maunakea Trails ATV
TOUR—SPORTS | FAMILY | This outfitter takes you on a beautiful trek through the coastal Hamakua rain forest, where you'll stop here and there to take in vistas of the ocean, famous local surf spots, and spectacular windward river valleys. Don't worry if you have never driven an ATV before. The professional guides will show you the ropes and present a detailed safety orientation for operation of the

high-flying Polaris ATVs. Prepare to get wet and muddy (that's the fun of it!) as you climb upcountry trails and learn a little Hawaiian history along the way. The highlight is reaching the private waterfall, where you can enjoy a snack and take a plunge in the icy water if you dare. You must be 18 with a valid driver's license to drive. You may also ride along if you don't want to drive. Children ages five and older are welcome. ⊠ *Grand Naniloa Hotel Hilo Lobby, 93 Banyan Dr., Hilo* ☎ *808/964–1000* ⊕ *www.kapohokine. com* ☜ *From $199.*

Biking

The Big Island's biking trails and road routes range from easy to moderate coastal rides to rugged backcountry wilderness treks that challenge the most serious cyclists. You can soak up the island's storied scenic vistas and varied geography—from tropical rain forest to rolling ranch country, from high-country mountain meadows to dry lava deserts. It's dry, windy, and hot on Kona's and Kohala's coastal trails, mountainous through South Kona, and cool, wet, and muddy in the upcountry Waimea and Volcano areas, as well as in lower Puna. There are long distances between towns, few bike lanes, narrow single-lane highways, and scanty services in the Kau, Puna, South Kona, and Kohala Coast areas, so plan accordingly for your weather, water, food, and lodging needs before setting out. ∎TIP→ **Your best bet is to book with an outfitter who has all the details covered.**

Big Island Mountain Bike Association
BICYCLING | Based in Hilo, this nonprofit group is dedicated to promoting safe mountain biking on the island. They have loads of recommendations. ☎ *808/961–8934.*

Hawaii Cycling Club
BICYCLING | This nonprofit club has tons of information on biking the Big Island, along with scheduled rides and events such as picnics. A free ride for members leaves Old Airport Beach Park in Kailua-Kona every Saturday at 7 am. ⊕ *www. hawaiicyclingclub.com.*

BEST SPOTS
★ Kulani Trails
BICYCLING | It has been called the best ride in the state—if you really want to get gnarly. The technically demanding ride, which passes majestic eucalyptus trees, is for advanced cyclists; muddy conditions prevail. To reach the trailhead from the intersection of Highway 11 and Highway 19, take Highway 19 south about 4 miles, turn right on Stainback Highway, continue 2½ miles, turn right at the Waiakea Arboretum, and park near the gate. A permit is required, available from the Department of Land and Natural Resources at Kawili Street and Kilauea Avenue in Hilo. ⊠ *Stainback Hwy., Hilo.*

Old Puna Trail
BICYCLING | A 10½-mile ride through the subtropical jungle in Puna, this trail leads into one of the island's most isolated areas. It starts on a cinder road, which becomes a four-wheel-drive trail. If it's rained recently, you'll have to deal with puddles—the first few of which you'll gingerly avoid until you give in and go barreling through the rest for the sheer fun of it. This is a great ride for all abilities and takes about 90 minutes. The ride ends at Haena Beach. To get to the trailhead from Highway 130, take Kaloli Road to Beach Road. ⚠ **Ride at your own risk; this is not a maintained trail.** ⊠ *Kaloli Rd. at Hwy. 130, Pahoa.*

EQUIPMENT AND TOURS
There are bike rental shops in Kailua-Kona and a couple in Waimea and Hilo. Many resorts rent bicycles that can be used around the properties. Most outfitters can provide a bicycle rack for your car, and all offer reduced rates for rentals

longer than one day. All retailers offer excellent advice about where to go; they know the areas well.

BikeVolcano.com

BICYCLING | This outfitter leads three- or five-hour bike rides through Hawaii Volcanoes National Park, mostly downhill, that take in fantastic sights from rain forests to craters. The company also coordinates and leads a cool ride to the 2018 eruption site in Puna. Equipment, support van, and food are included; pickup locations are in Hilo and Volcano (and Kona by request). Cruise passengers are welcome. ⊠ Hilo ☎ 808/934–9199, 888/934–9199 ⊕ www.bikevolcano.com ⊠ From $135.

Bike Works Kona

BICYCLING | The company caters to cyclists of all skill levels with race services, suggested rides for moderate to advanced riders, and rentals of deluxe road bikes, full-suspension mountain bikes, and high-end triathlon bikes. Their retail space in Kona's "Old" Industrial Area is huge and impressive. ⊠ 75-5660 Kopiko St., Kailua-Kona ☎ 808/326–2453 ⊕ www.bikeworkskona.com ⊠ From $25/day.

Hilo Bike Hub

BICYCLING | An enthusiast shop specializing in servicing bikes to fit the ruggedness of Hawaii's east-side terrain, this is a good resource for those wishing to mountain bike in these off-the-beaten-path areas. A sponsor of rides and local events, Hilo Bike Hub was instrumental in helping to establish Kulani Trails, part of the Waiakea Forest reserve, as an official mountain biking area. The shop also carries gear and accessories. ⊠ 318 E. Kawili St., Hilo ☎ 808/961–4452 ⊕ www.hilobikehub.com.

Mid Pacific Wheels

BICYCLING | The oldest bike shop on the Big Island, this community-oriented shop near the university carries a full line of bikes and accessories and rents mountain bikes for exploring the Hilo area. The friendly staff provides expert advice on where to go and what to see and do on a self-guided tour. They also carry a large selection of cycling accessories, bikes, and repair parts. ⊠ 1133C Manono St., Hilo ☎ 808/935–6211 ⊕ www.midpacificwheelsllc.com ⊠ From $35/day.

Body Boarding and Bodysurfing

According to the movies, in the Old West there was always friction between cattle ranchers and sheep ranchers. A somewhat similar situation exists between surfers and body boarders (and between surfers and stand-up paddleboarders). That's why they generally keep to their own separate areas. Often the body boarders, who lie on their stomachs on shorter boards, stay closer to shore and leave the outside breaks to the board surfers. Or the board surfers may stick to one side of the beach and the body boarders to the other. The truth is, body boarding (often called "boogie boarding," in homage to the first commercial manufacturer of this slick, little, flexible-foam board) is a blast. Most surfers also sometimes carve waves on a body board, no matter how much of a purist they claim to be. ■ TIP→ **Novice body boarders should catch shorebreak waves only. Ask lifeguards or locals for the best spots.** You'll need a pair of short fins to get out to the bigger waves offshore (not recommended for newbies). As for bodysurfing, just catch a wave and make like Superman going faster than a speeding bullet.

BEST SPOTS

Hapuna Beach State Recreation Area.
Often considered one of the top 10 beaches in the world, Hapuna Beach State Recreation Area offers fine white sand, turquoise water, and easy rolling surf on most days, making it great for

bodysurfing and body boarding at all levels. Ask the lifeguards—who only cover areas south of the rocky cliff that juts out near the middle of the beach—about conditions before heading into the water, especially in winter. Sometimes northwest swells create a dangerous undertow. ⊠ *Hwy. 19, near mile marker 69, just south of Mauna Kea Beach Hotel, Kohala Coast* ⊕ *dlnr.hawaii.gov/dsp.*

Honolii Cove. North of Hilo, this is the best body-boarding spot on the east side of the island. ⊠ *Off Hwy. 19, near mile marker 4, Hilo.*

Magic Sands Beach Park (White Sands Beach). This white-sand, shorebreak cove is great for beginning to intermediate bodysurfing and body boarding. Sometimes randomly, much of the sand here washes out to sea and forms a sandbar just offshore, creating fun wave conditions, only to "reappear" a few days later. Also known as White Sands, it's popular and can get crowded with locals, especially when school is out. Watch for nasty rip currents at high tide. ■TIP→ **If you're not using fins, wear reef shoes for protection against sharp rocks.** ⊠ *Alii Dr., just north of mile marker 4, Kailua-Kona.*

EQUIPMENT

Equipment rental shacks are located at many beaches and boat harbors, along the highway, and at most resorts. Body board rental rates are around $12–$15 per day and around $60 per week. You can also buy snorkeling equipment at one of the big-box retailers if you plan to be out every day, want to ensure sanitation, or need a perfect fit. Most also carry body boards.

Honolua Surf Company
WATER SPORTS | Surfboards, apparel, logowear, gear, sunglasses, and hats are available at these moderately priced surf shops. There are several locations statewide. ⊠ *Kona Shopping Village, 75-5744 Alii Dr., Kailua-Kona* ☎ *808/329–1001* ⊕ *www.honoluasurf.com.*

★ **Orchidland Surfboards and Surf Shop**
WATER SPORTS | This venerable shop in historic downtown Hilo—in business since 1972—carries a wide variety of surf and other water sports equipment for sale or rent. It stocks professional custom surfboards, body boards, and surf apparel. Owner Stan Lawrence, famous for his "Drainpipe" legacy, was one of the last people to surf that famous break before lava flows claimed the Kalapana area. Old photos and surf posters on the walls add to the nostalgia. Through the shop, he hosts surf contests and does the daily surf report for local radio stations. This surf shop is as authentic as they get. ⊠ *262 Kamehameha Ave., Hilo* ☎ *808/935–1533* ⊕ *www.orchidlandsurf. com* ➔ *From $15 body board/day, $25 surfboard/day.*

★ **Pacific Vibrations**
SURFING | Family-owned, this surf shop—in business since 1978—holds the distinction of being the oldest, smallest surf shop in the world. Even at a compact, sub-500 square feet, this place stocks tons of equipment, surf wear and gear, sunglasses, and GoPro cameras. Located oceanfront in downtown Kailua Town, it is tucked away in a vintage building, and is worth a stop just for the cool Hawaii surf vibe and to talk story with the friendly owners. The owners are activists in protecting local surf spots from development. ⊠ *75-5702B Likana La., at Alii Dr., Kailua-Kona* ☎ *808/329–4140.*

Caving

The Kanohina Lava Tube system is about 1,000 years old and was used by the ancient Hawaiians for water collection and for shelter. More than 56 miles of braided lava tubes have been mapped so far in the Kau District of the Big Island, near Ka Lae (South Point). About 45 miles south of Kailua-Kona, these lava tubes are a great experience for cavers of all age levels and abilities.

★ **Kula Kai Caverns**

SPELUNKING | Expert cave guides lead groups into the fantastic underworld of these caverns near South Point. The braided lava-tube system attracts scientists from around the world, who come to study and map them (more than 56 miles so far). Tours range from the Lighted Trail (in the lighted show cave, which is easy walking) to the Two Hour, a deep-down-under spelunking adventure that often takes closer to three hours and allows you to see archaeological evidence of the ancient Hawaiians. Longer, customized tours are also available; all gear is provided. Tours start at an Indiana Jones–style expedition tent and divulge fascinating details about the caves' geologic and cultural history. Reservations are required. ⊠ *Kula Kai Estates, Lauhala Dr. at Kona Kai Blvd.* ☎ *808/929–9725* ⊕ *www.kulakaicaverns.com* 🖃 *From $28.*

Deep-Sea Fishing

The Kona Coast has some of the world's most exciting "blue-water" fishing. Although July, August, and September are peak months, with the best fishing and a number of tournaments, charter fishing goes on year-round. You don't have to compete to experience the thrill of landing a Pacific blue marlin or other big-game fish. Some 60 charter boats, averaging 26 to 58 feet in length, are available for hire, all of them out of **Honokohau Harbor**, north of Kailua-Kona.

The Kona Coast is world-famous for the presence of large marlin, particularly the Pacific blue. In fact, it's also known as "Grander Alley" for the fish caught here that weigh more than 1,000 pounds. The largest blue marlin on record was caught in 1984 and weighed 1,649 pounds. In total, more than 60 granders have been reeled in here by top sportfishing teams.

For an exclusive charter, prices generally range from $600 to $950 for a half-day trip (about four hours) and $800 to $1,600 for a full day at sea (about eight hours). For share charters, rates are about $100 to $140 per person for a half day and $200 for a full day. If fuel prices increase, expect charter costs to rise. Most boats are licensed to take up to six passengers, in addition to the crew. Tackle, bait, and ice are furnished, but you usually have to bring your own lunch. You won't be able to keep your catch, although if you ask, many captains will send you home with a few fillets.

Honokohau Harbor's Fuel Dock

FISHING | Show up around 11 am and watch the weigh-in of the day's catch from the morning charters, or around 3:30 for the afternoon charters, especially during the summer tournament season. Weigh-ins are fun when the big ones come in, but these days, with most of the marlin being released, it's not a sure thing. ■ **TIP**➔ **In the foyer of the Kona Inn, look for some of the "granders" on display.** ⊠ *Honokohau Harbor, Kealakehe Pkwy. at Hwy. 11, Kailua-Kona.*

BOATS AND CHARTERS

Before you sign up with anyone, think about the kind of trip you want. Looking for a romantic cruise? A rockin' good time with your buddies? Serious fishing in one of the "secret spots"? A family-friendly excursion? Be sure to describe your expectations so a booking agent can match you with a captain and a boat that suit your style.

Bite Me Sportfishing Fleet

FISHING | **FAMILY** | This multifaceted sportfishing company offers a full fleet with shared, half-day charters, three-quarter-day, and invitational championships; they know how, when, and where to catch fish along the Kona Coast. They specialize in a family-friendly experience and can accommodate private parties of six or more. Lots of charters for different excursions are also available, and they follow catch-and-release practices to help sustain local fisheries. ■ **TIP**➔ **Bonus: they**

will share the catch with you so you can enjoy some while on the island, or they'll recommend a restaurant that can cook it for you. There's also a cool retail store where you can buy everything from logo T-shirts to hats. ⊠ *Honokahau Harbor, 74-425 Kealakehe Pkwy., Suite 17, Kailua-Kona* ☎ *808/936–3442* ⊕ *www.bitemesport-fishing.com* ⊠ *From $119.*

Bwana Sportfishing

FISHING | Full-, half-, three-quarter-day, and overnight charters are available on the 46-foot *Bwana.* The boat features the latest electronics, top-of-the-line equipment, and air-conditioned cabins. You get outstanding, quality tackle and lots of experience here. Captain Teddy comes from a fishing family; father Pete was a legend on Kona waters for decades. ⊠ *Honokohau Harbor, Slip H-17, 74-381 Kealakehe Pkwy., Kailua-Kona* ✛ *Just south of Kona airport* ☎ *808/936–5168* ⊠ *From $1,250.*

The Charter Desk at Honokohau Harbor

FISHING | With about 60 big-name boats on the books, this place will book just the right charter for you (even whale-watching cruises). Due to their location near the weigh scales, they know which boats are the most active and have the best daily catches. Captains will also weigh your catch, take photos, and give you souvenir tags to take home. ■**TIP→ You can make arrangements through hotel activity desks, but it's better to come here and look things over for yourself.** ⊠ *Honokohau Harbor Fuel Dock, 74-381 Kealakehe Pkwy., Kailua-Kona* ☎ *808/329–5735, 888/566–2487* ⊕ *www.charterdesk.com* ⊠ *From $499.*

Charter Locker

FISHING | Half- and full-day charter fishing trips on 36- to 53-foot vessels are offered by this experienced company. Featured boats include *Kona Blue, JR's Hooker, Strong Persuader,* and *Kila Kila.* Rates depend on the boat. ⊠ *Honokohau Harbor, 74-381 Kealakehe Pkwy., #16, Kailua-Kona* ✛ *Just south of Kona airport*

☎ *808/326–2553* ⊕ *www.charterlocker.com* ⊠ *From $395.*

Humdinger Sportfishing

FISHING | This father-son team brings more than five decades of fishing experience in Kona waters, and the expert crew are marlin specialists. Their 37-foot Rybovich, the *Humdinger,* features the latest in electronics and top-line rods and reels. ■**TIP→ They will let you keep your catch (except for billfish) and will even fillet for you.** Book online for discounts and specials; they sell out quickly, so plan ahead. ⊠ *Honokohau Harbor, 74-381 Kealakehe Pkwy., Slip B-4, Kailua-Kona* ☎ *808/425–9225, 800/926–2374, 808/425–9228 boat phone* ⊕ *www.humdingersportfishing.com* ⊠ *From $399.*

Jeff Rogers Charters

FISHING | One of Kona's friendliest "old salts," Captain Jeff has been leading personalized big game and other fishing charters since 1982. Using a few tricks of the trade (including targeting the bottom), he's able to find the right fish in the right place, nearly without fail. You may ask him to fillet part of your catch. Holder of six world records and six state records, Jeff has caught his share of marlin granders (over 1,000 pounds). Guests (no more than two) may share a charter to save costs through his special program, so check online for the list of available shares. ⊠ *73-4345 Oneone St., Kailua-Kona* ☎ *808/895–1852* ⊕ *www.fishinkona.com* ⊠ *From $375.*

Golf

For golfers, the Big Island is a big deal—starting with the Mauna Kea Golf Course, which opened in 1964 and remains one of the state's top courses. Black lava and deep blue sea are the predominant themes on the island. In the roughly 40 miles from the Kona Country Club to the Mauna Kea resort, nine courses are carved into sunny seaside lava plains,

Tips for the Green

Golf is golf, and Hawaii is part of the United States, but island golf nevertheless has its own quirks. Here are a few tips to make your golf experience in the Islands more pleasant.

■ Wear sunscreen, even in December. We recommend zinc-based, with a minimum SPF of 30; you should reapply on the 10th tee.

■ Stay hydrated. Spending four-plus hours in the sun and heat means you'll perspire away considerable fluids and energy.

■ Private courses may allow you to play at their discretion.

■ All resort courses and many daily-fee courses provide rental clubs. In many cases, they're the latest lines from Titleist, Ping, Callaway, and the like. This is true for both men and women, as well as left-handers, which means you don't have to schlep clubs across the Pacific.

■ Pro shops at most courses are stocked with balls, tees, and other accoutrements, so even if you bring a bag, it needn't weigh a ton.

■ Come spikeless—very few Hawaii courses permit metal spikes.

■ Resort courses, in particular, offer more than the usual three sets of tees, sometimes four or five. So bite off as much or little challenge as you like. Tee it up from the tips and you'll end up playing a few 600-yard par 5s and see a few 250-yard forced carries.

■ In theory, you can play golf in Hawaii 365 days a year. But there's a reason the Hawaiian Islands are so green. Better to bring an umbrella and light jacket and not use them than to not bring them and get soaked.

■ Unless you play a muni or certain daily-fee courses, plan on taking a cart. Carts are mandatory at most courses and are included in the greens fee.

8

Activities and Tours GOLF

with four more in the hills above. Indeed, most of the Big Island's best courses are concentrated along the Kohala Coast, statistically the sunniest spot in Hawaii. Vertically speaking, although the majority of courses are seaside or at least near sea level, three are located above 2,000 feet, another one at 4,200 feet. This is significant because in Hawaii temperatures drop 3°F for every 1,000 feet of elevation gained.

Greens Fee: Greens fees listed here are the highest course rates per round on weekdays for U.S. residents. Courses with varying weekend rates are noted in the individual listings. (Some courses charge non–U.S. residents higher prices.)
■ TIP→ Discounts are often available for resort guests and for those who book tee times online, as well as for those willing to play in the afternoon. Twilight rates are also usually offered.

Hamakua Country Club
GOLF | FAMILY | While the typical, modern 18-hole golf course requires at least 250 acres, this public course fits into just 19. Compact is the word, and with several holes crisscrossing, this place may require you to BYO hard hat. Holes run up and down a fairly steep slope overlooking the ocean—the views are spectacular. Cheerfully billed as an Old World golf experience, the course works on the honor system ("if no one is there, put your money in the slot") and the ninth green is square, but for 20 bucks (under 17 plays free), whaddaya expect? Most golfers prefer to walk, but there are carts available. ⊠ Hwy. 19 at mile marker 41, Honokaa ✛ 43 miles north of Hilo

☎ *808/775–7244* ⊕ *hamakuagolf.com* ✉ *$20; cart $13* 🏌 *Two sets of 9 holes, 4800 yards, par 66 (men), 74 (women).*

Hapuna Golf Course

GOLF | Hapuna's challenging play and environmental sensitivity make it one of the island's most unusual courses. Designed by Arnold Palmer and Ed Seay, it is nestled into the natural contours of the land from the shoreline to about 700 feet above sea level. There are spectacular views of mountains and sea (Maui is often visible in the distance). Holes wind through kiawe scrub, beds of jagged lava, and tall fountain grasses. Hole 12 is favored for its beautiful views and challenging play. ✉ *62-100 Kanunaoa Dr., Waimea (Hawaii County)* ☎ *808/880–3000* ⊕ *www.hapunabeachresort.com/golf* ✉ *$175, $125 after 1 pm* 🏌 *18 holes, 6875 yards, par 72.*

Hilo Municipal Golf Course

GOLF | Hilo Muni is proof that you don't need sand bunkers to create a challenging course. Trees and several meandering creeks are the danger here. The course, which offers views of Hilo Bay from most holes, has produced many of the island's top players over the years. Taking a divot reminds you that you're playing on a volcano—the soil is dark black crushed lava. ✉ *340 Haihai St., Hilo* ☎ *808/959–7711* ⊕ *www.hawaiicounty.gov/pr-golf* ✉ *$38 weekdays, $45 weekends; $20 cart* 🏌 *18 holes, 6325 yards, par 71.*

Kona Country Club

GOLF | Renovated in 2016, this William F. Bell–designed golf course is perched high above historic Keauhou Bay, with spectacular views of the sea from almost every hole. Stands of mature coco trees, several remarkable lava features, wide fairways, and challenging Bermuda greens make this course a classic Hawaii golf experience that's open to the public. The most prominent feature is the "blowhole" (*puka* in Hawaiian), fronting the par-4 13th tee, where seawater propelled through a lava tube formation erupts forcefully like a geyser—try timing your drive to penetrate the shooting water! In the winter months, golfers may also be treated to the sight of migrating humpback whales splashing and breaching within a tee shot of the shoreline. The View, the on-site restaurant, is a favorite of locals, whether they golf or not, and has some of the best sunset views on the Kona Coast. ✉ *78-7000 Alii Dr., Kailua-Kona* ☎ *808/322–2595* ⊕ *www.konacountryclub.com* ✉ *$180, $93 9-hole; $20 cart* 🏌 *18 holes, 6613 yards, par 72.*

Makalei Golf Club

GOLF | Set on the slopes of Hualalai, at an elevation of 2,900 feet, Makalei is one of the rare Hawaii courses with bent-grass putting greens, which means they're quick and without the grain associated with Bermuda greens. Former PGA Tour official Dick Nugent (1992) designed holes that play through thick forest and open to wide ocean views. Elevation change is a factor on many holes, especially the par-3 eighth, whose tee is 80 feet above the green. In addition to fixed natural obstacles, wild peacocks and turkeys can make for an entertaining game. ■ **TIP→ Check tourist and car rental guides for coupons and discounts.** ✉ *72-3890 Hawaii Belt Rd., Kailua-Kona* ☎ *808/325–6625* ⊕ *www.makalei.com* ✉ *$99, $79 after noon, $59 after 2 pm* 🏌 *18 holes, 7091 yards, par 72.*

Makani Golf Club

GOLF | Set 2,000 feet above sea level on the slopes of Hualalai, this course is out of the way but well worth the drive. In 1997, Pete and Perry Dye created a gem that plays through upland woodlands—more than 2,500 trees line the fairways. On the par-5 16th, a giant tree in the middle of the fairway must be avoided with the second shot. Five lakes and a meandering natural mountain stream bring water into play on nine holes. The most dramatic is the par-3 17th, where Dye created a knockoff of his infamous 17th at the TPC at Sawgrass. ✉ *71-1420*

Most of the Big Island's top golf courses are located on the sunny Kohala Coast.

Hawaii Belt Rd., Kailua-Kona ☎ *808/325–5044* ⊕ *makanigolfclub.com* ✉ *$119 with cart, bottled water* 🏌 *18 holes, 7075 yards, par 72.*

★ Mauna Kea Golf Course

GOLF | Originally opened in 1964, this golf course is one of the most revered in the state. It underwent a tee-to-green renovation by Rees Jones, son of the original architect, Robert Trent Jones Sr. Hybrid grasses were planted, the number of bunkers increased, and the overall yardage expanded. The par-3 third is one of the world's most famous holes—and one of the most photographed. You play from a cliffside tee across a bay to a cliffside green. Getting across the ocean is just half the battle because the green is surrounded by seven bunkers, each one large and undulated. The course is a shot-maker's paradise and follows Jones's "easy bogey, tough par" philosophy. ✉ *62-100 Kaunaoe Dr., Waimea (Hawaii County)* ☎ *808/882–5400* ⊕ *www.maunakeagolf.com* ✉ *$295,*

$225 after 11 am, $175 after 1:30 pm 🏌 *18 holes, 7250 yards, par 72.*

★ Mauna Lani Golf Courses

GOLF | Black lava flows, lush green turf, white sand, and the Pacific's multihues of blue define the 36 holes at Mauna Lani. The South Course includes the par-3 15th across a turquoise bay, one of the most photographed holes in Hawaii. But it shares "signature hole" honors with the seventh, a long par 3, which plays downhill over convoluted patches of black lava, with the Pacific immediately to the left and a dune to the right. The North Course plays a couple of shots tougher. Its most distinctive hole is the 17th, a par 3 with the green set in a lava pit 50 feet deep. The shot from an elevated tee must carry a pillar of lava that rises from the pit and partially blocks a view of the green. ✉ *68-1310 Mauna Lani Dr., Waimea (Hawaii County)* ☎ *808/885–6655* ⊕ *www.maunalani.com* ✉ *From $259, but dynamic pricing means greens fee fluctuates* 🏌 *North Course: 18 holes, 6057 yards,* par 72. South Course: 18 holes, 6025 yards, par 72.

Volcano Golf and Country Club

GOLF | Just outside Hawaii Volcanoes National Park—and barely a stone's throw from Halemaumau Crater—this is by far Hawaii's highest course. At 4,200 feet elevation, shots tend to fly a bit farther than at sea level, even in the often cool, misty air. Because of the elevation and climate, this Hawaii course features Bermuda and seashore paspalum grass putting greens. The course is mostly flat, and holes play through stands of ohia lehua (flowering evergreen trees) and multitrunk hau trees. The uphill par-4 15th doglegs through a tangle of hau. ☒ 99-1621 Pii Mauna Dr., off Hwy. 11, Volcano ☎ 808/967–7331 ⊕ www.volcanogolf-shop.com ☑ $62 with cart ⅂. 18 holes, 6106 yards, par 72.

★ Waikoloa Beach Resort

GOLF | Robert Trent Jones Jr. built the Beach Course at Waikoloa (1981) on an old flow of crinkly aa lava, which he used to create holes that are as artful as they are challenging. The par-5 12th hole is one of Hawaii's most picturesque and plays through a chute of black lava to a seaside green. At the Kings' Course (1990), Tom Weiskopf and Jay Morrish built a links-esque track. It turns out lava's natural humps and declivities replicate the contours of seaside Scotland. But there are a few island twists—such as seven lakes. This is "option golf," as Weiskopf and Morrish provide different risk-reward tactics on each hole. ■TIP→ Resort guests receive a lower rate. ☒ 600 Waikoloa Beach Dr., Waikoloa ☎ 808/886–7888 ⊕ www.waikoloabeach-golf.com ☑ From $150, including cart ⅂. Beach Course: 18 holes, 6566 yards, par 70. Kings' Course: 18 holes, 7074 yards, par 72.

Waikoloa Village Golf Course

GOLF | Robert Trent Jones Jr., who created some of the most expensive courses on the Kohala Coast, also designed this little gem 20 minutes from the coast. At a 450-foot elevation, it offers ideal playing conditions year-round; ask about summer rates. Holes run across rolling hills with sweeping mountain and ocean views. ■TIP→ The 9-hole sunset special starts at 3:30 pm. ☒ 68-1792 Melia St., Waikoloa ☎ 808/883–9621 ⊕ www.waikoloavil-lagegolf.com ☑ $113, $78 twilight, $50 sunset ⅂. 18 holes, 6230 yards, par 72.

Hiking

Ecologically diverse, Hawaii Island has four of the five major climate zones and eight of 13 subclimate zones—a lot of variation for one island—and you can experience almost all of them on foot. The ancient Hawaiians cut trails across the lava plains, through the rain forests, and up along the mountain heights. Many of these paths are still in use today. Part of the King's Trail at Anaehoomalu winds through a field of lava rock covered with ancient petroglyphs. Many other trails—historic and modern—crisscross the huge Hawaii Volcanoes National Park and other parts of the island. Plus, the serenity of certain remote beaches is accessible only to hikers. Check the statewide trail system website at ⊕ hawaiitrails.ehawaii.gov for up-to-date information on hiking trails.

Department of Land and Natural Resources, State Parks Division

HIKING/WALKING | The division provides information on all the Big Island's state parks and jurisdictions. Check online for the latest additions, information, and advisories. ☒ 75 Aupuni St., Hilo ☎ 808/961–9544 ⊕ www.dlnr.hawaii.gov/dsp/parks/hawaii.

BEST SPOTS

Hawaii Volcanoes National Park. Perhaps the Big Island's premier area for hikers, the park has more than 155 miles of trails providing close-up, often jaw-dropping views of fern and rain

Hiking Big Island Trails

- Trails on the eastern, or windward, side of the island are often wet and muddy, making them slippery and unstable, so wear good hiking shoes or boots.

- Bring plenty of water, rain protection, a hat, sunblock, and a cell phone (but be aware that service can be spotty).

- Always hike with a buddy or let someone know your plans.

- Don't eat any unknown fruits or plants, or drink unfiltered water from streams.

- Darkness comes suddenly here, so carry a flashlight if you'll be out after sunset.

- Always obey posted warning signs.

forest environments, cinder cones, craters, steam vents, lava fields, rugged coastline, and current eruption activity. Day hikes range from easy to moderately difficult, and from one or two hours to a full day. For a bigger challenge, consider an overnight or multiday backcountry hike with a stay in a park cabin (available en route to the remote coast, in a lush forest, or atop frigid Mauna Loa). To do so, you must first obtain a permit at the backcountry office in the Visitor Emergency Operations Center. ■TIP→ **Daily guided hikes are led by knowledgeable, friendly park rangers.** The bulletin boards outside Kilauea Visitor Center have the day's schedule of guided hikes. ✉ *Hwy. 11, 30 miles south of Hilo, Hawaii Volcanoes National Park* ☎ *808985–6000* ⊕ *www.nps.gov/havo.*

Kekaha Kai State Park. A 1.8-mile unimproved road leads to Mahaiula Bay, a gorgeous little piece of paradise, while on the opposite side is lovely Kua Bay. Connecting the two is the 4½-mile Ala Kahakai historic coastal trail. Midway between the two white-sand beaches, you can hike to the summit of Puu Kuili, a 342-foot-high cinder cone with an excellent view of the coastline. Mahaiula has picnic tables and vault toilets. It's dry and hot with no drinking water, so pack sunblock, hats, and extra water. Gates

close at 7 pm sharp. ✉ *Trailhead on Hwy. 19, about 2 miles north of Kona airport, Kailua-Kona* ⊕ *dlnr.hawaii.gov/dsp/parks/hawaii.*

Muliwai Trail. On the western side of mystical Waipio Valley, this trail leads to the back of the valley, then switchbacks up through a series of gulches and finally emerges at Waimanu Valley. Only very experienced hikers should attempt the entirety of this remote 18-mile trail, the hike of a lifetime. It can take two to three days of backpacking and camping, which requires camping permits from the Division of Forestry and Wildlife in Hilo. ✉ *Trailhead at end of Hwy. 240, Honokaa* ☎ *808/974–4221* ⊕ *hawaiitrails.ehawaii. gov.*

Onomea Bay Trail. This short but beautiful trail is packed with stunning views of the cliffs, bays, and gulches of the Hamakua Coast, on the east side of the island. The trail is just under a mile and fairly easy, with access down to the shore if you want to dip your feet in, although we don't recommend swimming in the rough waters. Unless you pay the entry fee to the nearby botanical garden, entering its gates (even by accident) will send one of the guards running after you to nicely but firmly point you back to the trail. ✉ *Trailhead on Old Hawaiian Belt Rd., just*

Hawaii Volcanoes National Park's 155 miles of trails offer easy to moderately difficult day hikes.

before botanical garden. ⊕ hawaiitrails. ehawaii.gov.

GOING WITH A GUIDE

To get to some of the best trails and hiking spots (some of which are on private property), it's worth going with a skilled, professional guide. Costs range from $95 to $259, and some hikes include full meals and refreshments and gear such as binoculars, ponchos, parkas, and walking sticks. The outfitters mentioned here also offer customized adventure tours.

★ Hawaii Forest and Trail

HIKING/WALKING | Since 1993, this locally owned and operated outfit has built a reputation for outstanding nature tours and eco-adventures. Sustainability, cultural sensitivity, and forging island connections are company missions. They have access to thousands of acres of restricted or private lands and employ expert, certified guides who are entertaining and informative. Choose an Endangered Native Habitats bird-watching tour, or journey deep into the Hakalau Forest National Wildlife Refuge. Other tours include a Hidden Craters adventure that leads you along private hiking trails on Hualalai Volcano, a Kohala waterfall trip, or the Kohala Canopy Zipline adventure. Their Summit and Stars adventure is a crowd favorite, but book well in advance. ✉ *73-5593A Olowalu St., Kailua-Kona* ☎ *808/331–8505, 800/464–1993* ⊕ *www. hawaii-forest.com* ✑ *From $149.*

★ KapohoKine Adventures

HIKING/WALKING | FAMILY | One of the largest outfitters on the island, locally owned KapohoKine Adventures offers a number of excellent hiking tours that depart from both Hilo and Kona. The epic full-day Elite Volcano Hike hits all the great spots, including now-quiet areas in Puna impacted by the 2018 eruption. Hikers will encounter a 40-foot wall of lava and follow it to the sea and an enormous black-sand beach. Also included are Kalapana, the Kaumana Caves, the Steaming Bluffs, and a tour of Hawaii Volcanoes National Park. The final stop at Volcano Winery features a wine tasting and Hawaiian barbecue dinner. Lunch is also included.

For highly advanced hikers, the company offers a private tour (minimum 7 guests) that takes you on a 20-mile, 10-hour hike into the Waimanu Valley, a remote location north of Waipio. The price is $3,385 and includes taxes, shuttles, gratuity, trail permits, meals, guides, and support gear. ✉ *Grand Naniloa Hotel Hilo, 93 Banyan Dr., Hilo* ☎ *808/964–1000* ⊕ *www.kapohokine.com* ✉ *From $259.*

Horseback Riding

With its *paniolo* (cowboy) heritage and the ranches it spawned, the Big Island is a great place for equestrians. Riders can gallop through upcountry green pastures or saunter through Waipio Valley for a taste of old Hawaii.

TOURS
Paniolo Adventures

HORSEBACK RIDING | Paniolo Adventures offers an open-range horseback ride on a working Kohala Mountain cattle ranch, spectacular views of three volcanoes and the coastline, and an authentic *paniolo* (cowboy) experience from 3,000 feet up. You don't ride nose-to-tail and can spread out and trot or canter if you wish: this is an 11,000-acre ranch, so there's room to roam. The company caters to beginning and experienced riders and offers special private rides as well. ✉ *Kohala Mountain Rd. (Hwy. 250) at mile marker 13.2, Waimea (Hawaii County)* ☎ *808/889–5354* ⊕ *www.panioloadventures.com* ✉ *From $69.*

Kayaking

The leeward (west coast) areas of the Big Island are protected for the most part from the northeast trade winds, making for ideal near-shore kayaking conditions. There are miles and miles of uncrowded Kona and Kohala coastline to explore, presenting close-up views of stark, raw, lava-rock shores and cliffs; lava-tube sea caves; pristine, secluded coves; and deserted beaches. There's even guided kayaking in a hand-built irrigation ditch dating from the early 1900s.

Ocean kayakers can get close to shore—where the commercial snorkel and dive cruise boats can't reach. This opens up all sorts of possibilities for adventure, such as near-shore snorkeling among the expansive coral reefs and lava-rock formations that teem with colorful tropical fish and Hawaiian green sea turtles. You can pull ashore at a quiet cove for a picnic and a plunge into turquoise waters. With a good coastal map and some advice from the kayak vendor, you might paddle by ancient battlegrounds, burial sites, bathing ponds for Hawaiian royalty, or old villages.

Kayaking can be enjoyed via a guided tour or on a self-guided paddling excursion. Either way, the kayak outfitter can brief you on recommended routes, safety, and how to help preserve and protect Hawaii's ocean resources and coral reef system.

Whether you're a beginning or experienced kayaker, choose appropriate location, distance, and conditions for your excursion.

Ask the outfitter about local conditions and hazards, such as tides, currents, and advisories, but also judge conditions for yourself and *never* launch in rough weather.

Beginners should practice getting into and out of the kayak and capsizing (called a *huli,* the Hawaiian word for "flip") in shallow water.

Before departing, secure the kayak's hatches to prevent water intake.

Use a line to attach the paddle to the kayak to avoid losing it.

Always use a life vest or jacket, and wear a rash guard and plenty of sunblock.

Carry appropriate amounts of water and food.

Don't kayak alone. Create a float plan; tell someone where you're going and when you will return.

BEST SPOTS

Hilo Bay. This is a favorite kayak spot. The best place to put in is at **Reeds Bay Beach Park.** Parking is plentiful and free at the bayfront. Most afternoons you'll share the bay with local paddling clubs. Stay inside the breakwater unless the ocean is calm (or you're feeling unusually adventurous). Conditions range from extremely calm to quite choppy. ⊠ *Banyan Way and Banyan Dr., 1 mile from downtown Hilo.*

Kailua Bay and Kamakahonu Beach. The small sandy beach that fronts the Courtyard King Kamehameha's Kona Beach Hotel is a nice place to rent or launch kayaks. You can unload in the cul-de-sac and park in nearby free or paid lots. The water here is especially calm, and the surroundings are historical and scenic. ⊠ *Alii Dr., next to Kailua Pier, Kailua-Kona.*

Kealakekua Bay State Historical Park. The excellent snorkeling and likelihood of seeing dolphins (morning is best) make Kealakekua Bay one of the most popular kayaking spots on the Big Island. An ocean conservation district, the bay is usually calm and tranquil. (Use caution and common sense during surf advisories.) Tall coral pinnacles and clear visibility surrounding the Captain James Cook Monument also make for stupendous snorkeling. Regulations permit only a few operators to lead kayak tours in the park. ⊠ *Napoopoo Rd. and Manini Beach Rd., Captain Cook* ⊕ *dlnr.hawaii.gov/dsp/parks/hawaii.*

Oneo Bay. Right in downtown Kailua, this is usually a placid place to kayak. It's fairly easy to get to. If you can't find parking along the road, there's a free lot across the street from the library and farmers' market. ⊠ *Alii Dr., Kailua-Kona.*

EQUIPMENT, LESSONS, AND TOURS

There are several rental outfitters on Highway 11 between Kainaliu and Captain Cook, but only a few are specially permitted to lead kayak trips in Kealakekua Bay.

Aloha Kayak Co.

KAYAKING | This outfitter is one of the few permitted to guide kayaking tours to the stunningly beautiful Kealakekua Bay, leaving from Napoopoo, including about 1½ hours at the Captain Cook Monument. The 3½-hour morning and afternoon tours include snacks and drinks, while the five-hour tour includes lunch. Local guides discuss the area's cultural, historical, and natural significance. You may see dolphins, but you must observe them from a distance only, as this is a protected marine reserve. Keauhou Bay tours are also available, including a two-hour evening manta ray tour. ⊠ *82-5674 Kahau Pl., Captain Cook* ☎ *808/322–2868* ⊕ *www.alohakayak.com* 🛒 *Tours from $99.*

★ Flumin' Kohala

KAYAKING | On this fascinating excursion, you take a slow-moving, cool ride through the engineering marvel known as the Kohala Ditch. Built mostly by manual labor in 1906, it brought precious water resources from the upcountry cloud forests of the Kohala watershed to the arid lands where sugarcane was grown. This kayak tour takes you over private property, where you will float through 10 concrete tunnels and seven elevated flumes in four-person, inflatable kayaks. Local guides raised in the area talk about the history of the ditch on a 3-mile tour of part of its currently operating 13.5 miles. The company is run by fourth-generation residents whose families were connected to the long-gone sugar industry. Allow about three hours and prepare to get wet. ✉ *55-517 Hawi Rd., Hawi* ☎ *808/933–4294* ⊕ *fluminkohala.com* ✉ *$142.*

★ Kona Boys

KAYAKING | On the highway above Kealakekua Bay, this full-service, environmentally conscious outfitter handles kayaks, body boards, surfboards, stand-up paddleboards, and snorkeling gear. Single-seat and double kayaks are offered. Surfing and stand-up paddleboarding lessons are available for private or group instruction.

One of the few companies permitted to lead tours in Kealakekua Bay, Kona Boys offer their Morning Magic and Midday Meander tours, two half-day guided kayaking and snorkeling trips with gear, lunch, snacks, and beverages. They also run a beach shack fronting the Courtyard King Kamehameha's Kona Beach Hotel, with everything for the beachgoer such as rentals of beach mats, chairs, and other gear. ■ TIP→ **The Kailua-Kona location offers Hawaiian outrigger canoe rides and SUP lessons.** ✉ *79-7539 Mamalahoa Hwy., Kealakekua* ☎ *808/328–1234 Kealakekua location, 808/329–2345 Kailua-Kona location* ⊕ *www.konaboys.com* ✉ *Rentals from $74.*

Ocean Safari's Kayak Adventures

KAYAKING | On the guided, 3½-hour morning sea-cave tour that begins in Keauhou Bay, you can visit lava-tube sea caves along the coast, then swim ashore for a snack. The kayaks are already on the water, so you won't have the hassle of transporting them. They also offer stand-up paddleboard lessons. ■ TIP→ **Book online for best availabilty.** ✉ *End of Kamehameha III Rd., Kailua-Kona* ⊹ *Next to Sheraton Kona Resort and Spa at Keauhou Bay* ☎ *808/326–4699* ⊕ *www. oceansafarikayaks.com* ✉ *From $49.*

Running

Ironman World Championship

RUNNING | Staged annually since 1978, the Ironman World Championship is the granddaddy of all triathlons. For about two weeks in mid-October, Kailua-Kona takes on the vibe of an Olympic Village as 2,000 top athletes from across the globe and their supporters roam the town, carb-loading, training, and prepping in advance of the world's premier swim-bike-run endurance event. The competition starts at Kailua Pier with a 2.4-mile open-water swim, followed by a 112-mile bicycle ride and a 26.2-mile marathon. The week prior is filled with fun community events such as the Underpants Run, in which locals and visitors—as well as well-known celebrities—run through town in only their knickers. ■ TIP→ **Only qualified athletes may participate, but if you are visiting during Ironman and want to volunteer, contact kona@ironmanvolunteers. com.** ⊕ *www.ironmanworldchampionship. com.*

Peaman Biathlon Series

RUNNING | Beloved by the community, Sean "Peaman" Pagett has been a Kona icon for decades, putting on no-cost biathlon events that are suitable for the whole family. Events begin at the pier at 8:08 am and have no sign-ups, just sign-outs. There are snacks and water at the finish, and Peaman always has awesome free prizes ready for the kids. ✉ *Kailua Pier, 75-5660 Palani Rd., Kailua-Kona* ☎ *808/938–2296* ⊕ *www.kona5k.com.*

Sailing

For old salts and novice sailors alike, there's nothing like a cruise on the Kona or Kohala Coast. Calm waters, serene shores, and the superb scenery of Maunakea, Mauna Loa, and Hualalai, the Big Island's primary volcanic peaks, make for a great sailing adventure. You can drop a line over the side and try your luck at catching dinner, or grab some snorkel gear and explore when the boat drops anchor in one of the quiet coves and bays. A cruise may well be the most relaxing and adventurous part of a Big Island visit.

Honu Sail Charters

SAILING | The fully equipped 32-foot cutter-rigged sloop *Honu* (Hawaiian for sea turtle) carries six passengers on full-day, half-day, and sunset sailing excursions along the scenic Kona Coast, which include time to snorkel in clear waters over coral reefs during the day tours and heavy *pupus* (appetizers) for the sunset excursion. This friendly outfitter allows passengers to get some hands-on sailing experience or just to kick back and relax. There are plenty of cushions and lots of shade. ⊠ *Honokohau Harbor, Kailua-Kona* ☎ *808/896–4668* ⊕ *www.sailkona.com* ⊠ *Tours from $100.*

Kohala Blue LLC

SAILING | Based at the Kawaihae South Small Boat Harbor, this company offers day sailing, sunset cruises, and humpback whale-watching (in season) aboard the 34-foot *Riva*. Owned and operated by Captain Steve Turner, the company focuses on sharing the wonders of the Kawaihae area, including the impressive Puukohola Heiau National Historic Site, the Puako reef, and views of Big Island volcanoes and even Maui's Haleakala. Private charters for up to six are available. ⊠ *Kawaihae Harbor South, Slip #8, 61-3527 Kawaihae Rd., Kawaihae* ☎ *808/895–1781* ⊕ *kohalablue.net* ⊠ *From $125.*

Scuba Diving

The Big Island's underwater world is the setting for a dramatic diving experience. With generally warm and calm waters, vibrant coral reefs and rock formations, and plunging underwater drop-offs, the Kona and Kohala Coasts offer premier scuba diving. There are also some good dive locations in East Hawaii, not far from the Hilo area. Divers find much to occupy their time, including marine reserves teeming with tropical reef fish, Hawaiian green sea turtles, an occasional and critically endangered Hawaiian monk seal, and even some playful spinner dolphins. On special night dives to see manta rays, divers descend with bright underwater lights that attract plankton, which in turn attract these otherworldly creatures. The best spots to dive are all on the west coast.

BEST SPOTS

Garden Eel Cove. Accessible only by boat, this is a great place to see manta rays somersaulting overhead as they feast on a plankton supper. It's also home to hundreds of tiny garden eels darting out from their sandy homes. There's a steep drop-off and lots of marine life. ⊠ *Rte. 19, near the Kona Airport, Kailua-Kona.*

Manta Village. Booking with a night-dive operator is required for the short boat ride to this area, one of Kona's best night-dive spots. If you're a diving or snorkeling fanatic, it's well worth it to experience manta rays drawn by the lights of the hotel. ■ **TIP →** **If night swimming isn't your cup of tea, you can catch a glimpse of the majestic creatures from the Sheraton's viewing areas.** (No water access is allowed from the hotel's property.) ⊠ *78-128 Ehukai St., off Sheraton Kona Resort and Spa at Keauhou Bay, Kailua-Kona.*

Pawai Bay Marine Perserve. Clear waters, abundant reef life, and interesting coral formations make protected Pawai Bay

Hawaii's Manta Rays

⊙

Manta rays, one of Hawaii's most fascinating marine-life species, can be seen on some nighttime diving excursions along the Kona and Kohala Coasts. They are generally completely harmless to divers, though of course no wild animal is totally predictable. If you don't want to get wet, head to the beach fronting the Mauna Kea Beach Hotel, on the Kohala Coast, or to the Sheraton Kona Resort and Spa at Keauhou Bay, where each evening, visitors gather by the hotel's lights to watch manta rays feed in the shallows.

■ The manta ray (*Manta birostris*), called the devil fish by some, is known as *hahalua* by Hawaiians.

■ Its winglike fins, reaching up to 20 feet wide, allow the ray to skim through the water like a bird gliding through air.

■ The manta ray uses the two large, flap-like lobes extending from its eyes to funnel food to its mouth. It eats microscopic plankton, small fish, and tiny crustaceans.

■ Closely related to the shark, the manta can weigh more than 3,000 pounds.

■ Its skeleton is made of cartilage, not bone.

■ A female ray gives birth to one or two young at a time; pups can be 45 inches long and weigh 20 pounds at birth.

Marine Preserve ideal for diving. Explore sea caves, arches, and lava-rock formations and dive into lava tubes. An easy, boat-only dive spot is ½ mile north of Old Airport. (No shoreline access to protected Pawai Bay is available due to its cultural and environmental significance.) ⊠ *Kuakini Hwy., north of Old Kona Airport Park, Kailua-Kona.*

Puako. Just south of Hapuna Beach State Recreation Area, beautiful Puako (a small oceanfront town) offers easy entry to some fine reef diving. Deep chasms, sea caves, and rock arches abound with varied marine life. ⊠ *Puako Rd., off Hwy. 19, Kailua-Kona.*

EQUIPMENT, LESSONS, AND TOURS

There are quite a few good dive shops along the Kona Coast. Most are happy to take on all customers, but a few focus on specific types of trips. Trip prices vary, depending on whether you're already certified and whether you're diving from

a boat or from shore. Instruction with PADI, SDI, or TDI certification in three to five days costs $600 to $850. Most instructors rent dive equipment and snorkel gear, as well as underwater cameras. Most organize otherworldly manta ray dives at night and whale-watching cruises in season.

Aggressor Adventures

BOATING | For those divers who want an extended experience, the luxurious 80-foot *Kona Aggressor II* offers week-long liveaboard diving charters. Plying waters along the west coast, the yacht takes you to the vast, untouched southern Kona Coast, where divers can explore the sea life that thrives among fantastical arches, bommies (outcrops of coral reef), pinnacles, lava tubes, and more. Meals are included, as are filled tanks, weights, and weight belts. ⚓ *Departs Saturday from Kailua Pier, Kailua-Kona* ☎ *706/993–2531* ⊕ *aggressor.com/destination/kona* ▨ *From $2,935 for 4-person cabin.*

The Kona Coast's relatively calm waters and colorful coral reefs offer excellent scuba diving.

Big Island Divers

DIVING/SNORKELING | This company offers several levels of certification as well as numerous excursions, including night dives, two-tank charters, and in-season whale-watching. ✉ *74-5467 Kaiwi St., Kailua-Kona* ☎ *808/329–6068* ⊕ *bigisland-divers.com* ✆ *From $149.*

Jack's Diving Locker

SCUBA DIVING | Good for novice and intermediate divers, Jack's has trained and certified tens of thousands of divers since 1981, with classrooms and a dive pool for instruction. Four boats that accommodate up to 18 divers and six snorkelers visit more than 80 established dive sites along the Kona Coast, yielding sightings of turtles, manta rays, garden eels, and schools of barracuda. They even take you lava tube diving. Snorkelers can accompany their friends on the dive boats or take guided morning trips and manta night trips, and dolphin-watch and reef snorkels. Combined sunset/night manta ray dives are offered as well. ■**TIP**→ **Kona's best deal for scuba newbies is Jack's pool and shore dive combo.** ✉ *75-5813 Alii Dr., Kailua-Kona* ☎ *808/329–7585, 800/345–4807* ⊕ *www.jacksdivinglocker.com* ✆ *Tours from $155 certified divers, $275 intro divers.*

Kohala Divers

SCUBA DIVING | The Kohala Coast's gorgeous underwater topography of lava tubes, caves, vibrant coral reefs, and interesting sea life makes it a great diving destination. This full-service PADI dive shop has been certifying divers since 1984. A one-day intro dive course has you in the ocean the same day. A four-day, full certification course is offered, too. The company also rents any equipment needed for boat or shore excursions and takes divers to the best diving spots on their fully outfitted, comfortable, 46-foot Newton dive boat. The cute retail shop is packed full of everything needed for diving and snorkeling, as well as clothing, beach gear, and gifts. ✉ *Kawaihae Harbor Shopping Center, Hwy. 270, Kawaihae* ☎ *808/882–7774* ⊕ *www.kohaladivers.*

com ✉ *Two-tank dive $159, certification from $250.*

Nautilus Dive Center

SCUBA DIVING | Across from Hilo Bay, Nautilus Dive Center is the oldest and most experienced dive shop on the island. It offers a broad range of services for both beginners and experienced divers. Owner Bill De Rooy, with his calm, reassuring manner, has been diving around the Big Island since 1982, personally certifying more than 2,000 divers. He's known for helping nervous guests feel comfortable in the water. He can provide you with underwater maps and show you the best dive spots in Hilo, and also offers PADI instruction, one- and two-tank dives, and snorkeling tours. ✉ *382 Kamehameha Ave., Hilo* ☎ *808/935–6939* ⊕ *www. nautilusdivehilo.com* ✉ *Certification from $480.*

Torpedo Tours

SCUBA DIVING | Owner-operators Mike and Nikki Milligan, both dive instructors, love to take divers out on their 40-foot custom dive boat, the *Na Pali Kai II.* They specialize in small groups, which means you'll get personalized attention and spend more time diving and less time waiting to dive. Morning excursions feature two-tank dives. Both snorkelers and divers can try the torpedo scooters—devices that let you cover more area with less kicking. Certified divers should try the spectacular Blackwater Night Dive. ✉ *Honokohau Harbor, 74-425 Kealakehe Pkwy., Kailua-Kona* ☎ *808/938–0405* ⊕ *www.torpedotours.com* ✉ *Dives from $129.*

Skiing

Where else but Hawaii can you surf, snorkel, and snow ski on the same day? In winter, the 13,796-foot Maunakea (Hawaiian for "white mountain") usually has snow at higher elevations—and along with that, skiing. No lifts, no manicured slopes, no faux-alpine lodges, no après-ski nightlife, but the chance to ski some of the most remote (and let's face it, unlikely) runs on the planet.

Ski Guides Hawaii

SKIING/SNOWBOARDING | With the motto "Pray for pineapple powder," Christopher Langan of Mauna Kea Ski Corporation is the only licensed outfitter providing transportation, guide services, and ski equipment on Maunakea. Snow can fall from Thanksgiving to June, but the most likely months are February and March. With "springlike" conditions, some runs can be 2 miles long and offer 2,500–4,500 feet of "vertical." You may be able to see Haleakala, Kilauea Crater, and Mauna Loa from this surreal place. The price per person is for a daylong experience that includes lunch, equipment, guide service, transportation from Waimea, and a four-wheel-drive shuttle back up the mountain after each ski run. ☎ *808/885–4188* ⊕ *www.skihawaii.com* ✉ *$450; ski or snowboard rentals $50 per day.*

Snorkeling

A favorite pastime on the Big Island, snorkeling is perhaps one of the easiest and most enjoyable water activities for visitors. By floating on the surface, peering through your mask, and breathing through your snorkel, you can see lava-rock formations, sea arches, sea caves, and coral reefs teeming with colorful tropical fish. While the Kona and Kohala Coasts boast more beaches, bays, and quiet coves to snorkel, the east side around Hilo is also a great place to get in the water.

If you don't bring your own equipment, you can easily rent all the gear needed from a beach activities vendor, who will happily provide directions to the best sites for snorkeling in the area. For access to deeper water and assistance from an experienced crew (to say nothing of typically great food and drink), you can opt for a snorkel cruise. Excursions generally range from two to five hours; be sure to ask what equipment and food is included. ■TIP→ **Use a few drops of baby shampoo on your mask for a perfect, cheap, and easy-on-the-eyes defogger.**

BEST SPOTS

Carlsmith Beach Park. This calm group of lagoons is a great place to bring kids. Freshwater springs might cloud your mask and keep the water cool, but you'll see lots of turtles and tropical fish here. There are showers, a lifeguard, and picnic tables. ⊠ *1815 Kalanianaole Ave., 10 min. east of Hilo on Hwy. 137.*

Puako Tide Pools. There's a large shelf of extensive reef and tide pools at this sleepy beach town along the Kohala Coast, where you'll find fantastic snorkeling as long as conditions are calm. ⊠ *South end of Puako Beach Rd., Puako, off Hwy. 11.*

Kahaluu Beach Park. Since ancient times, the waters around Kahaluu Beach have provided traditional throw net–fishing grounds. With super-easy access, the bay offers good swimming and outstanding snorkeling, revealing turtles, angelfish, parrot fish, needlefish, puffer fish, and many types of tangs. ■TIP→ **Stay inside the breakwater and don't stray too far, as dangerous and unpredictable currents swirl outside the bay.** ⊠ *Alii Dr., Kailua-Kona.*

Kealakekua Bay State Historical Park. This protected Marine Life Conservation District is hands-down one of the best snorkeling spots on the island, thanks to clear visibility, fabulous coral reefs, and generally calm waters. Pods of dolphins can be abundant, but they're protected under federal law and may not be disturbed or approached. Access to the area is restricted, but a few companies are permitted to escort tours to the bay. ■TIP→ **Overland access is difficult, so opt for one of the guided snorkel cruises permitted to moor here.** ⊠ *Napoopoo, at end of Beach Rd. and Hwy. 160, Captain Cook.*

Magic Sands Beach Park. Also known as White Sands or Disappearing Sands Beach Park, this is a great place for beginning and intermediate snorkelers. In winter, it's also a prime spot to watch for whales. ⊠ *Alii Dr., Kailua-Kona.*

EQUIPMENT, LESSONS, AND TOURS

Body Glove Cruises

SNORKELING | FAMILY | A good choice for families, this operator has a waterslide and high-dive platform that kids love. On the daily Snorkel and Dolphin Watch Adventure, the 65-foot catamaran sets off for stunning Red Hill in uncrowded South Kona from Kailua-Kona pier. The morning snorkel cruise includes breakfast and a barbecue burger lunch, with vegetarian options. A three-hour historical dinner cruise to Kealakekua Bay is a great way to relax, watch the sunset, and learn about Kona's history. It includes a Hawaiian-style buffet, complimentary cocktail, and live music. (A lunch version is also available.) Seasonal whale-watch cruises and all dolphin snorkel cruises guarantee you will see the featured mammals or you can go again for free; the company implements a NOAA-approved Dolphin SMART policy on all of their cruises. Children under five are always free. ⊠ *75-5629 Kuakini Hwy., Kailua-Kona* ☎ *808/326–7122, 800/551–8911* ⊕ *www.bodyglovehawaii.com* ⌦ *From $138.*

★ Fair Wind Cruises

SNORKELING | FAMILY | In business since 1971, Fair Wind offers morning and afternoon snorkel trips into breathtaking Kealakekua Bay. Great for families with small kids, the custom-built, 60-foot catamaran has two 15-foot waterslides, freshwater showers, and a staircase descending directly into the water for easy access. Snorkel gear is included, along with flotation equipment and

Continued on page 252

SNORKELING IN HAWAII

Molokini Crater

The waters surrounding the Hawaiian Islands are filled with life—from giant manta rays cruising off the Big Island's Kona Coast to humpback whales giving birth in the waters around Maui. Dip your head beneath the surface to experience a spectacularly colorful world: pairs of milletseed butterflyfish dart back and forth, redlipped parrotfish snack on coral algae, and spotted eagle rays flap past like silent spaceships. Sea turtles bask at the surface while tiny wrasses give them the equivalent of a shave and a haircut. The water quality is typically outstanding; many sites afford 30-foot-plus visibility. On snorkel cruises, you can often stare from the boat rail right down to the bottom.

Certainly few destinations are as accommodating to every level of snorkeler as Hawaii. Beginners can tromp in from sandy beaches while more advanced divers descend to shipwrecks, reefs, craters, and sea arches just offshore. Because of Hawaii's extreme isolation, the island chain has fewer fish species than Fiji or the Caribbean—but many of the fish that live here exist nowhere else. The Hawaiian waters are home to the highest percentage of endemic fish in the world.

The key to enjoying the underwater world is slowing down. Look carefully. Listen. You might hear the strange crackling sound of shrimp tunneling through coral, or you may hear whales singing to one another during winter. A shy octopus may drift along the ocean's floor beneath you. If you're hooked, pick up a waterproof fishkey from Long's Drugs. You can brag later that you've looked the Hawaiian turkeyfish in the eye.

Picasso Triggerfish

Milletseed Butterflyfish*

Yellow Tang

Moorish Idol

Hawaiian Whitespotted Toby*

Saddleback Wrasse*

Redlip Parrotfish

Hawaiian Turkeyfish*

Zebra Moray Eel

Stocky Hawkfish

Green Sea Turtle (Honu)

Spotted Eagle Ray

*endemic to Hawaii

POLYNESIA'S FIRST CELESTIAL NAVIGATORS: HONU

Honu is the Hawaiian name for two native sea turtles, the hawksbill and the green sea turtle. Little is known about these dinosaur-age marine reptiles, though snorkelers regularly see them foraging for *limu* (seaweed) and the occasional jellyfish in Hawaiian waters. Most female honu nest in the uninhabited Northwestern Hawaiian Islands, but a few sociable ladies nest on Maui and Big Island beaches. Scientists suspect that they navigate the seas via magnetism—sensing the earth's poles. Amazingly, they will journey up to 800 miles to nest—it's believed that they return to their own birth sites. After about 60 days of incubation, nestlings emerge from the sand at night and find their way back to the sea by the light of the stars.

SNORKELING

Many of Hawaii's reefs are accessible from shore.

The basics: Sure, you can take a deep breath, hold your nose, squint your eyes, and stick your face in the water in an attempt to view submerged habitats . . . but why not protect your eyes, retain your ability to breathe, and keep your hands free to paddle about when exploring underwater? That's what snorkeling is all about.

Equipment needed: A mask, snorkel (the tube attached to the mask), and fins. In deeper waters (any depth over your head), life jackets are advised.

Steps to success: If you've never snorkeled before, it's natural to feel a bit awkward at first, so don't sweat it. Breathing through a mask and tube, and wearing a pair of fins take getting used to. Like any activity, you build confidence and comfort through practice.

If you're new to snorkeling, begin by submerging your face in shallow water or a swimming pool and breathing calmly through the snorkel while gazing through the mask.

Next you need to learn how to clear water out of your mask and snorkel, an essential skill since splashes can send water into tube openings and masks can leak. Some snorkels have built-in drainage valves, but if a tube clogs, you can force water up and out by exhaling through your mouth. Clearing a mask is similar: lift your head from water while pulling forward on mask to drain. Some masks have built-in purge valves, but those without can be cleared underwater by pressing the top to the forehead and blowing out your nose (charming, isn't it?), allowing air to bubble into the mask, pushing water out the bottom. If it sounds hard, it really isn't. Just try it a few times and you'll soon feel like a pro.

Now your goal is to get friendly with fins—you want them to be snug but not too tight—and learn how to propel yourself with them. Fins won't help you float, but they will give you a leg up, so to speak, on smoothly moving through the water or treading water (even when upright) with less effort.

Flutter stroking is the most efficient underwater kick, and the farther your foot bends forward the more leg power you'll be able to transfer to the water and the farther you'll travel with each stroke. Flutter kicking movements involve alternately separating the legs and then drawing them back together. When your legs separate, the leg surface encounters drag from the water, slowing you down. When your legs are drawn back together, they produce a force pushing you forward. If your kick creates more forward force than it causes drag, you'll move ahead.

Submerge your fins to avoid fatigue rather than having them flailing above the water when you kick, and keep your arms at your side to reduce drag. You are in the water—stretched out, face down, and snorkeling happily away—but that doesn't mean you can't hold your breath and go deeper in the water for a closer look at some fish or whatever catches your attention. Just remember that when you do this, your snorkel will be submerged, too, so you won't be breathing (you'll be holding your breath). You can dive head-first, but going feet-first is easier and less scary for most folks, taking less momentum. Before full immersion, take several long, deep breaths to clear carbon dioxide from your lungs.

If your legs tire, flip onto your back and tread water with inverted fin motions while resting. If your mask fogs, wash condensation from lens and clear water from mask.

TIPS FOR SAFE SNORKELING

- Snorkel with a buddy and stay together.
- Plan your entry and exit points prior to getting in the water.
- Swim into the current on entering and then ride the current back to your exit point.
- Carry your flippers into the water and then put them on, as it's difficult to walk in them, and rocks may be slippery.
- Make sure your mask fits properly and is not too loose.
- Pop your head above the water periodically to ensure you aren't drifting too far out, or too close to rocks.
- Think of the water as someone else's home—don't take anything that doesn't belong to you, or leave any trash behind.
- Don't touch any sea creatures; they may sting.
- Wear a T-shirt over your swimsuit to help protect you from being fried by the sun.
- When in doubt, don't go without a snorkeling professional; try a guided tour.
- Don't go in if the ocean seems rough.

Green sea turtle (Honu)

Surfing is popular on the Big Island.

prescription masks. The 4½-hour cruise is known for its delicious meals; 3½-hour snack cruises are offered, too. For ages seven and older, the company also operates the *Hula Kai* snorkel cruise, a 55-foot luxury hydrofoil catamaran that takes guests to several remote South Kona locations. Their five-hour morning snorkel cruise includes a gourmet breakfast buffet and barbecue lunch. ✉ *Keauhou Bay, 78-7130 Kaleiopapa St., Kailua-Kona* ☎ *808/322–2788, 800/677–9461* ⊕ *www.fair-wind.com* 🖅 *From $149.*

Sea Quest

SNORKELING | Careful stewardship of the Kona Coast and its sea life is a major priority for this company, which offers catamaran charters and other snorkeling excursions. Trips leave from Keauhou Bay and head to Captain Cook Monument and other points south. ■**TIP→ Book five days in advance for $10 off.** ✉ *78-7138 Kaleiopapa St., Kailua-Kona* ☎ *808/329–7238* ⊕ *www.seaquesthawaii.com* 🖅 *From $88.*

Snorkel Bob's

SNORKELING | You're likely to see Snorkel Bob's wacky ads in your airline in-flight magazine or rack cards. The company offers a wide selection of rental gear packages and options; they often run specials, so be sure to ask. They also rent beach chairs and flotation devices. There are two Big Island locations, one in Kona and one at Mauna Lani. ■**TIP→ If you happen to be traveling interisland, you can rent your gear on one island and return it to another.** ✉ *75-5831 Kahakai St., Kailua-Kona* ☎ *808/329–0770, 800/262–7725* ⊕ *www.snorkelbob.com* 🖅 *From $38/week.*

Stand-Up Paddleboarding

Stand-up paddleboarding (or stand-up paddling; SUP for short), a sport with roots in the Hawaiian Islands, has grown popular worldwide in recent years. It's available for all skill levels and ages, and even novice stand-up paddleboarders can get up, stay up, and have a great time paddling around a protected bay or exploring the gorgeous coastline. All you need to get started is a large body of calm water, a board, and a paddle. The workout tests your core strength as well as your balance and offers an unusual vantage point from which to enjoy the beauty of island and ocean.

BEST SPOTS

Anaehoomalu Bay Beach. In this well-protected bay, it's usually fairly calm even when surf is rough on the rest of the island, though trades pick up heartily in the afternoon. Boards are available for rent at the north end, and the safe area for stand-up paddling is marked by buoys. ⊠ Off Waikoloa Beach Dr., south of Waikoloa Beach Marriott, Kohala Coast.

Hilo Bay. At this favorite among locals, the best place to put in is at **Reeds Bay Beach Park.** Most afternoons you'll share the bay with local paddling clubs. Stay inside the breakwater unless the ocean is calm (or you're feeling unusually adventurous). Conditions range from extremely calm to quite choppy. ⊠ Banyan Way and Banyan Dr., 1 mile from downtown Hilo.

Kailua Bay and Kamakahonu Beach. The small, sandy beach that fronts the Courtyard King Kamehameha's Kona Beach Hotel is great for kids; the water here is especially calm and gentle. If you're more daring, you can easily paddle out of the bay and along the coast for some great exploring. ⊠ Alii Dr., next to Kailua Pier, Kailua-Kona.

EQUIPMENT AND LESSONS

★ **Hypr Nalu Hawaii**

WATER SPORTS | SUP master Ian Foo is the king of the stand-up paddleboard in downtown Kailua-Kona. At his small oceanfront shop across from the pier, a family affair, he stocks surfboards and paddleboards, all beautifully custom-made with veneer finishes and gorgeous hardwoods such as rosewood and applewood. Hypr also offers OC1 (outrigger canoe, one person) lessons, rentals, active ocean gear, and a great line of logo apparel. Foo and his fitness-minded family are serious and enthusiastic about ocean sports and are awesome teachers. If you rent or take a lesson, there's a very good chance you will fall in love with one of their iconic boards; luckily, they ship worldwide. Rentals for surfboards and paddleboards are weekly only, and rates vary by type. ⊠ 75-5663 Palani Rd., Unit K, Kailua-Kona ☎ 808/960–4667 ⊕ www.hyprnalu.com ✎ Instruction from $110; 2-hour outrigger rentals from $95 for OC1 and $135 for OC2.

Ocean Sports

WATER SPORTS | This outfitter at the Waikoloa Beach Marriott rents equipment, offers lessons, and has the perfect location for easy access to the bay. Ocean Sports also operates rental shacks at the Whale Center Kawaihae, Queens' MarketPlace, and Anaehoomalu Bay. They can also set you up with cruises, dives, and charters elsewhere on the island. ⊠ Waikoloa Beach Marriott, 69-275 Waikoloa Beach Dr., Waikoloa ☎ 808/886–6666 ⊕ www.hawaiioceansports.com ✎ SUP rental $50/hr, body board $5/hr, snorkel gear $25/day.

Submarine Tours

Atlantis Submarines

TOUR—SPORTS | FAMILY | Want to stay dry while exploring the tropical undersea world? Climb aboard the 48-passenger Atlantis X submarine, anchored off Kailua Pier, across from Courtyard King Kamehameha's Kona Beach Hotel. A large glass dome in the bow and 13 viewing ports on each side allow clear views of the aquatic world more than 100 feet down. They take you to a pristine, 25-acre

Passengers aboard the Atlantis submarine can visit the aquatic world without getting wet.

coral garden brimming with sea creatures of all kinds. This is a great trip for kids and nonswimmers. ■TIP→ **Book online for discounts and specials.** ✉ *75-5669 Alii Dr., Kailua-Kona* ☎ *808/326–7939, 800/381–0237* ⊕ *www.atlantisadventures.com* 📧 *$114.*

Surfing

The Big Island does not have the variety of great surfing spots found on Oahu or Maui, but it does have decent waves and a thriving surf culture. Local kids and avid surfers frequent a number of places up and down the Kona and Kohala Coasts of West Hawaii; some have become famous surf champions. Expect high surf in winter and much calmer activity during summer. The surf scene is much more active on the Kona side.

BEST SPOTS

Honolii Cove. North of Hilo, this is the best surfing spot on the eastern side of the island. It hosts many exciting surf contests. ✉ *Off Hwy. 19, near mile marker 4, Hilo.*

Kahaluu Beach Park. Slightly north of this beach park and just past the calm lagoon filled with snorkelers, beginning and intermediate surfers can have a go at some nice waves. *Alii Dr., Kailua-Kona.*

Kohanaiki. Also known as Pine Trees, this community beach park is among the best places to catch waves. Keep in mind that it's a very popular local surf spot on an island where there aren't all that many surf spots, and be respectful. ✉ *Off Hwy. 11, Kohanaiki entrance gate, about 2 miles south of Kona airport, Kailua-Kona.*

Old Kona Airport Park. This park is a good place for catching wave action. A couple of the island's outfitters conduct surf lessons here, as the break is far from potentially dangerous rocks and reefs. ✉ *Kuakini Rd., Kailua-Kona.*

EQUIPMENT, LESSONS, AND TOURS

★ Hawaii Lifeguard Surf Instructors

SURFING | This family-owned, lifeguard-certified school helps novices become wave riders at Kahaluu Beach Park and offers lessons for more experienced riders at Kona's top surf spots. A two-hour introductory lesson has one instructor per two to four students, and is gentle and reassuring. Private instruction is available as well. If the waves are on the smaller side, the school converts to stand-up paddleboard lessons for the same prices as surfing. ⊠ 75-5909 Alii Dr., Kailua-Kona ☎ 808/324–0442, 808/936–7873 ⊕ www.surflessonshawaii.com ☑ From $75.

Ocean Eco Tours Surf School

SURFING | Family owned and operated, Kona's oldest surf school emphasizes the basics and specializes in beginners. It's one of a handful of operators permitted to conduct business in Kaloko-Honokohau National Historical Park, which gets waves even when other spots on the west side are flat. All lessons are taught by certified instructors, and the school guarantees that you will surf. If you're hooked, sign up for a three-day package. There's an authentic soul surfer's vibe to this operation, and they are equally diehard about teaching you about the ocean and having you standing up riding waves on your first day. Group, private, and semiprivate lessons available. ⊠ Courtyard King Kamehameha's Kona Beach Hotel, 75-5660 Palani Rd., Suite 304, Kailua-Kona ☎ 808/324–7873 ⊕ www.oceanecotours.com ☑ From $99.

Tennis

Many of the island's resorts rent rackets, balls, and shoes and allow nonguests to play for a fee. On the Kohala Coast, try the Fairmont Orchid Hawaii, the Hilton Waikoloa Village, and Waikoloa Beach

Marriott. In Keauhou, there's Holua Tennis and Pickleball Center; in Kailua-Kona, you can play at the Courtyard King Kamehameha's Kona Beach Hotel and the Royal Kona Resort. There are also several free public courts on both sides of the island. Call the County of Hawaii Department of Parks and Recreation (☎ 808/961–8311) for information about public courts.

Edith Kanakaole Tennis Stadium

TENNIS | The stadium is used for large events, but there are public courts in the same complex. ⊠ Hoolulu County Park, Piilani and Kalanikoa Sts., Hilo ☎ 808/961–8720.

Higashihara Park

TENNIS | You can play for free at this nearly always uncrowded park near Honalo. ⊠ Off Hwy. 11 before Honalo, Kailua-Kona.

★ Holua Tennis and Pickleball Center

TENNIS | This is by far the nicest tennis center in Kona town, with 11 beautiful, tournament-quality courts (seven lighted) and even a pickleball center. Daily TennisCize, drop-in play, lessons, and a pro shop (with shoe and racket rental) are available. There's ice-cold water on every court, a very nice shower and changing room, and a breezy lounge with vending machines. The center also hosts major tournaments and actively supports the local tennis community. ⊠ 78-7190 Kaleiopapa St., Kailua-Kona ☎ 808/322–6090 ⊕ www.holuatennisandpickleballcenter.com.

Old Kona Airport Park

TENNIS | A community tennis organization nicely maintains the courts here.
■ TIP→ It can get very hot midday, so bring water. Plan on using hats, sunscreen, and long-sleeve rash guards to play comfortably. ⊠ North end of Kuakini Hwy., Kailua-Kona ☎ 808/961–8561.

8

Activities and Tours TENNIS

Humpback whales are visible off the coast of the Big Island between December and April.

Whale- and Dolphin-Watching

One of the most highly anticipated experiences for visitors to the Hawaiian Islands from December through May is seeing humpback whales, which return annually. They travel south about 3,000 miles in as few as 40 days, making only limited stops along the way. Leaving the icy Alaska waters in fall, they migrate here to mate and give birth (the following year) in warm waters off Hawaii. Once here, they do not feed. In 2014, the population of migrating humpbacks was thought to range between 8,000 and 10,000 individuals, with varying levels of arrivals in subsequent years. They live to be about 50 years old. Behaviors that you might witness include splashes, spy-hops, blowhole sprays, tail whacks, and the most spectacular of all—leaping barrel rolls. Toward the end of the season, you may see mothers showing newborn calves the ways of the world. Humpbacks tend to stick close to shore, so you will often witness them from many accessible locations, especially along the Kohala Coast.

Eighteen species of dolphin live here year-round, including spotted, spinner, rough-toothed, and bottlenose. Be sure to choose excursions that respect the natural boundaries of dolphins and that don't disturb or impact their resting states.

■ TIP→ **If you take a morning cruise, you're more likely to see dolphins.** *In addition to the outfitters listed below, see Snorkeling for more outfitters that offer whale- and dolphin-watching cruises.*

TOURS

Captain Dan McSweeney's Whale Watch Learning Adventures

WHALE-WATCHING | Captain Dan McSweeney, self-described whale researcher and conservationist, offers three-hour trips on his double-decker, 40-foot cruise boat. In addition to

Be Dolphin SMART

Dolphin Smart

The idea of swimming with Hawaii's wild spinner dolphins may seem like an amazing experience, but in actuality it's neither ecologically advisable nor safe for the animals. Oh, and did we mention that it's illegal to feed, chase, harass, or swim too closely to wild dolphins? Instead, visitors should follow the Dolphin SMART guidelines ⊕ *sanctuaries.noaa.gov/ dolphinsmart* developed by NOAA, Whale and Dolphin Conservation, and the Dolphin Ecology Project. These guidelines break down the cans and cannots when it comes to wildlife, and the rules are proudly followed by most tour operators and businesses; if you're looking into a company that does not follow these practices, we suggest you look elsewhere.

S is for Stay Away. People must stay at least 50 yards from dolphins at all times.

M is for Move Cautiously Away. Move away cautiously from dolphins who are showing signs of disturbance.

A is for Always Put Your Engine in Neutral. Always put your boat engine in neutral when dolphins are near. The same can be said for humans—put yourself in neutral and stop to think about the negative impact you may have by getting too close.

R is for Refrain. This means refrain from swimming with, feeding, or touching dolphins.

T is for Teach. Share your knowledge with others.

Keep these guidelines in mind for Hawaii's other protected species such as sea turtles, humpback whales (and other whales and dolphins), and Hawaiian monk seals.

humpbacks (in winter), he'll try to show you dolphins and some of the six other whale species that live off the Kona Coast throughout the year. McSweeney guarantees you'll see whales or he'll take you out again for free. ✉ *Honokohau Harbor, 74-381 Kealakehe Pkwy., Kailua-Kona* ☎ *808/322–0028, 888/942–5376* ⊕ *www. ilovewhales.com* ✍ *$120.*

Hawaii Nautical

WHALE-WATCHING | An NOAA-designated "Dolphin SMART" operator, this company practices strict guidelines for viewing protected marine animals, including dolphins and whales. You can be assured that you'll enjoy a wonderful ocean tour, see plenty of animals, and not be a part of harming or impacting the animals' activities or habitats. Excursions include affordable powerboat cruises, catamaran snorkel sails, and even a pampering yacht adventure that takes a maximum of six guests to Pawai Bay or Makalawena. Private charters are also available, but prepare to splurge. ✉ *74-425 Kealakehe Pkwy., Slip I-10, Kailua-Kona* ☎ *808/234– 7245* ⊕ *www.hawaiinautical.com* ✍ *From $79.*

Zipline Tours

One of the few ways to really see the untouched beauty of the Big Island is to fly over its lush forests, dense tree canopies, and glorious rushing waterfalls on a zipline. You strap into a harness, get clipped to a cable, step off a platform, and then zip, zip, zip your way through paradise. Most companies start you out easy on a slower, shorter line and graduate you to faster, longer zips. It's an exhilarating adventure for all ages and, between the zipping, rappelling, and suspension bridges, has been known to help some put aside their fear of heights (at least for a few minutes).

Kapohokine Adventures

ZIP LINING | In addition to offering volcano hikes, waterfall swims, and helicopter tours, this company does zipping exceptionally well, in combinations or via à la carte adventures. It has one of the longest ziplines on the island, at 2,400 feet, as well as the only all-dual-track zip, which means you'll be able to traverse the eight stations more quickly and have a friend at your side the whole way. You'll soar over the lush rain forests of Hilo's Honolii River gorge, complete with waterfalls, and get views of volcanoes in the distance. If you want to get muddy, try the Zip and Rip, which combines ziplining with an ATV adventure. Those wishing to splurge can't do better than the Heli-Zip, combining an aerial tour with a zipline. This is the one big-name celebrities have been known to book, so you might share the platform with someone famous. Tours depart from both Hilo and Kona. ⊠ *Grand Naniloa DoubleTree by Hilton, 93 Banyan Dr., Hilo* ☎ *808/964–1000* ⊕ *www.ziplinehi.com* ⊠ *From $189.*

Kohala Zipline

ZIP LINING | Located in the canopy of the Halawa Gulch in North Kohala, this tour features nine zips and five suspension bridges for a thrilling, within-the-canopy adventure in the forest. You'll bounce up to the site in a six-wheel-drive, military-style vehicle. Two certified guides accompany each small group. Designed for all ability levels, the Kohala Zipline focuses on fun and safety, offering a dual line for efficient, confident braking.

You'll soar more than 100 feet above the ground and feel like a pro by the last platform. A quickie lesson in rappelling is included. Zip and Dip tours (combining zipline, nature walk, lunch, snacks, and waterfall swim) are available. ⊠ *54-3676 Akoni Pule Hwy., Kapaau* ☎ *808/331–3620, 800/464–1993* ⊕ *www.kohala-zipline.com* ⊠ *From $189.*

Umauma Zipline Experience

ZIP LINING | This is the quickest, most adventurous way to see 14 waterfalls, including the dramatic Umauma Falls, as you soar overhead via nine ziplines (four are dual). Suspension bridges take you over rain forests, gorges, grottoes, and lava tubes in the beautiful Hakakau region on the Hamakua Coast. You can also opt for the Waterfall Rappel and River Experience and rappel down a waterfall and over caves to the river. ⊠ *31-313 Old Mamalahoa Hwy., Hakalau* ☎ *808/930–9477* ⊕ *umaumaexperience.com* ⊠ *From $191.*

Photo Credits

Front Cover: Danita Delimont Creative / Alamy [Description: Kilauea lava flow near former town of Kalapana, Big Island, Hawaii, USA]. **Back cover, from left to right:** Fominayaphoto/Shutterstock, Marek Poplawski/Shutterstock, Maridav/Shutterstock. **Spine:** aquatic creature/Shutterstock. **Interior, from left to right:** Shane Myers Photography/Shutterstock (1). Fremme/Shutterstock (2). Big Island Visitors Bureau (3) **Chapter 1: Experience Maui:** Ademyan/Dreamstime (6-7). Blakerandall81/Dreamstime (8). Swaengpic/ Dreamstime (9). Michael DeFreitas North America / Alamy (9). Melissa Burovac (10). Kailua village business improvement District (10). Barsik/ Dreamstime (10). Kilauea Military Camp (10). George Burba/Shutterstock (11). Michael Hanano / Shutterstock (12). Anita Gould/Flickr, [CC BY-NC 2.0] (12). Big Island Gravity (12). Samantoniophotography/Dreamstime (13). Picturist21/Dreamstime (13). Vacclav/Dreamstime (14). Icemanj/ Dreamstime (14). Phillip B. Espinasse/Shutterstock (14). John Elk III / Alamy (15). Hawaii Tourism Authority (HTA)/Cameron Brooks (20). Big Island Visitors Bureau (BIVB)/Kirk Lee Aeder (20). Hawaii Tourism Authority (HTA)/Tor Johnson (20). Hawaii Tourism Authority (HTA)/Anna Pacheco (21). Christopher Mazmanian/Shutterstock (21). Big Island Visitors Bureau (BIVB) / Kirk Lee Aeder (22). Island of Hawaii Visitors Bureau (IHVB) / Tyler Schmitt (22). emperorcosar/Shutterstock (22). Png-Studio/iStockphoto (23). Hawaii Tourism Authority (HTA) / Tor Johnson (23). Martinmark/Dreamstime (24). Dana Edmunds 2014 (24). Hawaii Tourism (24). Magdanatka/Shutterstock (25). Big Island Visitors Bureau (BIVB) / Kirk Lee Aeder (25). Pr2is/Dreamstime (26). Ancha Chiangmai/Shutterstock (26). Marilyn Gould/Dreamstime (26). Tpower70/Dreamstime (26). Vfbjohn/ Dreamstime (26). Big Island Visitors Bureau (BIVB) / Kirk Lee Aeder (27). Eddygaleotti/Dreamstime (27). Caner CIFTCI/Dreamstime (27). Elmar Langle/iStockphoto (27). Koondon/Shutterstock (27). Temanu/Shutterstock (28). Hawaii Tourism Authority (HTA) / Brooke Dombroski (28). Lost Mountain Studio/Shutterstock (28). Alla Machutt/iStockphoto (28). Mongkolchon Akesin/Shutterstock (28). Hawaii Tourism Authority (HTA) / Heather Goodman (29). Hawaii Tourism Authority (HTA) / Heather Goodman (29). Hawaii Tourism Authority (HTA) / Dana Edmunds (29). Hawaii Tourism Authority (29). olgakr/iStockphoto (29). Cathy Locklear/Dreamstime (33). HVCB (34). Thinkstock LLC (35). Linda Ching/HVCB (37). Sri Maiava Rusden/HVCB (37). Leis Of Hawaii @ leisofhawaii.com (38). www.kellyalexanderphotography.com (38). Leis Of Hawaii @ leisofhawaii.com (38). Leis Of Hawaii @ leisofhawaii.com (38). Leis Of Hawaii @ leisofhawaii.com (38). www.kellyalexanderphotography.com (38). Tim Wilson/Flickr, [CC BY-NC 2.0] (39). Polynesian Cultural Center (40, 1-5). Dana Edmunds/ Polynesian Cultural Center's/Alii Luau (41,1-3). Oahu Visitors Bureau (41). **Chapter 3: Kailua-Kona and the Kona Coast:** atommy/Shutterstock (79). Mariusz S. Jurgielewicz/Shutterstock (89). Marek Poplawski/ Shutterstock (109). Hawaii Tourism Authority (HTA) / Heather Goodman (111). Cornforth Images / Alamy (115). **Chapter 4: The Kohala Coast and Waimea:** Georgeburba/Dreamstime (119). instacruising/ Shutterstock (137). Georgeburba/Dreamstime (143). **Chapter 5 :The Hamakua Coast With Maunakea:** Ujjwalstha/Dreamstime (153). Russ Bishop / Alamy (159). Cornforth Images / Alamy (160). JMP Traveler/ iStockphoto (168). **Chapter 6: Hilo:** emperorcosar/Shutterstock (171). Tpower70/Dreamstime.com (183). **Chapter 7: Hawaii Volcanoes National Park, Puna, and Kau:** Maridav/Shutterstock (193). INTERFO-TO Pressebildagentur / Alamy (198). Big Island Visitors Bureau (202). Russ Bishop/age fotostock (203). Janice Wei/iStockphoto (205). Cornforth Images / Alamy (206). SuperStock (207). Linda Robshaw / Alamy (207). MNStudio/ Dreamstime (220). **Chapter 8: Activities and Tours:** WaterFrame / Alamy (223). CAMERON NELSON (227). Russ Bishop / Alamy Stock Photo (235). MNStudio/Dreamstime (238). Andre Seale / Alamy (244). Shane Myers Photography/Shutterstock (247). Gert Vrey/iStockphoto (248). SPrada/iStockphoto (250). sweetlifephotos/iStockphoto (251). Blaine Harrington III / Alamy (252). David Fleetham / Alamy (254). Stephen Frink Collection / Alamy (256). **About Our Writers:** All photos are courtesy of the writers.

Every effort has been made to trace the copyright holders, and we apologize in advance for any accidental errors. We would be happy to apply the corrections in the following edition of this publication.

Notes

Notes

Notes

Notes

Notes

Notes

Fodor's BIG ISLAND OF HAWAII

Publisher: Stephen Horowitz, *General Manager*

Editorial: Douglas Stallings, *Editorial Director;* Jill Fergus, Jacinta O'Halloran, Amanda Sadlowski, *Senior Editors;* Kayla Becker, Alexis Kelly, Rachael Roth, *Editors*

Design: Tina Malaney, *Director of Design and Production;* Jessica Gonzalez, *Graphic Designer;* Mariana Tabares, *Design and Production Intern*

Production: Jennifer DePrima, *Editorial Production Manager;* Elyse Rozelle, *Senior Production Editor;* Monica White, *Production Editor*

Maps: Rebecca Baer, *Senior Map Editor;* Henry Colomb and Mark Stroud (Moon Street Cartography), David Lindroth, *Cartographers*

Photography: Viviane Teles, *Senior Photo Editor;* Namrata Aggarwal, Ashok Kumar, Carl Yu, *Photo Editors;* Rebecca Rimmer, *Photo Intern*

Business and Operations: Chuck Hoover, *Chief Marketing Officer;* Robert Ames, *Group General Manager;* Devin Duckworth, *Director of Print Publishing;* Victor Bernal, *Business Analyst*

Public Relations and Marketing: Joe Ewaskiw, *Senior Director Communications and Public Relations;* Esther Su, *Senior Marketing Manager*

Fodors.com: Jeremy Tarr, *Editorial Director;* Rachael Levitt, *Managing Editor*

Technology: Jon Atkinson, *Director of Technology;* Rudresh Teotia, *Lead Developer;* Jacob Ashpis, *Content Operations Manager*

Writers: Karen Anderson, Kristina Anderson

Editors: Linda Cabasin, Douglas Stallings

Production Editor: Elyse Rozelle

7th Edition

ISBN 978-1-64097-300-8

ISSN 1934–5542

SPECIAL SALES

This book is available at special discounts for bulk purchases for sales promotions or premiums. For more information, e-mail SpecialMarkets@fodors.com.

PRINTED IN CANADA

10 9 8 7 6 5 4 3 2 1

About Our Writers

 Karen Anderson is a Kona resident who enjoys horseback riding in the hills of the Big Island. She is the managing editor of *At Home, Living with Style in West Hawaii* and has written for a variety of publications including *West Hawaii Today, Big Island Weekly, Hawaii* magazine and the Kona-Kohala Chamber of Commerce. She's also the best-selling author of *The Hawaii Home Book, Practical Tips for Tropical Living*, which received an award for excellence from the Hawaii Book Publishers Association. Her monthly editor's column and chef/restaurant profiles are known throughout West Hawaii. For this edition, Karen updated Travel Smart, Hilo, and Hawaii Volcanoes National Park, Puna & Kau.

 Kristina Anderson has been writing professionally for more than 25 years. After working as an advertising copywriter and creative director in Southern California for more than a decade, she moved to Hawaii in 1992, freelancing copy and broadcast for Hawaii agencies. Since 2006, she's written for national and regional publications, most notably for *At Home in West Hawaii* magazine, which profiles a variety of homes—from coffee shacks to resort mansions—and for USAToday.com Travel Tips. She also fills in here and there as a substitute teacher, which keeps her busy, as does being a single mom to two teenage boys. When there's time, she paddles outrigger canoes competitively and plays tennis very noncompetitively. For this book, Kristina updated Experience, Kailua-Kona & the Kona Coast, The Kohala Coast & Waimea, The Hamakua Coast with Maunakea, and Activities & Tours.